General Sir David Richards was commiss
in 1971. He has served in the Far East, Germany, East Timor, Sierra Leone, and Afghanistan, where he commanded ISAF between May 2006 and February 2007. A graduate of the Staff College, Camberley (1984), his staff appointments include being Chief of Staff of the Berlin Infantry Brigade, an instructor at the Staff College, Colonel Army Plans in the Ministry of Defence, Chief Joint Force Operations, Assistant Chief and then Chief of the General Staff. He commanded 3rd Regiment Royal Horse Artillery, 4th Armoured Brigade, and the Allied Rapid Reaction Corps. He was appointed Chief of the Defence Staff in October 2010.

Dr Greg Mills heads up the Johannesburg-based Brenthurst Foundation. From 1996–2005 he was National Director of the South African Institute of International Affairs. He headed up the Prism strategic analysis group for General Sir David Richards in Kabul in 2006, was seconded as Strategy Adviser to the President of Rwanda in 2008, has served as a member of the Danish Africa Commission from 2008, and deployed twice during 2010 to Regional Command (South) in Afghanistan in an advisory capacity. He is the author of a number of books and articles, most recently of *Why Africa is Poor – And What Africans Can Do about It* (Penguin, 2010).

VICTORY AMONG PEOPLE

Lessons from Countering Insurgency and Stabilising Fragile States

EDITED BY DAVID RICHARDS AND GREG MILLS

FOREWORDS BY STANLEY MCCHRYSTAL,
JUAN MANUEL SANTOS, JOHN A KUFUOR
AND SØREN PIND

Strengthening Africa's Economic Performance
www.thebrenthurstfoundation.org

Published in 2011 by Royal United Services Institute
for Defence and Security Studies (RUSI)
Whitehall, London SW1A 2ET, UK

A co-publication with the Brenthurst Foundation
PO Box 61631, Marshalltown 2107, South Africa

ISBN (HB) 0-85516-158-2
ISBN (PB) 0-85516-163-9

A full CIP record for this book is available from the British Library
A full CIP record for this book is available from the Library of Congress

Library of Congress catalog card: available

Printed and bound in Great Britain by Stephen Austin and Sons Ltd.
Camera-ready copy edited and supplied by RUSI

CONTENTS

ACRONYMS AND ABBREVIATIONS

ABP	Afghan Border Police
AFRC	Armed Forces Revolutionary Council (Sierra Leone)
AFRICOM	US Africa Command
AMIS	African Union mission in Sudan
AMISOM	African Union Mission in Somalia
ANA	Afghan National Army
ANC	African National Congress
ANP	Afghan National Police
ANSF	Afghan National Security Forces
ARENA	Alianza Republicana Nacionalista
AUC	Autodefensas Unidas de Colombia
AVIPA	Afghanistan Vouchers for Increased Production in Agriculture
BNP	Bangladesh Nationalist Party
BRN	Barisan Revolusi Nasional
BSAP	British South Africa Police
CAR	Central African Republic
CCAI	Centro de Coordinación de Acción Integral
CDF	Civil Defence Forces
CEB	Christian Base Community
CENTCOM	US Central Command
CIAT	International Oversight Committee for the Transition
CIC	Council of Islamic Courts (Somalia)
CNDP	National Congress for the Defence of the People
COIN	Counter-insurgency
DAC	Development Assistance Committee
DAS	Departamento Administrativo de Seguridad
DCDC	Development, Concepts and Doctrine Centre
DDR	Disarmament, demobilisation and reintegration
DfID	Department for International Development
DIGGS	Demography, infrastructure, geography, governance and security
DNI	Director of National Intelligence
DRC	Democratic Republic of the Congo
DRU	Unified Revolutionary Directorate
ECOMOG	ECOWAS Monitoring Group
ECOWAS	Economic Community of West African States
ELF	Eritrean Liberation Front
ELN	Ejército de Liberación Nacional
EPLF	Eritrean People's Liberation Front

EPRDF	Ethiopian People's Revolutionary Democratic Front
ERA	Eritrea Relief Association
FAR	Forces Armées Rwandais
FARC	Fuerzas Armadas Revolucionarias de Colombia
FARDC	Forces Armées de la République Démocratique du Congo
FATA	Federally Administered Tribal Areas
FDLR	Forces Démocratiques de Libération du Rwanda
FEDEMU	Federal Democratic Movement of Uganda
FMLN	Frente Farabundo Martí para la Liberación
FNLA	Frente Nacional para a Libertação de Angola
FRELIMO	Front for the Liberation of Mozambique
GDP	Gross domestic product
GEMAP	Governance and Economic Management Assistance Programme
HIPC	Heavily Indebted Poor Countries
HuJI-B	Harkat-ul-Jehad-al-Islami Bangladesh
ICC	International Criminal Court
IED	Improvised explosive device
IMATT	International Military Assistance and Training Team
IMF	International Monetary Fund
IO	Information operations
IRA	Irish Republican Army
ISAF	International Security and Assistance Force
ISI	Directorate for Inter-Services Intelligence
JMB	Jama'atul Mujahideen Bangladesh
JRG	Revolutionary Government Junta
JSOTF-P	Joint Special Operations Task Force – Philippines
LRA	Lord's Resistance Army
M-19	Movimento 19 de Abril [
MINURCAT	United Nations Mission in the Central African Republic and Chad
MoD	Ministry of Defence
MONUC	United Nations Mission in the Democratic Republic of the Congo
MONUSCO	United Nations Organization Stabilization Mission in the DRC
MPLA	Popular Movement for the Liberation of Angola
NAC	North Atlantic Council
NCO	Non-commissioned officer
NGO	Non-governmental organisation
NPRC	National Provisional Ruling Council
NRA	National Resistance Army
NSC	National Security Council
NSP	National Solidarity Programme
OECD	Organisation for Economic Cooperation and Development
ONUSAL	UN Observer Mission in El Salvador
OPO	Ovambo People's Organisation
PAD	People's Alliance for Democracy
PDC	Christian Democratic Party
PJHQ	Permanent Joint Headquarters
PLAN	People's Liberation Army of Namibia
POK	Pakistan Occupied Kashmir
PRT	Provincial Reconstruction Team
PSYOPS	Psychological Operations
PULO	Patani United Liberation Organisation (Thailand)
RCD	Rassemblement Congolais pour la Démocratie
RC-S	Regional Command South

RDF	Rwanda Defence Force
RENAMO	Resistência Nacional Moçambicana
RhAF	Rhodesian Air Force
RKK	Runda Kumpalan Kecil (Thailand)
RPA	Rwanda Patriotic Army
RPF	Rwanda Patriotic Front
RSLAF	Republic of Sierra Leone Armed Forces
RUF	Revolutionary United Front
SADF	South African Defence Force
SAM	Surface-to-air missile
SAS	Special Air Service
SHIRBRIG	Standby High Readiness Brigade for United Nations Operations
SLA	Sierra Leone Army
SLP	Sierra Leone Police Force
SLPP	Sierra Leone People's Party
SPLA	Sudan People's Liberation Army
SRSG	Special Representative of the Secretary-General
SSR	Security sector reform
SWA	South West Africa
SWAPO	South West African People's Organisation
TFG	Transitional Federal Government
TPLF	Tigray People's Liberation Front
TRC	Truth and reconciliation commission
UAV	Unmanned aerial vehicle
UDI	Unilateral Declaration of Independence
UFM	Uganda Freedom Movement
UIC	Union of Islamic Courts
ULIMO	United Liberation Movement of Liberia for Democracy
UNAMID	United Nations-African Union Mission in Darfur
UNAMIR	United Nations Assistance Mission for Rwanda
UNAMSIL	United Nations Mission in Sierra Leone
UNDP	United Nations Development Programme
UNICEF	United Nations International Children's Fund
UNISOM	United Nations Operation in Somalia
UNITA	União Nacional para a Independência Total de Angola
UNITAF	Unified Task Force (Somalia)
UNMIL	United Nations Mission in Liberia
UNMIS	United Nations Missions in Sudan
UNOSOM	United Nations Operation in Somalia
UNPROFOR	UN Protection Force (Bosnia)
UOR	Urgent Operational Requirement
UPDA	Uganda People's Democratic Army
UPDF	Uganda People's Defence Force
USAID	United States Agency for International Development
USDA	United States Department of Agriculture
ZANLA	Zimbabwe African National Liberation Army
ZANU	Zimbabwe African National Union
ZAPU	Zimbabwe African People's Union
ZIPRA	Zimbabwe People's Revolutionary Army

ACKNOWLEDGEMENTS

A compendium is inevitably the end product of great teamwork. Not only have all the sixteen authors willingly gone the extra mile in delivering their excellent chapters in timely fashion, but the editing and production team led by Adrian Johnson and his colleagues Lindsay O'Sullivan and Anna Rader at RUSI, as well as Terence McNamee at the Brenthurst Foundation, have demonstrated both precision and professionalism (not to say some humour) despite the ratcheting time pressures always associated with such a task. The editors would also like to pay special thanks to President Juan Manuel Santos, President John A Kufuor, Minister Søren Pind and General Stanley McChrystal for adding their personal insights.

Finally, this volume is dedicated to the men and women, both military and civilian, who have given so selflessly to the task of building peace in fragile and, at times, violent situations. This volume hopefully will help not only to inform their actions, but highlight their role and personal sacrifices for those who stay at home.

FOREWORDS

Every insurgency is different. Iraq is not like Afghanistan and Afghanistan is not like the Congo. The specific tools and approaches required to counter insurgency will vary according to the political and social context, the nature of the adversary, and the purpose of the mission. But we do not have to reinvent the wheel. Several key principles can be drawn both from our recent hard-earned experience in the field and the reinvigorated study of insurgency, past and present, in universities and staff colleges.

No insurgency can be defeated by military means – if there is a first principle, that probably comes closest to it. Without a political accommodation, the wellspring of social or economic grievance that fuels insurgencies will never dry up. Of the other principles, several bear mention. In all insurgencies, the population is the vital ground, so to understand people's needs and insecurities you have to live among them. Fight the insurgent aggressively, but never exceed the force that is required to do the job. Force densities are critical, but so is the balance between local and foreign forces. The public information war is the counter-insurgents' strong suit, so do not shirk from the fight: the insurgents' venal acts will turn the population against them if the information they receive is accurate and from a trusted source. Diplomacy and development has to be regionally and not nationally focused: insurgency typically does not recognise national borders. Bad governance is the best recruiting sergeant for the insurgents' cause.

These are just some of the principles percolating throughout this unique and wide-ranging volume, which offers an appraisal of current thinking about counter-insurgency and stability operations, and reviews lessons and case studies from South and Central Asia, Latin America and Africa. The fact that several contributors have hands-on operational experience is only one reason why this volume stands out from the burgeoning literature on contemporary insurgency. Another is the contributions of General Sir David Richards, current Chief of the Defence Staff. Co-editor of the book with Dr Greg Mills, General Richards draws on his exceptional command experience in two very different theatres of conflict, Sierra Leone (in 2000–01) and Afghanistan (2006). The environments could hardly be more different, but the challenges faced by these two missions, especially in setting the conditions for stability over the long term, share important similarities. The same is true of low-intensity insurgencies – such as Thailand and Uganda – and the more bloody and intractable conflicts in the Congo and Kashmir. These rich and detailed case studies, which also include essays on Bangladesh, former Rhodesia, Rwanda and Colombia, are complemented by thematic papers on information operations, the role of special forces and the economic side of counter-insurgency, as well as particular emphasis on the current Afghanistan campaign.

No recent study of counter-insurgency can claim the same breadth and diversity of cases and perspectives as this volume. *Victory Among People* shall remain a vital reference for practitioners well into the future.

General Stanley McChrystal US Army (Rtd)
Former Commander ISAF and Commander of US Forces Afghanistan

I have always been convinced that real results in combating violence in the globalised world of the twenty-first century can only be achieved through international co-operation, by assessing the experiences and lessons learned elsewhere.

As minister of defence between 2006 and 2009, I sought the advice of experts from the United Kingdom, Israel and the United States, among others, to strengthen our intelligence capabilities, develop the concept of joint operations at the highest level and support and consolidate the advances made by our armed forces. At the same time, our soldiers and policemen produced the greatest results in the history of our struggle against subversive organisations and their terrorist actions.

We also studied the best military doctrine generated by field experience of commanders that set the theoretical pillars for what we now know as counter-insurgency theory. Classics such as *Strategy: the Indirect Approach* by Basil Lidell Hart; *Counterinsurgency Warfare* by David Galula; *Defeating Communist Insurgency* by Sir Robert Thompson; *Guerrilla Warfare* by Mao Zedong; and *People's War, People's Army* by General Vo Nguyen Giap, are required reading and the basis of modern counter-insurgency.

Within this framework of international co-operation in the fight against factors of violence such as terrorism and drug-trafficking, I find this book, by Dr Greg Mills and General Sir David Richards, Chief of the UK Defence Staff, on counter-insurgency in various countries – including Colombia – especially valuable.

Colombia's experience in countering insurgency illustrates how much leadership and policy counts, and that history and culture are not destiny.

Over the past decade, we have learned important lessons. Armed forces have to be properly equipped, funded and led, in order for them to materialise the goals that politicians set. Soldiers should not be put in harm's way without the tools and political backing to get the job done properly. We have learnt also of the critical role that intelligence – and counter-intelligence – plays in this fight, and how special forces, in particular, can help to turn the insurgent tide. Security is critical in providing the space in which reconstruction and social and economic development can occur. Security begets development and vice versa, but development is impossible without a measure of security. I like to quote the Romans, who said that security is the first law of the republic. It is not the only law, but, without security, any other undertaking is almost impossible.

And just as development should be focused on reducing inequalities – the gap between rich and poor in our society – we have to find the means to ensure that all people have the opportunity to find formal employment, a goal which requires close alignment between the private sector and government policy. Overall, government must ensure it is not indifferent to the needs of less-privileged sections of the population.

State- and institution-building is an indispensable aspect of this process. In our case, the state has had to be extended into some of the most inaccessible areas, where topography, geography and poor investment in roads and telecommunications combined to make contact with remote communities difficult. This goes hand-in-hand with building systems of taxation to provide a sustainable base for national development.

Between 2002 and 2010 President Álvaro Uribe led a massive effort to restore the country's security and strengthen the state's control over the entire territory. The so-called 'Democratic Security' policy received the overwhelming support of the Colombian people, who were tired of being intimidated by illegal armed groups, and the backing of the business sector, which contributed to safety through a tax whose proceeds went to this objective.

During President Uribe's second term, it was my responsibility as minister of defence to lead a process we called 'Democratic Security Consolidation', in which we aimed to make all our armed forces' operational successes irreversible. We established a comprehensive state presence in the liberated areas, not only with soldiers and police, but with judges, teachers, health services, and, in general, with all the social services of the state.

The alignment of the military and police effort with judicial capacity, socioeconomic development and institutional strengthening is the key to success. The irreversibility of the achievements so far, considering protection as a strategic centre of gravity, and the respect for human rights above tactical considerations, are equally important principles.

I emphasise the issue of human rights and international humanitarian law, because we made their observance the pillar of legitimacy of our armed forces. Colombia has shown that it is possible to strike terrorist insurgents and militias without violating humanitarian principles.

In the government of President Uribe, and now in my administration, we understand security not as an end in itself but as the means for the state to reach all Colombians equally, and to promote prosperity for all.

After eight years of advances in security; that have significantly weakened – but not yet defeated – the narcoterrorist groups; that have reduced the murder rate in the country to its lowest level in thirty years; and that have allowed Colombians to travel in their country without fear of kidnapping; we can dream of a better future.

My objective, in the government that began on 7 August 2010, is to build on the achievements of 'Democratic Security' to move into a new era of 'Democratic Prosperity'.

The aim of 'Democratic Security' has been to protect each and every Colombian. 'Democratic Prosperity' seeks to give every Colombian an equal opportunity to enjoy their constitutional rights and share in the prosperity that such security has made possible.

At the same time, our armed forces – who continue fighting illegal armed groups –are ready to co-operate and share their experience with other countries which are going through circumstances similar to those we went through a few years ago.

Regional and international diplomacy – as I said at the beginning – is critical in building a team-approach to solve these problems, and help providing the development and material resources. But we also know that, while international partners are important, long-term stability is fundamentally the responsibility of domestic actors. Our disarmament, demobilisation, and reintegration programme, to which more than 50,000 former guerrillas and paramilitary combatants have signed up, is a case in point.

This volume not only provides us with a clear analytical framework to better understand the origins and dynamics of conflict, but the tools to assist in their successful resolution. It is an operational guide, reflecting the practical experience of many of the contributors, including the co-editors, in senior posts in national and multilateral missions.

Victory Among People: Lessons from Countering Insurgency and Stabilising Fragile States is a major and exceptional contribution to the literature on countering insurgencies and stabilising states in jeopardy.

Juan Manuel Santos
President of the Republic of Colombia

There can be no prosperity in Africa unless its many conflicts are resolved – this is one of the founding ideas of the African Union in 2002. It is no less relevant today, both within our continent and in war-torn regions throughout the world.

Although the responsibility for ending armed conflict must rest, first and foremost, with the local parties involved, there will always be a role for regional and international organisations to assist the parties on the road to recovery. My own country, Ghana, has played a key role in several peacekeeping missions and we are working to build our 'peace-building' capacity within Africa in order to promote conflict resolution and sustainable development. In the 1990s, West Africa was synonymous with brutal civil war and poor governance. But, now, some of the worst affected countries, such as Liberia and Sierra Leone, are moving towards a more stable and prosperous future.

These two case studies form part of this remarkable compendium, which examines the evolution of insurgencies and stabilisation operations over the past three decades. *Victory Among People* rightly identifies the population as the vital prize. Without winning them over to your cause, you stand no chance of success, whether you are the host government or an international assistance force. This is only one of many invaluable insights found in this book, making it a must-read for anyone interested in global peace and security.

John A Kufuor
Former President of Ghana
Member of the Brenthurst Foundation Board

There are more than forty fragile states worldwide, where more than 600 million people live, many in conditions of extreme poverty. These states constitute one of the most significant challenges to global peace and security. Not only are they threats to their regions, but a combination of inequality and hopelessness can, with the spark of political radicalism, foment acts of violence and terrorism further afield.

Of course, the varying reasons for fragility and failure need to be disaggregated and understood if we are to stabilise such environments. We also need to make external forms of assistance – whether they be military or economic – less of an inexact science, by measuring effects and by better aligning aid, for example, to the development of the private sector. Without a vibrant private sector, there will not be sustainable growth, and without growth, little hope of stability. We need to find the means to turn this vicious circle into a positive one.

This volume contains a wealth of information for the policy-maker and analyst alike. In gathering case studies and lessons from Latin America, Asia and Africa, it provides a unique window on current thinking. With insights from a range of senior military and civilian practitioners, it is more than just a review of contemporary insurgency and stability operations, but also a guideline for greater success.

Søren Pind
Minister for Development Co-operation of Denmark

INTRODUCTION:
CONTEMPORARY INSURGENCY

Greg Mills and David Richards

Conventional war is a thing of the past. Such is one lesson from Afghanistan and Iraq. This appears true even for those countries that possess a considerable array of conventional weaponry. Why should they risk everything in a conventional attack, if they can instead achieve their aims through the use of proxies, or through economic subterfuge and cyber-warfare?

Lessons from Afghanistan and Iraq are contained in the experiences, a decade earlier, of the ill-fated international intervention into Somalia. The dusty, bloody and chaotic streets and markets of Mogadishu taught that considerable advantages in technology and military firepower are by themselves not enough, and can be countered by relatively rudimentary 'Kalashnikov' weaponry. It also showed, again, that the military cannot by itself win the battle, but only hold the ring enabling the local actors to make the right decisions about their future. If they do not want to – *or cannot* – make these, then the military's role is largely superfluous. Insurgencies are beaten by local actors and local governments, not foreigners, and victory requires at least as much political will as it does military might.

Such assertions raise two issues for states of the Western alliance. The first concerns their force posture, training and equipment over the next generation. The threat of proxy warfare suggests that land forces and equipment to counter asymmetric warfare – mine-proof vehicles, helicopters and other transports, intelligence, and special forces – will be at a premium. And whilst it is a long-term guarantee against the unthinkable, it is uncertain what the tactical value of nuclear deterrent is against an irrational and nihilistic foe.

The second is a more pressing, yet ongoing point: how to repair those states that serve both as flashpoints of conflict and harbours for terrorist activities. This is as much a long-term issue as it is an immediate challenge in countries in Africa, including Somalia and Guinea, but especially in Afghanistan. To this Afghan dilemma, a choice has been advanced as a solution: get in deeper in working out a political and development solution; or get out by focusing on the security aspect alone, turning Afghanistan into a counter-terrorist operation. The answer to this dilemma holds solutions for countries elsewhere on the path from fragility and conflict to sustainable development, just as it points to the nature of future war on which this compendium is focused.

On Future War and Warfare[1]
To ensure the fundamental safety of any nation, it is necessary to establish what it *needs* before establishing what can be afforded. If, as is likely, there is a gap, this should be recognised as a risk that a government is – *or is not* – prepared to carry. This need, of course, depends on the threat assessment.

From the end of the Cold War to 2005, the number of armed conflicts fell by 40 per cent. The number of major conflicts (involving battle deaths of more than 1,000 people) dropped even more significantly, by 80 per cent. Wars between countries fell to just 5 per cent of all conflicts. Most conflict now occurs in the poorest countries of the world, and as income rises, the risk of conflict declines. Unsurprisingly, most conflict now takes place in Africa, though that too is in decline (see Figure 1). By the end of the 1990s, more people were being killed in sub-Saharan Africa than the rest of the world combined.[2] In this, indirect deaths, including disease and malnutrition, are estimated to account for more than 90 per cent of all war-related fatalities.

Figure 1: Incidence of Conflict in Sub-Saharan Africa, 1989–2005.

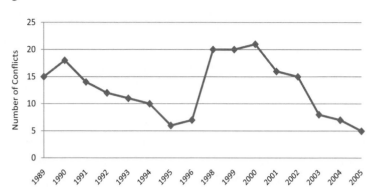

Correspondingly, the period since 1946 is the longest for hundreds of years of there being no war between the major powers. Colin Gray may be right in contending that the basics have not changed much, and that war will still be with us, driven by interests, personalities and politics today as ever before.[3] Though diminished, the threat of conventional wars still remains: most notably in Asia, not least given the resource needs and ambitions of China, Japan and India; and especially on the Korean peninsula, given unresolved issues of nationalism and ideological struggle.

But, as is advanced above, if the last twenty years is anything to go by, most conflicts are likely to be so-called 'small' wars, between ill-defined often non-state opponents, fighting for complex sets of causes ranging from greed to deeply entrenched grievances, fought at a low intensity employing mostly small arms and simple but deadly bombs. These are most likely to be fought not over territory but over ideas and symbols, among rather than between peoples.[4] For the last twenty years, with the notable exception of Iraq (1991 and 2003) and possibly the Ethiopian-Eritrean border conflict, wars involving conventionally equipped massive armies have virtually become a thing of the past. Warfare today has gone back to being a task of the light infantry and modern cavalry, where numbers (and getting them there) are the important enabling aspect, along with other critical assets of intelligence, surveillance, local knowledge, and a suite of niche skills and resources aimed at meeting the basic needs of the people amongst whom the conflict plays out. Even state-on-state war is likely to look like something that the West is trying to do in Afghanistan, rather than some hot version of the Cold War. Belligerent states – unless the employment of mass manoeuvre becomes an asymmetric attraction to them because their opponents have done away with 'traditional' combat power available to alliances – will likely use proxies, guerrillas, terrorists, cyber-warfare *et al* to achieve their aims rather than mass air, sea and land operations.

The British armed forces' Development, Concepts and Doctrine Centre (DCDC) recognises the primacy of the modern insurgency in its mapping of global strategic trends to 2040. A combination of exclusion from the benefits of globalisation, climate change, political fragility and a burgeoning population will create, the DCDC has highlighted, a volatile mix in parts of the developing world which will constitute around 85 per cent of the global population in 2040 (Europe will shrink to just 6 per cent), and especially in Africa. Whereas the global population will increase from 6.9 billion (2010) to almost 8.8 billion (2040), creating all sorts of social and resource pressures, in some areas these trends will be exacerbated by shifting demographics. For example, the median age in sub Saharan Africa will be approximately twenty-four, whereas in Europe it will be around forty-seven. Such stresses are compounded by competition for resources driven by both external requirements (for minerals and hydrocarbons) and internal demand (for food, water, and energy). Nearly 70 per cent of the world's population will, by 2040, be located in areas of environmental stress, notably in sub-Saharan Africa, and South, Central and East Asia. Nearly 30 per cent of the world will face water scarcity in these areas.

Resource scarcity, the DCDC observes,[5] will stunt development, and lead to poverty, instability and conflict. Coupled with effects of climate change, there will be humanitarian crises and increasingly uncontrollable internal and external migration. Many of these stresses will occur in the pressure-cooker of African and other developing-world cities. By 2025, more than 50 per cent of sub-Saharan Africa's people, by then numbering around 1 billion, will be living its cities, up from just 15 per cent in 1950. According to a 2010 UN-Habitat report, the number of people living in African cities will triple over the next forty years. Already 200 million sub-Saharan Africans live in slums, the highest number world-wide.[6] The fastest-growing city, Kinshasha, is forecast to increase by nearly 50 per cent over the next decade. The waves of Congolese already, today, walking to and from their capital each day in search of work reinforces this point. With people moving to the cities in search of a better life, escaping grinding rural poverty, a combination of overcrowding, poor services and dashed expectations could, if not adequately addressed, prove a hugely destabilising cocktail.

Critically, perceptions of inequality and associated grievances could, the DCDC notes, result in increased instability and societal tension. Of the twenty most unequal countries measured in terms of the Global Peace Index's Gini figures (Equatorial Guinea, Angola, Afghanistan, Gabon, Republic of Congo, Democratic Republic of the Congo, Chad, Sudan, Belize, Lebanon, Iraq, Syria, Myanmar, Qatar, Bahrain, Libya, Bhutan, Oman, Saudi Arabia and North Korea),[7] seven are in sub-Saharan Africa. Afghanistan is the third most unequal, just ahead of Angola and Equatorial Guinea. It is not poverty *per se* that is apparently problematic, but rather when dearth lives cheek by jowl with excess.

The 2040 DCDC report concludes that the incidence of armed conflict is likely to increase, underpinned by an unstable transition to a multipolar world, widespread global inequality heightening grievances, population increases, resource scarcity and the adverse consequences of climate change. While future conflict will remain unpredictable and violent, its character will continue to evolve and present new challenges. In an environment where the differences between state, state-sponsored and non-state adversaries *will* blur, while technology will remain important, people, the report argues, are likely to provide the asymmetric edge when responding to both expected and unexpected challenges.

As Afghanistan illustrates, and wars from the Congo to Liberia confirm, the modern insurgency is fought among the people even if it may be supported without. The choice of weapons is determined by availability and practicality: ammonium nitrate bombs, AK-47s, rocket propelled grenades, mobile phones and the Internet. Thus defence should respond to the new strategic, and indeed economic, environment by ensuring much more ruthlessly that our armed forces are appropriate and relevant to the context in which they will operate rather than the one they might have expected to fight in previous eras. Too much emphasis is still placed on what the US Defense Secretary Robert Gates has described as 'exquisite' and hugely expensive equipment.

Yet many defence establishments have not yet fully adapted to the security realities of the post-Cold War world and this complex and dangerous new century. Operating among, understanding and effectively influencing people requires mass – *numbers* – whether this is 'boots on the ground', riverine and high-speed littoral warships, or unmanned aerial vehicles (UAVs), transport aircraft and helicopters. Investing in intelligence and strike capacity through special forces provides critical assets and force enablers in any counter-insurgency. It may be even more central to a counter-terrorist operation, stood further off. But they have to be used judiciously, not as an end in themselves: tools shaping the political context. We will also need to focus more activity on reinvigorating 'traditional' special forces (so-called 'white' special forces), in focusing on civic defence and socioeconomic aspects of communities.

And while the military will have to be able to fight and win battles in such complex and hostile environments, this is insufficient for success.

Beyond Equipment

While it undoubtedly has a kinetic dimension, as is intimated above, dealing with the modern insurgency is a profoundly political and developmental task. It is as much about governance as guns, and providing jobs and economic security as military activity. It is also critically about getting the 'information operations' or, more plainly put, marketing and public affairs dimension of the campaign correct – something that the Taliban, amongst other, have wittingly or not played to maximum advantage through the global media.

Modern war is to be fought as much in the fourth estate as on the battlefield. As John Mackinlay contends, 'Rather than confronting the dissident narrative head on by challenging it in the same networks and news propagation systems ... future operations will have to engage disaffection on the ground at a very local level. The emerging theme would be that local beats global.'[8] This emphasises a range of actions beyond military and stability operations to ensuring longer-term development needs in undergirding a modern society.

In charting actions across this virtual battle space, 'the news footage and the endless refrain of occupation ... has turned individual members of migrant communities in Europe from spectators to activists.'[9] 'Engaging and animating' populations in ways that are not easily militarily countered is a strategy of the insurgent in asymmetric warfare, one that demands the management of external expectations, guarding against and preparing for insurgent 'spectaculars' (so-called 'propaganda of the deed'), and sensitively both carrying out and portraying counter-insurgent actions. It is much more than about attack and defence, of guns and rockets; but about the aspirations, fears and faces of people.

Managing the softer side of an insurgency through development efforts and diplomacy, along with defence, is critical. Yet development through donor assistance is something that has proven very difficult to get right, especially (but not only) in fragile states. Although the period of recovery of fragile states is generally at least as long as the period of decline (and mostly much longer, up to thirty years in cases[10]), donor constituency concentration spans are usually much shorter.

The comparative success of the Marshall Plan in Europe proves the value of large-scale assistance, but only among those countries that want peace and which possess the inner trappings of successful societies and economies – an educated workforce with knowledge of how to operate and use modern infrastructure and all its software and hardware. Fundamentally, they have to want to develop – which makes local ownership not just critical, but absolutely fundamental to the success of any mission.

Certainly, improved development spending and its close co-ordination with military activity – expedited through institutions such as the Afghan Policy Action Group established in 2006 to enable focus on Afghan Development Zones – should help. In this there is a constant need for foreign actors to guard against choosing local favourites – local actors who are both amenable and believed to be able to deliver the country from chaos. Favouring personalities over process inevitably stakes too much on individuals and their political fortunes. And their status as the darling of the foreigners may expose and ultimately undermine them more than it assists in countering insecurity.

Development, like politics, is primarily local. And it is often rooted in socioeconomic injustice and inequality as much as it is ideological in nature. Yet satisfying local grievances is at best only partly a job for external development and military effort. While it can blunt the edge of short-term economic collapse or humanitarian disasters, donor assistance has never proven a way to develop any country in the longer term.

Indeed, the most important lesson learnt over and over again in stabilisation and counter-insurgency operations is for the political deal to be right: the international, regional and local compacts which the tools of defence, diplomacy and development can support. Where the political deal is unrealistic or badly conceived, then only trouble, failure and costly disappointment is likely to follow. One of many lessons of Afghanistan is that political relationships have often been clumsily handled.

Further lessons relearned again and again in COIN operations have concerned the establishment of local forces and the manner in which they have integrated their actions with international counterparts. The creation of local capacity does not end there. Embedding international support in critical areas of state organisation is also important in getting the country functioning and reinstating the traditional drivers of growth in the economy and fixing key infrastructure.

For all of the assets – from highly impressive people to money and technology available to international forces – it is remarkable how difficult the international community has found just getting the basics right: reinstating electricity (and keeping ahead of demand), fixing roads and railways, and stabilising the economy. Again, local ownership and the setting of priorities are key to success. If they are only recalcitrant reformers, foreigners have to learn to hold them to task while ensuring always the carrot of long-term partnership if they deliver – and not abandoning them when they actually do so.

Back to the Future

Britain's then-Foreign Secretary David Miliband noted in September 2009 that Afghanistan represented 'the laboratory of so much that we will be doing in the future.'[11] No doubt the spectre of conventional conflict will always remain, but if defence planning is about assessing likelihoods and making hard choices, the future is about countering instability and insurgencies in poverty-stricken environments. The laboratory of Afghanistan is, in military terms, more the Boer than the Cold War. It is about dealing with an insurgency amidst continuous international scrutiny against a poorly armed yet resourceful foe, always playing to their strengths of local character against foreigners, and underdog status. It is back to the future.

If Afghanistan is the laboratory of conflict, of meeting the interlocking challenges of state-collapse, radicalisation, population growth, social inequality and hopelessness, then that future has to be met with a different posture than the armed forces possess today. It is one less about hi-tech than troop densities and logistics; knowledge rather than high-altitude intelligence and information; and small-steps rather than strategic sweeps. It is fundamentally about putting people, not technology, first.

Recalling Churchill's dictum that 'The further backward you look, the further forward you can see', by scrutinising contemporary insurgencies and stability operations, this volume's purpose is to offer short-hand case-studies but, more importantly, lessons to be followed and avoided by the range of actors involved; whether militaries, donors or multilateral agencies. Our contributors have been given considerable latitude to draw on the experiences (often their own) of those countering as well as those employing insurgency.

The thematic contributions to this book examine the role of information operations, intelligence and special forces, as well as the all-important governance dimension to counter-insurgency. The selection of regional case-studies is rich and diverse, and includes current African conflicts, such as the Democratic Republic of the Congo, Uganda and Somalia, as well as countries that are in a post-conflict stability phase, such as Liberia and Sierra Leone; intractable struggles in Asia, such as Kashmir, Afghanistan and Southern Thailand; and other conflict environments that do not fit neatly into any hard and fast categories, such as Colombia and Bangladesh.

Such is the diversity of experience and perspective our contributors bring to bear in their analyses, it was inevitable that we might differ on some of the arguments and conclusions made here. Instead of trying to force an artificial consensus on what is a highly contentious subject, we have sought to encourage vigorous debate and even constructive disagreement in order to further our understanding of what is required to stabilise fragile states.

In the end, and despite their varied origins and distinct characteristics, the case studies examined in this volume did generate several common themes.

The Primacy of Politics

As insurgencies are profoundly political in nature, so too must be the process of countering them. Where counter-insurgency campaigns succeed or fail will be primarily down to the quality of the political processes, ranging from the arguments that inspired intervention to the local and regional political situations.

The Military and Stabilisation

The military has a role in not only pressing the insurgent to co-operate, but in establishing the conditions in which development can take root. But there is a need to guard against confusing short-term actions with the requirements for longer-term stability.

Stabilisation and Development

The development dimension to post-conflict recovery is the core of state sustainability. Yet this aspect has been most problematic, with very limited returns on vast expenditure. Execution has lagged well behind planning, and it has typically been very difficult not only to meet basic services, but also instil the governance conditions necessary for development. Better measurement of the effects of aid expenditure – and the activities of NGOs – is necessary not only to ensure that money is prudently spent, but that there is an overt governance and development aspect to such expenditure, which goes beyond narrow fiduciary controls.

Unintended Consequences
Care must be taken to avoid (or at least manage) the unintended consequences of international engagement, such as the impact of donor spending on local power-brokers.

Risks and Rewards
Accepting an element of risk can bring success – not just in military actions (including the manner in which local parties are engaged), but also with development actors.

Regional Diplomacy
The regional diplomatic component is similarly critical to the campaign, from Rwanda/Congo to Colombia/Venezuela, Pakistan/Afghanistan/India, Sierra Leone/Liberia, Iraq/Iran, Sudan/Uganda/Congo, to Thailand/Burma. The limited attention span of contemporary political actors coupled with a failure to appreciate this dimension has delivered sub-par results in most cases.

Messaging and the Fourth Estate
The message of the international community – of partnership with the choices made by local actors – has to be clear, co-ordinated and consistent, as is the setting of clear 'red lines' for the locals at a higher, strategic level. These should make clear the extent to which the international community is willing to go – and be pushed.

Knowledge, Culture and Incentives
While knowledge of local conditions and cultural mores is crucial in understanding constraints and opportunities, care should be taken not to overstate this 'cultural' aspect in favour of hard intelligence and to realise that local actions are intrinsically shaped by incentives and disincentives. Knowledge of operating conditions has to include the nexus between criminal and political groups, and of the overall local 'operating system' of politics, personalities, tribe, religion, power and money.

Duration and Co-ordination
External assistance has often proven fragmentary, duplicative, unco-ordinated and very short-termist. Yet local knowledge of the permanence of foreign commitment and local government presence – from schools to police-stations – has improved security.

Local Ownership
Success fundamentally demands the host population's *ownership* of the campaign.

Countering contemporary insurgencies has, all too often, been delegated to the military as the only agency capable of operating in these environments. But this cannot – and will not – achieve success. Victory among people[12] is instead down to managed co-operation between all arms of government over a sustained long-term timeframe with politics at the forefront at all times.

A SOLDIER'S PERSPECTIVE ON COUNTERING INSURGENCY

David Richards*

There was a time when the word 'COIN' in British military circles conjured up images of soldiers in the Malayan jungle, or in Aden's dusty souks, or on the streets of Northern Ireland. For years these campaigns provided the backbone for the study of counter-insurgency (COIN) at the army's Staff College. However, the most recent campaigns in Iraq and in Afghanistan's Helmand Province have challenged any notion that COIN is 'low intensity' or something other than war. These campaigns have shown that dealing with irregular adversaries can be every bit as intense as combat in warfare in the conventional sense.

Intensity is not, however, the central issue. At the heart of COIN is the inherent asymmetry between a government and all the measures at its disposal on the one hand, and the insurgent on the other. Insurgency and COIN are two sides of a very complex form of warfare in which a group or groups have resorted to violence by taking up arms to solve their grievances and achieve their political objectives. There are some insurgencies that want to replace an existing government, others to secure their position and the status quo, and, more recently, a combination of these where we have seen groups emerge to challenge nascent post-conflict governments and to

* The author wishes to acknowledge the key role played by Colonel Alexander Alderson in the writing of this chapter.

fight those trying to establish order. For the state concerned and the international community supporting it, and without fully-fledged political processes or the necessary capacity for effective governance and security, dealing with the challenge of violent insurgency is particularly difficult.

Today, what we refer to as hybrid threats – what Frank Hoffman describes as any simultaneous and adaptive employment of conventional weapons, irregular tactics, terrorism and criminal behaviour in the same space to obtain political objectives[1] – are seeking to exploit what they see as the vulnerabilities of governments and their armed forces. There is no indication that this form of challenge will abate. Terrorism and subversion are the obvious methods of attack, made more difficult to counter because insurgent groups hide behind and blend into the very population security forces seek to protect. The use of terrorist attacks on the population provides the focus through which such groups can exploit their most effective weapon: the influence that they can extend through mass communications. As General Sir Frank Kitson, one of the most important figures of British COIN, once observed, the 'main characteristic which distinguishes campaigns of insurgency from other forms of war is that they are *primarily concerned with the struggle for men's minds*'.[2]

Although the insurgency in Afghanistan is now the principal focus of attention, it is not the only insurgency under way around the world and we should not forget that insurgency is an attractive way to challenge authority. The bloody Naxalite insurgency spreading across parts of India is an example of an insurgency that has a sense of hopelessness and economic envy at its core. These are powerful instincts that today can be inflamed and communicated to other similarly dispossessed groups across the world at the touch of a button. This is the aspect of COIN that makes winning the battle of ideology, or 'hearts and minds' – the term famously coined by General Sir Gerald Templer in Malaya – so important. Templer believed that 'the answer lies not in pouring more troops into the jungle, but in the hearts and minds of the people'.[3] While the term 'hearts and minds' has been somewhat discredited, we should be clear that only genuine improvements in the lot of the dispossessed and viscerally envious – what I referred to as an upward trajectory of progress when I commanded ISAF in 2006 – will prevent such conflicts eventually affecting our own lives.

COIN is warfare. It is distinctly political, not primarily military, and it involves the people, the government and the security forces. These include the police, the armed forces, paramilitary forces and auxiliaries. The latter category is an important part of the overall solution because it gives local people, through locally raised forces, a role to play in their own security. In overall terms, the strength of the relationship between these three groups – people, government and the security forces – generally determines the outcome of the campaign. If the population gets behind the government, the government tends to win. This relationship of people, government and the security forces was famously coined by Clausewitz, the famous Prussian theorist of war, and it provides a useful framework against which we can examine several closely related questions: what have we learnt from recent operations, and have these lessons changed over the past fifty years? What does this mean for strategy, and for tactics, and how should we approach future operations?

The Security Dimension: Adjusting to Wars for the People
The last ten years have seen some remarkable developments in military capabilities. British armed forces, like many of our European and American allies, now field some of the most sophisticated equipment ever developed. Our soldiers, sailors, airmen and marines are trained to an unprecedented standard and technology has radically altered our intelligence-gathering and surveillance capabilities. Our people are linked today in a way simply not possible in previous generations which means decision-making and the exchange of intelligence and information can be lightning fast. Although this can have its

drawbacks, armed forces are now able to generate and benefit from greatly increased tempo in military operations. Commanders, both on the ground and far removed from the theatre of operations, have access to a great deal of information to help them make split-second decisions.

These developments are important and our armed forces are now so much more capable than the Cold War forces that we sent to enforce and then support peace in the Balkans. And yet it is important to recognise that these changes have not in themselves proved decisive in either of the two major wars in this century in which British forces have been engaged. We may have benefited from the products of the technological revolution of the 1990s, but the levels of *military* success envisaged then, and embodied for example in terms such as 'Shock and Awe', 'Network-Centric Warfare', and 'Rapid Decisive Operations', have not materialised.

One stark reason is that the context in which advanced military capabilities are now employed – with the exception of the invasion of Iraq in 2003 – is very different from that for which they were originally intended. First, today's campaigns are almost unavoidably operations among the population.[4] De facto, these are wars for the population, and they are complicated because those who threaten society live, hide and operate within it. This means that understanding what the population is, and what its norms, values, concerns and expectations are, has value beyond being able to locate, identify and track a conventional enemy's tanks and aircraft. Secondly, today's armed forces now operate in a complex, combined, joint, inter-agency and multinational environment. This is where success is measured by how confident the population is that it is secure, not how much of the enemy's combat power has been destroyed; where progress is measured in terms of sustained political and economic development, not how many insurgents have been killed or detained.

Operating among and for the population has been a feature of COIN since the end of the Second World War, when the spread of

Communism challenged existing orders. During the Cold War, the population *per se* was a factor that was all too easy to forget in what was a very Industrial Age approach to war. In the last four years, however, the emphasis has shifted away from an enemy-centric approach to one that recognises the central role the population plays in COIN. To use General David Petraeus's phrase, the population is the prize and it must be protected. While confronting and neutralising insurgents is an important aspect of the campaign – after all, the insurgent cannot be given a free hand – it is not the only part of the campaign. Making this transition was an important step in Iraq in late 2006, and then in Afghanistan in 2009 when General Stanley McChrystal gave the campaign its population-centric focus.

What Have We Learnt?

If we needed reminding, the major UK interventions in the first decade of the twenty-first century have reinforced the simple truth: the principal task for security forces in COIN is to secure the population from violence. Without security, the political process will be unable to function and the likelihood of conflict resolution is slim. Bernard Fall said of the Viet Cong insurgency in the late 1950s that a government which is losing to an insurgency 'is not being outfought; it is being out-administered'.[5] As the 'surge' in Baghdad in 2007 and then Iraqi-led operations in Basra in 2008 showed so clearly, effective security operations are needed to create the 'political space' for governance to be re-established, and for the government to then out-administer the insurgents.

From this central task of securing the population, several key elements are now recognised in British circles as essential. The latest doctrine captures them to emphasise their importance. They are: the need for presence and with it the need for mass; the need for intelligence; the need for continuity in approach and the maintenance of understanding; the value of partnering with local forces to build their capacity and capability; and the need to educate forces so that they understand not just conventional approaches but those best-suited to the complexity of the COIN problem. None of these would be a surprise to any successful counter-insurgent from the past, but the importance of each has been borne out by operations in Basra and Helmand. In both cases, it is clear that risks taken with some of them brought challenges that proved difficult but not impossible to overcome as campaigns developed.

Effective security measures need a permanent security presence. Security forces have to live and work among the population, which means that they cannot 'commute to work'. In Iraq this approach – adopted by necessity because of troop levels – failed in part because, until late 2006, the Iraqi security forces were not in a position to assume security responsibilities themselves. They were unable to contain the insurgents and terrorists intent on destabilising the country. Despite this, the intention remained for coalition forces, including the UK contribution, to pull back to large central operating bases, to lower their profile and to hand over security responsibilities to Iraqi forces as they stood up. The move from small patrol bases, spread out among the population centres, to large, isolated main bases meant the security forces had to travel to their areas of operation. This provided the insurgents with greater opportunities to use their favoured tactics of ambushes and the weapon of choice: improvised explosive devices (IED).

To compound the problem, security forces became isolated from the very population their primary task was to protect, so once a patrol had moved on, the population was left open to insurgent intimidation and violence. This produced a counterproductive spiral of action-counter-action, where measures we introduced to protect our forces – for example more heavily armoured vehicles, or tactics that limited time on the ground to reduce the chances of being ambushed – further isolated forces from the population. Insurgents were free to dominate normal life and public confidence in security operations dropped. In turn, this further limited the opportunity security forces had to gain information and intelligence from the population about the insurgents and local needs, and this then limited opportunities to make concrete advances in confronting the insurgent and improving conditions generally for the population as a whole.

The way to avoid these problems is to establish a continuous security presence. However, the trouble comes when security forces have moved in to re-establish control of an area. Insurgents can be relied on to fight hard for control of the population. This was evident in Baghdad in 2007 when US and Iraqi forces moved into insurgent-controlled neighbourhoods. There was a vicious spike in violence which subsequently dropped as security measures started to have an effect, and the people realised that they were not going to be abandoned again. From a UK perspective, we saw this in Basra in March 2008 when Iraqi forces, supported by the US and UK, moved to regain control of the city in Operation *Charge of the Knights*. After some days of fierce fighting, security was established and Baswaris soon started to identify insurgents, arms caches and IEDs, and general confidence started to improve after a very difficult few months.

Clearly, the ideal is not to cede control to the insurgent in the first place. This is easier said than done, particularly if we accept that one reason for the emergence of an insurgency is the inability of a government to extend its authority over the country as a whole. The key factor is the government's determination to re-establish control, and for it to make clear that protecting the population is of primary concern and that its security forces are there to stay. This means mass (numbers) and in the early stages of establishing security, many more policemen and troops are generally required than are needed to maintain 'normal' security. But what does this mean in practical terms? Today in Helmand Province, the British task force operates alongside two US Marine Corps task forces, and it benefits from levels of combat power well beyond the scale the UK can provide. Higher ISAF troop numbers, much stronger Afghan National Security Forces (ANSF), and increasing political momentum at district and provincial level are now having an effect that was not possible even as late as 2009. Armed with a comprehensive campaign plan, one galvanised by General Petraeus, and with the requisite resources now in place, the situation is hopeful.

Good intelligence, on which all sound military operations are built, is essential in any form of warfare but especially so in COIN. Insurgents try not to stand out, so they have to be identified and separated from the population, and the population safeguarded from military operations to neutralise insurgents. This needs accurate and timely intelligence because without it security operations risk being blunt, blundering and indiscriminate. This was the case in the early years in Malaya and Northern Ireland, and we saw the difficulties of operating without good intelligence in Iraq. The difference comes, however, when the population starts to gain confidence in the security forces and the government those forces represent.

Building up the intelligence picture depends as much on the very low-level, local pattern of life as it does on intelligence from the intelligence agencies and the most sophisticated technical methods. This ties in very closely with the idea of continuity, where units build up a detailed understanding of their area and can start to recognise what is unusual, or still better, when the local population has the confidence to offer up information. It goes without saying that this requires soldiers from an international force, and civilians working with them, to have a sound working knowledge of the local culture and language, so that they can actively build relationships with the population and have some understanding of what is going on. Besides gaining basic information, one of today's challenges is sharing intelligence, particularly on multinational operations where national legislation may place limits on doing so. Nevertheless, these issues have to be overcome because experience has shown us many times before that intelligence must be integrated at every level of command, and across and between agencies engaged in COIN.

For much of the British Army's history, its soldiers have trained and then fought alongside local forces. The need for capable local forces which can maintain effective security has not changed. They remain central to the plan in Afghanistan, and were so in Iraq. In both cases considerable effort and resources have been needed to give them the capability to maintain the longer-term security for their own countries. This requires a very 'hands on' approach. Building effective forces is much more than simply teaching soldiers what to do and then expecting them to go out and confront violent and often fanatical adversaries. In Iraq, we formed small Military Transition Teams, responsible for training and advising the Iraqi Army. In Afghanistan, as part of General McChrystal's plan to build the ANSF, we have moved beyond training and mentoring towards a full partnership with our Afghan counterparts. Forging a trust-based relationship has proved to be a crucial part of the development process. Having British soldiers and marines training and fighting alongside first their Iraqi allies and now the Afghan National Army and the Afghan National Police provides a clear statement of intent: that our forces are prepared to take exactly the same risks, and face the same dangers, as those fighting for their own country.

Both partners benefit from this approach. British forces provide expertise and the many enabling capabilities such as medical support, firepower and intelligence, which the ANSF are still developing. Their British partners benefit from what they learn from their Iraqi and Afghan counterparts, and the improved local knowledge and greater understanding of an area and its people that comes with effective partnering. Embedding our soldiers in this way is not, however, risk-free. They have to operate independently from the main body of their battalion or regiment, and their day-to-day safety depends on that all-important bond of mutual trust between local forces and British troops. This can, and indeed has, broken down with tragic results, but this is very much the exception. However, the British soldier can be relied on to get on with people, and the approach of working closely with local forces is proven and continues to pay dividends. After all, training and developing the host nation's security forces and partnering and mentoring them on operations are essential parts of ensuring that the host nation can sustain long-term security without recourse to foreign assistance.

Everything we have learnt again about COIN confirms that it is a complex, challenging business; one, experience has shown, best not learnt on the job. Education and training are necessary to attune the approach of those who have to counter insurgency to the problems and more effective ways of dealing with them. After all, it is the practitioners who need to have the knowledge and confidence to adapt doctrine and the tactics they have been taught to meet the challenges they face; the education and training system requires keeping up with developments in the outside world.

Over thirty years of security operations in Northern Ireland equipped the British Army with a very responsive, highly adaptive training organisation that has the agility to respond quickly – often within twenty-four hours – to emerging trends in the theatre of operations. This approach served UK forces well while they were in Iraq and has been outstanding as the campaign in Afghanistan has evolved. The battle to neutralise the threat from the IED, for example, has focused the attention of military trainers, scientists and intelligence analysts, but it has been the agility imbued by our approach to training that has been important. It has inculcated the flexibility and pragmatism needed to adjust doctrine and drills quickly to match, or better still get ahead of, the insurgent. This is one way we can prevent doctrine from becoming dogma, as J F C Fuller so colourfully described:[6]

> To be seized upon by mental emasculates who lack virility of judgment, and who are only too grateful to rest assured that their actions, however inept, find justification in a book, which, if they think at all, is in their opinion, written in order to exonerate them from doing so.

Implications for Strategy and Tactics

We cannot ignore the fact that strategy and tactics must be derived from political objectives. Is the campaign in question in the national interest? Sir Robert Thompson, writing based on his extensive experience in Malaya during The Emergency and on his time advising the US in Vietnam in the early 1960s, made clear that the first requirement of government was to have a clear political aim. This was 'to establish and maintain a free, independent and united country which is politically and economically stable and viable'.[7] While he conceded that this aim might be too broad to be immediately achievable, his next point remains highly relevant to today:[8]

> In newly independent or underdeveloped territories it is essential to recognize that an insurgent movement is only one of the problems with which such governments are faced ... It would be futile to succeed in defeating the insurgency, especially by military means alone ... if the end result is a country which is not politically and economically viable, and which might therefore fall to the [insurgents] at any moment in the future, perhaps without a shot being fired.

The approach to COIN has to be broad-based enough to provide for the security and the political and economic viability of the country in question.

We cannot separate tactics from the strategy required for the campaign as a whole. One should follow from the other and a strategy that matches means and ways to objectives will keep the approach balanced. Balance is important, particularly since military tactics alone will not create the conditions for success, though effective military operations are needed to establish and maintain security. The key – and the central challenge – is to develop and then resource a comprehensive plan that addresses security, governance and development in equal measure. This is not new. There are several notable examples where plans have been developed that address the steps required in a comprehensive way: the 1950 Briggs Plan for Malaya; the plan which underpinned the Omani campaign in Dhofar in 1970; and more recently the 2007 Crocker-Petraeus Joint Campaign Plan in Iraq. Now the ISAF plan for Afghanistan reflects the concurrent requirements to improve the three strands of governance, security and development.

Keeping the campaign's plan and resources in balance, experience shows, helps avoid one aspect of the campaign from being unduly pressured beyond a level we can reasonably expect. Security operations, for example, are difficult and soldiers can expect to have to deal with a myriad of problems for which there may be no obvious or straightforward answers. Get the force levels right, and many of those challenges can be avoided. In future people-centric conflicts, delivering success will often need mass, whether it is the right number of troops and support helicopters, sufficient intelligence sensors or sufficient small ships. As we found in Iraq, forces that are designed primarily to conduct short conventional warfighting operations tend to compensate for what historically would be viewed as a shortage of troops with huge firepower. The bias of the equipment programme towards these capabilities over the last sixty years bears this out. But in wars among the people, when counter-insurgents resort to using a lot of firepower – often delivered from the air *in extremis* as a result of insufficient manpower – they are almost certainly losing. It is important, therefore, to have enough troops to retain the tactical initiative and to provide the enduring routine security without which, as I have emphasised, the population will not have the confidence to reject the insurgent or spoiler. Whether they are the host nation's forces – the ideal – or allies, enough soldiers are needed in the first place to train local forces quickly and efficiently.

With the right force levels in place, it is much more straightforward to use the right balance of tactics without recourse to firepower *in extremis*. ISAF operations in Afghanistan have highlighted the difficult balance to be struck between pursuing the insurgent, on the one hand, and safeguarding the population on the other. In April 2010, ISAF introduced guidance to reduce civilian casualties while still enabling ISAF to use force when necessary. It was needed because ISAF's use of force was causing civilian casualties and this threatened the mission. The challenge was to make soldiers think about what should be done, not just what could be done. They had the rules of engagement to use lethal force; the question they had to answer was should they use them as a situation developed or was there another way to bring things under control?

This opens up the need to be generally manoeuvrist in COIN, not just in pure military terms but in focusing on the intellectual and psychological aspects of the campaign, not just the physical; people and ideas are more important than holding ground or hunting the insurgent. The aim should be to create the conditions for government success using less force and more subtlety, and not just through COIN's classic tactics of cordons, searches, patrols, ambushes and surveillance work. Again, this is easier said than done, as the Taliban's IED campaign in central Helmand showed all too painfully. The proliferation of cheap, readily made, often highly sophisticated IEDs became a major challenge for several years. However, the fielding of an impressive range of counter-IED technologies and the combination of outstanding soldiering from the UK task force and special forces, careful intelligence work, and the essential work by the Provincial Reconstruction Team gradually turned the situation around. By mid-2010, once the balance was right in terms of forces, tactics, intelligence and political and developmental support at provincial and district level, it was possible to make clear, if still fragile, gains.

Approaching Future Operations

A pragmatist might answer the question of how to approach future operations 'with care'. Much depends on the first principle of COIN which is 'Political Purpose has Primacy'. If governments decide it is in the national interest to undertake a future COIN campaign, or one perhaps characterised in terms of a more general stabilisation operation, then Iraq and Afghanistan provide several prompts that if followed should help avoid some of the painful challenges those involved faced.

The first point to recognise is that countering insurgency takes time: time to restore security; time to get political processes back on track; time to address the root causes of whatever real or perceived grievance prompted the insurgency; and time to change the perceptions of those involved, in the theatre of operations, regionally, internationally and at home. Time is one of the many resources that COIN requires – the overall bill may be less if one prepares properly and acts in a timely manner – yet the time available to politicians may well be less than that which is needed to restore security and to resolve the problem. Heavy domestic media and public opinion are also factors that serve to foreshorten political timelines.

One important challenge for any future campaign to overcome is the historical propensity to struggle in the early stages. Most campaigns have not got off to the most promising start, and that inevitably takes time to resolve. The most notable exception is the Omani campaign in Dhofar between 1970 and 1976, where the plan was written using the doctrine available at the time and coloured by a great deal of experience from past campaigns. As Major General Tony Jeapes, one of the main protagonists, later noted:[9]

> The Dhofar War was a classic of its type, in which every principle of counter-insurgency operations built up over the previous fifty years in campaigns around the world by the British and other armies, often by trial and error, was employed. It was probably only the third campaign after Greece in the 1940s and Malaya in the 1950s and early 1960s to be won against a Communist armed insurrection.

Jeapes's point about principles opens up the wider issue of the utility of doctrine. Until David Petraeus introduced his new Field Manual into the US COIN debate in 2006, it was difficult to see whether doctrine had any influence on campaign design or conduct in Iraq. By late 2010, doctrine was featuring strongly both in discussion and in shaping the approach in Afghanistan, and a great deal of effort continued to be applied to getting the thinking about COIN right before defaulting to developing military tactics and action. Doctrine is not, however, just about producing books. Doctrine has to be taught to keep the ideas it contains alive. We cannot expect commanders and their staff to be immediately comfortable with what can be, as experience has shown, a most challenging form of warfare if we do not attune their minds to its theory and its pitfalls.

Revising courses at the Joint Services Command and Staff College and our service arms schools is one response, but much effort has gone into ensuring that our forces have a broader intellectual preparation for COIN and stabilisation operations. This has included, for example, developing a small cadre of officers and non-commissioned officers familiar with the language, history and culture of Afghanistan and its region, who provide skilled advice to our commanders in the field. Conscious that the British Army needed a focal point for stabilisation and COIN, it established its own Afghan COIN Centre in 2009 to develop new doctrine and tactics and to educate soldiers and their civilian counterparts in current thinking. Once again, the idea of such a centre is not new; one was set up in the Malayan Emergency in 1949, another in Kenya, and the US military established one in Iraq in November 2005. The British COIN Centre has had a remarkable effect on our understanding and our approach. It has focused our thinking about COIN and it has made extensive use of our own recent and historical experience, and that of our allies, to develop very relevant and often much-needed responses to problems as they have emerged in Afghanistan, or in terms of more general strategic and operational issues at home. These have been articulated in a wide range of pamphlets, lectures, lessons and multimedia products tailored for each specific audience.

The theory contained in doctrine is, as all good theories are, relatively straightforward. The challenge is that the context continues to evolve. The legal and administrative frameworks in which operations now take place is constantly changing; the accelerated effect of globalised communications and media has to be addressed actively to reflect the myriad interests in the myriad of audiences both at home and in the theatre of operations; and insurgents continue to develop their networks, tactics, use of mass media and fundraising. This last point brings in the complex and challenging issue of the presence and often close interaction of organised, highly sophisticated criminal activity with major insurgency. Crime thrives in unstable environments where governments struggle to maintain order, and sophisticated insurgent groups need funding to pay their fighters and to fund their recruiting, training and equipment programmes. This nexus of crime and insurgency means that, if we needed to be reminded, military measures alone are not enough, and developing the host nation's police force to impose security needs to be in parallel with developing its law enforcement capability.

Against this backdrop of change, which most now recognise as becoming increasingly complex, the British Army's latest doctrine lays out principles which reflect not just contemporary challenges but longstanding ideas based on a great deal of experience. The challenge for our doctrine writers remains that of providing a framework of principles that is robust enough to absorb change so that it remains relevant. Accepting that every insurgency is *sui generis*, the doctrine provides just such a framework: recognise the political dimension; employ co-ordinated government action; integrate intelligence from a wide range of sources; develop and maintain an understanding of the cultural, social and political situation, not just the military; secure the population; neutralise the insurgent, physically and psychologically; gain and secure popular support; operate in accordance with the law and use minimum force; prepare for the longer term; and learn and adapt.

In 1969, the British Army published *Counter-Revolutionary Operations*,[10] which established a broad-based approach to military operations in the face of an insurgent or revolutionary threat. It built on Sir Robert Thompson's experience in Malaya and Vietnam, in that it introduced principles for government not just military action. The doctrine was very clear that 'the outstanding lesson from past revolutionary wars is that no single programme – political, military, psychological, social or economic – is sufficient by itself to counter a determined revolutionary movement'. The first requirement was, therefore, for a national – not just a military – plan. Such a plan would in all probability require emergency legislation to be passed to support the campaign; and a wide range of political, social and economic measures to be implemented to 'gain popular support and counter or surpass anything offered by the insurgents'. This needed an effective organisation to be set up to co-ordinate civil, police and military action at all levels; an integrated national intelligence service to be established; the police and armed forces built up to establish and maintain security; and imposing whatever control measures were necessary 'to isolate the insurgents from popular support'.[11] All this should sound very familiar because little has happened to challenge the efficacy of such a model, and we can see the elements it contains in ISAF's approach in Afghanistan.

The institutional challenge we face, however, is that the model laid out in military doctrine since 1969, and in due course embodied in campaign plans in Iraq and Afghanistan, is that it is really doctrine for a government response. It is a model for a politically led, whole-of-government approach of which the military contribution is one part. Military doctrine may address the needs of the military planner and the military practitioner, but all contributing parties should be familiar with the tenets of COIN if practice is to match the theory. Political primacy and co-ordinated government machinery are central to effective COIN, certainly if concepts such as the 'Comprehensive Approach' are to have any campaign effect at all. Lord Ashdown spoke in 2008 of the need for such co-ordination in the context of Afghanistan:[12]

> First we have to agree a strategy. Even the wrong one would be better than what we have at present, which is none. Second we have to give whoever it is in charge of the international effort, the authority to bash heads together and co-ordinate action, especially when it comes to international aid. Third, we have to co-ordinate military action with our political aims. Lastly, we have to have priorities, and the ability to concentrate on them.

Much has changed since then but the need remains to address the priorities he noted. In the period of withdrawal from empire, British colonial administrations could call on civil servants who themselves had served in the armed forces. The world has moved on and today's challenge is to institutionalise a whole-of-government approach, if necessary with doctrine, that not just the military espouse, but the political and inter-agency communities understand and support as well. The response required is one that efficiently orchestrates all of the military, civilian, multinational and host nation elements of the Comprehensive Approach. We established the Policy Action Group in 2006 in order to bring greater co-ordination to Afghan and international efforts. Chaired by President Hamid Karzai, the Group provided the forum in which the key issues could be debated and the strategy or way ahead agreed. Co-ordinating the international effort in a campaign as complex as Afghanistan is a huge task, but one that cannot be carried out in a vacuum. Experience shows that the work of the host government and its allies benefits from the appointment of a high-profile and authoritative individual with responsibility for co-ordinating the international effort in its support.

Difficult, But Not Impossible

Writers on COIN have pointed out consistently that establishing or re-establishing security is important but it is only one part of the overall task. General Sir Frank Kitson summed it up neatly when he said, 'There can be no such thing as a purely military solution because insurgency is not primarily a military activity'.[13] However, what Kitson said, along with that other influential COIN practitioner-turned-theorist, Sir Robert Thompson, was that effective security operations enabled the necessary political activity needed to resolve the problems that had caused the insurgency. Without effective security, there could be no hope that the insurgency would be countered. This has not changed, and there are no shortcuts to achieving it. While other means continue, a government's first responsibility is to establish effective security for its people.

The British armed forces continue to adapt to the challenges of war in Afghanistan. Self-critically however, this 'transformation in contact' is still too localised and not yet fully in our bloodstream. While certainly a great deal of work is under way, the population-focused, often subtle and certainly hi-tech ways of fighting that we now take for granted in places like Helmand are still to be taken into the core of the armed forces, as we train and equip for generic operations. Understanding the vital role of the Royal Navy and Royal Air Force in such conflict is taking too long. Our US allies, by contrast, have made a great deal of progress. Having only six years ago abjured nation-building and counter-insurgency as things 'real' armies did not stoop to do, they now give stabilisation operations the same doctrinal weighting as those related to conventional offensive and defensive operations. In many ways, Afghanistan is a signpost to the future: it is a testing ground for us and our enemies. How we deal with the threat posed by violent extremism more generally, often embedded in dangerously radicalised states, is an issue that will dominate politicians and military officers for the foreseeable future. However, our armed forces cannot focus exclusively on a single version of conflict; traditional forms of state-on-state warfare cannot be discounted. The lesson from the last ten years is that armed forces will still have to be able to contribute to important stabilising activity in fragile and failed states. Building that capability is best not done on the job.

If there is one thing we have to keep reminding ourselves, it is that countering insurgency may be difficult but it is not impossible. The fact remains that it is complicated. There is no escape from that because it is a complex, intractable mix of factors of which security is but one, and where political, social and economic factors may well be far more important in the longer term. However without security they will be difficult to improve. The costs of all these countermeasures go well beyond the many more policemen, soldiers and auxiliaries needed to restore security. Security forces and those they are there to safeguard have to face a wide range of often indiscriminate and hugely destructive threats and attacks. This is the case until security and the normal political process are restored, lives improved and, to paraphrase General Sherman, the legitimate object of a more perfect peace is achieved.[14]

COUNTERING INSURGENCIES BY PREVENTING INSURGENCIES

Paula G Thornhill

Insurgency and counter-insurgency are fundamentally about a government's legitimacy to rule. Insurgents will exploit a government's lack of legitimacy to seize political power through the use of armed force.[1] Successful governments understand this dynamic, identifying fault lines within their states and striving to manage them responsibly. Counter-insurgency's (COIN) inherently political nature offers a useful way to assess fault lines and to anticipate eruptions along them by analysing a number of key factors. After all, one of the most tangible manifestations of a state's failure to manage its fault lines and lose legitimacy is to see fighting emerge along these lines. Awareness of these fault lines, an understanding of how competitors for power might exploit them,[2] and devising an effective plan to manage these divisions could prevent an insurgency from erupting in the first place. Thus by effectively identifying, analysing and managing COIN factors prior to the break-out of violence, governments could possibly prevent insurgencies altogether.

All nations have fault lines. The key to a government's legitimacy is to manage them peacefully. This is a significant challenge given the complexities of governing. For strategists dealing with this challenge, COIN theory provides a useful framework for a number of reasons.

First: it identifies those key factors that, when managed well, underscore a government's legitimacy and which, if managed poorly, can lead to violent political change. These factors include demography, infrastructure, geography, governance and security (DIGGS).

Second: it reminds leaders of the critical role external intervention can play in dealing with fault lines. It also reminds external governments that intervention is about *assisting* host-nation governments (or in some cases, insurgents).

Third: it highlights the importance of three planning variables (time, violence and victory) to governments and insurgents alike when fighting has erupted along a fault line.

Fourth: it reminds policy-makers that legitimacy rests with a nation's population. A government 'wins' its legitimacy every day by responding to its population's needs.

By successfully addressing these key COIN factors, a nation is better positioned to prevent insurgency altogether. In other words: a government can prevent insurgencies by pre-emptively applying a COIN template to identify and address its population's needs. This approach allows a government to peacefully manage its nation's fault lines.

COIN and the Identification of Fault Lines

The COIN literature is abundant and growing. It has received considerable attention since America's 2001 invasion of Afghanistan and 2003 invasion of Iraq, and includes now-classic texts, as well as some noteworthy new additions.[3] From these works, we can parse five elements and their components that are essential for the identification and management of fault lines within (and on) a state's borders: demography, infrastructure, geography, governance and security (see Table 1).

Demography

Insurgencies and counter-insurgencies are fundamentally about the unique needs of a population. Preventing and countering insurgencies hence requires a basic understanding of the size, distribution and key characteristics of a nation's population. David Galula argues that the larger the population, the harder it is to control; conversely a small, concentrated population usually favours government control.[4] Hence the size of a population may be relevant to preventing the growth of insurgency. A second consideration is differentiation within the population group – in other words, mapping the racial, ethnic and religious profile of the nation, and any sub-national groups contained therein.[5] For instance, does it include communities that distinguish themselves from others based on learned cultural practices, language or belief systems (such as concepts of God, views of the afterlife, ideas about sacred and profane, rules of conduct and methods of worship)?[6]

How a population then organises based on commonalities or cleavages along racial, ethnic and religious lines is also crucial to understand. How conducive are these societal structures to discipline? How coherently are they organised? And how easily might these structures be integrated into others? Assuming a government is inclined to do so, answering these questions could help it devise more integrative strategies for its various demographic groups.[7]

Conversely, if a group feels particularly disadvantaged by the government, it could represent a target population for co-option

Table 1: COIN Factors and their Essential Components.

Factors	Components
Demography	Population size/distribution, racial/ethnic/religious composition
Infrastructure	Road, electricity, water, port systems
Geography	Location, size, configuration, terrain, climate, borders
Governance	Political community, political system, leadership, policies
Security	Physical security (including intelligence), economic security

by insurgents. Indeed, how that group might be integrated could have a major impact on the outcome of an insurgency. Afghanistan historically offers an excellent example of this. During the Soviet occupation, for example, several disparate groups successfully united in an insurgency against the Soviet/Afghan government alliance. But after the Soviet defeat, the alliance quickly dissipated and old rivalries re-emerged shortly thereafter.[8]

Infrastructure

A second COIN factor for policy-makers and strategists to consider is a nation's physical and communications infrastructure. Infrastructure literally connects a nation together, facilitating the movement of people and economic goods. Through roads, railways, ports, telephone cables and other networks, a government can reach out more effectively to its population. However, underdeveloped or degraded national infrastructure can conversely be exploited by insurgents. As a basic rule, the worse a nation's infrastructure, the better an insurgent's operating environment.[9] This is generally for two reasons: the lack of robust infrastructure may indicate a more fractured national population, whose fault lines insurgents may probe; and insurgents are more able to isolate elements of a nation's population, win it over and eventually control it.

Moreover, as C E Callwell noted almost a century ago in his book *Small Wars*, the lack of robust infrastructure immensely complicates any COIN operation.[10] Because of the great distances and variable terrain that often characterise insurgent environments, the resupply of food, water and ammunition becomes a dominant operational consideration. The lack of infrastructure can also make COIN forces much more vulnerable because their supply lines present vulnerable points to attack and it is more difficult to concentrate government forces.[11] In short, the lack of infrastructure is usually both an indicator of significant fault lines and an important advantage for any insurgents.

Geography

Geography is not just a backdrop for counter-insurgency, but is a key factor in the assessment of national fault lines. In COIN, management of fault lines requires a government to understand the physical geography of its nation-state and the impact of the terrain on governance and security. It is particularly important to consider the landscape from the perspective of possible insurgents. Clausewitz was one of the first strategists to point this out when he noted in *On War* that terrain that was 'rough and inaccessible' favoured the insurgents.[12] Indeed, Galula contends that geography might play the overriding role in determining the outcome of a revolutionary war. Of the COIN experts, he provides the most systematic discussion of geographic factors when examining its impact on insurgency. The factors he examines are location, size, configuration, terrain, climate and borders.[13]

The location of a country matters greatly to an insurgency's eventual success or failure. A geographic location that isolates a country by natural barriers or sits in a region where other countries would likely oppose an insurgency usually favours the existing government. The size of a country also matters: generally, the larger a country, the more difficult it is for a government to protect and control its territory. But a country that lends itself to geographic compartmentalisation (for example, Malaya) tends to favour the counter-insurgent. Moreover, difficult terrain within a country usually favours the insurgent. Bard O'Neill explains that rugged terrain is associated with successful insurgent operations because it hinders government operations and provides inaccessible safe havens for the insurgents. In Indochina, the dense jungle was a tremendous advantage for the North Vietnamese and Viet Cong forces; the rugged mountains in Afghanistan similarly favour the Taliban.[14] Conversely, the existence of, or close proximity to less-rugged, more favourable areas of terrain facilitates government command and control.

Climatic factors are also important, although there is a disagreement in the literature. Galula believes that understanding a nation's climate is essential to an effective COIN strategy, and asserts that government forces are better able to operate under tough climatic conditions because of superior logistics and facilities. While O'Neill agrees that understanding climate is important, he asserts that bad weather, such as heavy snow or rain, works to the insurgents' advantage. Because their logistical needs are less than the government's forces, O'Neill believes the insurgents' relative combat effectiveness is greater under demanding conditions.

Finally, Galula reminds us of the importance of borders, both internal and international. As he notes, any border tends to favour the insurgents because they can exploit administrative and security disconnects. He contends that international borders in particular are easily exploited and, if neighbouring countries favour an insurgency, these borders can prove decisive to its outcome.[15] Border administration and control thus becomes one of the most important and problematic COIN factors.

Governance

How successfully a government meets its population's needs and manages its nation's fault lines determines its legitimacy to govern and its corresponding ability to prevent insurgencies.[16] O'Neill defines legitimacy as those existing aspects of politics that are considered moral (right or wrong) by the governed population or selected elements thereof.[17] This assumes that the more legitimate a government is, the more inherently stable it is likely to be, and hence the more resilient it will be to any insurgent activities.[18] O'Neill identifies four key elements of politics that underpin a government's legitimacy and conversely represent potential fault lines: political community, political system, leadership and policies.

A political community consists of those individuals interacting on a regular basis to make and execute binding decisions on a society.

The inclusiveness of this community and its ability to reach out to the myriad demographic groups of a nation-state can be a major contributor to regime stability.

O'Neill views a political system as the composite of rules, values and structures that comprise the basic framework for making and executing binding decisions, such as autocratic or pluralistic systems. Some of the twentieth century's most dramatic examples of successful insurgencies have been the identification of an existing political and economic system as a fault line by Marxist groups and the successful toppling of that system through violent means. The strength of the administrative bureaucracy is also an important part of this system, since it runs the state on a daily basis. Insurgents can exploit weak bureaucracies to their own advantage, but a strong bureaucracy can sustain weak, faltering leadership for a considerable length of time.[19]

O'Neill classifies leadership as those senior authorities possessing values consistent with the political system. A fault line can emerge between specific leaders whose behaviour is viewed as inconsistent with the expectations of its political community. This is a comparatively easy fault line for insurgents to exploit, as these leaders come to personify the disconnect that exists between a population and its government.[20]

Policies include the social, economic and political principles for governance: are they inclusive or discriminatory? Discriminatory policies against a demographic group create a readily accessible fault line for insurgents to exploit. They may seek changes to other aspects of governance, but this would be the way to precipitate a legitimacy crisis.[21]

In short, it is paramount that policy-makers and strategists recognise that insurgencies may be caused by a failure in one or more of these aspects of governance. If the existing government is seen as consistent and fair, it may be considered effective at governing a nation-state. Perceived inconsistencies or discriminatory practices by the governed population in any of these areas could become major fault lines easily targeted for exploitation by an insurgent group.

Security

In COIN theory, a symbiotic relationship exists between good governance and good security. Security focuses on ensuring a population's physical *and* economic security. The former broadly encompasses internal and external security as well as the associated intelligence apparatus. The latter covers secure production and exchange of goods and services.

Physical Security (Internal)

Internal security depends on the size, competency and professionalism of a government's police force. This force should provide sufficient security to enable other aspects of society to function. The police force tends to be the first organisation to perceive instability within a nation, including sensing when a fault line might erupt violently. This was the case, for example, in Algeria in 1954 when the Algerian police warned that an insurgency was brewing a year before the French government actually took measures to address it.[22]

An effective police force must in turn be supported by good intelligence and a fair judiciary. Effective intelligence operations can detect insurgent threats to the government and population before a mature insurgency materialises. How the government subsequently deals with these insurgents is equally important. An impartial, incorrupt judiciary must support the police and government policies in order to ensure fairness under the law.[23]

Conversely, shortcomings in any of these areas – the size, competency or professionalism of a police force, the intelligence apparatus or the judiciary – put, at a minimum, the credibility of a nation's internal security apparatus at risk. At the extreme, corruption in one or more of these institutions could provide an important unifying point for insurgents.

Physical Security (External)

A sufficiently large, competent and professional military is critical to protecting a nation from external threats and from mismanaged fault lines along its borders. Should an insurgency break out, this same military will have a decisive bearing on the conflict's outcome. Under these circumstances the military must be large enough to take on the insurgent force, be highly adaptive to successfully counter the insurgents' tactics, and maintain loyalty to the government throughout the conduct of COIN operations. The first two are challenging because they could require rebalancing and retraining a nation's military in wartime. The latter is particularly important and difficult to sustain during a lengthy and costly counter-insurgency.[24]

Similar to police operations, effective intelligence is essential to a successful counter-insurgency. In fact, timely, actionable intelligence is arguably the decisive factor in COIN operations. This intelligence is focused on gleaning detailed demographic information, understanding its nuances, and then crafting an effective strategy that eventually will win back the people's trust. Although straightforward in theory, this is a very difficult mission to execute during counter-insurgency operations.[25]

Economic Security

Economic security is another essential component of a nation's overall security environment. It is one of the most tangible manifestations of a population's belief that it can move freely to meet its material needs by equitably producing, distributing and consuming goods and services. Thus, it is inextricably tied to a secure physical environment. If a population lacks confidence in its physical security, it is virtually impossible to encourage the interaction in the marketplace essential to a functioning economy. Moreover, the population must believe in the openness and fairness of the marketplace. A government's failure to meet either of these conditions could easily create an economic fault line for insurgents to exploit by turning institutionalised economic discrimination into a rallying point for the population.[26]

Gauging Potential Insurgency

Using these COIN principles, policy-makers and strategists can execute a 'quick look' assessment of their nations' fault lines that includes evaluating their current or potential volatility (see Table 2 below).

Such analysis requires reflection and honesty on the part of the policy-makers, which are often difficult to muster. However, even with this significant limitation, it could be sobering for national leaders to contemplate the demands and strains of waging a counter-insurgency operation if an analysis revealed the

Table 2: Fault Line Management – A Quick Look Assessment.

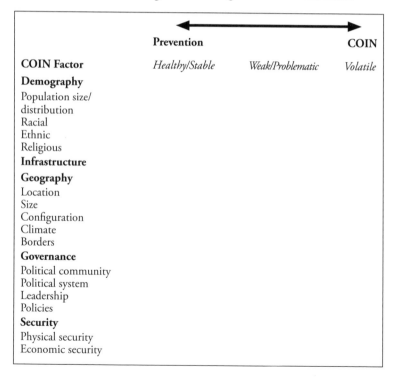

COIN Factor	Prevention ←————————————→ COIN		
	Healthy/Stable	*Weak/Problematic*	*Volatile*
Demography			
Population size/ distribution			
Racial			
Ethnic			
Religious			
Infrastructure			
Geography			
Location			
Size			
Configuration			
Climate			
Borders			
Governance			
Political community			
Political system			
Leadership			
Policies			
Security			
Physical security			
Economic security			

possibility of an emergent insurgency along one of its weak or volatile fault lines. At a minimum, they would need to weigh the costs and benefits of bridging their nation's fault lines peacefully (whether through internal actions or external assistance from other nations, international governmental organisations or non-governmental organisations) against potentially waging a long counter-insurgency. This is the basic overlap of countering and the prevention of insurgency. By analysing COIN factors in order to identify problematic or fractured fault lines prior to violence breaking out, and acting to address some of the most egregious problems, an insurgency might be prevented altogether.

Intervention by External Governments

Arguably, an external government considering involvement in either preventing or countering an insurgency along one or more fault lines should go through a similar analytical process. This would help reveal the extent of the challenge before them and should remind external governments that their actions are focused on providing *assistance* to bolster another government's legitimacy – not to reinforce their own (see Table 3).

The analysis should also suggest the levels of commitment, likelihood of success and the corresponding lines of action necessary for a successful intervention, whether preventing or countering an insurgency. A successful intervention should have multiple

Table 3: Fault Line Management – External Assistance.

	Preventing Insurgency	Countering Insurgency
Internal Management/ Conflict	Ensure/sustain government's legitimacy	Restore government's legitimacy
External Assistance/ Intervention	Provide *assistance* to foster current government's legitimacy	Intervene to *assist* in restoring current government's legitimacy

components such as improving governance, providing economic assistance, supporting infrastructure projects and building host-nation security forces. These lines should be executed under an integrated strategy involving national, international and non-governmental resources with an overall objective of assisting the enhancement of the host government's legitimacy.[27]

If a nation is already countering an insurgency, external governments should also account for one additional factor – what is the likelihood of another nation offering external assistance to the insurgents? External assistance is generally vital to the ultimate success of an insurgency. As Jeffrey Record states in *Beating Goliath*, external support 'is certainly no guarantee of victory', but there are very few examples of an unassisted, victorious insurgency against governments not already on the verge of collapse.[28] Therefore, the possibility of external support of insurgent forces should be considered by an outside government before it decides to provide assistance to a faltering government.

As a general rule, external assistance in preventing insurgency (such as building partner capacity) is cheaper and less likely to inspire external support for insurgents than an external intervention in counter-insurgency. Ironically, however, the management of non-volatile fault lines is regarded as a low priority for providers of external assistance, even though these may be the source of future insurgency. In other words, when external assistance could be of the greatest value to stabilising a nation, it is generally in the shortest supply. Using US military assistance as an example, a 2006 RAND report concludes that an early modest investment in many places to help host nations manage security fault lines is very cost effective. Yet, especially when compared to direct COIN actions in Iraq or Afghanistan, the US spends very little on broad-based, preventive military assistance programmes.[29]

Considering all these factors, an integrated external assistance strategy clearly requires a long-term commitment to the host nation. Due to competing domestic and foreign demands, varying views of the challenge, the long time horizon, and the uncertainty of success, there are often limitations to the provider nation-state's resources, leadership and political will, which hence undermine the success of a prevention or COIN effort. Based on these limitations, a supporting government should offer external assistance if it meets four conditions:

1.   It is willing to assist rather than dominate the host nation
2.   It is confident it can sustain its efforts in a way that enhances the legitimacy of the host-nation government
3.   It understands that expenses (in money and lives) are likely to increase as fault line management moves from prevention of insurgency to COIN
4.   It recognises the complexity of the undertaking and is willing to exercise considerable patience before seeing tangible outcomes.

Strategies for Fault Line Management: Key Variables
When fault lines are assessed as problematic or volatile, handling them effectively is of great importance to the affected government's legitimacy. Government strategies to deal with such fault lines need to be formulated according to three key variables: time, violence and victory. These concepts are critical because they matter deeply both to a government and to (would-be) insurgents, but for very different reasons.

Time
Insurgents and governments generally have very different time horizons. A government's perspective on the amount of time available to address a problematic or volatile fault line is a function of whether or not it is preventing or countering an insurgency. In prevention, a government tends to have more time to manage fault lines if a population believes key issues are being addressed and

security is tolerable. Would-be insurgents, however, will be looking for opportunities to exploit these fault lines at the same time and will strive to exacerbate instability by undermining any government initiatives to address the fault lines.

Once a violent struggle has emerged, however, a government's time horizon is shorter than the insurgents'. This is especially true when it comes to the restoration of security and essential services to a population. Indeed, a well-established, direct correlation exists between this capability and the overall effectiveness of a COIN campaign.[30] Insurgents will be much attuned to this and craft a strategy to do everything possible to extend the insurgency's time horizon. As T E Lawrence noted, 'our cards were speed and time, not hitting power'. Mao's protracted struggle is the most famous example of time being used by insurgents to maximise strategic advantage. In a protracted struggle, every day an insurgency survives is strategically important.[31]

Violence

One advantage insurgents have is the ability to systematically integrate varying levels of violence into their strategy from the outset. Initially, this allows insurgents to deceive the targeted government about their objectives. As Galula points out, as fault lines become more volatile, governments tend to accept higher levels of violence as 'normal' rather than as indicators of a possible insurgency.[32] Hence, governments are less inclined to take more decisive COIN actions early in a conflict. The lagging reaction of French and Algerian authorities to escalating violence in Algeria epitomises this. Their tendency to underestimate the significance of violent activity in Algeria in the early and mid-1950s ceded strategic advantage to the insurgents.[33]

Put on a continuum, when a fault line violently erupts, governing authorities tend to assume a greater level of stability then frequently exists. They are more likely to see early violence as criminal activity than as an act of war and therefore do not tend to consider the need to counter an insurgency at this point. This gives strategic advantage to the insurgents – they are executing early phases of their strategy often before a government recognises the insurgency, much less has crafted a strategy to counter it.

Victory

Finally, while legitimacy conferred by the population is the objective of both the governing authorities and the insurgents, the measures of victory are very different. 'Victory' for governing authorities would ideally occur without any fighting; and the successful management of fault lines would remove any insurgent claims to legitimacy. If unsuccessful, a government must be able to identify the fault line(s) that has violently erupted as early as possible and work to manage it effectively. Most importantly, this requires the restoration of physical security. It must also encompass improved governance through activities such as better or restored public services. In the process, the government must also be able to discern who the insurgents are, which insurgents are irreconcilable and which can be reintegrated into the population. All of this requires the government to fight the insurgents while reasserting its legitimacy with the population. When this approach is well executed, the insurgency will eventually dissipate.[34]

For insurgents, the mere act of fighting is a 'victory'. As mentioned previously, the longer they can sustain this capability, the better it is for the insurgents' cause. By simultaneously reminding a population of a government's ineffectiveness through violent activities while reaching out to that population through the provision of essential services and security, insurgents begin to demonstrate their legitimacy to govern. In this sense, insurgents are executing what J C Wylie calls a 'cumulative strategy' – they 'win' with each victory they accumulate through individual acts of violence against a government. In this way, they incrementally erode a government's legitimacy.[35] Fighting in any form is a victory for insurgents, as long as it does not alienate the majority of the population. The 'virtuous cycle of violence' for the insurgents is thus: the more acts of violence insurgents commit against government forces, the more victories they accumulate; the more victories they accumulate, they better able they are to offer viable alternative security and governance models to the population; and the better security and governance insurgents provide, the more likely they are to win over the population. Most importantly, as noted above, the insurgents have the luxury of time, so they can determine the frequency with which they repeat this cycle. Executed effectively several times – and without challenge – the insurgents may be able to eventually wrestle the legitimacy and ability to govern away from the existing authorities and assert their right to govern in its stead.

Conclusion

All nations have fault lines. The key to a government's legitimacy is to identify, understand and manage these fault lines peacefully. This is a significant challenge given the myriad complexities of governing. For policy-makers and strategists grappling with this challenge, COIN theory provides a useful framework because it is fundamentally about legitimacy. Thus COIN theory helps:

1. Identify those key factors that, when understood and managed well, underscore a government's legitimacy; and when managed poorly can prompt a group of individuals to seek political change through violence. These factors include demography, infrastructure, geography, governance and security

2. Remind policy-makers and strategists of the critical role external intervention can play in dealing with fault lines – prior to and after violence breaks out. Further, it also reminds external government planners that intervention is about *assisting* either governments or insurgents in asserting

their legitimacy to rule, not winning on behalf of the intervening nation. External governments should intervene only when they have a good understanding of the fault lines in the nation-state they are assisting, and the resources and commitment to make a difference. Without meeting all of these conditions, the intervention could easily fail

3. Highlight the importance of three planning variables – time, violence, and victory – to governments and insurgents alike when fighting has erupted along a fault line. A government sensitive to these variables will work assiduously to craft a strategy that denies insurgents strategic advantage by moving quickly to stop violence and recapture legitimacy. Conversely, insurgents will strive to exploit these three elements to their strategic advantage. The longer and more violent their struggle against governing authorities, the more likely they are to assert their own claims to legitimacy

4. Most importantly, emphasise to policy-makers and strategists that legitimacy to govern rests with their nations' populations. Governments 'win' their legitimacy every day by understanding and responding to their populations' myriad needs.

By successfully monitoring and addressing these key COIN factors, a nation is better postured to avoid an insurgency altogether. This is the irony of COIN prevention: one of the best ways for a government to prevent insurgencies is to pre-emptively apply the same template used to respond to COIN to identify and address its population's needs. This allows a government to peacefully manage a nation's fault lines on behalf of its entire population.

FROM INSURGENCY TO STABILITY TO DEVELOPMENT: IN AFGHANISTAN AS AFRICA

Anthony Arnott and Greg Mills[*]

> The military is inherently corrosive to development, but necessary too. It's a bit like treating cancer with chemotherapy. You try and kill the disease – the insurgent – before the patient – Afghanistan.
>
> (US Marine General, Kabul, May 2010)[1]

About the same size in landmass as East Timor, Kuwait or Slovenia, there is little in Zabul province, Afghanistan. Its bleak, dusty moonscape is punctuated only by green islands of orchards along the two main rivers. But it cannot produce enough to feed its 275,000 people. And it certainly does not add value to these goods. Moreover, there is just a trickle of USAID-provided electricity to the capital Qalat – enough for a few hours a day of basic services, but little else.

Only 10 per cent of Zabul's men are literate, and under 1 per cent of its women. The province's governor, Muhammed Ashraf Nasari, holed up in his residence in Qalat, said in April 2010 that nearly 70 per cent of positions in his administration remain unfilled due to a lack of skills.[2] He complained also of neglect. He had been visited once over the preceding year by a minister from Kabul, and just

---

[*]   This article reflects the results of research conducted during April–May 2010 in Kandahar with the Prism Group. Grateful appreciation is expressed to Major General Nick Carter, Brigadier General Dickie Davis, and the head of the Prism Group, Colonel Ewen McLay, for their kind professional assistance during this secondment. All views remain the authors' alone.

for two hours. And his annual budget of $28 million offered little latitude for imaginative action, if there was any about.

It is a perfect environment for the insurgent. Not only is there a lucrative target in the form of Highway One, which links Kandahar with Kabul, running right through the territory, but its 63 km southern border with Pakistan makes it an ideal transit range for Taliban. But they are not all imported. To the contrary: a combination of a lack of job opportunities, weak central authority, Pashtun tribal alienation from Kabul, and growing unhappiness about corruption make this region a perfect recruiting ground. As one businessperson in Kandahar who had been forced to close his plastics factory put it:[3]

> I had a meeting with my 85 staff. I did not want to tell them they were to lose their jobs as they were very poor and I knew that they would not have any food for their families. I said to them that I would try to find them jobs with others. I told them three times, and eventually people stood up and said that they did not have professions and that if the government did not provide jobs for them they would have to go up to the mountains to fight.

Indeed, Afghanistan's conflict is beset with fault lines. The split between urban and rural populations equates roughly with the divide between those who favour modernising influences and forms of governance, and those who prefer a more traditional version of it, where religion and tribe is to the fore. In this, however, there is widening inequality, between the haves and have-nots, between those who play the game of nepotism for reasons of power and personal financial advantage, and those who are left out of the game altogether. There are further geographic differences, also fuzzy, between Pakistan and Afghanistan; a border that separates states but divides a nation. And in the conflict's resolution, there are differences too between defining military success and political victory; and between ensuring stability and development, which may not mean the same thing.

There has been impressive economic growth since 2002, estimated at an average of around 12 per cent per annum during the 2000s, peaking at 30 per cent in 2003. But as much as 80 per cent of this has been driven by the donors, and much has been Kabul-centric (as any visit to the city testifies). A thriving bubble of traffic, new shops, wedding palaces and restaurants, it was estimated that the capital, designed for fewer than 600,000 people, by 2010 housed more than ten times this number as homes literally climbed their way up the city's grey-brown surrounding hills in chaotic heaps.

For the majority of Afghanistan's 28 million people the living situation remained much the same – desperate. More than half the population still lived below the poverty line, unemployment was at least 40 per cent, and the average annual income was around $460. Its Gini coefficient ranked it as the third most unequal country in the world, with only Angola and Equatorial Guinea worse. Afghanistan imported ten times more than it (officially) exported. Government revenues were under $1 billion while expenditure was nearly $3 billion. The sustainability of this situation was, by 2010, compounded by the huge annual expenditure (estimated at $8 billion) on the Afghan National Security Forces, a tab picked up then primarily by the US government.

Yet the international community was seen by many not to be uplifting Afghans *per se*, but rather creating an environment benefiting a small political dynasty. Donors had got into the bad habit of identifying, analysing and proposing, but seldom implementing solutions to obvious problems. And when they did, they spent money on projects that were hopelessly conceived from a commercial standpoint, such as the Bost Airport complex in Lashkar Gah in Helmand. There, $52 million was spent (mostly by USAID, partly by the United Kingdom's Department for International Development, DfID) on an airport that handled just one civilian flight a day by May 2010. The carrier, Pamir Airways, it seemed, contrary to their slogan, were somewhat hesitantly 'flying to globalisation'.

A walled area demarcating a planned agro-industrial park sat forlornly on one side of the Lash runway, expecting investment that seemed unlikely to appear without someone else subsidising it; at which point it would cease to be good business but speculative politics. Moreover, the long-term viability of the airport was dubious, too, given the creation of massive air infrastructure (including a 12,000 foot runway) nearby at Camp Bastion, which presumably will one day be handed over to the Afghanis.

The same had happened in Kandahar City, where the industrial park sat largely vacant to the southwest of the city. A world-class USAID-installed site capable of housing 150 businesses across 33 acres remained idle because probably the most important of all industrial services – electricity – had not been supplied. Adjacent to the park was an Indian-built cold storage facility, capable of taking 5,000 tonnes of produce. The problem was, again, electricity and the small matter of an absence of produce. Build, it seemed, and they would not necessarily come, illustrating if nothing else that it would help to know what businesspeople – like Afghanistan's citizens – wanted first, and then act on it. This only increased local frustrations. As a representative of the Kandahar Industrial Agency put it, 'Our meetings with donors are usually very interesting. They take lots of notes.'

Yet, by 2010, Western-led forces were much better placed than at any time during the preceding decade to deal with Afghanistan's security challenges. The number of International Security Assistance Force (ISAF) troops surpassed the 140,000 mark, the numbers in the south (56,000) virtually equalling those countrywide just four years earlier. More troops and more focus has meant that ISAF has been able to get its troop-to-population densities better aligned to doctrinal aspirations of twenty to twenty-five counter-insurgency troops (ISAF and Afghan National Security Forces) per 1,000 population. And critical enabling assets such as helicopters have increased tenfold in the south in four years. Along with improved mine-proof vehicles, better training and understanding of local conditions and actors, and improved targeting, intelligence, reconnaissance and communications, have all greatly improved ISAF combat power.

By 2010 there was additionally a much greater understanding of the local tribal, familial and personality dynamics. For one, there was nascent appreciation of the symptoms of the insurgency and jihad and the underlying motives, notably the difference between urban and rural communities – violence is often used in the latter to protect a way of life and define manhood. And there was widespread appreciation of the importance of governance and development as facilitators of long-term change. As ISAF's then-Deputy Commander Lieutenant General Nick Parker put it in May 2010, the military was 'mowing the grass'.[4] Unless other lines of operation including governance and the economy, politics and regional/international diplomacy were linked, the grass (the insurgency) would simply grow back.

All of this was illustrative of the refinement in ISAF's counter-insurgency strategy, summed up as 'Shape' (public opinion, and targeting Taliban leadership through mainly special forces activity), 'Clear' (the insurgent through military means primarily – or, if the 'Shape' has been well handled, this could become the 'Steal', where troops take the ground virtually uncontested), 'Hold' (the security situation) while one 'Builds' (the economy and enables political reconciliation). Partnership with the Afghan government was seen as crucial throughout these stages, described in terms of their intended effect in separating out the insurgents from the civilian population in Figure 1.[5] Even so, it is the last phase – 'Build' – that no-one has still got particularly right in a post-conflict environment, whether in Africa, Afghanistan or anywhere else. The practice has not matched advances in the theory, even though lessons have been distilled and apparently learnt *ad infinitum*.[6]

This chapter reviews the challenges in building an economy in countries transitioning from conflict to peace, defined here as 'fragile

Figure 2: Separation of Insurgents from the Population.

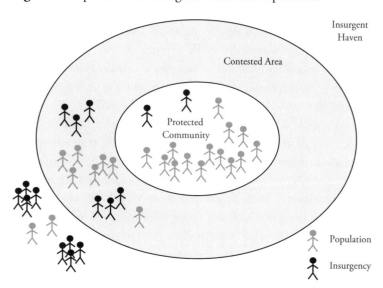

states', and considers what might be required to stabilise beyond the short-term aim of militarily countering insurgencies in places such as Afghanistan.

Developments in International Strategy

In Afghanistan, the international strategy to counter the insurgency has rolled out in three stages: first, improving security by protecting local communities and ensuring freedom of movement. This 'bubble' of protection is gradually expanded, using manoeuvre and special forces units primarily in the so-called 'contested area' where the insurgent operates, and later into the 'havens' where the insurgent resides.

The second stage has been that of stabilisation ('Hold'). Led by the Provincial Reconstruction Teams (PRTs), a set of stabilisation measures – including cash-for-work programmes, improved basic services (notably roads) and, critically, better governance – slot in immediately behind the military as part of an overall 'District Development Plan'. A variation on the 'protected villages' theme of Malaya and Rhodesia (or US 'strategic hamlets' and Portuguese 'Aldeiamentos'), it was in effect what General David Richards aimed to achieve in Afghanistan in 2006/7 with the 'ink-spot' strategy employing focused security and development action in Afghan Development Zones.

At the same time, however, some aspects of stabilisation were unsteady – especially electricity. For example, Kandahar City offered a unique development solution. Yet in April 2010 its inhabitants received just 16 megawatts,[7] just enough electricity to give each resident around six hours of daily power for a single light bulb. There were critical socioeconomic aspects to this. The Kandahar water supply was, for example, dependent on fifteen electrically powered pumps. A surge of power was a necessary (if not sufficient) condition for businesses to take root and, critically, by improving the quality of living, to give locals a stake in Taliban clearout. For want of $300 million annually – the same as putting 300 US troops[8] in the theatre for a year – ISAF battled bureaucratic obstacles during 2010 to get agreement on funding for delivering even another 20 megawatts of power.

But perhaps the even bigger issue rested on understanding what was to follow the stabilisation phase. In this, there are seven specific challenges.

The first is to synchronise short-term stability initiatives with longer-term development needs and strategies. There is a danger, for example, that humanitarian assistance could undermine Afghan farmers by deflating prices; or increase yields through massive, sudden extension schemes, which would not only be unsustainable, but also not followed up by the creation of markets in which to sell such goods. By 2010, more than 37,500 Afghan farmers in the south had benefitted from the 'Food Zone' alternative livelihoods scheme, along with a further 50,000 farmers reached under the US-funded AVIPA

(Afghanistan Vouchers for Increased Production in Agriculture) seed and extension project.[9] While the alternative livelihoods programmes such as AVIPA and the Food Zone offered a carrot of institutionalised governance to the rural areas, often bringing Kabul into contact with rural people for the first time, they were missing the developmental aspects of post-harvest handling, beneficiation, marketing and sales so crucial to establishing a value chain. As an agriculture ministry official in Kabul put it, AVIPA and the Food Zone 'are absolutely not sustainable. At some point things will have to give … [AVIPA] is run by a bunch of beltway bandits.'[10] Or as another with extensive experience in the pomegranate and grape industry in the south put it: 'They [AVIPA] have not understood what works in terms of crops, and what is needed after harvesting.'[11]

The second challenge is that donor strategies are not harmonised, and sometimes fragmentary and conflicting, rather than complementary. Three seed programmes in Helmand and Kandahar with different lead nations are a case in point. This may also be one impact, paradoxically, of over-resourcing, where there is more money to spend than good projects and local capacity, leading *inter alia* to 'engagement fratricide' by overloading fragile local systems of governance. By 2010, the international community was spending more than $100 billion annually on Afghan assistance. This includes more than $10 billion in development aid annually, amounting to $333 per Afghan man, woman and child per year. In some areas, such as the restive southern provinces, this concentration has been much higher. Yet given the lack of development impact – measured by the existence of an economy outside that supported by donor money – it may have been better (and considerably more efficient) if the international community had just bombed the country with bundles of money. Of course, not every Afghan receives this aid. Much of it goes into just a few hands. And much is spent on consumptive areas of investment, rather than productive ones aimed at expanding business and creating jobs.

The scale of the failure and wastage is staggering, even among hardened aid workers. 'Aid expenditure in Afghanistan is highly distributive', said one in Kabul. 'There is too much money. It is so gross in its volume that the effort is mostly to disperse it rather than disperse it in a wise, sustainable way.'[12] And where donors create jobs, this is normally in services, most notably construction. But sustainability is problematic, especially when the gush of donor funding is inevitably cut. As one Afghan policeman notes in this regard, 'The return of the international community [on its aid to Afghanistan] has been very poor. I would be very angry if I was them. I would look closely at my partners.'[13]

There are, however, some examples of success in this area. The World Bank-sponsored National Solidarity Programme (NSP) is a regional development programme dispensing $200 million per year. It deliberately steers clear of the big projects in preference of smaller-scale, community-led ones, typically offering around $200 per household. Not only does this method enable greater efficiency, but it also empowers local communities through democratically elected decision-making bodies called Community Development Councils. To date there have been over 40,000 community 'sub-projects' completed.

Third, much of the aid expenditure is spent getting it to the people, rather than actually hitting the ground. This is partly down to the high security and personnel costs in Afghanistan (where, for example, many civilians are on six weeks in/two weeks out contracts) and the sheer inaccessibility of the terrain.

Fourth, aid has never proven an effective way to develop any country, let alone Afghanistan. We should not believe that Afghans will behave differently to other politicians in assessing their choices, or that the country should develop differently to any other. Afghans are no different in the manner in which they respond to incentives – and disincentives – of donors.

This problem is, too, perhaps best illustrated by the civilian-led (and thus apparently more attuned to civilian needs) Helmand

PRT in achieving bang for buck. Despite much experience and having carefully devised outreach strategies, the PRT has achieved remarkably little stability and development for its annual budget of nearly $500 million. True, much of this money never hits the ground, being held up by bureaucracy (especially the US Commander's Emergency Response Program funds), and much is expended on private security. Nevertheless, the returns are still poor.

Fifth, aid programmes are by and large antithetical to economic development since they are often led by people either unfamiliar with or hostile to business.

Combined with a pathological tendency to *examine* rather than to *do*, attempts to create jobs in Afghanistan (as elsewhere) follow a pattern: an idea followed by a scoping study, normally backed up by a consultative process, an evaluation process producing a commission to conduct fieldwork to deliver a detailed report, 'workshopped' along the way by various representative constituents and appraised by peer reviewers in 'deep-dive longitudinal' processes. And the product has to be matched by a business plan, after a period involving at least one turnover of donor staff, is condemned to the shelf and forgotten when the idea is revived later – and the process started over again.

The traditional route of an entrepreneur with a good idea, borrowing money and starting a business, is lost in the focus on easy money, where talent is diverted to tapping soft donor money. The businessman or woman is seldom anywhere near this process. This results, too, in good ideas becoming international NGO causes rather than business cases.

Sixth, as highlighted above, aid has a deleterious impact on normal economic practices, diverting entrepreneurship towards the donors. Not only do the better qualified and skilled head for donor salaries (which, as a guide, are around twice as high in the managerial ranks in Kabul as businesses), but businesspeople feed off the economy.[14] This is not surprising in an economy in which there are few other productive alternatives. And the pestiferous impact does not end there: the grand contracts that go with donor and military expenditure (estimated at $330 billion for the US alone from 2001–10), reinforce bad governance practices.

For example, the principal host-nation transport contract to support ISAF totaled $2.16 billion in 2010,[15] providing 70 per cent of goods consumed by US troops in the field. The 6–8,000 truck missions monthly work out at over $25,000 per truck, per mission. Although there were eight main contractors in 2010, these missions are sub-contracted to others: Commander Ruhallah, who dominates the private security business along Highway One, guards 3,500 trucks per month at up to $1,500 per truck. He contracts to Watan Risk Management, a firm closely connected to the Kandahari powerbroker Ahmad Wali Karzai, the half-brother of President Hamid Karzai, which is run by Ahmed Rateb Popal and Rashid Popal, two of his cousins. Colonel Matiullah Kahn is a leading private security contractor in Uruzgan Province, north of Kandahar, whose 2,000-strong militia controls the highway between Kandahar and Tarin Kowt, Uruzgan's capital. He reportedly charges between $1,500 and $3,000 per truck to pass through using 'his' road. Trucking offers the ultimate lucrative protection racket. In the words of one logistics manager, 'You buy the security from the very people who will attack you if you don't.'[16]

Seventh, and finally, the size of foreign inflows has an inevitable upward pressure on the afghani (Afghan currency), making its exports less competitive, keeping the economy wedded to commodity exports and addicted to foreign inflows of money and imports.

All this means that the Taliban can continue to thrive in areas of low income and poor living conditions, where there is apparently little alternative to a grim subsistence lifestyle.

A View from the Trenches

Every country's development depends on its ability to sell things to others. By definition these have to be things others want to buy. On-the-ground interviews with traders in bazaars in Spin Boldak, Lashkar Gah, Kabul and Kandahar in April and May 2010 provide an idea of the scale of the challenge.

Very few Afghan-produced goods were on sale, and virtually no manufactured goods – save for clay pots, sweets, cool drinks, matches, reed-brushes and soap. Even seasonally adjusted, the absence of basic vegetables and staples was most notable in Helmand, the supposed breadbasket of Afghanistan. Apart from limited supplies of rice, cucumbers and melons, nearly all staples were imported: oil from the UAE and Tajikistan; flour from the US (aid being resold) and Pakistan; sugar from the US; rice from Pakistan and India; and potatoes, tomatoes, onions, apples, oranges and beans, all from Pakistan. Traders all cited their principal problems as, in order, high prices (they made on average $2 daily profit), a shortage of electricity (especially for refrigeration, the traders using ice instead), and security. Traders said that Pakistani rice, for example, was around $0.30 cheaper per kilogramme than the Afghan product, and 'better quality'; and cooking oil $1 cheaper per 20 litres from outside.

When asked why no items were sourced from Afghanistan, the most common responses were that Afghan goods were of an inferior quality, expensive and less abundant.[17]

When asked what the biggest challenges facing their communities were, Kandaharis overwhelmingly listed unemployment, an absence of stable electricity and high prices as their biggest concerns.[18] Yet in Kandahar the Canadian government has focused its aid money on education, health care and the restoration of irrigation. The international community is guilty of acting on what they *think* the local population need.

These are not just academic concerns. Take Timorshah, a young metalworker in Kandahar City who has been making gates, burglar bars and other items for the local market. His steel comes from Pakistan and Iran, his welding rods from China and his power is supplied by a small generator humming nearby. His profit, usually around 20–30 per cent, he says, is declining due to high prices. Or take the kebab seller who works near the governor's palace, and who uses an electric fan to fuel his cooking fire. The harder it blows, the greater the profit. Each megawatt hour (using Sri Lanka as regional benchmark) can add up to $1,740 to the economy. Thus one megawatt capacity could, using this benchmark, add $15 million to the economy over the course of a single year.

A sample survey conducted in Kandahar City in May 2010[19] of traders in agricultural equipment found normal seasonal patterns in prices and demand. The Afghan portion of their business remained much the same, though they acknowledged short-term benefits of seed, fertiliser and equipment via AVIPA purchases. The biggest constraints cited were security. The second problem was the cost of transport, due to a lack of drivers willing to go out to the rural areas. Foreign agency agreements with Pakistani traders were seen as a further impediment, especially to the quality of their product. Finally, a lot of agri-business has been set up with donor money. Yet those businesses doing best are those that pre-existed this flow of funds. The newcomers were unhappy about the lack of training that they have received from the donors, while the longstanding traders were unhappy with the market distortion it has created.

Kabul-based traders said that 95 per cent of all food consumed in Afghanistan was imported in the non-producing season. Even during the summer months, Afghanistan is still heavily dependent on external supplies. An estimated 170 trucks travel daily into the Kabul market, including 120 from Pakistan (forty-five of which carry potatoes), a handful from China, Iran and Uzbekistan, and the remainder from inside Afghanistan. This falls to 120 trucks during the summer.[20]

Afghanistan is not helped by the relatively high value of the afghani, boosted by aid inflows, making it expensive to export (penalising the producer) and cheap to import (favouring the elites and the traders). By comparison, the Pakistani rupee has steadily declined in value from parity with the afghani to nearly half of its value. Virtually no country has developed and diversified its economy without a cheap and stable currency, and Afghanistan will likely be no exception.

So What Economy?

Despite the abundance of advisers, the Afghan economy remains very badly understood. There are few reliable statistics, and little detailed knowledge of many key aspects:

- The micro and macroeconomics effects (such as on currency value) of aid
- The extent of the credit and financing system
- The use of more than one currency, including barter in goods such as opium[21]
- The extent of the penetration of the *hawala* money transfer system and the scale of remittances
- The scale of illegal trade
- The scale of corruption (we know that bribes, for example, account for up to 50 per cent of the value of land transfers and, according to one foreign businessman, 'The culture here is to take bribes and give bribes'[22])
- The scale of the black market economy (estimated at between 40 and 60 per cent of the overall economy)
- The barriers to trade
- The deterrent effect of instability on prospective investment
- The return of some two to three million refugees from Pakistan.

What is known, however, is that Afghanistan's export economy traditionally relied, before the Communist takeover in 1978, on smuggling and arbitrage (leveraging tariff differentials with the region), opium, agriculture, and some oil and gas. Today, agriculture employs 80 per cent of the workforce. There have been dramatic improvements in production post-Taliban. The country's cereals output was, by 2010, more than twice the 2001 level of 2 million tonnes.

Yet around 400,000 people today receive food aid in Afghanistan. Not only does this contradict the intention to ultimately reduce external dependency and ensure domestic development, but it is also a sober indication of the likelihood of Afghanistan supplying its neighbourhood.

Afghanistan has two major long-term comparative economic and development advantages: power and minerals. The country is well endowed with natural resources including gas, oil, gold, copper, chrome, iron, zinc, granite, marble and coal. For example, there are around 300 documented copper deposits countrywide.[23] The US Geological Survey has estimated that Afghanistan has as much as 36 trillion cubic feet of natural gas, and 3.6 billion barrels of oil and condensate reserves. During the 1980s, natural gas sales accounted for $300 million a year in export revenues (56 per cent of Afghanistan's total), mostly to the Soviet Union, with 3 billion cubic feet of annual exports. With the withdrawal of Soviet troops in 1989, the fields were capped to prevent sabotage by the mujahideen, although today some small-scale gas production continues. Apart from the May 2008 $2.8 billion agreement with China to develop the world-class (high grade at 2.3 per cent Cu) copper reserves at Aynak in Logar Province, little has happened due to the security situation. The giant iron ore deposit at Haji Gak in Bamyan, originally discovered in 1911, remains undeveloped. These two investments alone could create an estimated 45,000 jobs, as well as providing a revenue dividend to government, to say nothing of the uranium deposit at Khanishin in

Helmand, the Kundulayn copper resource in Zabul Province, or the Hai Alam iron find in Kandahar. Advisers in the Geological Survey division in Kabul estimate the potential revenue at $3–4 billion per annum, about the same as the country has received on average in aid since 2001.[24] In all, approximately 170 mines operate in Afghanistan today. Most of these are artisanal, and in coal, marble, semi-precious gems and salt, representing less than $40 million in annual value.

However, we should expect little to happen in minerals until the government changes its unattractive mining regime and the security situation improves. Currently, there is no automatic transfer of title between exploration rights and mining rights. The latter is subject to a bidding process, fraught with governance concerns. Moreover, as per the China Metallurgical Group Corporation investment in Aynak, the royalty fee expectation (at 18.5 per cent of gross) is unrealistically high. This is especially so given the almost total absence of infrastructure – notably power and rail – necessary for large-scale mining projects. In the opinion of experts, the provinces should be given a greater say in the distribution of exploration and mining rights and, subsequently, in benefitting from them.

Nonetheless, with China's continuously rising appetite for resources and given, too, the presence of so many untapped opportunities under Afghanistan's soil, the country will, with stability (and perhaps even without it) attract interest in this sector.

Despite its current situation, Afghanistan also possesses enormous hydro-power potential, which could not only feed local demand, but regional demand too. For example, Pakistan had a 2010 power deficit of 6,000 megawatts out of a requirement of 16,000 megawatts.

How to help Afghanistan realise this positive future is the key challenge for the international community, and if it is not met then the blood and treasure expended in ousting the Taliban will have been wasted. An earlier generation approached this problem differently: the $100 million spent on the Helmand Valley and Kajaki Dam schemes from the 1950s are enduring testimony to the focus, half a century ago, on leaving behind tangible schemes which could make long-term differences to people's lives. No doubt they both, especially the Helmand Valley Water Project, created a number of social ills, including the movement of nomadic tribespeople to permanent settlements to the southwest of Lashkar Gah, the costs of which the country is still paying today. Because the contemporary pacifier does not apparently do big infrastructure, today the focus is on governance – the 'soft' infrastructure aspect – which is easier to deliver, though more difficult to measure in terms of its impact, and certainly much less able to meet the local population's hunger for growth.

And there is something else. All of the talk about a better future for all Afghans is empty when one views the role of the elites in running Afghanistan for their benefit and brazenly extracting wealth, often at the expense of the people.

The Water in which the Guerrilla Swims

At the conclusion of a meeting with Spin Boldak's border police generalissimo Abdul Razziq in April 2010, his aide walked across the large room and turned on the satellite television. Up popped a programme on hair care for South Asians, 'Zing Hottie'. The presenters contrasted markedly with the scene just down the road at the border in Weish – a dusty, busy frontier town, termed 'Razziqistan' on account of the Afghan Border Police (ABP) chief's extensive security and business interests.

Razziq was in loose control of the border area from Nimruz province, near Iran on the West to Zabul on the East. The 3,700 ABP men under his command clearly revered him. Only thirty-three years old, he was anointed into the job by a combination of tribe and circumstance. A power-broker of note, dancing between our meeting and another with village elders and maliks, he provided security (of a sort) to Spin and surrounding areas. But he was clearly in on the game, without which he would not be able to access the patronage that ensured his local support and greased the wheels of local government, however wobbly it was.

'General' Razziq clearly illustrates Afghanistan's (and the West's) dilemma. Crack down on corruption and get rid of him, and the region could quickly degenerate. Keep him there, and the best one can hope for is to gradually wean him off corrupt practices. And the wily if wide-eyed generalissimo, of course, knows that the international forces are not going to be there forever, so he is also hedging his bets. It does not help in this regard that US President Barack Obama telegraphed in July 2011 his country's likely drawdown.

A key element in fighting any insurgency is separating the insurgent from the population. It is, to borrow from Mao, to alienate them from the sea in which the guerrilla swims. This is difficult where there are complex webs of tribal and familial loyalties. But that has not been the only reason why the insurgents are fighting against Kabul and ISAF, both of which are seen as foreigners by many of the Pashtun-dominated Taliban. There have also been religious or ideological motivations, rites of passage and financial reasons, with many Taliban being paid to fight. The going rate circa 2010 was $200 per month.

Increasingly there has appeared to be another reason: unhappiness with a lack of progress since the fall of the Taliban in 2001, and corruption and widening inequality. Corruption has taken many forms, from backhanders to policemen at dozens of formal and informal checkpoints, racketeering, drug trafficking, and nepotism in the big international contracts. Many of the key contractual players have been very closely related to each other, by marriage and by tribe, and to the bigwigs in Kabul. Governance and government has not, in Afghanistan, always meant the same thing.

In this respect Afghanistan operates no differently from many other states, notably some in Africa – along the lines of the 'politics of the belly', a primordial lust for power along crude racial, tribal, party, and familial lines, with patronage the key mechanism (and reason) for delivery. In this the government and business elite use their positions and influence to enrich themselves, families or kinsmen, where 'Material prosperity ... is one of the chief political virtues rather than being an object of disapproval.'[25] In this, 'In most African countries, the state is no more than a decor, a pseudo-Western façade masking the realities of deeply personalised political relations [where] legitimacy is firmly embedded in the patrimonial practices of patrons and their networks.'[26]

In this system corruption is institutionalised, as politics – like wealth – is kept closely in the family. As one Canadian police mentor has put it: 'Tribalism is underneath everything; every glance, every knowing look, every payment, every invitation, everything that happens is linked to tribal connections.'[27] Everything from policing appointments through investigations and prosecutions has been highly politicised. Given that the political elite makes these decisions, they in effect become above the law.

As in Sierra Leone and the Congo, instead of making long-term investments in productive areas of the economy, this system focuses on plunder – on creating short-term income-generating opportunities for personal benefit, based on consumption rather than production, and on extortion rather than taxation. As one US colonel observes in this respect: 'The culture of patronage starts at the top. People pass on up to the leadership, and cut down to their tribe.' Or as a senior Afghan official puts it: 'It is impossible to separate the Taliban from the power-brokers and the government. They make money in it together. It is nothing less than a mafia.'[28]

As is highlighted above, there are many means to this end: from punitive bribery of the local population, through to the benefits of security, logistics and other contracts. But mostly it is achieved through the absence of government vision, policy and plans for governance and socioeconomic development, and through the absence of the rule of law. Instead of being preoccupied with creating economic absorptive capacity, the government is concerned with ensuring security and distributing profits – in a word, on foreign relations (for continued aid) and local patronage and politics (to maintain control). Moreover, the economic system has been characterised by widening inequality, fuelling grievances alongside greed. Improvement to the life of the average Afghan has been limited, even though the success of any foreign and reform effort is ultimately to be measured by the extent of such benefit.

In this, the government, the power-brokers and the Taliban have all been intent on creating their own demand – setting the circumstances that allow them a role and revenue-creating opportunities, an Afghan form of racketeering. This has been exacerbated by a lack of central leadership authority and capacity.

In these circumstances, the best the coalition can hope for is to patch the security situation together, focusing on incapacitating the Taliban while bolstering and building the Afghan National Security Forces hoping that they can, over time, take the lead. This leaves behind the possibility that Afghanistan will quickly collapse without foreign troops and largesse. In turn, this ushers in the possibility of Taliban redux, the return of a government which promises to restore law and order, even if it is of the brutal extremist Islamic sort.

Perhaps the best way to imagine the choices confronting the international community is to think of oneself in the midst of a campaign as long (or perhaps longer) than the First or Second World Wars: what would be the one aspect that demanded changing to ensure circumstances changed permanently for the better? The answer should be to change the nature of the sea, as Mao might have put it, in which the guerrilla swims. In this case it means getting rid of the warlords, or breaking the power of the power-brokers. And it also means getting the basics right.

Getting the Basics Right
Countries transitioning from conflict have the overall challenge of providing a satisfactory long-term policy and governance framework,

while in the interim ensuring that there is sufficient visible change and economic opportunity to maintain stability. There is a very long road ahead if these states, from Afghanistan to Zimbabwe, are to function effectively according to liberal democratic and economic norms. But patience is limited.

Success in their development relies on sustaining a virtuous cycle, in which economic recovery and political stability are mutually reinforcing. Indeed, economic recovery has a number of political jobs to do: in the short run, it needs to placate or neutralise political opposition (both ex-combatants and those in the parliamentary legislature); build support for government in both the non-urban areas and the capital; and signal a return of confidence and change for the better.

The recovery process also has an economic dimension. Firstly, it must return per capita GDP to pre-war levels (adjusted for population growth and changed commodity prices). This is best done by restoring the traditional engines of any economy – natural resources and agriculture are usually key – to full production. Secondly, it must build the revenue base of the government to levels that allow public investment and service delivery to normalise. Thirdly, it must increase labour absorption to promote political and social stability and reduce poverty. Lastly, it must build the minimum infrastructure base for a modern economy, which requires focusing on power, roads and ports. Economic growth prospects must thus be viewed in the context of shorter- and longer-term constraints.

Shorter-term constraints are those that could most easily be addressed through direct policy action and could improve the prospects for short-term economic growth and political stability and human security. These include infrastructure such as roads and power. Usually, the limited capital-raising capacity and execution capacity of the government means that private sector involvement in infrastructure provision will be needed. But to bring about such participation, these governments have to improve another capacity: the ability to transact effectively with potential providers.

Despite their limited execution capacity, these governments should not stop leading and directing donor contributions, as opposed to adopting the agenda and preferences of the donor community. In particular, the institutional weakness of the donor community for comprehensive and all encompassing policy plans quite unrelated to capacity or political needs needs to be resisted. This is achieved by superimposing on such comprehensive plans a clear and short set of government priorities. Further, donor relations management needs to be addressed. Complex donor-imposed processes need to be attempted only after careful consideration: once embarked upon, such processes should be managed by dedicated units and *not* by line managers.

In terms of agriculture, a key requirement here is to establish secure land rights for those who use it productively; this means tackling the problem of absentee owners, and making land available to new farmers.

The extreme lack of capacity in the government below the ministerial level also needs to be addressed. Technical resources from third parties have to be properly used and integrated. This illustrates the need for sound *transacting capacity*. This capacity should include both planning as well as the capability for negotiation.

Longer-term constraints centre on the structural economic issues that need to be addressed over the longer term, without which any economy will be unable to effectively compete internationally and prosper. These include the need to establish an appropriate legislative/regulatory framework, and ensure systems of institution- and capacity-building and transparency. This stresses, too, the importance of sound macroeconomic policies, including competitiveness. The central bank must be authoritative and respected and not seen as captured by financial or political elites. Full currency convertibility is essential for such an open economy, and needs to include the full and unambiguous absence of all forms of currency controls.

Efforts to grow beyond the economy's traditional extractive base will be severely hampered by the absence of a proper banking system. Basic transactional, store of value and credit functionality needs to be built up. The financial system must be equitable – therefore policy should aim towards building an inclusive financial sector. In the short run, *remittances* are an important area of work.

There is also an overall need to create a competitive environment through, for example, ensuring diversity of supply. Similarly, openness to the international economy is key, and as it increases, alternative forms of taxation (other than customs) have to be found.

Conclusion: Learning to Flip the COIN
The following aspects of the political economy of fragile states need to be continuously thought through by the would-be stabiliser.

Aid: What is the link between short-term stability initiatives and longer-term development patterns on the role and space for entrepreneurship, and on currency values and competitiveness?

Political Elites: Do they distort market conditions? If so, how and to what extent? Do they inhibit economic competitiveness? What can be done to mitigate this? What is the effect of the international community's engagement (and contracts) on their role and influence?

Transport and Trade: Are there factors that constrain freedom of movement and of goods, relating to 'soft' infrastructure – people, policies, permits and processes?

Infrastructure: Are there 'hard' aspects significantly inhibiting economic activity? Why have they not been fixed? What is the impact of repairing them – are there vested interests that will be affected and if so, how?

Prices: What are the factors influencing prices? Are there actions that can influence these, and what would be the effect?

Goods and Services: Where are these acquired from? Why are they imported, and who benefits from this? Are there tariffs and other regimes (such as transport) that make this more or less profitable?

Regional Interests and Opportunities: What are the regional economic interests? What is the impact – in political and other respects – of strengthening or lessening these? How might these effects be achieved? Are there opportunities that have been neglected?

The International Community: How does international action affect the economy? Does it make it more or less competitive? What can be done to lessen its worst effects?

In answering these questions, getting the economic dimension to stability operations right requires addressing the following:

Focus on the Population Centres, Build a Sense of Inevitability of Change

In the case of Afghanistan, tribal and familial loyalties have helped to ensure loyalty to the Taliban cause, as well as the Pashtuns' traditional antipathy to outsiders, whether Afghan or foreign. It is a misnomer (and a common failing in counter-insurgency campaigns) to think of the Taliban as the minority: think of them rather as the population, and a winning strategy is one that changes that population's perceptions and behaviour.

ISAF's war against the Taliban and the system of governance that underpins their support can only be won, in the short term, by building a sense of the inevitability of change, especially in these centres. The population has to feel that things are changing for the better, that the government is a force for good. Hence the need for short-term spending on electricity along with actions that bring about a sense of such change, yet minimise long-term developmental distortions. Hence the need, too, for actions which deal with the governance conundrum, and not just from the bottom up.

Realise that the Elites Create their Own Demand

A huge influx of foreign donor funds from which local opportunists profit may be a means of short-term stability but is not a recipe for long-term governance and development. Again, in the case of Afghanistan, it is the system itself that is pernicious, and the main predators are not necessarily the insurgents, but rather a tightly-knit group of warlords – now known as the power-brokers – who profit from the continuation of conflict and the injection of international funds. They create their own demand.

Instead of taxes being imposed by and paid to Kabul, Afghans have been indirectly taxed continuously by those who themselves have to pay for their positions. And presumably the Taliban are pleased to hear that many of the key contractual players are very closely related to each other by marriage and tribe, and to the bigwigs in Kabul. Pashtun perceptions of their continued impunity and links to the top in Kabul play right into Taliban hands. This compounds the growing resentment of a lack of progress, corruption and widening inequality since 2001.

Of course, such a system is how Afghanistan has 'worked' from time immemorial. But it is just this level of grievance about the lack of governance and about the warlords that brought the Taliban to power in the mid-1990s. Unless ISAF can assist in changing this game, Afghans will continue to suffer and peace will remain elusive, no matter the number of soldiers installed in-theatre or insurgents eliminated. The existence of a parallel government undermines the Afghan government's writ and authority. By diluting the power-brokers, too, this offers a political path that is not tribal (one of the features endearing the Taliban to the marginalised, by moving against the tribal grain).

One means to do this involves the reviewing of donor contracts to local actors, employing a scorecard to change their behaviour, to invest more of the proceeds locally – to simply spread the wealth a bit better and more productively. Such a scorecard would insist either that contractors need a certain number of points to be eligible or receive a discount on their tender. This would be dependent on their score in a number of categories, including local ownership, female participation in management, records of tax payments, employee equity, local procurement and the employment of disabled employees.

Stop Going 'Tribal' on Stability Operations
What is a Kandahari likely to think – scratching out a living in the dusty city environs, where 800,000 fellow citizens make do with just 15 megawatts of electricity supply, and the security situation remains fragile at best, caught in the pincer between the Taliban and common criminals – when just 20 kilometres down the road are 25,000 international forces at the Kandahar Airfield living in comparative splendour with 100 megawatts of electricity?

The debate over Kandahar's electricity quickly became a tribal power struggle in the international community between those who saw it as providing fuel for the warlords and bad governance (and thus were against it), and those who understood its short-term counter-insurgency benefits. There is no gainsaying the need for a long-term power solution for the city, which involves upgrading the Kajaki Dam and other hydro facilities in Arghandab valley and elsewhere, along with power line and transformer rejuvenation. But 'perfect' should not be the enemy of 'good enough' in any stabilisation campaign, no less in Afghanistan as elsewhere. Bridging the gap between today and tomorrow benefits the economy, quality of life and, critically, the impression of security. More electricity to Kandahar has thus not only to be measured in terms of peak power, but also by stability of supply and a reduction in the frequency of outages, both of which, if successfully implemented, can lead to greater commercial productivity. It means that people can read at night, with improvements to education and in other aspects of quality of life. And it could reinforce government and international donor credibility. The bottom line is that it shows that the international community can deliver – and quickly – and are not just note-takers; and that the governor and government listen to the people and can deliver on their concerns, which is especially important at a time when many in the population are running scared because of the declining security situation.

But this raises a more profound question for post-conflict and developing countries at large: how to quickly create a sustainable surge of electricity? Diesel is expensive and can create problematic unintended governance consequences around the supply of fuel, for example. The international community has found it very difficult to offer a mid-level answer that goes beyond the local (generators) and yet is sustainable and relatively cost-effective when compared to diesel.

The industrial-scale rollout of micropower systems (defined as those producing up to 100 kilowatts) and development of a medium-power, non-diesel response offers great possibilities in the developing world, especially in fragile states. Hydro is the most common form of renewable energy used in this regard. It can be a cheap and simple solution. Water moves along a power canal or pipe, known as a penstock, which is usually the most expensive part of the construction. Each one-metre drop generates about one kilowatt of electricity. A small TV uses about 65 watts of electricity; a computer uses 300 watts. In a village of 100 homes, a 10-kilowatt generator can provide 100 watts to each home – enough to power a TV and two small light bulbs.[29] About 160 micro-hydro plants have, for example, been installed in Afghanistan in recent years.[30]

Micro-hydro systems potentially complement photovoltaic solar energy systems when water flow is seasonal or sporadic, though these systems are expensive and produce direct current, which has to be converted into alternating current with a resultant energy loss. By comparison, a 30 kilowatt hydro plant has been installed in Afghanistan for around $100,000.

In such an environment there are few clear wins, and it is careless to not exploit such opportunities to the full. The issue is not one of cost and resources, but the plethora of parochial agendas creating sufficient friction to paralyse these projects. With no coherence from the political level downwards, many of these projects stand alone and die alone. Again, the question of whether these projects would be better supported by the wider ISAF effort if the leadership were inherently more adept and familiar in these matters raises its head.

Align the Region with Small Steps
It is difficult, if not impossible, to imagine how Afghanistan's issues of state-building could be solved without Pakistan contributing positively to this task. How might this be encouraged? Until now, the preference has been to focus on meeting processes (which have delivered little) rather than small, functional steps, which could encourage a wider process of engagement.

While a lot has been achieved in this regard (such as the increase in trade from $40 million to $1 billion in a decade), much more can be done. This is partly dependent on improved policy, and partly on reduced prejudice. There needs to be continuing focus on reducing (or preferably eliminating) the incentives for smuggling, notably the tariff differential between Pakistan and Afghanistan. At the same time, there needs to be much greater focus on creating the opportunities for trade through, for example, the curtailing of transloading requirements (moving cargo from one form of transport to another), and the instituting of regularised exchanges between chambers of commerce and between journalists. Other Afghan constraints to be managed include high transportation costs (a result of both transport policy and the security premium), and the rising value of the afghani relative to the Pakistani rupee.

Pakistan does not just create a strategic headache, but one that pervades all levels, down to the tactical. Not only does the insecurity in the border regions allow insurgents to permeate with ease; the absence of law allows the tenuous (at best) passage of trade to be corroded by corruption – a truck of potatoes typically paying around 200 Rupees ($60)[31] in bribes during the relatively short passage from Quetta to Spin Boldak. Additionally, since the route to Islamabad runs usually through Delhi, the diplomatic relationship has to account for these sensitivities and maintain the delicate balance of power, ensuring that India does not establish too much influence in Afghanistan.

Fold Stability into Development, Build an Economy

While insurgents can provide some form of justice and security, they cannot do development. But until now the international community can justifiably have been accused of delivering only short-term vectored responses, where visible totemic large-scale development projects are largely ignored, yet critical to changing the perception of the international community as 'note-takers' and providers of little else.

There is little doubt that while security can provide a boost to economic growth, such growth is imperative for security. As one Kandahar businessman has put it: 'As a representative of the private sector, I believe that if the economy gets better, security problems will be reduced by 50 per cent. ... But today no-one is sure that they will get back home when they go out at night.'[32]

It would be useful for ISAF to think continuously about what the Taliban would like it (and the Afghan government) to be doing – or not doing.[33] The Taliban is said to be poised at a moment akin to Germany in 1942: they cannot win unless the other side has lost. That said, focusing only on countering the insurgency will inevitably be counterproductive in the longer term, since it means cutting deals and seeking balances of power with those whose modus operandi and interests are antithetical to good governance and Western interests, and which ultimately depend on and amplify tribalism, corruption, nepotism, inequality and violence of the sort the insurgents thrive on. Of course, some rapid expenditure (such as that on electricity) is necessary to encourage a change in perceptions, but much more has to be done to change the country's operating system – its governance software – without which the fatal flaws to the international campaign will persist.

The record on countries being changed from outside in a positive and lasting way is, at best, mixed. Many of the governance changes made to Africa by colonialism proved to be ill-fitting, hence the fifty ensuing post-independence years of widespread instability. Subsequently, however, those African countries that have performed better have been able to instil or adapt modernising reforms within an African version of government and cultural context. In the same way, much of Southeast Asia has been able to import lessons of successful economic modernisation from elsewhere and adapt these positively to their own ends. Indeed, the waning of tribalism as the potent organising social force along with openness to ideas from outside is a critical determinant of post-colonial and post-conflict success, as is the presence of a determined, reform-minded and technically competent leadership. Whether the international community can encourage this path will be decisive in whether Afghanistan will stand on its own two feet and not collapse with the inevitable international withdrawal.

Hold Donors and NGOs Accountable

The question here is simply: how does one achieve this when both have proven remarkably elusive in this regard? For example, QuODA (Quality of Official Development Assistance), a tool created by the Centre for Global Development's Nancy Birdsall and the Brookings Institution's Homi Kharas, compares the quality of aid for thirty-one countries and multilateral agencies, and more than 150 aid agencies.[34] The tool considers aid efficiency in four dimensions: maximising efficiency (spending aid in countries where it has the most potential to help); fostering institutions in recipient countries (co-ordinating spending with local priorities and budgets); reducing burdens (for example, cutting back on official visits and paperwork); and transparency and learning (achieved by sharing useful data on aid spending).

It is not the first to attempt to establish an aid efficacy template. Indeed, their efforts are on the back of considerable work over the past decade, including the OECD's Development Assistance Committee (DAC) 1991 criteria, and the later Paris and Accra Declarations.

The five DAC criteria have been widely used in the evaluation of development initiatives – efficiency, effectiveness, impact, sustainability and relevance. They have also been subsequently adapted for the evaluation of complex emergencies, becoming a set of seven criteria: relevance/appropriateness, connectedness, coherence, coverage, efficiency, effectiveness and impact.[35]

In March 2005, over 100 countries met in Paris and agreed to draw up a concrete scheme to achieve aid effectiveness, setting out twelve indicators and concrete targets. The Paris Declaration is based on five principles: local ownership, alignment of aid (with national strategies), harmonisation, results-orientated aid and mutual responsibility. In September 2008, more than 1,700 participants including more than 100 ministers and heads of agencies from developing and donor countries, emerging economies, UN and multilateral institutions, global funds, foundations and eighty civil society organisations attended the third high-level forum on aid effectiveness, hosted by the government of Ghana in Accra. The meeting adopted the Accra Agenda for Action, which focuses on aid predictability, ownership, the importance of partnering country systems and aligning conditionalities with recipient country needs, untying aid, reducing aid fragmentation and introducing transparency in mutual assessment reviews. These were to be in place by 2010, involving 'stronger parliamentary and citizen engagement and ... complemented with credible independent evidence.'[36]

The theme of aid efficiency in fragile states and conflict situations has been taken up by the Accra Forum, among others. The African Development Bank has established a fragile states facility, in addition to a post-conflict facility set up in 2003 to help such states both clear debt arrears with multilateral financial institutions and re-engage with the international community. Participants at the Accra Forum agreed that the development community understood that effective aid was most needed in fragile countries that could not afford the luxury of fragmented aid and high transaction costs. They stressed the need for quick disbursement of aid, with a focus on rebuilding state institutions and addressing poor people's basic survival needs. The Forum also called for aid agencies to develop flexible and streamlined procedures for aid delivery, including pooling for aid delivery, avoiding parallel projects and the division of local labour.[37] But all this is mainly focused on how money should be spent rather than on evaluating how well it is spent. As a result they are focused on process, rather than measurement of impact.

Thus it may be appropriate to investigate establishing a scorecard for aid and NGO effectiveness, including quantitative (and not just qualitative) assessments, such as jobs, business indicators, bureaucratic efficiencies, infrastructure, tax revenue, security and impact on marginalised communities (women, the disabled and youth). This should go beyond the notion simply of 'doing no harm', too often the benchmark for efficacy of international assistance. A threshold could be set which a project must score over in order to be continued. While donors might guard against negative assessments by setting their sights low, such a low-value project in terms of potential impact would then be judged against other priorities.

The importance of the primacy of politics sits at the heart of COIN, yet it is soldiers who find themselves in charge of this multinational effort, adaptable and capable as they are. Military men and women are finding themselves in roles that have traditionally been the domain of diplomats and politicians. New military structures, such as the British Army's Military Stabilisation Support Group, are being established to offset the absence of other governmental departments. We acknowledge that insurgency is largely rooted in economic and political spheres, therefore it would follow that the organism that is COIN should have the arms, legs, even heart of the military, but the brain should be that of an economist and politician. Whilst some progress has been made in this field through the appointment of a NATO Senior Civilian Representative, there is still work to be done.

Get the Politics Right

Finally, corruption, jihad, violence, instability, a preference for isolation and resistance to modernisation and reconstruction are all symptoms of Afghanistan's insurgency. The underlying causes, however, likely run deeper and concern urban/rural divisions, widening income inequality, tribal identity and lineage, concepts of *torbornwalli* (promoting intense competition between cousins often resulting in violence and vendettas) and *pashtunwali*, the habituation of violence, caste conflict and the role of martial experience as a rite of passage. Indeed, perhaps it should be asked if there is an ideological insurgency, or a clash of cultures exacerbated by the (financial) opportunities present?

This means, too, dealing with the representation deficit. In much of post-colonial Africa, to take another example, the moratorium on border changes imposed by the Organisation for African Unity coupled with weak systems of governance and fractured (and often fractious) nationhood has meant that governments have not had to respond to the disciplines imposed by contended frontiers, including the raising of armies and taxes. Coupled with an African moratorium on the discussion about its colonial borders, African leadership has not been encouraged to adhere to these disciplines and to extend governance to the edge of these frontiers. Hence rule of the capital and its surrounds was equated with national authority, even though this did not reflect realities on the ground.

In Afghanistan, Kabul's ongoing disinterest in the affairs of the provinces, especially those of the south, is a major constraint on extending national governance. The executive style of governance has led the capital to prefer to deal with the provinces by proxy power-brokers, such as the president's appointment of his half-brother.

For example, as noted above, just one minister visited Kandahar's neighbouring province, Zabul, in the twelve months prior to April 2010, and then for just two hours. The governor of Kandahar regularly complained in 2010 that 'I have never heard a minister cancel his trip to Europe. But they do so regularly to Kandahar. And then if they come, they only do so to [the ISAF base at] Kandahar Airfield for a few hours.'[38] Additionally, the 351-seat Afghan bicameral parliament[39] is essentially dysfunctional, its two-house system a fob to Western notions of liberal democracy rather than a reflection of its functionality.

In sum, any basis for economic success in fragile states, from Afghanistan to those in Africa, like the reasons for their failure, must be profoundly political.

SPECIAL OPERATIONS AND INSTABILITY: A MILITARY INVESTMENT STRATEGY

Michael A Lewis

While military commanders conducting counter-insurgency operations (COIN) in Afghanistan and Iraq call for more troops, and doctrinal studies advocate high troop-to-population ratios, critics continue to challenge the enormous costs associated with a large-scale strategy of military intervention. At a current aggregate cost to the US of $1,086 billion and, for 2011, a projected commitment of nearly 150,000 troops,[1] the counter-insurgency operations in Afghanistan and Iraq represent a significant drain on the strategic resources of all nations involved. When assessed from a per capita standpoint, the average estimated cost to the US of $390k per deployed soldier in 2006 and an average casualty rate of over 600 per month for the years 2004–07[2] combine to represent the staggering costs – in both blood and treasure – associated with major counter-insurgency efforts.

For the US and its allies, these operations also represent a questionable investment in national security. From a cost-benefit perspective, the large-scale counter-insurgency commitments undertaken by the US in the twenty-first century have failed to significantly advance the counter-terrorism agenda, and have challenged the viability of full-scale counter-insurgency as an affordable method for mitigating threats to national security. Additionally, the personnel and material costs, when combined with the challenges of a large and long-term military commitment, result in a decline in the ability to respond to other crisis situations.

Finally, the negative consequences of a large-scale intervention can significantly overshadow any short-term gains and ultimately increase the threat from violent extremists.

In contrast, smaller engagements focused on a developmental approach toward building host nation capability and capacity are more cost-effective, less politically risky, and designed to yield enduring results. However, this type of approach, when conducted in reaction to a fully developed insurgency, rarely provides immediate results and therefore fails to satisfy the need for measurable success and attributed victory. This makes a developmental approach less attractive to results-minded military and civilian decision-makers compelled to justify expenditures with quantifiable results. Ultimately, a pre-emptive security strategy that balances precise and measurable offensive actions with diplomatic, economic and military developmental programmes provides a more economically and politically palatable option that yields both short-term and enduring results. The most important guiding factor, however, is that any programme intended to strengthen the position of a standing government and reduce the long-term cost to the sponsoring nation must be implemented with a conscious effort to minimise the overt role of the sponsor and focus on working by, with and through the host nation.

The US military, by capitalising on expeditionary capability, organic security resources and international relationships, continues to play a significant role in countering instability and building capacity. Special operations forces, with highly developed skills and a focus on long-term engagement, provide a contemporary solution with a strong historical record. Special operations forces offer a distinct advantage derived from their small footprint, tremendous versatility, and relative low cost when compared with conventional forces and equipment. Special operations teams are equipped to provide training and advice to security organisations within the framework of the target country's military and political apparatus or, should the political and security situation dictate, conduct unilateral operations to directly target threat organisations and infrastructure. As demonstrated in countries as varied as Colombia, Yemen, and the Philippines, special operations teams paired with host nation military, police and government security forces can exponentially improve host nation capabilities without significantly undermining the legitimacy of existing government organisations.[3]

This chapter is not intended to minimise the heroic efforts of the numerous international forces committed to establishing stability in Iraq and Afghanistan, nor will it provide a universal prescription for attaining international stability. Rather, from a US special operations perspective, it is intended to champion a strategy that combines the small footprint and high impact of special operations direct action, with the low-cost, enduring effects of indirect special operations to address the threat from violent extremist organisations – without the significant costs and risks levied by a large-scale counter-insurgency strategy.

Special Operations Defined

It is important to begin with some definitions. First, and most difficult, is a definition of *special operations*. US joint military doctrine states:[4]

[Special operations] are operations conducted in hostile, denied, or politically sensitive environments to achieve military, diplomatic, informational, and/or economic objectives employing military capabilities for which there is no broad conventional force requirement. These operations often require covert, clandestine, or low-visibility capabilities. SO [special operations] are applicable across the range of military operations. They can be conducted independently or in conjunction with operations of conventional forces or other government agencies and may include operations by, with or through indigenous or surrogate forces. SO differ from conventional operations in degree of physical and political risk, operational techniques, mode of employment,

independence from friendly support, and dependence on detailed
operational intelligence and indigenous assets.

While publicly the term often conjures up images of camouflaged
jungle warriors, black helicopter raids and clandestine operations
to capture or kill ruthless terrorists, the reality is much more wide-
ranging. Within US doctrine, special operations include twelve core
tasks: Direct Action, Civil Affairs Operations, Special Reconnaissance,
Psychological Operations, Foreign Internal Defense, Information
Operations, Unconventional Warfare, Counterterrorism,
Counterproliferation of Weapons of Mass Destruction, Security
Force Assistance, Counterinsurgency, and Activities Specified by the
President or Secretary of Defense.[5] In simple terms, most of these
tasks can be broken down into those that are conducted *against an
enemy* and those conducted *in support of a partner.*[6]

Adding to the confusion surrounding special operations units
and missions, the terms 'black special operations forces' and 'white
special operations forces' are often used in news reports and other
publications. With no foundation in US doctrine or regulation, the
terms are colloquialisms loosely used to distinguish either different
types of special operations, or specific units. The dichotomous
relationship between the colours 'black' and 'white' is also used to
distinguish between overt vs covert[7] or direct vs indirect. Black usually
describes units that operate under tight security classification to
protect their tactics, techniques and personnel from compromise and
exploitation. The term is also used to describe units that are focused
specifically on direct action, unilateral counter-terrorism missions.
White comprises those units or activities that operate more overtly
and conduct predominately partnership missions, such as foreign
internal defence and unconventional warfare. Considering the lack of
a doctrinal definition and the fact that most special operations units are
prepared to conduct any combination of direct/indirect or overt/covert
operations, the black/white descriptor is not particularly informative.

Based on the military efforts in Iraq and Afghanistan over the last decade, it is reasonable to assess that the distinct line that once existed between special operations and conventional operations during the Cold War period is rapidly blurring. With a new focus on building partnership capacity – targeted efforts to improve the collective capabilities and performance of the Department of Defense and its partners[8] – individual services within the US military are clamouring to reorganise training and organisational structures to support the mission of advising and assisting foreign security forces and also to work with other national and international agencies. Foreign internal defence and its seemingly polar opposite, unconventional warfare,[9] are traditionally the realm of special operations units because of the importance of cultural and linguistic skills, specific training in military-to-military engagement, and a primary focus on building long-term local and regional relationships that enhance future co-operation. Using size as a discriminating factor, the following definition suggests a better demarcation:[10]

> The successful conduct of special operations relies on individual and small unit proficiency in a multitude of specialized, often nonconventional combat skills applied with adaptability, improvisation, innovation, and self-reliance. The small size, unique capabilities, and self-sufficiency (for short periods of time) of special operations forces operational units provide the United States with feasible and appropriate military responses. These responses may not entail the degree of political liability or risk of escalation normally associated with employment of inherently larger or more visible conventional forces.

Despite the detail and eloquence of the above definition, the distinction between conventional/non-conventional and regular/irregular capabilities and activities is, at best, amorphous. While volumes could be written to argue the definitions of these contradictory terms, it is more instructive to look at the actual application of military power and the situations where a particular capability provides the greatest benefit to the management and reduction of instability. The challenge is for planners and policy-makers to determine where and when it is most appropriate to employ special operations forces. The criteria to inform this decision include operational risk, strategic and political sensitivity, and overall complexity of the operation.

Before addressing these criteria, it is important to consider one of the core special operations truths: *humans are more important than hardware.*[11] At the core of special operations capability is the individual operator. Special operations units are composed of military personnel that are specially selected and assessed, empowered with extensive training, and employed strategically, often with little or no external support. Whereas many conventional military units derive their utility from the technology they employ, the value of special operations forces comes from the people. In his monograph, 'A Theory of Special Operations', Robert Spulak suggests that what distinguishes special from conventional forces is the capability to assess individuals for specific attributes such as creativity, flexibility, adaptability and maturity, and the resultant high average distribution of these attributes across the special operations population. In contrast, conventional forces are constrained by larger, less-specific selection criteria and, while not devoid of personnel with similar attributes, the proportion is significantly lower across the force.[12] For example, a self-determined selection process could allow special operations units to select individuals with demonstrated operational and leadership experience resulting in a population that is statistically more mature than the conventional force. Whereas the specific criteria for selection vary across the individual components of the special operations community, the prevailing characteristic of all such organisations is a cultural disposition towards *collective individuality*.

Collective individuality, a seemingly self-contradictory phrase, describes a person who thrives on being unique, resists absolute authority, abhors institutional processes and consistently looks for ways to work outside the system while simultaneously valuing teamwork, loyalty and an unwavering dedication to accomplishing the mission. These individuals thrive on overcoming Clausewitzian friction by avoiding doctrinal solutions and working outside standard military or political bureaucracies. While often interpreted as rebellious and counter to good order and discipline, this characteristic frequently yields results that are better tailored to the idiosyncrasies of a specific situation. It is precisely this quality that empowers special operations forces to find unique, bottom-up solutions to complex problems, but often alienates them from conventional, top-driven military organisations.

In order to further discuss the role of special operations forces in countering instability, it is important to first outline both the offensive and the developmental roles of the military as an element of foreign policy and strategic outreach. For the purposes of this chapter, and the specific goal of countering instability, the abovementioned core tasks are compressed into two simple categories. Firstly, 'direct': tasks to address the needs of operations conducted unilaterally and which have near real-time empirical results. Secondly, 'indirect': those activities conducted in conjunction with a partner and designed to have enduring, but sometimes difficult to measure, results.

The Direct and Indirect Approaches

As stated in the US National Security Strategy of 2010:[13]

> The United States must reserve the right to act unilaterally if necessary to defend our nation and our interests, yet we will also seek to adhere to standards that govern the use of force. Doing so strengthens those who act in line with international standards, while isolating and weakening those who do not.
>
> Where governments are incapable of meeting their citizens' basic needs and fulfilling their responsibilities to provide security within their borders, the consequences are often global and may directly threaten the

American people. To advance our common security, we must address the underlying political and economic deficits that foster instability, enable radicalization and extremism, and ultimately undermine the ability of governments to manage threats within their borders and to be our partners in addressing common challenges.

Arguably, the greatest threat to international security on the scale of probability/severity emanates from violent extremist organisations that draw their disciples from unstable regions of the world and plan their attacks from safe havens in failed or failing states. These transnational organisations are not confined to the boundaries of nation-states, nor do they usually respond to traditional strategies of deterrence.

The US approach, entitled 'Building Partnership Capacity',[14] resembles previous partnership strategies intended to develop allies in the context of a wider bipolar power struggle. The difference, of course, is in the logic behind the strategy. During the Cold War, other nations were pursued based on their geographic location; embraced for their potential as an instrument of power projection; and evaluated by the strength of their anti-communist character. Full partnership with the US today, however, requires a rejection of violent extremism, an internal security structure that precludes the existence of global terrorist organisations, and a respect for human rights.

As a world power, the United States essentially has two options for addressing threats from global extremism: direct operations targeted at the specific organisation, its support network and associated infrastructure; or indirect approaches, aimed at shaping the environment and reducing the factors that promote instability and support radicalisation. While the former draws on the tremendous expeditionary military capability of the US and its allies, the latter relies on a much more nebulous combination of strong diplomacy, copious development aid and multilateral engagement bounded by the assumption that 'no one nation—no matter how powerful—can meet global challenges alone.'[15] Which strategy, or combination of strategies, best serves the national interest is the critical question.

The important distinction between the two strategies is in the characterisation of goals and intentions. The direct strategy assumes a basic inability of a foreign state to adequately address security issues within its own borders to the satisfaction of the projecting power. Therefore, the military intervention – with or without international charter, or host nation acquiescence – is undertaken to achieve unilateral objectives; any resultant benefits to the host nation are considered ancillary.[16] The goal is the destruction or disruption of a perceived threat, and the intention is self-interested and immediately rewarding. Examples of the direct approach include unilateral cruise missile strikes or the use of unmanned aerial vehicles to identify and disrupt extremist safe havens. Special operations roles include all elements of the find, fix, finish, exploit and analyse (F3EA) model that includes focused intelligence collection, a network of interlinked organisations and partners, direct action raids and targeting methods, and a continuous cycle of reassessment and reaction. These efforts are usually conducted under strict operational security and employ assets from all elements of the national military and civilian counter-terrorism community. The primary focus is not on changing the environment, but rather on influencing the actors within. According to Admiral Eric Olson, the commander of the US Special Operations Command, 'The direct approach is urgent, necessary, chaotic and kinetic, and the effects are mostly short term. But they are not decisive. Enduring results come from the indirect approaches… It is the efforts to shape and stabilize the environment that impact the enemy in the long term. This is truly "draining the swamp," rather than simply attempting to capture or kill all of the "alligators."'[17]

In contrast to the direct approach, the indirect strategy rests on the assumption that there is greater efficiency, as well as national and international acceptance, in the support of a sovereign nation's internal security forces to maintain stability. In this developmental strategy, external forces are used in a supporting role, at most. Optimally, these forces would be limited to a capacity-building role outside an area of open hostilities. The goal of this approach is empowerment of the host nation, and the intention is overtly altruistic yet simultaneously self-interested.

At the heart of the indirect approach is the concept of surrogate warfare or, more specifically, the employment of proxy forces to accomplish tasks that the sponsor nation is either unwilling or unable to accomplish. Kelly Smith observes that surrogate warfare is not a new strategy, nor is it solely the realm of special operations forces.[18] The US has employed surrogates in conflicts from the American Revolutionary War, through the Second World War, and up to and including the ongoing operations in Afghanistan and Iraq. Successful employment of surrogates requires a relationship that acknowledges the requirement to satisfy the operational needs of the surrogate as well as those of the sponsor.[19] Contemporary literature describes surrogate warfare as a process of working 'by, with, and through' a host nation force.

Travis Homiak, in his essay 'Expanding the American Way of War', provides an excellent abstract explanation of the strategies of 'by, with, and through'. He describes the level of military commitment on a continuum that is highest when working 'with' indigenous forces, and lowest when objectives are accomplished 'by' indigenous organisations without direct support or impetus from the external agent.[20] The salient consideration, at all levels of commitment, is the subordination of direct military goals to the importance of always prominently portraying the face of the host nation government. This reinforces the local public's perception of their own security forces, limits the adverse effects of third-party intervention, and ensures that the operations are generally aligned with the objectives of the host nation.

For example, from 1980–87, US Special Forces teams working in El Salvador and through a training centre in Honduras provided training and development that increased the size of the El Salvadoran military from a force of 8,000 to 54,000, directly contributing to the defeat of the communist insurgency. Constrained by congressional limits on the number of US forces and a direct prohibition against participating in combat operations, US objectives were accomplished 'through' and 'by' the Salvadoran military.

However, these indirect approaches are not without significant risks. Operationally, working as a small team of advisers requires confidence in the indigenous force's ability to effectively conduct the tactical portion of their operation, while still maintaining the ethical and moral posture required to obtain or sustain the support of the population. Small adviser units in austere conditions working with inadequately trained and equipped forces face the risk of being overwhelmed by enemy forces, with little expectation of support from their own country. The level of confidence in the ability of the host nation forces to operate successfully and in the adviser units to negotiate these risks is inversely proportional to the required level of direct involvement.

Additionally, the investment of national blood and treasure in order to support the security and stability of an emerging government requires a long-term commitment. The intervening nations must be prepared to endure numerous challenges and setbacks – most significantly, the potential for dissonance between the goals and intentions of the host nation and those of the supporting governments. In Yemen, US support is focused on training, intelligence and military support to enable counter-terrorism operations against Al-Qa'ida operatives.[21] Critics charge the Yemeni government with exploiting the emphasis on counter-terrorism to implement increasingly repressive tactics including attacks on protestors, postponement of elections and arbitrary arrests of foreign journalists.[22]

On a daily basis, special operations forces from the US employ the indirect approach by co-ordinating or conducting foreign internal defence, civil affairs and security force assistance operations in over sixty countries. Efforts focus on improving internal security organisations, enhancing local infrastructure and developing relationships between governments and the people they serve. These engagements take several forms, and include everything from individual soldier skills training to direct liaison with US and host nation diplomats and government agencies. One country may see special operations civil affairs personnel conducting medical, dental or veterinary civic action programmes alongside non-governmental aid organisations and local police and military forces. Concurrently, in another country, a small team of special operators may conduct advanced military training for a host nation counter-terrorism unit, and ethics and leadership training for the unit leaders. By working within the constraints and limitations of the host nation, special operations forces provide individual and collective training opportunities and humanitarian assistance that enhance the capabilities of the host nation, while simultaneously adding a level of professionalism and competence that indirectly attends to many of the root causes of instability. Again, fundamental to each of these engagements is the principle of promoting the host nation while minimising the overt presence of the US.

Considering that some regions and countries are not receptive to external engagement, and unilateral targeted elimination efforts are rarely decisive, a combined strategy that includes indirect and direct approaches is essential. By accepting a global leadership role, the US and other ideologically aligned nations need to balance their own security needs with the sovereign rights of other countries. A role that is too active, and fails to consider the effects of hegemonic behaviour on the governments and populations that potentially spawn extremist organisations, is fundamentally counterproductive.

Afghanistan: Size Matters

As a contemporary example of different indirect and direct approaches, consider the US and NATO strategies for Afghanistan.

In October 2001, US Army Special Forces and US Air Force Combat Controllers, broken into small teams, linked up with the Afghan Northern Alliance to advise and assist with the overthrow of the Taliban regime. As part of a classic unconventional warfare mission, the special operators provided close air support, tactical and operational planning assistance and logistics to the Afghan fighters. While the US played a significant role in the Taliban defeat, the intent was to reinforce the actions of the Northern Alliance and establish the legitimacy of Hamid Karzai, the future president. Although the initial operations involved kinetic strikes and combat operations, the approach – unconventional warfare – was essentially indirect and arguably very effective. Over the next few years, however, the strategy changed. US military units, conventional and special, focused their efforts on destroying remaining Taliban elements and capturing Al-Qa'ida leadership. Even though these operations occasionally included members of the fledgling Afghan military, the focus was essentially direct and unilateral.[23] Without a cohesive strategy and defined long-term goals, these efforts applied significant pressure to Al-Qa'ida and the Taliban, but failed to adequately address the overall Afghan environment or strategic goals of the US and partner nations. This led to a renewed focus on strategy following the US presidential election of 2008.

Next, consider the two competing approaches that constituted the political debate in 2008–09. The two strategies were characterised as the COIN option and the counter-terrorism option. The COIN option centred on a nation-building approach that included aid, support to government institutions, establishment (or re-establishment) of democratic processes, and a large influx of foreign troops intended to establish security while concurrently preparing the Afghan security forces for eventual takeover. This essentially constituted the status quo, with a shift in emphasis to full-scale inter-agency nation-building as well as a larger military presence. In contrast, the counter-terrorism option reflected more of a military isolationist approach whereby the US would severely reduce the number of committed forces, sustain aggressive diplomacy, and retain the option to attack any insurgent or terrorist entities that posed a threat to US or international security. In simple terms, this type of strategy rested on the ability to maintain near real-time surveillance to enable cruise missile strikes, manned and unmanned aircraft attacks, and small unit raids – with or without the explicit consent of the Afghan government.

When viewed in cost-benefit terms, the two contrasting strategies represent on the one hand a long-term, 'all-in' investment plan, and on the other a short-term, highly focused, but lower-cost alternative. In reality, with the US increasing its deployment by 30,000 troops alongside a continuing pursuit of Taliban and Al-Qa'ida fighters, the chosen course has actually become a hybrid. Unfortunately, the synergistic effects of the combined approaches have been overshadowed by the enormous (and visibly so) commitment of NATO troops and foreign development agencies. The critical principle of promoting the host nation while minimising the overt presence of the US and NATO is virtually impossible. As T E Lawrence cautioned, 'Do not try to do too much with your own hands. Better the Arabs do it tolerably than that you do it perfectly. It is their war, and you are to help them, not to win it for them. ... under the very odd conditions of Arabia, your practical work will not be as good as, perhaps, you think it is'.[24]

Today, US and NATO troops are fully immersed in all aspects of Afghan security and development – from training land, air and police forces, to fighting the insurgency with tens of thousands of troops alternating between combat operations and humanitarian outreach. Simultaneously, a large counter-terrorism force conducts direct action raids and directs kinetic strikes against high-value Taliban and Al-Qa'ida targets. While the long-term intent of this COIN strategy is sound, and the methods and considerations included in the latest military doctrine are appropriate, the costs and detrimental effects of the methods actually used undermine the investment. As stated in US Army Field Manual 3-24, 'A COIN effort cannot achieve lasting success without the HN [host nation] government achieving legitimacy.'[25]

Considering research on historical COIN operations that validates the need for substantial ground force to population ratios,[26] why is a large-scale intervention strategy a poor investment? Fundamentally, the answer has nothing to do with the theory and everything to do with the size. When a third-party nation – or group of nations – dispatches tens of thousands of troops into another nation's territory, the impact is more likely to be destabilising rather than stabilising. When conducted in a country such as Afghanistan with a long history of resistance to occupation, the effects are exponentially greater.

First, when large counter-insurgent operations are initially conducted with a preponderance of foreign forces, the perceptive line between liberator and invader is very slim.[27] When, after several years, collateral damage continues and the number of foreign forces increases rather than decreases, it becomes easier to believe a narrative of long-term occupation.

Second, when operations conducted by national security forces usually include support from foreign aircraft, weapons and intelligence, it is hard to gain confidence in the ability of host nation security forces to act alone.

Third, when a large democratic nation, such as the US, deploys large numbers of troops, the public and politicians become acutely sensitive to casualties. This results in the imposition upon the COIN operation of restrictive and counterproductive measures such as heavily armoured vehicles, large fortified base camps, and rigid, bureaucratic mission-approval processes. Imagine the perception of a local Afghan who sees insurgents in his village at night and during the day watches heavily armed troops in combat vehicles visit his village and try to convince him, paradoxically, that the area is now safe.

Fourth, when politicians, media, and military leaders speak in terms of the US or NATO 'winning' or 'losing', and are unable or unwilling to accept imperfect results from the host nation institutions, the Afghan government is effectively immune from responsibility. This leaves countries like the US culpable for the success and failure of the entire counter-insurgency effort, and ultimately casts the role of the Afghan government simultaneously as both puppet and incompetent.

Finally, the technological and force advantages provided by NATO forces have actually elevated the capabilities of the insurgent adversaries to a level that exceeds the future capabilities of the government security forces. By employing advanced tactics, equipment and force-protection measures, NATO forces have outclassed the Taliban and Al-Qa'ida in nearly every confrontation. However, through a cycle of battlefield evolution – further enabled by external benefactors and an influx of foreign fighters – the insurgent forces have developed their capabilities to a level that now demands of NATO forces advanced mine-resistant vehicles, hundreds of fixed- and rotary-wing aircraft, sophisticated signals intelligence and a sky full of unmanned surveillance drones. How many of these hi-tech solutions will be left behind for the Afghan National Army?

Given these factors, no matter how many more additional forces are employed, the chances for a clean exodus become smaller while the costs in blood and treasure continue to grow. US doctrine states that 'long-term success in COIN depends on the people taking charge of their own affairs and consenting to the government's rule. Achieving this condition requires the government to eliminate as many causes of the insurgency as feasible.'[28] But what if one of the primary causes of the insurgency is the presence of the counter-insurgents?

The Philippines: An Indirect Approach

Consider a country comprised of numerous ethnic, political and geographical divisions with a history of colonisation and a deeply rooted resistance to foreign occupation, fuelled by the shared trauma of violent invasion and sustained exploitation. Add to this a central government incapable of providing sufficient political goods – including security – to all of its citizens. And within this mix, consider a Muslim extremist group with ties to Al-Qa'ida. The result is a very difficult counter-terrorism situation that – when combined with a strict constitutional government focused on fighting internal insurgents while prohibiting direct foreign participation in combat operations – describes not Afghanistan, but the Philippines. The Philippine Islands have had a strong Muslim presence since the fifteenth century that has been targeted by Spanish Catholics, overwhelmed by American democracy-building in the early twentieth century, and marginalised by the Philippine government ever since. The proclaimed defeat of the Muslim uprising in 1913, and the frequently violent nature of American military occupation throughout the archipelago, cultivated seeds of resistance in the southern islands. These sprouted into movements for Muslim independence from central government and a palpable prejudice against the US. While of vital importance to its Pacific ally, these Muslim liberation movements are a secondary concern to the US because of their localised objectives. However, the Philippine Abu Sayyaf group is perceived to be a direct threat.[29] This political conundrum illustrates some of the challenges with the indirect approach and provides a case study for the value of special operations.

In 2002, the southern Philippine island of Basilan was a recognised safe haven for Abu Sayyaf and other violent extremist organisations. The Armed Forces of the Philippines' operations had been largely unsuccessful due to several environmental factors, including the overwhelming poverty of the predominately Muslim villagers, the lack of support from the central government, and the mistrust of government forces that existed among the local population. These factors also contributed to the influence the anti-government insurgents maintained over the local people. Upon arrival of the

US Joint Special Operations Task Force – Philippines (JSOTF-P),[30] special operations forces and their conventional support elements expanded their mission from purely military training and assistance to include conducting population surveys to determine the needs of the island communities. In an effort to merge the existing US development approach with a counter-terrorism/COIN strategy, US forces focused efforts on using development projects, including road construction and medical programmes, to improve the relationship between the government forces and the semi-autonomous communities and villages scattered throughout Basilan, Jolo and greater Mindanao. They effectively drove 'a wedge between the people and the insurgents.'[31] On Basilan, using funds and support from the US, JSOTF-P enabled the Philippine armed forces along with local labourers using locally procured materials to dig wells, improve schools, mosques, and hospitals and even build sanitation facilities.[32] With the Philippine armed forces providing security and the US supporting positive development, the local population became more supportive of government efforts, developed trust in the security forces and discounted the legitimacy of the terrorists. Simultaneously, US training of security forces enabled host nation military direct operations that resulted in capture or elimination of fifty-six terrorists.[33]

Within two years, and with a US investment of hundreds rather than thousands of troops, the presence of Abu Sayyaf in Basilan was virtually eliminated, the population began to support government counter-terrorism efforts, and the Philippine armed forces were able to significantly reduce the military commitment to the island and focus efforts elsewhere on the archipelago.[34] Equally if not more important to the US is that the elimination of another terrorist safe haven and the increased capacity of the Philippine military will keep Abu Sayyaf off balance and focused on immediate survival, rather than planning for and conducting attacks against international targets.[35]

What distinguished the US special operations effort in the Philippines from any other conventional military approach? Fundamentally, it was a combination of the willingness and initiative to work outside the normal system, the small but extremely versatile operational elements and the intent to develop long-term relationships that would endure for decades – not just until the terrorists leave or the exercise ends. Special operations forces identified the shortcomings in the standard US development strategy that ostensibly supported the larger political goals of the host nation, yet failed to ameliorate the underlying conditions fomenting the insurgency. Instead, they implemented focused, specific measures to directly enhance the capability of the host nation armed forces. Concurrently, from a US strategic perspective, the small size and limited involvement of the JSOTF-P minimised any political and popular blowback from the participating nations or the international community as a whole. While by no means directly comparable to the challenges caused by the intervention in Afghanistan, efforts in the Philippines show the value of engaging early with a small footprint and a focus on capacity-building. Therefore, as a case study for indirect efforts against transnational terrorists, it is a model example.[36]

Conclusion

As extremist networks seek to capitalise on the conditions present in weak and failing states, and the governments of those countries are either unwilling or unable to mitigate the threats to other nations, countries such as the US will find themselves increasingly focused on a comprehensive and collaborative security approach. Combining the unilateral application of direct force with the persistent benefits of building partnership capacity yields a strategy that provides both immediate and long-term advantages. However, as the large military operations in Iraq and Afghanistan draw down, domestic and international pressure will likely prevent another large-scale military intervention. Therefore, it will become increasingly important for concerned nations to develop strategies that maximise effects while minimising the overall military commitment.

Special operations forces, as both primary actors and supporting enablers, are equipped with regional knowledge, integrated intelligence and exceptional access. They provide both a direct and indirect alternative to large conventional formations. Targeted accessions and specialised training combined with a culture focused on innovative approaches to mission accomplishment make special forces the logical choice in complex situations where there is high operational risk and strategic and political sensitivity. Most importantly, with appropriate authority and requisite access, special operations forces can serve as an active tool for wielding all elements of national power and influence. When employed early, special operations forces provide an investment strategy with exponential benefits that will ultimately compound over time.

INTELLIGENCE IN LOW-INTENSITY CONFLICTS: LESSONS FROM AFGHANISTAN

Adam Cobb*

An old saw has it that during the Cold War the enemy was easy to find, but hard to kill. In low-intensity conflicts the enemy is easy to kill, but hard to find. Unconventional wars are referred to as intelligence-led efforts for good reason. However, the kind of intelligence required in each category differs because the strategic objects are different. Additionally, not all low-intensity conflicts are the same. On the contrary, they span the full gamut of strategic possibilities: from state-sponsored proxy wars in third-party territories (Vietnam and Afghanistan in the Cold War); to anti-colonial insurgency (Algeria); separatist terrorism (the IRA and ETA); international intervention to quell anarchy in failed states (Liberia, Sierra Leone, Haiti, Somalia); to counter-insurgency following externally imposed regime change in a hostile environment (contemporary Iraq); to counter-insurgency following externally imposed regime change in a culturally diverse hostile environment within an all but failed state that is contested by multiple nations that transcend state boundaries (Afghanistan). This

* I would like to thank the following Afghanistan combat veterans who have helped shape my thinking: Kelly Alexander, Mike Barbee, Mike Lewis, and past and present students of mine at the Air War College and the Marine Corps Command and Staff College. I would especially like to thank Rachel Kingcade of the USMC's superb Gray Research Center for her unrelenting research support on this project. The views presented however are mine alone and do not reflect the position of the US government.

chapter will confine itself to discussing the intelligence challenge in
the latter case, because it is the most challenging and continues to be a
contemporary strategic conundrum.[1]

Typically, military intelligence in conventional warfare is concerned
with locating the enemy and identifying its size, disposition, readiness,
and, if possible, discerning its intent (the holy grail of military
intelligence). Simply put, intelligence is about targeting. In low-
intensity conflict where an external power imposes regime change in a
failed state over extreme geographic and cultural barriers, intelligence
takes a vastly more complex turn. Knowledge of every aspect of the
political, economic, ethnic, social and cultural landscape, through
history to the present, is vital to create or choose a viable partner and to
monitor progress in the execution of the war to a successful conclusion.
In this kind of conflict, the intelligence challenge is primarily about
intent; not just of the enemy, but also of every actor that is party to
the conflict. This is a profound challenge. It is, counter-intuitively,
both ultimately strategic and fundamentally tactical. It is strategic in
the sense of needing to know how all the parts fit the whole (broadly
defined) and tactical in the sense that such knowledge is largely derived
at the local level and means different things to different actors.

Intelligence in this kind of conflict is not so much about collection
as it is about analysis. If the analytical lens is incorrectly focused,
no amount of information will help win the war. On the contrary:
the plethora of information in today's wired battle space will simply
overwhelm good people trying their hardest to do a good job.[2] Analysts
must be able to sift vast quantities of data. In order to do that effectively,
they must have strong historical, cultural and strategic judgment that
is acquired over years of experience in and around the territory of
interest, in order to turn that raw information into knowledge of the
complex social world they seek to dominate. Collection is important,
but secondary to analysis. Culturally aware analysts must drive
collection requirements in order to get the right data upon which to
exercise judgment. This in turn raises questions about the divisions

between collectors and analysts across some parts of the US intelligence community. In intelligence of this kind, 'Clausewitzian genius' is the ability to see through the patterns and the discontinuities from the local to the global level in complex overlapping alien cultures, and find seams along which war aims might be prosecuted either politically or by the use of precise force. This kind of warfare is complex, nasty, expensive and long.

This raises an important point in understanding the study and application of intelligence and its role in warfare. While it can be usefully studied in isolation, intelligence cannot be fully appreciated in the absence of knowledge about the strategy it seeks to serve or the resources dedicated by a government to the fulfilment of that strategy. Thus the conduct of warfare is dependent upon the interplay of all three arms of what might be called the 'iron triangle of warfare' – intelligence, strategy and resources.[3] The arms of the triangle must be in agreement and mutually supportive. If not, the object of the war will be impossible to obtain.

This chapter contends that the arms of the US 'iron triangle' in Afghanistan are currently not in alignment. The resources the US is willing to expend do not support the current strategy, and significant evidence suggests that the intelligence system has never quite mastered the considerable difficulty of adapting to the new demands placed on it since the initial invasion. Further, US resources devoted to the war in Afghanistan were set to diminish in 2011 but that date may have been pushed out to 2014. It follows that the strategy, and thus the intelligence requirements for the war, will also change. It will be argued here that it would be prudent both to accept that these changes are inevitable (due to the parlous public accounts of the US, public opinion about both these accounts and the war in Afghanistan, and concomitant executive action to remedy both public policy challenges), and to build a plan to anticipate the new reality, rather than merely react when the inevitable crunch comes. The good news is that away from Afghanistan and Iraq, the US has been engaged for some years in a much more effective and sustainable fight in the Horn of Africa and the Philippines that may come to be viewed as a model for reform. US military *doctrine* (the much favoured counter-insurgency doctrine) should not continue to act as a substitute for a national *strategy* for winning a global war against radical Islamic extremists.

Background to the Conflict

As the forgoing suggests, even characterising the war in Afghanistan is a complex exercise. In reality there are multiple wars in Afghanistan between different groups: between the coalition (ISAF – International Security Assistance Force) and Al-Qa'ida; between the allies and the Taliban; a proxy war between Pakistan and India for strategic depth and influence with 'Afghans', China and the US;[4] between the US and Iran for regional influence (another proxy war); between Pashtuns and most other trans-state groupings (Tajik, Hazara, Uzbek, and so on); as well as intense competition based on mutual suspicions between so-called 'frenemies' such as the US and Pakistan,[5] and friends, the US and India.[6] This chapter deals primarily with only a small part of the wider conflict and its consequences, namely US policy towards Afghanistan. When broken down into its parts, the problem is clearly much more than a question of countering an insurgency. But – in the absence of a coherent regional policy, a robust inter-agency mechanism for state-building, an acceptable model of governance able to resolve demands of competing groups, an incorruptible electoral mechanism, and the ability to moderate the behaviour and policies of regional powers – merely applying a military doctrine to counter an insurgency will only address a symptom of the problem. This is why so many COIN advocates talk about military force being marginal compared to all the other tasks of good governance. Yet the fact is the US is unable to achieve these wider tasks cited, given a range of powerful factors including past failures in Afghanistan, the growth of anti-US forces, the loss of resolve and the state of the public accounts.

The US invaded Afghanistan in direct response to the unprovoked surprise attack mounted by Al-Qa'ida in September 2001. The initial action had three goals: capturing Osama Bin Laden 'dead or alive'; preventing Afghanistan from being used as a staging ground for future attacks on the US and its interests (as it had been throughout the 1990s); and eliminating Al-Qa'ida. Global public opinion was strongly in support of the American response.

However, a range of factors complicated matters. Afghanistan was ruled by the Taliban, who had fought their way to dominance over the myriad warring groups that were left in the wake of the Soviet retreat. They were (and remain) the strongest and best organised of all the nations, political networks, terrorist networks, crime syndicates and warlords that exist within the territory of Afghanistan. All these groups straddle international boundaries into adjacent states.[7] Pashtun by birth, Islamic extremist by indoctrination, the Taliban did not then, nor do they today, pose a direct threat to the US however culturally alien and politically unsavoury they may be in the eyes of Western society. In addition to their politics, their tribal custom of *pashtunwali* was also a factor that encouraged them to provide sanctuary to the transnational terror network that came to be known as Al-Qa'ida when it escaped to Afghanistan from Sudan in the 1990s. When the US invaded Afghanistan, its fight against Al-Qa'ida necessarily became a fight against the Taliban as well. Small groups of US Special Forces, allied with indigenous rivals to the Taliban, toppled the regime and retook the country in a matter of weeks. Badly mauled, Al-Qa'ida and the Taliban melted into the population to wait, re-equip, reorganise, and plan their return via a classical insurgent campaign. Many escaped US forces by slipping across the border into Pakistan's lawless Federally Administered Tribal Areas (FATA), which became a new safe haven for their activities.

The outward appearance of rapid and near-complete success had a range of consequences that have subsequently complicated US strategy. First, the job was not complete. Osama Bin Laden was at large, and

Al-Qa'ida was not broken. While Afghanistan itself was no longer a safe haven in the way it once was, the war had prompted the enemy to create new safe havens in Pakistan that were largely outside of US reach. Second, as each day of Al-Qa'ida's survival passed, it appeared to their fellow travellers the world over that the terrorists had got away with their atrocity against the last remaining superpower. For those who might wish the hegemon and its allies ill, the lesson was impossible to miss. Third, fresh attention was placed on the deep problems of daily life in Afghanistan. There was a natural reaction to want to try and aid the situation. Mission creep, from eliminating Al-Qa'ida to building a stable Afghanistan to creating a democracy, had begun. Fourth, the strategic pause in Afghanistan was the perfect opportunity for those in the Bush administration who wanted to add Iraq to the US response to 9/11. Fifth, the resulting change in US strategic priorities shifted resources and attention away from the unresolved situation in Afghanistan. Sixth, once weapons of mass destruction were dropped as the rationale for the Iraq war, and the spread of democracy became the *post-bellum casus belli*, mission creep in Afghanistan accelerated. Yet all the while, the war in Afghanistan was an 'economy of force operation', concentrated on fixing and eliminating the enemy – largely via air strikes called in by small patrols searching along enemy lines of communication away from population centres. Seventh, presidential candidate Barack Obama had campaigned on the war of necessity in Afghanistan taking priority over the war of choice in Iraq. The rise of US COIN doctrine and its initial success in Iraq set the stage for a change in the US approach in Afghanistan once the new Obama administration came into office in 2009.

US Intelligence in the Afghan Theatre Pre-2009

The approach to military intelligence on Afghanistan mirrored the course of US strategy. During the economy of force period, military intelligence was focused on traditional tasks associated with the prosecution of discrete enemy targets and the challenge of force protection as the ISAF mission grew. Changes in emphasis occurred as different NATO commanders rotated through the headquarters in Kabul. While conducting an intelligence review in January of 2009 the new commander of Central Command (CENTCOM), General David Petraeus, discovered that at that time ISAF 'had not directed intelligence collection toward economic, social and political issues of the Afghan tribes and villages'.[8] This assessment was reinforced by a review instigated by General Stanley McChrystal after he took command in June of that year. Review members observed, 'Intelligence collection was in a shambles. The military understood relatively little about the Afghan people. It could not measure how the Taliban's propaganda campaign of fear and intimidation affected the population.'[9] As troop strength increased, so did improvised explosive device (IED) attacks. Theatre intelligence assets were consumed by the pressing requirement to get on top of the IED threat and continue to hunt down enemy forces.

Things did not fare much better at the strategic level. When Major General John M Custer was the director of intelligence at US CENTCOM,[10]

> He grew angry at how little helpful information came out of the NCTC [National Counter Terrorism Centre]. In 2007, he visited its director at the time to tell him so. 'I told [Vice Admiral John Scott Redd] that after 4 ½ years, this organization had never produced one shred of information that helped me prosecute three wars!'

The intelligence prioritisation also reflected the operational stance at the time, which had not yet adopted a COIN approach. Nevertheless, according to one of his top intelligence advisers, the state of intelligence at the time of his review 'was a forehead-smacking moment for Petraeus ... The problem was obvious. He needed to fix the intelligence shortcomings immediately ... Petraeus decided to create his own intelligence agency inside CENTCOM'.[11] From this, the

Af-Pak Center of Excellence was created in Tampa, which has grown dramatically since its inception (and at the time of writing was due to move into a brand new 270,000 square foot facility).[12]

Petraeus's intelligence adviser at the time, Derek Harvey of the Defense Intelligence Agency, is credited with revolutionising military intelligence as it pertains to COIN. 'The insurgency's resources, leadership, financing, freedom of movement, popular support and group cohesion all had to be measured. No such metrics had existed'.[13] These findings were also reflected in the McChrystal review that discovered that '70% of the intelligence requirements were enemy-centric'.[14] Of the ninety different metrics collected at the time, few paid attention to the populace. 'Harvey wanted to expand [the metrics collected] to 500' to better reflect the complex requirements of a population-centred COIN strategy.[15]

Harvey is also credited with creating what became known as the 'AfPak Hands' programme. The US military personnel system is ruthlessly resistant to change – though often for a lot of very sensible reasons – and it has come under criticism for the two-year assignment cycle that ensures personnel are rotated out of a job they have only just begun to master. By contrast, the AfPak Hands programme invites volunteers to devote five full years of their career to learning a relevant language and undertaking a series of deployments between the region and AfPak centres in Tampa and the Pentagon. While there are a number of concerns with the programme, it is an important initiative designed to provide the military with the kinds of expertise that could help answer the deeper cultural intelligence requirements that were missing when both Generals Petraeus and McChrystal conducted their respective reviews.[16] In some respects AfPak Hands is reminiscent of the British Army in India.

Afghanistan is perhaps one of the world's most complex cultural geographies. Adopting a population-centric approach, as General McChrystal did when he took command, placed a further premium on wider and deeper situational awareness than the intelligence system was providing at the time. When President Obama was presented with a map depicting tribal culture in Kandahar, which reportedly resembled 'a crazy quilt of overlapping colors that represented a piece of modern art [that] would almost require a PhD in Afghan culture for an American to comprehend', he was heard to remark, 'what makes us think that given that description of the problem, that we're going to design a solution to this?' As Bob Woodward observed with considerable understatement, 'the Taliban lived this, putting the US at a strategic disadvantage'.[17]

The Flynn Review

The ISAF intelligence chief, Major General Michael Flynn, personally co-wrote the most damning indictment of the conventional approach to intelligence in this complex low-intensity conflict. In an unusual move, General Flynn issued his commander's directive on 'Fixing Intel' in the form of a Washington, DC think tank working paper:[18]

> Eight years into the war in Afghanistan, the U.S. intelligence community is only marginally relevant to the overall strategy. Having focused the overwhelming majority of its collection efforts and analytical brainpower on insurgent groups, the vast intelligence apparatus is unable to answer fundamental questions about the environment in which U.S. and allied forces operate and the people they seek to persuade.

US intelligence analysts are 'ignorant of local economics and landowners, hazy about who the powerbrokers are and how they might be influenced, incurious about the correlations between various development projects ... and disengaged from people in the best position to find answers'.[19] This had created a situation where, according to General McChrystal, 'Our senior leaders – the Chairman of the Joint Chiefs of Staff, the Secretary of Defense, Congress, the President of the United States – are not getting the right information to make decisions'.[20] For example, 'in a recent project ordered by the White House' – presumably the Obama review – 'analysts could barely scrape together enough information to formulate rudimentary assessments.'[21] The report urges, 'The urgent task before us is to make our intelligence community ... "relevant".'[22]

The Flynn report goes to significant lengths to stress that the intelligence enabling the targeting of the enemy is effective. Rather, the key intelligence weakness is moving beyond kinetic operations to understanding the highly disaggregated cultural geographies within each of the 398 districts across the thirty-four provinces of Afghanistan (which is about the size of Texas). Not surprisingly, the report discovered that the most effective intelligence practices could be found primarily at the tactical level of war.[23] This makes sense in so far as intelligent, adaptive and able field commanders will do whatever they need to do to accomplish the mission. But it also demonstrates the complexity of Afghanistan, where knowledge of local issues is vital to local operational outcomes. As any commander who has been there will say, generalising between tribes, valleys or districts in Afghanistan is a complicated business.[24] It is hard to aggregate data that has meaning above the local level. In a COIN fight, '[T]he best information, the most important intelligence, and the context that provides the best understanding come from the bottom up, not from the top down.'[25] This is certainly true in Afghanistan.

Flynn and his co-authors note that some units have become very adept at pushing intelligence officers down to the company level, training infantrymen to be collectors, and a range of related programmes to collect 'white' or cultural/societal intelligence. But they go on to highlight the disconnection between the tactical, operational and strategic levels of military intelligence. 'We were unable to find significant information in official reports and summaries reaching headquarters level ... Moving up through levels of hierarchy is normally a journey into greater degrees of cluelessness'.[26] They continue on this theme, quoting an operations officer of a US task force who complained that the intelligence fusion centre had no data on the population in his area of operations: 'I don't want to say we're clueless, but we are.'[27]

The report makes a series of unconventional recommendations to leverage the good work they observed in the field, including empowering analysts to move freely between commands looking for patterns within the ground-level data, and creating open source stability operations information centres (SIOCs) designed to create substantive written reports and provide comprehensive situational awareness across data sets. At the regional command level, the authors argue the SIOCs should be placed under the State Department's representatives responsible for development programmes.[28]

Taken together, their assessment and recommendations make it very clear that the US military intelligence system is exceptionally well configured for counter-terrorist operations, but woefully inadequate for the Afghan counter-insurgency mission. President Obama explicitly rejected a COIN strategy. The military resisted the president and has continued to mount a combination of direct and indirect operations aimed at COIN objectives. What is also interesting is that strategic intelligence has been highly effective. So taken together, tactical and strategic intelligence are working well: it is the operational or theatre level where the breakdown occurs, at least in the case of US Afghan strategy. More specifically, it would appear from the evidence that the bureaucracy of intelligence, at least in the US model, has not caught up with advances at the sharp end of the military instrument. Due to the nature of the threat, there are in fact two spears in the American arsenal. The first we have examined; we now turn to the next.

Strategic Intelligence

The threat of non-state extremist terrorism in the US has radically changed the size and structure of the intelligence community and has required a very different approach to strategic intelligence to that of the past. There has been an incredible expansion of strategic intelligence capabilities since 2001. By one simplistic measure, more than 17 million square feet of office space for 'top-secret intelligence work' is under construction, or has been built since 2001. That is the equivalent of four and a half Pentagons.[29] More than 854,000 people have top secret security clearances (it is estimated that 31 per cent, or 264,000, of whom are contractors), 206 new classified organisations have been created, meaning that in total '1,271 government organizations and 1,931 private companies work on programs related to counterterrorism, homeland security and intelligence in about 10,000 locations across the United States'. For the first time in history the complete US intelligence budget numbers were released. In 2009, military and non-military intelligence spending was $80.1 billion dollars.[30] Defense Intelligence Agency personnel numbers have swelled from 7,500 (2002) to 16,500 (2010), not including contractor support that is likely be as much as four times that number – if not more. The list of code names for specific, highly classified 'Special Access Programs' is in excess of 300 pages. 'There's only one entity in the entire universe that has visibility on all SAPs – that's God', quips James R Clapper, the Director of National Intelligence.[31]

The Intelligence Reform and Terrorism Prevention Act of 2004 was the legislative vehicle that created the Office of the Director of National Intelligence (DNI), which was designed to be the co-ordinating authority across the seventeen different organisations that comprise the intelligence community.[32] However, the DNI does not have budgetary control of the whole community; a key weakness in the new arrangements established in the wake of the 9/11 Commission's recommendations.[33] This could be changing: DNI James Clapper announced on 1 November 2010 that he had 'secured at least a conceptual agreement with the secretary of defense to take the national intelligence program out of the defense budget. We plan to do that by 2013. I mention that because I think that is one specific way to accrue more authority to ODNI in the oversight and execution of that funding.[34] The 2004 reforms dispensed with the foreign/domestic intelligence divide – for example, by creating the National

Counterterrorism Center as an all-source analysis organisation. The scale of the challenges that the strategic intelligence enterprise faces on a daily basis is staggering: 'Terabytes of foreign intelligence information come in each day, vastly exceeding the entire text holdings of the Library of Congress, which is estimated at 10 terabytes. [The] National Counterterrorism Center's 24-hour Operations Center receives 8,000 to 10,000 pieces of counterterrorist information, roughly 10,000 names, and 40-plus specific threats and plots, every day.'[35]

Ultra hi-tech intelligence platforms are at the heart of many US strategic intelligence programmes, and they are routinely used in low-intensity conflicts. From space-based reconnaissance satellites, to battle space robots (drones on land and in the air), to airborne electronic warfare and land movement radar, to phenomenal computing power driving searches of data collected by these and a remarkable array of other means, the US brings a great deal of raw intelligence power to the table.

In Afghanistan, for example, the incredible capability of the Real Time Regional Gateway has been used extensively. It can take data intercepted by any means, 'store it, and make it instantly available to intelligence analysts and operators allowing the US to react quickly in response to the enemy'. Director of National Intelligence McConnell explains the power of this capability in simple terms; 'they talk, we listen. They move, we observe. Given the opportunity, we react operationally'.[36] It is notable that this system, like many in the strategic category, is designed to provide information for counter-terrorism targeting (known as the 'sensor to shooter kill chain'). But they do not offer the understanding of the social environment needed in counter-insurgency.

Criticisms have also been made of the post-2001 growth of organisations involved, the use of contractors, and the sheer scale of the strategic intelligence system. Redundancy is useful in intelligence work: different agencies have different information needs, and can see the same data point in a variety of different and useful ways. But there is little doubt that the system is too large to be effectively controlled. Lieutenant General (Rtd) John R Vines, 'who was asked [in 2009] to review the method for tracking the Defense Department's most sensitive programs was stunned by what he discovered':

> 'I'm not aware of any agency with the authority, responsibility or a process in place to coordinate all these interagency and commercial activities,' he said in an interview. 'The complexity of this system defies description. Because it lacks a synchronizing process, it inevitably results in message dissonance, reduced effectiveness and waste,' Vines said. 'We consequently can't effectively assess whether it is making us more safe.'

Admiral Dennis Blair later said, 'as we so often do in this country ... the attitude was, if it's worth doing, it's probably worth overdoing.'[37] Frequently, strategic assets are essentially searching for a single individual with a bomb strapped to their side. It is much worse than a needle in a haystack: it is a silver needle in a stack of three million stainless-steel needles.[38] Given the odds, it is probable that, occasionally, a terrorist will be lucky. The howls of outrage following the discovery of the 'underwear bomber' pointed to some of the problems inherent in a culture that relies so heavily on technology for security. America was built on innovation in science and technology. There is a deep seam running through the culture that more resources and more technology can solve any problem. There is no doubt that it is better to have the vast capabilities that the US possesses than not. However, the counter-terror threat is inherently a human challenge, and the literature is clear that human intelligence has long been a weakness in US intelligence. And recent evidence suggests, the literature has not kept up with developments on the ground.

> It is worth noting that significant improvements have been made in HUMINT in recent years in Afghanistan and across the border in FATA. Nizam Khan Dawar, a tribesman from North Waziristan, said in

a phone interview, 'The number of agents for the CIA has been increasing considerably in recent months ... Mysterious people disguised as Taliban militants are behind these attacks, guiding the drone missiles.' The report continues, 'A Taliban commander in North Waziristan said the militant group is trying to unmask the spies that have been guiding the strikes'.[39]

The CIA's Afghan counter-terrorism pursuit teams have partnered with 'the agency's paramilitary wing, known as the Special Activities Division', which used:[40]

> [B]order bases to build and manage networks of ethnic Pashtun informants who cross into Pakistan's tribal belt. In combination with near-constant surveillance from U.S. drone aircraft in the skies, the informants have enabled the CIA to identify the whereabouts of al-Qaeda and Taliban leaders. At the same time, the border-hugging bases have reduced the CIA's dependence on Pakistan's Inter-Services Intelligence directorate, a mercurial spy service that has helped track down dozens of al-Qaeda and other insurgent leaders but is also considered a secret supporter of the Afghan Taliban. For years, the ISI restricted CIA operatives to Pakistani bases in the tribal belt and strictly controlled access to its sources in the region. As a result, the Americans were kept largely in the dark about the presence of al-Qaeda and Taliban forces on that side of the border.

These are impressive outcomes and they need to be enhanced not just in the border areas, but wherever the US and its allies are fighting 'by, with, and through' local partners. Importantly, the local partner is not the Afghan government, but Pashtun tribesmen. Additionally, this is yet again an example of counter-terrorism, not counter-insurgency.

At 854,000 personnel and with a budget of more than $80 billion a year, the US intelligence community is bigger than the rest of the world's intelligence services combined. Does it deliver a proportionally superior product? The vast majority of the work done within the intelligence community is technical, not analytical. Strategic judgments are made by a very small cadre of senior decision-makers that, on average, do not amount to more than the 1 per cent at the top of each of the seventeen agencies that comprise the intelligence community. Of those agencies, the Office of the Director of National Intelligence is charged with taking a community-wide view and presenting it to the president and his top national security advisers. With around 1,200 staff, the Office amounts to 0.14 per cent of the intelligence community. It is not possible to survey the quality of the work, but the numbers give a glimpse into the imbalance between technical and analytical capabilities in the US intelligence system.

If there is a quantitative imbalance between technical and analytical work, could there be a qualitative imbalance also? In the absence of an exhaustive investigation into the quality of the intelligence community's work (which would require reading all of its highly classified reports), this proposition is impossible to prove. Therefore, it is a matter of opinion, but one worth serious thought. It could be that what is missing in intelligence work dependent on hi-tech capability is not so much new systems and methodologies, but the deep learning and broad knowledge through which data gets critically assessed by the analyst. Diagnostic and quantitative systems and methods support – but do not supplant – a critical mind. Therefore, the most important quality is the ability of the analyst to see linkages and patterns where others see chaos. No new systems or methodologies have made critical thinking and seasoned professional judgment redundant. This is not to suggest that the intelligence community does not have highly educated, culturally adept, and strategically nuanced analysts. The Flynn review is proof that it does: but it is also proof that they are clearly in the minority.

Given the quality of assessments released to the public and the academic work of former analysts, there is strong evidence that it exists at the strategic level too. But where is the reporting on the mismatch between intelligence, budgets and strategy in the US approach to Afghanistan? There is no doubt that some in the intelligence community are seeing and reporting these disconnects, given that they are so glaring. But for all the money, people and emphasis on technical wizardry, the US strategic community seems comparatively light on alternative strategies for success in Afghanistan. When tasked with giving the new president alternative courses of action during the strategic review in 2009, by their own admission, the most senior Pentagon leaders repeatedly failed.[41] As Woodward's account makes clear, the president was continually frustrated with long time lines forced on him by the Pentagon. Announcing the review's findings, President Obama insisted on summer 2010 as the drawdown date. However, the Pentagon is now citing 2014 in various media. They could not come up with more than one idea – COIN. The irony is that the military talks COIN, but it is really not doing COIN at all: it is doing counter-terrorism. This goes beyond intelligence and into the realm of the intelligence-budget-strategy iron triangle.

Intelligence and Strategy

The focus of Obama's strategy as declared in 2009 is on Al-Qa'ida, not the Taliban; the core aim is to transfer responsibility to Afghan security forces; and Pakistan takes centre stage. Based on his success in Iraq, General Petraeus, with the support of Chairman of the Joint Chiefs Admiral Michael Mullen and Secretary of Defense Robert Gates, never presented the Obama administration with any option other than an Afghan surge. The military plan was packaged as COIN, but it does not have the manning, the resources or the time to be effective – as defence leaders indeed argued repeatedly in National Security Council meetings with the president. In fact, the additional troops are conducting large-scale counter-terrorism operations in addition to a major escalation of the covert war in FATA over the border.

There are problems with the strategy. First and foremost among them is Pakistan. Despite the fact that anti-government forces have mounted dozens of successful attacks on Pakistani military facilities, intelligence facilities and leaders, and for a time gained control of the Swat Valley, the Pakistani national security establishment is still absorbed with India as the greater threat. In a society vulnerable to fantastic rumour, even the president believed that the anti-Pakistani Taliban were a creation of the CIA and Indian intelligence services.[42] This is a common view the author has heard from Pakistani officers. Is Pakistan a dubious ally? Pakistan complains about US drone strikes against the Taliban, but also hosts the base from which they are launched. It profits from the US supply convoys stretched across its two access lines into Afghanistan, yet has shown that it will cut those vital supply lines to make a political point. In 2009, the Pakistani military mounted intense operations against anti-government forces in South Waziristan, but not against Al-Qa'ida and Afghan Taliban in North Waziristan. Nevertheless, the US is reluctant to push Pakistan too hard, for fear that the government will collapse and the radicals will take over a territory with 166 million people and a number of nuclear warheads.

With the best intelligence in the world, the United States cannot alter two critical facts in the war in Afghanistan. It cannot improve the quality of the government in Kabul or its acceptance among the people, and it cannot make Pakistan change its policy on supporting terrorists. Pakistani claims that it does not support terrorism are weak in the face of a body of evidence to the contrary and former president Pervez Musharraf's recent admission that these activities took place. Bruce Riedel's assessment of Pakistan in 1999 was that it was 'behaving as a rogue state in two areas – backing Taliban/Osama Bin Laden and provoking war with India [in the Kargil crisis]'. President Bill Clinton complained to Nawaz Sharif in 1999 about Pakistan's role in tacitly supporting the Taliban and Osama Bin Laden.

Following the Mumbai attacks, 'The CIA received reliable intelligence that the ISI was directly involved in the training for Mumbai'. Woodward continues, 'An upset Bush asked his aides about contingency plans for dealing with Pakistan'. When DNI McConnell briefed President-elect Obama, Pakistan was presented as the foremost national security challenge to the US. President Obama assessed the role of Pakistan in Afghanistan thus: 'we need to make clear to the people that the cancer is in Pakistan ... we need to excise the cancer in Pakistan'.

For the enemy, Pakistan, with its nuclear weapons, is a much richer prize than Afghanistan, which makes the situation for the US and its allies so much more acute. Additionally, the strategic imbalance of dedicating $1 billion of military effort per Al-Qa'ida operative in Afghanistan in 2010 seems to fulfil Bin Laden's desire to drain America of its blood and treasure, and thus, in the long run, its will to fight.

Conclusion

Adopting a new approach will not be without costs. The US has to move past its zero-defect approach to counter-terrorism. By virtue of the time it will take to win this struggle, there will be a concomitant rise in the success rate of enemy attacks on the US (and European) homeland. American life may come to resemble, in very small part, British life during the Troubles in Northern Ireland. Despite the best intelligence system in the world, it is inevitable that a terrorist will again achieve a strike on the US homeland at some point. That is the nature of this war. It will not be a sign of weakness, as indeed various domestic demagogues will inevitably seek to paint such an attack once it happens.

The enemy has been breathtakingly stupid in its terror operations, killing many more Muslims than anyone else. This, in turn, has turned public opinion against extremism throughout the Muslim world and enhanced the power of the extremists' 'near enemies', namely governments from Riyadh to Jakarta. There is good evidence to suggest that a major shift has already taken place among radical extremist intellectuals. As Lawrence Wright writes about Dr Fadl's rejection of violent jihad:[43]

People hate America, and the Islamist movements feel their hatred and
their impotence. Ramming America has become the shortest road to
fame and leadership among the Arabs and Muslims. But what good is
it if you destroy one of your enemy's buildings, and he destroys one of
your countries? What good is it if you kill one of his people, and he kills a
thousand of yours? ... That, in short, is my evaluation of 9/11.

Once one of the foremost advocates of violent jihad, Fadl, like
Noman Benotman and a number of others, have come to see the
hopelessness of the struggle in its violent form.[44]

The Afghan Taliban are now in negotiations with Kabul and the
US.[45] It has been driven to the negotiating table by the unrelenting
counter-terrorism operations on both sides of the Afghan border since
January 2010. But it is not really the Taliban with whom we should be
negotiating. Ironically, the best political advice on Afghanistan comes
from one of our dubious allies in this fight. General Musharraf, in a
Churchillian assessment, summed it up thus:[46]

> Now you try to negotiate with so-called 'moderate Taliban,' but there is
> no such thing as a moderate Taliban. There are Taliban and Pashtuns. But
> as I have always said: All Taliban are Pashtun, but not all Pashtun people
> are Taliban. Again, you should reinforce the ancient Pashtun clans who are
> not ideologically aligned with the Taliban to govern Afghanistan and to
> fight the Taliban. That's my strong advice.

In the long run, America will win because the allure of what it stands
for is far more attractive than what is offered by the enemy. The
US and its allies must capitalise on its strengths in unconventional
warfare and counter-terrorism intelligence capabilities if it is to cost-
effectively answer the threat over the many years still ahead in the
long war against Al-Qa'ida.

THE ROLE OF MEDIA OPERATIONS

Christopher Vernon

Western militaries have been generally slow to accept that the information battle must necessarily sit near the epicentre of operational thinking. This snapshot of the British Army's experience – illuminated by my own personal experiences in the field, first as the UN military spokesman in Bosnia in 1995 and more latterly as the British Army spokesman for the invasion of Iraq in 2003 – attempts to chart some of the key stages in the journey. Australian counter-insurgency (COIN) expert David Kilcullen emphasises the importance of information as a line of operation:[1]

> We [the West] typically design physical operations first, then craft supporting information operations to explain our actions. This is the reverse of Al-Qaeda's approach. For all our professionalism, compared to the enemy's, our public information is an afterthought. In military terms, for Al-Qaeda the 'main effort' is information; for us information is a 'supporting effort'.

The Evolution

A recent study of British COIN doctrine over the last half century shows that it was not until the publication of 'Land Operations: Counter Revolutionary Warfare' in 1969, which contained a chapter on 'Public Relations' (PR), that any attempt was made to address how the media was handled. With its non-military sounding ring, this 'PR' label in many ways set the scene for the effective military mindset on the subject for the two following decades.

Northern Ireland

In Northern Ireland, after some frequently naïve media forays in the very early days of the troubles in the 1970s, the British Army was obliged to adopt closely controlled, centralised information practices. Troops on the ground were not generally authorised to speak to the media, with the only real conduit being at the Force Headquarters level , and more often than not, at the political Northern Ireland Office level. Further, the authorised spokesmen were civil servants, so the bona fide voice of the military was seldom heard. It is understandable that the military was required to toe a strictly controlled 'party line' as a national operation of a democratically accountable military in support of the civil power on sovereign soil, and against a backdrop of acute political sensitivity. However, the perceptions of the key target audience (moderate nationalist and loyalist citizens), who seldom actually encountered the regular British Army, was not helped by an impression of an aloof and distant entity.

The Falklands

Beyond a few front-line journalists (who, despite being defence correspondents, found themselves closely controlled in terms of content and copy release timelines), the main source of public information on the Falklands War was a daily formal press briefing in London. This was delivered by a rather grey civil servant with a style and voice reminiscent of the government bulletins of the Second World War. This arrangement was judged in hindsight to have been perhaps a little too quaint for 1982.

The 1991 Gulf War

The Gulf War in 1991 saw some embedding of journalists with front-line troops (with greater reporting freedoms) and some effective front-line footage, and generally improved military efforts to co-ordinate and shape media matters, but it was really too short an episode to force the pace of change.

The Balkans

It was with the experience of the Balkans in the 1990s, with UK participation in UN and NATO operations, that things moved on. The looser national controls of a multinational military environment resulted in a more candid and fulsome engagement with the media – both at the international and local levels. In a way that had not previously been the case, proper resources and significant numbers of dedicated media staff officers were allocated to the task and, importantly, public relations evolved to be termed 'media operations', becoming at the same time a recognised component of the overall military effort and wider military lexicon. Further, greater science began to be applied to the subject with planned contingency lines, and assessment and analysis of different target audiences, with commensurate varied and subtle messaging. Though hints of amateurism continued to survive, it was clear nonetheless that a transformation was under way.

Significant in this advance was the recognition and emphasis given to media operations by senior commanders and their adoption of spokesmen to engage the media on their behalf. This was in effect a manifestation of the army's senior echelon's realisation that the media age was upon them. For much of 1995 I worked in Bosnia as the spokesman for the British Commander of the UN Protection Force (UNPROFOR), Lieutenant General Rupert Smith. His approach to the media proved novel and contentious. He diligently avoided correspondents unless the significance of an event truly merited the force commander's involvement. At the same time, this by no means meant that he underestimated the importance of a mature and professional relationship between the UN and the media. On the contrary, he allowed Alex Ivanko (the UN civilian spokesman) and me to fully engage with the media on his behalf, speaking with his full authority. He was not, however, entirely invisible to the media. In fact, he regularly entertained selected correspondents to discreet dinners at the UN HQ (somewhat ironically, Tito's former residence) at which he spoke frankly, but on the strict understanding that anything he said constituted 'background' in media terms: in other words, it was to provide context, but was not for use. This approach worked well. Lieutenant General Smith did not become a media star with all the dangers and disadvantages that such a standing necessarily implies. Instead he spoke sparsely, but on the record when the occasion justified, while allowing himself and his views to be known discreetly by the serious players in the international press corps in Sarajevo. The success of this approach suggests, I would contend, that it provides a viable blueprint for senior military commanders at the operational (theatre) level of command.

The relationship that gradually evolved between the international media professionals and the UN spokesmen in Bosnia warrants comment. On the one hand, the media 'needed' the daily UN press briefings as a vital component of the story. On the other hand, the UN 'needed' the media to maintain the international focus on the operation. Importantly, the relationship was based on an understanding of trust and mutual respect. This might surprise many, because traditionally the military tends to be wary of the media – often without any real justification. However, it need not be the case if both sides work at rubbing along together in the full understanding of each other's very different roles and requirements. To illustrate the symbiotic nature of the relationship, trusted senior correspondents were confidentially forewarned prior to the NATO air campaign of August 1995. Subsequent footage of the destruction of Bosnian Serb trenches around Sarajevo, beamed live from the roof of the Holiday Inn, certainly sapped morale in Pale and Belgrade, while Western capitals took heart at some progress after a long and difficult summer that had included the tragedy of Srebrenica. And the trusted media had their shared scoop.

Technological developments were also a key driver for change at this time. Advances in satellite communications and digital data transmission, coupled with the advent of the twenty-four hour news channels (like CNN) meant that journalists were reporting live from the ground, compelling military actors in theatre and home governments in capitals to keep pace. The later NATO intervention in Kosovo demonstrated, perhaps for the first time, an excellent synergy and unity of effort between the very visible military spokesmen on the ground and the lead civilian spokesman, Jamie Shea, at NATO headquarters in Belgium.

During the late 1990s, under the NATO mandate in Bosnia, the term 'Information Operations' (IO) entered Western military doctrine. This rather ambiguous expression tended to muddy the waters over the next decade. Information operations were in fact just Psychological Operations (PSYOPS) and could, and should, have remained termed as that. PSYOPS – with its dark connotations – were, however, deemed an unacceptable term for broadly consensual peace support operations and a less sinister nomenclature was required. The term 'information operations' would, in my opinion, have been better given to the collective capabilities of media and psychological operations as a distinct effort to fuse and harmonise the two disciplines. But, driven by a military fear of being seen to manipulate the media (a view conveniently propagated as much as anyone by the media itself), media operations and information operations remained separate and unco-ordinated capabilities. So stark was the divide that in many military headquarters a very definite firewall was placed between the two branches. It did not help that media operations were seldom ever viewed as military mainstream business. Often staffed by well-meaning reserve officers with civilian media experience but little military knowledge, or by regular officers with little or no experience in the media arena, media operations were seldom able to gain a full seat at the commander's table. Rather, it developed a reputation as a discretionary, 'soft and fluffy' non-core discipline.

Iraq

The 2003 intervention in Iraq proved a major milestone along the evolutionary path. Both the US and UK made great strides forward. I was attached to the British divisional headquarters as the spokesman for the commander, Major General Robin Brims, becoming Chief of Media Operations across the British land component. I was authorised by London to speak on the record to the media from Kuwait in early March 2003, some two weeks before the operation was launched. This was a time of acute political sensitivity in the UK as the government sought to gain a second UN Security Council Resolution, an affirmative vote in parliament and popular domestic support. Consequently, I found myself walking something of a political tightrope. It was absolutely critical during this period to be fully conversant with the ongoing political dynamics in London, Washington and New York, because whenever I was interviewed questions would inevitably be posed on macro-political issues. For example, US Defense Secretary Donald Rumsfeld had stated publicly that if the British did not participate then the US could, and would, go it alone. I was asked what I thought of that statement on the BBC's flagship current affairs programme, *Newsnight*. Having anticipated the question, I replied that while this was probably accurate, the US military on the ground would much prefer our help which, with a significant ground division, would make their task much easier.

The point here is that an official military spokesman at the operational level has to be thinking across the broad range of issues from the strategic military/political through to the tactical issues on the ground. S/he also has to anticipate and be prepared to go it alone without reference. I often found myself explaining events and answering questions over the following three months that were well advanced of where the operation sat and military planners focused. Further, key to any success I might have enjoyed – and certainly this was the view of the British commander on whose behalf I spoke – was my credibility as a mainstream regular army commander and staff officer, and not as a media specialist (although I did have some experience in that latter forte). In other words, it was more important that I was fully conversant with the art of war than with media studies.

A key innovation of the Iraq campaign was a strategic decision to embrace an unprecedented level of embedded media at every level of the military force. Conceived by the civilian media practitioners in the Pentagon and Ministry of Defence, the initial military response was lukewarm. The mutually beneficial nature of the 'embed' contract was that embedded reporters would be given considerable access and freedom to report, within the bounds of operational security, while being provided physical security with their host unit – but they could not wander away from that unit. Hundreds of non-embedded reporters were also accredited, who would be free-wheelers across the battle space. Conceptually, this was to create a broad-ranging picture of the operation at every level: from the tactical infantry section, through to the operational-level CENTCOM headquarters in Doha, Qatar. Equally, US and UK headquarters had media operations staffs that were fully manned and, to a large degree, integrated with the core general staff at every level.

Did this arrangement work? There is no doubt that an unprecedented amount of front-line reality footage was produced, which served to, if nothing else, inform the global and regional audiences of the realities of war. However, the bigger picture and the degree of informed analysis that it had been hoped would flow from the reporters embedded at the higher headquarters level was, on balance, disappointing. The requirement for intense, visual coverage tended to prevail. A more mature, in-depth explanation of the operation generally failed to materialise. In many ways, this reflected the gradual demise of the war correspondent and the growth of the generalist reporter in recent times. The complexity of modern, effects-based, high-intensity warfare is a complex business (as is COIN) and, understandably, difficult to fathom for any layperson. Competent reporters as they were, it was, for the majority, a subject way beyond their generalist media skills-base.

There were some other novel concepts employed during the campaign that merit mention. In the planning and rehearsal phase in Kuwait in February 2003, the British planning staff had identified two key elements to their plan: the port of Umm Qasr and the oil infrastructure of southern Iraq. Security and control of these two facilities would be critical to post-conflict reconstruction and the future economic viability of Iraq. The term 'media optic' was coined and plans hatched to fly additional media teams to these locations once they were under coalition control. The results varied. At Umm Qasr it backfired, as the resistance was greater than expected and the media were flown into a fierce fight between allied forces and Fedayeen Saddam ('Saddam's Men of Sacrifice') fighters. The hoped-for pictures of an early and obvious success to be beamed around the world (and to Baghdad) did not in the end come to fruition. Rather the opposite: coalition forces were shown to be slugging it out and progressing very slowly to take the first fairly small Iraqi population centre. This did not, as the media reported, bode particularly well for Basra and Baghdad. Conversely, the second media optic, the critical gas and oil separation plants of the southern Iraqi oil infrastructure – which had been rigged to explode – were quickly secured and the media effect maximised. Pictures of this notable success were indeed flashed around the world as planned.

The embedding concept was refined as the campaign unfolded. The London and Washington media planners had been exclusively preoccupied with their national audiences, and thus the embedded reporters were almost entirely from Western media outlets. This pool was widened in-theatre when major regional broadcasters like Al Jazeera were also embedded and embraced by the coalition. Key regional audiences and obscure media outlets were actively sought out. For example, Iranian national TV was not resourced to stay at the Hilton, which was the Coalition's main Press Information Centre and, in consequence, missed the regular press briefings held there. They were tracked down late in the day in a back-street hotel in Kuwait City, where I gave them a one-hour interview to attempt to explain the Western perspective. They were, I recall, unfailingly polite, gracious and grateful. The British Embassy in Tehran estimated that a very significant Iranian audience of many millions watched the interview, and that it constituted their only exposure to a foreign Western spokesman regarding what was happening in their neighbouring country.

Co-ordination between the US and UK media operations staffs worked well, with excellent liaison and discussion at all levels. Differences of approach – like the British decision to go public and accept the legal obligations of an 'occupying power' before the US – while not fully resolved, were at least discussed. The parochial UK effort was well co-ordinated from tactical military level to the strategic political level. The in-theatre civilian government media advisers made strenuous efforts to keep the Ministry of Defence, Foreign Office and Cabinet Office news staffs in London fully briefed (and vice versa) and efforts were fully synchronised. If, for example, the British prime minister was due to be giving a statement in the House of Commons on a certain day, the military spokesmen in Iraq and Qatar would go quiet to allow the full media focus to shine on London.

Information Maturity after Iraq and Afghanistan

As the insurgency in Iraq dragged on, protagonists on both sides increasingly grasped the significance of the media battle.

For Al-Qa'ida, in the words of one of its senior leaders, Ayman Al-Zawahiri: 'We are in a battle and that more than half of this battle is taking place in the battlefield of the media… [We] are in a media battle for the hearts and minds of our Umma'.[2]

For US forces, it was illustrated by the following statements: 'The information environment is just as much part of the battlespace as the physical environment, and commanders at all levels must plan to operate in both environments simultaneously'. (Lieutenant General Odierno, commander, Multi-National Corps, Iraq, 2007.)[3]

And also: 'Traditionally in the course of conventional operations we use information operations to explain what we are doing, but in COIN we should design operations to enact our influence campaign'. (David Kilcullen, then advisor to General Petraeus, Iraq, 2008.)[4]

And here for the first time I refer to 'influence'. As COIN doctrine in both the US and UK has evolved since 2003, influence has become a critical feature. As defined in the British Army field manual on COIN:[5]

> Counterinsurgency is about gaining and securing the support of the people both in the theatre of operations and at home. Influence Activity therefore underpins everything which British forces undertake because counterinsurgency is as much about the battle of perceptions as it is about military operations targeted against insurgents.

As influence doctrine has evolved, so has the definition of the interaction between information and media operations. The worry about media manipulation remains, but there now is an acceptance that the two activities are separate but closely related and with significant overlap. Further, the spectrum of the information operations package has been expanded to include broader influence activity beyond PSYOPS, to include activities such as Key Leader Engagement and Electronic Warfare. And the significance of the Internet to both disciplines is fully appreciated and utilised. This quasi-merger could go further, but nonetheless reflects considerable progress. The organisation of most Western military headquarters will now include the media operations staff closer to the centre of proceedings, at least conceptually, if not always physically. The army field manual again:[6]

Media operations are an essential part of any commander's ability to understand and influence local, regional and wider audiences. They must be coordinated and synchronized with other aspects of influence activity.

As Western influence doctrine has evolved, so too has counter-influence thinking and the role of media operations within it. The insurgent, unconstrained by the niceties of the truth and democratic accountability, and helped by an often austere information environment and an unsophisticated audience, makes use of propaganda, misinformation and disinformation through local and global media channels in masterly fashion – and often at an impressive tempo. Time and time again, coalition forces have been out-manoeuvred in this arena. Slow reaction and rebuttal caused by an unnecessary requirement to gain clearances and co-ordinate the narrative through a layered chain of command are still prevalent and need to be dispensed with. This was a key deduction from our media and effects analysis cells in southern Afghanistan in 2006, where I was chief of staff. To counter this, we simply instructed a sharp, savvy spokesman, equipped only with a mobile phone, operating in the tactical operations centre, to get our side of the story out quickly to key local radio stations, which were the primary conduit for news. In time, whenever the Taliban detonated an improvised explosive device against NATO troops with collateral civilian casualties, we said so within minutes, while the Taliban spokesman in Quetta was yet to get on air. Subsequent target audience analysis established that this move had significantly shaped local perceptions in our favour. The point here is that the very simplest of counter-influence measures can work, once one moves beyond a 'safety first' or 'umbrellas up' approach to interaction with the media.

The journey from public relations through media operations and to the current, all-encompassing 'influence' doctrine has been a long, and at times difficult, journey. The major lesson that I draw from this case study, and my own experience, is that, despite contradictory agendas, a proactive and engaged relationship with the media best serves the military purpose. And while there remains room for improvement, media operations are now at least firmly established as a key component of current British COIN (and broader military) doctrine. Putting it into practice will, as ever, be the hard part.

FAILURE TO COMMUNICATE: 'PRODUCING' THE WAR IN AFGHANISTAN

David Betz

In July 2006 the then International Security Assistance Force (ISAF) commander, General Sir David Richards, now Britain's Chief of Defence Staff warned, 'Afghanistan is a good and winnable war but, at the pace we are proceeding, we need to realise that we could actually fail here.'[1] Approaching the end of 2010 at the time of writing, it is difficult to show greater optimism: 'good governance' in Afghanistan is a term dripping with irony; the security forces are many years away from being able to stand on their own; and the support of NATO populations for the continuance of the campaign, including in America where it has always been the most buoyant, is waning.

It is sometimes said that we have been here before, in Iraq; that 'lost war' was turned around. There is some justification to this view, but to it must be appended some caveats. The capacity for central governance, a self-sustaining economy, and a reasonably vibrant society in relatively literate, urban, technocratic and educated Iraq is far greater than in Afghanistan, which possesses few readily exploitable resources, a largely uneducated population and a society fractured – even more so than Iraq – by myriad regional, tribal, ethnic, linguistic and other divisions.[2] Also, the Afghan campaign is already ten years old – meaning there is a decade's worth of broken promises to make good, in a hurry – and underlying all of this is a looming clash of political expectation and military reality with respect to campaign progress. If it works, and if it follows the trend it did in Iraq, the ongoing surge of 30,000 extra American troops will only begin to produce results in the summer of 2011 and *substantive* results in the 2014–18 timescale; but before then, 'positive trends' will need to be demonstrated if political will is not to falter and end the campaign prematurely.

How did we arrive at this muddle? Why, despite the 'surge' and significant evidence of tactical and operational improvement,[3] is strategic defeat still the most likely eventuality? This chapter argues, based in large part on field research in Afghanistan,[4] that above all there has been a failure to communicate:

- A message of *purpose*, which answers the oft-asked 'why are we there?' question amongst Western audiences
- A message of *resolve*, on which Afghans can bet their lives that ISAF will remain there until the Taliban is beaten or compelled to reasonable compromise
- A message of *what success will look like*, which is accompanied by a compelling rationalisation of the cost.

What we have instead is an ambiguous strategic narrative, a perception of crumbling resolve, and an increasing apprehension in the populations of ISAF-contributing countries that even if the war is 'winnable', it is 'not worth it'.

Theatre of War

Students of insurgency will not be surprised at this turn of events because it has long been understood that 'big nations lose small wars' not because their forces are defeated in the field, but because their domestic will becomes exhausted. This is the master narrative of American failure in Vietnam, and French failure in Algeria, for instance – it was also, to an extent, the *leitmotif* of the USSR's misadventure in Afghanistan and is rapidly becoming NATO's.[5] The basic effect was pithily encapsulated by Colin Powell:[6]

[The American people] ... are prepared to take casualties. Even if they see them on live television, as long as they believe it's for ... a cause that is understandable ... They will not understand it, if it can't be explained.

There is good reason to argue, however, that the effect is even more palpable now because of the emergence of a global 'mediascape' which is more dense, ever-present and pervasive than has existed before.[7] Academic social scientists such as Manuel Castells argue that 'The conflicts of our time are fought by networked social actors aiming to reach their constituencies and target audiences through the decisive switch to multimedia communication networks.'[8] Soldiers such as General Richards concur: 'Conflict today, especially because so much of it is effectively fought through the medium of the Communications Revolution, is principally about and for People – hearts and minds on a mass scale.'[9] And US Secretary of Defense Robert Gates, arguably the most important defence official in the world, laments:[10]

It is just plain embarrassing that al-Qaeda is better at communicating its message on the internet than America. As one foreign diplomat asked a couple of years ago, 'How has one man in a cave managed to out-communicate the world's greatest communication society?'

Good question. Increasingly, scholars and statesmen speak of 'mediatised' wars, voicing an apprehension that the centre of gravity of the wars they are in exists in the perception of the conflict more so than its material actuality. No one has captured this more eloquently than the British general Rupert Smith, who offers this arresting simile of war as theatre:[11]

We are conducting operations now as though we are on stage, in an amphitheatre or Roman arena. There are two or more sets of players – both with a producer, the commander, each of whom has his own idea of the script. On the ground, in the actual theatre, they are all on the stage and mixed up with people trying to get to their seats, the stage hands, the ticket collectors and the ice-cream vendors. At the same time they are being viewed by a partial and factional audience, comfortably seated, its attention focused on that part of the auditorium where it is noisiest, watching the events by peering down the drinking straws of their soft-drink packs – for that is the extent of the vision of a camera.

Perhaps we might assay an answer to the question posed by Secretary Gates by looking at it through the conceptual framework of theatre commander as producer.

The Script

The most strategically debilitating aspect of the Afghan campaign has always been the incoherence of the mission's purpose. There is nothing unusual about mutable war aims, but the hard fact is that the question 'why are we in Afghanistan?' has never really settled in public consciousness. As an American officer in ISAF Joint Command described it, we drifted into it: 'We entered Afghanistan after September 11 for one limited reason – to get Bin Laden and punish those who attacked us and those who sheltered them. And then we just … stayed.' But war needs a firmer plot than this, a 'strategic narrative'; without it, everything else – policy, strategy, action – lacks foundation.[12] A senior ISAF official charged with public affairs described it as the 'central core' while, unfortunately, averring that 'we've lost it … and the international audience has grown lost and uncommitted.'

The campaign in Afghanistan suffers from a diversity of narratives and audiences, including the home populations of the coalition, Afghanistan's neighbours, Muslims worldwide, and the Afghans (who are also divided). For the United States, the war is about 9/11, punishing the perpetrators and preventing the cancer of Al-Qa'ida – which once metastasised in Afghanistan – from rooting there again.

For most of the rest of the coalition, the war is about the coherence of NATO and the relationship with the United States.[13] Meanwhile, the Afghan elite is generally making hay while the sun shines, skimming off what it can of the money the war brings in; not for nothing did a cultural adviser in Regional Command South (RC-S) describe the roots of the insurgency as 'Cashtunwali and the Dollarzai'.

One can see why, therefore, a strategic narrative is elusive; it is very difficult practically to construct a single resonant and mutually supportive message for each audience because all have their own priorities, particular historical beliefs, ideals and strategic circumstances. That said, without it there is nothing to make the story cohere. As the interlocutor noted above summed it up: 'It's like a film being directed by twenty directors. If you can actually get the film finished it will be a miracle – and it will be dull.'

Ideally, one might imagine strategic communications as a spotlight emanating from the highest political authority illuminating everything in the 'theatre of operations', right down to the tactical level. But with ISAF, imagine not one spotlight but dozens, all focusing where and when they will – the 'theatre' will be well illuminated, but what is one supposed to be looking at? How does the theatre commander create narrative order out of this?

The Crew

Not by himself, obviously – after all, the producer does not make the film on his own. Sadly, the disco-ordination of the ISAF information campaign, the 'crew' as it were, is one of the most evident things about it. Whereas 'integrated plans should be the engine of the communications activity', in reality, said a highly placed interviewee at the heart of the campaign, 'they are not'. Some communicators are doing good work, but much of it is 'stove-piped', unco-ordinated with other efforts, producing unexploited 'one-offs', which may in fact cause more Afghan exasperation than anything else, as promises made (or intimated) fail to be kept, and initiatives announced with great fanfare fail to materialise or be sustained.[14] The implications were sharply outlined by a high-ranking American officer at ISAF HQ:

> The reason that the public is losing interest is because we don't know the end state. What is the *internal* political solution? What is the *external* political solution? We haven't thought that through … we get busy and we don't do sufficient political reconnaissance. The key thing is to develop a strategy of influence – we don't have one … We need a political strategy – we don't have one.

Western publics generally have a superficial and skewed view of the campaign. This is not surprising: their governments are also ill-informed.[15] Moreover, the Western media is interested in exciting stories about fighting, not 'stabilisation'; they operate according to the dictum 'if it bleeds it leads', which can make things seem worse from afar than they are up close.

And yet one cannot simply lay the blame at the feet of the media, because the fact is that some governments have positively welcomed public ambivalence and lethargy about military commitments abroad in the hope that this means they will remain off the electoral menu.[16] More broadly, there has been little or no public engagement with a number of uncomfortably plausible suppositions:

1. That, for the European members of NATO, participation in ISAF does not protect them from terrorism on the streets at home as much as it exacerbates the alienation and radicalisation of their substantial Muslim populations from which political violence is erupting[17]
2. That ISAF's own supply chain fuels a nationwide protection racket run by warlords and power-brokers, and is a significant source of Taliban income[18]
3. That for nearly ten years, for a complex of bureaucratic, political

and strategic reasons, the war has been fought in a series of discrete chunks memorably described as 'mowing the grass' rather than in a progressive 'clear, hold, build' manner which might actually defeat the insurgency.

The last point is a particularly bitter pill to swallow. Probably the best face that can be put on it was captured by a senior officer in RC-S: 'This is the third time I've been out and it's been particularly intense, but I think that we *now* have all the pieces right.' Hopefully the pieces are now in place, at the beginning of year ten; yet one must not underestimate the height of the mountain to be climbed. It is a classic dilemma of political marketing with a martial twist: how to sell something which is old and discredited (such as a defeated governing party) as new and exciting?

But the bottom line is that strategic communications in the campaign are not joined up; integrated plans and synchronisation are inadequate. As a result, said one information operations practitioner: 'Unity of command here is not sufficient for every sub-unit commander to understand the intent of the commander and his method'. Perhaps the most important reason for this is that, as a senior officer at HQ RC-S put it, the campaign is radically Balkanised:

> [N]ations do not see their soldiers as contributing to the NATO mission but in terms of narrow national perspective. This nationalist perspective of course makes it very difficult for the public to understand the strategic goal of the NATO mission; they see their soldiers dying for nothing.

In various forms, this idea was repeated in most interviews conducted for this chapter. Where there should have been a streamlined effort and a single coherent message consistently reinforced, there was a multiplicity of often contradictory messages. Inefficiency is built into the system: 'this HQ is too slow', one ISAF official put it simply. ISAF has the feel of a Frankenstein monster composed of diverse body parts gathered from dozens of sources, some strong, others weak, tied together with crude stitching and given life by an electric jolt which struck on 11 September, ten years ago – an animating force which is gradually dissipating. Thus it does not move with swift agility and precision; it lurches.

The Name on the Marquee

According to Morris Janowitz, there are three archetypes of officership: the heroic leader, the military manager, and the military technologist; in the American tradition, he offers Curtis LeMay, George Marshall, and Hyman Rickover as respective examples of each.[19] In practice, most officers are a blend of these types. Is there now a fourth type, the military communicator? It stands to reason; if we really are at the cusp of the Information Age why should it not, as other ages did, produce a corresponding archetype of generalship?

Many of our interlocutors drew attention to certain qualities of the ISAF commander General David Petraeus; particularly his political acuity, televisual and personal charisma, and enormous credibility with diverse audiences that enable him to make complex arguments convincingly. As it was put to us, it is only the commander, ultimately, who can *characterise* the conflict, to crystallise it, in some sense to embody its direction and purpose in the minds of observers, and *contextualise* the events, good or bad, that occur in its conduct – particularly the death and injury of one's own soldiers to the home audience and unintended civilian casualties to the local audience. As an interlocutor in Public Affairs HQ ISAF put it, 'We have an incredible leader and an incredible spokesman. He is the commanding general and the commanding spokesman.'

History's spotlight clearly shines very brightly upon General Petraeus. It is interesting, therefore, to consider how he himself views his role as commander. On taking command of ISAF, General Petraeus used Frederick Remington's famous painting 'Stampede' as a visual metaphor:

I use this painting to describe what we do. I use this image to tell you what I am comfortable with. The painting depicts an outrider galloping full tilt over rough terrain at the height of a violent storm while steering a wilful mount and guiding a sometimes frightened and unthinking herd to its destination. It represents getting the job done despite the challenges. Some of these cattle will get out ahead of us – that's fine – we will catch them up. Some cattle will fall back and we will have to circle back and get them – that's fine – we will bring them on. We must be comfortable with this environment of uncertainty, challenge, risk, danger and competing agendas. We need to accept it. But we need to do more than simply hang onto the saddle. We must master our mount and we must flourish in the apparent chaos and competing ends. I am comfortable with this. It is a privilege to be part of the 'Kabul Stampede' – kick on!

As with Rupert Smith, it probably does not do to interrogate the simile too deeply, but rather to try to understand the overarching message: the nature of the information environment must be accepted because, like the weather, it is what it is – chaotic, uncertain; and yet, also like the weather, it is something which is not merely endured but *exploited* for advantage as part of the military art. The commander and his army who can manage this best, who can find comfort in apparent chaos will, all things being equal, wear the laurels in the end. One should also not draw too rigidly the distinction between archetypes, recognising that the ideal is probably a combination of types and that the emergence of a new type does not obviate others. Nonetheless, it would seem the case that in this age, in our 'overcrowded information marketplace',[20] consumers – that is to say, citizens – need and demand guidance, if only because if you lose your own population they will demand you come home and your own treasury will stop signing the cheques. Thus a new archetype: the general explainer.

But again with Afghanistan we need to consider this in the context of ISAF's multinational composition. Can the ISAF commander perform the role of star, or 'spokesman in chief', for all contributing nations? The British government has struggled to put a British case for the campaign that resonates with its public. Indeed, there is an increasing apprehension in government that operations in Afghanistan worsen security by aggravating relations with the Muslim minority.[21] If this is the case with the United Kingdom, which views itself as the staunchest American ally and is the second largest contributor to ISAF, it is very likely that this is a strategic calculus which applies across the coalition.

The real problem is that political guidance has been lacking. It is a dreadful failure of political leadership, and an inversion of strategic logic, when the onus of explaining 'why we are there' seems to rest most heavily on the theatre commander. The question is perfectly legitimate, but as Canadian General Andrew Leslie lamented, it is not really within the power of the soldier to answer:

> I often get asked … why are you there? … We're there because you sent us … as a soldier, it's not my job to explain why *you* sent us. Soldiers don't do that. We tell you what we're doing, we tell you how we're doing it, but we should not be in the position of explaining to the people of Canada why we're there. The responsibility for that lies with the political leadership and those who sent us.

A problem with Smith's simile of theatre commander as producer is that it ascribes to him more powers of control than he actually possesses (or should possess). Perhaps commander as 'star' (or perhaps an amalgam with producer) would be more accurate most of the time; but on the big issues, on strategic narrative, 'supporting actor' is probably the most correct term. One gets the feeling widely within ISAF that senior commanders feel they are 'holding the bag' for decisions made (or not made) above them. If one does liken the campaign in Afghanistan to a film, its nearest relation might be the Howard Hughes-produced, John Wayne vehicle, *The Conqueror* – a film so awful that Hughes not only refused to have his name on the marquee, he spent $12 million buying back every copy distributed so that there could be no marquee at all.

The Audience

After ten years it is surprising that there remains any rosy tint in the glasses through which ISAF views the Afghan government. This is not to say that commanders on the ground are naïve. In fact, as King notes, General Nick Carter's appreciation of the political terrain in RC-S where he was in charge is astute and open-eyed:[22]

> ...he knows that NATO and the international community have generated the regime and therefore, in part, the very insurgency which it has come to suppress. Political authority – generated and sustained by Western money – flows down these fragmented patrimonial chains to create hatred and mistrust and finally insurgency at the local level.

Yet political authorities in ISAF nations are, by and large, in denial about the ability (or desire, for that matter) of the government of Afghanistan to rule in a manner congenial to the defeat of the insurgency (let alone in a manner we would recognise as democratically representative and transparent).[23] Perhaps one reason why sufficient 'political reconnaissance' has not been done is that it is implicitly understood that if it were, the conclusions drawn – that an 'Afghan solution' would look a good deal messier than Western voters would think worth the price – could explode the foundation of the campaign.

Thus, lacking a credible strategic narrative which resonates with home audiences, ISAF is forced into reactive mode, structuring its response to events as they occur – a straight line route to the surrender of the initiative. Rather than acting proactively, the main focus of messaging efforts is the mitigation of effects, above all casualties (one's own as well as others'). In other words, strategy (such as it is) devolves into endless, obsessive debate over deaths and injuries: how can they be reduced? Again, this is an entirely worthy concern, but it is not actually the crucial question at hand – the 'casualty conundrum', as it were, is more 'what are they for?'. In fact, the public is asking: not 'can the war be won?' to which the theatre commander can assay an answer on the basis of his military judgment, but 'is it worth it?' which is a more pernicious question that no military man is in a position to answer.

On the whole, ISAF also has a poor understanding of the disposition of the Afghan population. The profile of the coalition forces does not lend itself well to the development of a sophisticated sense of public mood. It is practically impossible to fight a 'war amongst the people' without actually being amongst them.[24] The influx of 30,000 more troops into theatre may alleviate some of the difficulties; however, given the high threat environment, it is the case that movements and patrols are conducted in a tactical manner, often under armour, which works against meaningful engagement with the population. Contrast this with the British campaign against the IRA in Northern Ireland in which it was also considered difficult to gauge the mood of the population: in that case the security forces spoke the local language, and shared a common history and a similar culture. Or, indeed, consider how past imperial enterprise was conducted, not so much through military force as through policemen, colonial administrators and engineers – intrepid, highly experienced men, often with intimate knowledge of the language, history, culture and politics of the countries in which they served.[25]

The Afghanistan Assessments Group based at ISAF HQ conducts field surveys, opinion polling and questionnaires throughout the country, producing detailed reports on a monthly basis. Yet on the whole, according to an interviewee in ISAF HQ at the centre of the information operations campaign, both the volume of information and the granularity of analyses were lacking: '… there are just not enough people analysing the disposition of the population and fusing it in a way that the commander can use.' The debate on how to utilise

Taliban atrocities for propaganda effect provides a good example of how this lack of data affects decision-making.

When General Petraeus took over ISAF he announced that he wanted to hang the Taliban's atrocities 'around their necks'. Is this a good idea or a bad one? Publicising the Taliban's intimidation tactics might just help them to intimidate the population better. On the other hand, some research suggests that the Taliban are sensitive to reports that they have killed innocent civilians;[26] thus publicising has the effect of forcing them onto terrain where they are uncomfortable – a sensible tactic. Or perhaps, as a highly placed interlocutor on his third tour put it:

> You don't have to publicize every event but you do need to publicize their excesses. Particularly when they commit acts which are clearly un-Islamic, for it is on their allegedly superior religiosity that they base their authority. For instance, the provincial director of tribal affairs in Zabol, Ata Jan, who was assassinated by the Taliban recently: when his wife intervened to beg for her husband's life while brandishing the Koran they killed her too. As a result of this the Karoti tribe armed themselves against the insurgents to remove them from their territory.

Almost certainly, General Petraeus (who by all accounts possesses a preternatural understanding of media and messaging) means to differentiate audiences: demonise the Taliban internationally, thereby buoying up support from that quarter; but locally avoid building them up for the reasons stated above. Be that as it may, the point which stands out about all these arguments is that they are more or less theoretical: there is no actual data which tells us that Afghans respond to these things positively or negatively. This is what we do not do well. As the interviewee quoted above continued:

> I think that what we really miss here is atmospherics. You need to work out what matters to the people from what people are talking about in

the tea shops. Because what we do too much of here is tackling things that *we* think are important.

It is approaching common wisdom that the Taliban is beating NATO hands down in the information campaign. Former Secretary of Defense Donald Rumsfeld acknowledged this in a Council on Foreign Relations speech in 2006,[27] his successor Robert Gates, as noted earlier, reiterated the point in 2008, and the former UK Chief of Defence Staff, Air Chief Marshal Sir Jock Stirrup, reached a similar conclusion:[28]

> [I]n one particular area [the Taliban have] had the better of 2008: information operations. They've beaten us to the punch on numerous occasions, and by doing so they've magnified the sense of difficulty and diminished the sense of progress. This is down in part to their skill, and in part to our own failings.

The Taliban's superiority at information operations is widely taken as read. In actuality, though, the situation is complex: Taliban information operations are not that good, say some analysts; their message is one which, by and large, Afghans do not welcome and they are not terribly effective at delivering it;[29] and their style of governance is one which the vast majority of Afghans, including Pashtuns, have declared they do not want to have repeated. From a political marketing perspective, this position is not much better than ISAF's – worse in some respects. They do possess certain advantages, however.

First, they have high *coercive credibility*: there is a high fidelity of message coherence between what they say and what they do. In the words of an interlocutor in HQ RC-S where much thought has gone into countering Taliban intimidation:

> In some respects the Taliban are very effective at influence. They have certain levers which we do not. They use fear very effectively. They don't

need to kill 100 people to get their message across. They just have to kill one and the other ninety-nine will go along.

The coalition forces in this respect have it much tougher. The promise 'anyone who co-operates with the infidels is dead' is ninety-nine times more efficient than the promise 'everyone who co-operates with the government will be protected'. Even if it is true that the Taliban's argument alienates and dispirits the population, it is still an effective mechanism of control. This is analogous to the truism 'destroying is easier than building' – ultimately the Taliban too will have to face the problem of building; destruction, however, is sufficient now for the proximate goal of undermining ISAF.

The second advantage is the insensate action of the international media which systematically distorts perspective, making mountains out of molehills and molehills out of mountains in accordance with viewer bias and editorial perception of what sells.[30] Examples of the 'echo chamber' in action are legion but consider this recent very apposite one which occurred during our field research: on the ninth anniversary of 9/11, a small fringe church in Florida planned to burn some Qur'ans in protest. The story of this event, before it even occurred, was broadcast around the world, repeated every thirty minutes on twenty-four hour news; evidence, said the Taliban, that the whole of the Western world was against Muslims, which in turn required the intervention of the theatre commander to decry the affair. Truly, to quote Walt Kelly's famous 'Pogo' comic, 'we have met the enemy and he is us'.

To close this section, as we saw in the previous one, the key thing is to characterise the conflict in a way that can be understood, to give context to what happens within it so that the purpose of sacrifices can be realised, and to know one's audience and let them draw their own conclusions about the cost-benefit ratio. On none of these can ISAF be said to be 'firing on all cylinders'.

Conclusion

Ideally, one might conclude, as did one of our interlocutors, all strategic communications should be 'down and in' from the highest political authority to the men at both ends of the very tip of the spear: 'narrative is simultaneously linear and, paradoxically, circular. Messaging has to be cohesive from bottom to top; to be otherwise is potentially quite dangerous.' The deeper truth may be, however, as Neville Bolt has wrote in a 2010 *RUSI Journal* article, that strategic communications as we have come to know it is dead.[31] There are no certainties: no stable audience, no clear-cut enemy, nor for that matter any seamless ally, or reliable home support. All is in flux and the implications of what we see now in Afghanistan with respect to the adaptation of armed forces to the task of 'producing the war' go well beyond the current contingency.

The disorder of the strategic communications campaign is curious given the importance which has been placed upon it by senior commanders and their political masters. There can hardly be any who have not used the term 'war of ideas' in order to describe the security environment after 9/11; that being the case, why the underdevelopment? Reasons no doubt include traditional ills of bureaucracy and vested interest, as well as a lack of a 'strategic communications champion' and the time lag between operational experiences translating into capability in the institutional army. Nonetheless, the situation is remarkable: if logistics or intelligence, or some other vital line of the campaign, were in as much of a state alarm bells would be ringing.[32]

The problem, if a single one is to be identified, with strategic communications in this campaign is the paucity of strategy behind it. In the course of this research, speaking with numerous clever and committed senior officers and officials, we experienced a certain 'contact high', a feeling that maybe the campaign could be brought to a successful resolution – not 'victory', by any means, but a result which we could live with. On sober second thought, however, the high inevitably fades. The fact is that, as no small number of our interlocutors admitted, there is still no real discernible political strategy; we are in a cul-de-sac of our own making, tied to a regime which has little interest in governing in a manner congenial to our interests, and unable to talk with the Taliban, uninterested as they are in dialogue when it seems possible they will get their way without it.

The main thing on the line is credibility, or put differently, pride. Great powers do not care to be humiliated. Moreover, there is the matter of the bill which amounts now to many billions of dollars and thousands of soldiers killed or grievously, life-changingly injured. How can that sacrifice be requited? What benefit has the undoubted gallantry of the troops in theatre brought to their respective nations? For that matter what has it brought the Afghans? Failure in Afghanistan will be humiliating, and painfully awkward for those who must answer the question of soldiers' mothers, fathers, daughters and sons: 'what was it for?' Looking past Afghanistan, one lesson which ought to be learned is that of governing one's expectations of members of broad coalitions assembled for the purpose of lending the campaign a veneer of international support, and to weigh that advantage against the effect on unity of effort.

Negotiating our way out of this dilemma will be difficult, to say the least. At the end of the day, any marketing campaign whatever its nature – political, commercial or military – depends upon the existence of a saleable product. Clarity about what we are 'selling' – the desired end state, in other words – is required urgently. And if a way is to be found it will not be in conventional thinking or by conventional means. If that was ever possible at all, after almost ten years with the patience of the Afghan and home populations attenuating, it is not possible now. Fresh thinking is required, reducing the expectations of what we can achieve while simultaneously broadening our beliefs in what the Afghans might achieve for themselves – all the while letting go, leaving the 'theatre' with the grace and dignity of an old thespian. Fancy footwork indeed.

ETHIOPIA AND ERITREA: THE FAILURE OF COUNTER-INSURGENCY

Christopher Clapham

The victories in May 1991 of the Eritrean People's Liberation Front (EPLF) and the Tigray People's Liberation Front (TPLF) over the government of Ethiopia are among the most stunning triumphs in the history of insurgent warfare, capable of standing comparison to those of the Viet Minh and Viet Cong in Vietnam, or indeed of the People's Liberation Army in China.

This was no ragtag bunch of guerrillas winning out over a ramshackle government army. Ethiopia has a formidable military tradition allied to a strong sense of hierarchy and discipline, entrenched in the social structures of the northern parts of the country from which the 2,000 year old Ethiopian state historically derives. Its armed forces were generally efficient and well trained, capable of deploying modern weapons including a substantial air force, and during the late 1970s and 1980s fielded a total strength of some 300,000–350,000 men. It was backed to the hilt by one of the world's then superpowers, the Soviet Union, which supplied it with virtually limitless hardware and with senior professional advisers, though without committing any of its own troops. The Ethiopian army fought, almost until the end, with discipline and dedication. It follows that the insurgents were in their turn every bit as formidable, and must indeed count amongst the greatest guerrilla armies in the history of the world.

Conflicts in countries such as Somalia and the Democratic Republic of the Congo have promoted a view of African armies and guerrillas alike as ill-disciplined factions led by predatory 'warlords', often guided by bizarre beliefs, and concerned largely with plunder. This was a very different affair, and holds lessons both for insurgents and for counter-insurgency warfare that are of much wider applicability.

Background

Ethiopia was the sole indigenous African state to maintain its independence through the era of colonial conquest, an honour that it owes to its own long-established tradition of statehood, to the spectacular topography especially of its northern regions (which likewise provided ideal terrain for guerrilla operations), and to the leadership of a series of exceptional late nineteenth century emperors, the greatest of whom, Menilek, was able in 1896 to put into the field an army of some 120,000 men – most of them armed with modern rifles – to defeat an invading Italian would-be colonising army. Not only did Ethiopia maintain its own independence, it took advantage of its military strength and international contacts to extend its territory massively during the period of the colonial partition, especially over regions south of the modern capital of Addis Ababa. Only in the north was it significantly constrained by the Italian colony of Eritrea, which was carved out in 1890 from the northern tip of the historically Ethiopian highlands, along with a strip along the Red Sea coast and a western zone extending to the Sudan. It was from Eritrea in 1935–36 that the Italian fascist regime launched an assault that resulted in the Italian conquest and five-year occupation of Ethiopia. The Italians were ejected in the early years of the Second World War by a British force with substantial assistance from the Ethiopian resistance, and an independent Ethiopian government under Emperor Haile Selassie was restored. The Italian invasion, coupled with plausible historical claims over at least the highland areas of Eritrea and a measure of local support, enabled Ethiopia to secure the 'reunification' of Eritrea with the 'motherland' in 1952, following a decision by the newly established United Nations, in which the backing of the United States was critical.

The Ethiopian administration of Eritrea was, however, disastrous. After fifty years of Italian rule, followed by a decade of British administration, Eritrea had acquired an identity of its own. Though the territory was ethnically divided, with Muslims and Christians each accounting for about half of the population, Eritreans had become used under British rule to a fairly open political regime, for which there was no room in the imperial autocracy to which they were subjected. Many Eritreans, especially in the Muslim areas, had not wanted to join Ethiopia in the first place, and the rapid suppression of the federal arrangement which had been intended to provide them with local self-government left even Christians with a sense of exclusion. At its simplest, Eritrean separatism derived from blocked political aspirations which soon took the form of armed revolt. The first shots were fired in the western Muslim lowlands in 1961, and by the mid-1960s the Ethiopian government was facing a significant though still largely Muslim insurgency, to which it could respond only by force on the one hand, or by simple inducements to local community leaders on the other.

But analogous problems confronted the imperial government in Ethiopia proper, where aspirations, especially of increasing numbers of urban and educated Ethiopians, encouraged by the surge of nationalism elsewhere in Africa, likewise found no outlet in an anachronistic and highly personalised regime based on the palace. Students in particular looked to Marxism as an ideology of evolution, and their ideas spread to the junior officer corps of the army, into which many of them were unwillingly recruited. In 1960 an attempted coup d'état led by the commander of the imperial guard was suppressed, but by 1974 the level of dissent was too great to contain. A prolonged series of upheavals eventually led to the takeover of power by a committee of junior officers, known as the *Derg*, and the aged emperor was deposed, imprisoned, and eventually murdered.

Revolutionary Marxism and Counter-Insurgency

One might plausibly suppose that a revolutionary Marxist regime would be far better placed to cope with insurgency than the monarchy that it displaced. The old order was rapidly swept away, many of the leading officials in the imperial government being summarily executed, and the new regime introduced a series of wide-ranging reforms designed to tackle the inefficiencies and abuses that had led to the revolution. Chief among these was the nationalisation of land, and its redistribution through peasants' associations that were organised throughout the countryside. The removal of the heavy burden of landlord exactions from which many peasants suffered provided the new regime with instant support, while the peasants' associations gave it an administrative structure that was far more effective than the previous system of governors and headmen. Equivalent urban dwellers' associations were established in the towns. An ideology of revolutionary nationalism, reminiscent of the Jacobins of the 1789 French Revolution, assured everyone an equal place in a dynamic new order. Vicious in-fighting between rival Marxist factions created an initial impression of chaos, but by 1977 the dominant clique in the *Derg*, led by Major Mengistu Haile Maryam, had succeeded in killing its opponents and assumed control. An invasion of southeast Ethiopia from Somalia, in an attempt to take advantage of the situation to incorporate the ethnic Somali inhabitants of the region into the Somali Republic, was decisively defeated by an army whose numbers were swollen by peasants eager to defend the regime that had given them control over their own land, assisted by Soviet weapons and advice and by substantial Cuban engagement. In the process, Ethiopia cast off its longstanding alliance with the United States and shifted into the Soviet bloc, which was far better attuned to the attitudes of its new rulers.

The Soviet role was significant, but should not be exaggerated. An alliance with one of the world's superpowers greatly increased the *Derg*'s self-confidence, and gave it a profound belief in eventual victory derived from the conviction that Marxism-Leninism had mapped out the road that Ethiopia was destined to take. The weapons, supplied from the apparently limitless stocks that the USSR retained in its own armouries, were essential. Soviet military advisers were provided, but there is nothing to suggest that the actual conduct of counter-insurgency operations owed much to their guidance, not least because their own assumption that the application of enough soldiers and enough weaponry would necessarily overcome insurgent resistance (a doctrine that was even then, of course, being tested to destruction in Afghanistan) closely coincided with the attitudes of the Ethiopian military. The actual conduct of operations was firmly in Ethiopian hands, and the Ethiopian government proved capable of maintaining its autonomy from its Soviet protector whenever its own vital interests were threatened; as has often happened in such situations, the superpower's commitment to its local client provided that client with significant leverage over its protector. The fact that the *Derg* was overthrown less than two years after the fall of the Berlin Wall, and just months after the collapse of the USSR itself, readily lends itself to the conclusion that the outcome of the insurgencies was simply a knock-on effect of global upheavals, but this would be misleading. This war was overwhelmingly a local affair, and the key sources of victory and defeat are to be found in the Ethiopian government and its opponents.

Critical to the outcome were attitudes to governance that are deeply embedded in Ethiopian political culture, and which were only strengthened by revolution. The societies of northern highland Ethiopia – the region from which the country's tradition of statehood is drawn – are exceptionally dependent on conceptions of hierarchy. Through them runs the belief that effectively exercised power is legitimate, that authority is to be revered, and that orders are (at least publicly) to be obeyed. These assumptions evidently underlie the country's military prowess, and the often outstanding heroism of its armies. But at the same time, they leave little if any place for the arts of 'politics': for compromise, bargaining, negotiation. To question or even discuss the orders of a superior is to challenge his authority. While chains of command are extremely clear, opportunities for collaboration between equals are correspondingly weak, and the system as a whole is permeated by a lack of trust. The carryover of these features into the new regime was particularly evident in the early years of the revolution, when the initially collegiate character of the *Derg* rapidly broke down into a series of factional conflicts, in which the penalty for being on the losing side was invariably death. The first chairman of the post-imperial government, Aman Andom, was a general of Eritrean origin who favoured a negotiated solution to the Eritrean war, a stance that within a few months led to his execution. The logic of such a system is that the most ruthless strongman inexorably rises to the top, an outcome perfectly embodied in Mengistu Haile Maryam. In the aftermath of his accession, resistance both in the army and among the intellectuals who had provided much of the inspiration for the revolution was relentlessly purged.

While the conduct of the former imperial regime had been mitigated by the traditional restraints of family and religion, and by a growing sense of its own weakness, no such qualms affected the new rulers. They had, in their own eyes, swept away everything that was rotten in the 'feudal' government they had overthrown, and created in its place a new Ethiopian state founded on equality and justice, in which any patriotic citizen could find a place. Several leading members of the regime, including Mengistu himself, were drawn from the previously suppressed and despised peoples of southern Ethiopia, who were at the same time the principal beneficiaries of the revolutionary land reform. Any opposition could only be drawn from 'reactionaries' bent on maintaining their former privileges, deluded factionalists seeking to displace the legitimate revolutionary order, or 'narrow nationalists' serving the interests of their own ethnic groups rather than those of the nation as a whole. There was no basis of compromise with any of these people, and no need for it either. Given that the revolutionary government was committed to the creation of a prosperous and united Ethiopia, that it was supported by the toiling masses who had thrown off the yoke of feudalist oppression, and that it was allied to one of the world's great superpowers, what could stop it?

The Insurgents

What could, and eventually did, stop it were two insurgent armies that in many ways mirrored the regime against which they fought. The first and most important of them, the EPLF, started as a breakaway faction from the Eritrean Liberation Front (ELF), the original group formed to fight against Ethiopian control of Eritrea, and drawn largely from Muslims in the western lowlands, adjacent to Sudan, where it had its base areas. The EPLF drew its leadership mostly from highland Christian Eritreans, and was alienated by the ELF's limited appeal to highlanders, dependence on support from Arab regimes, and military ineffectiveness. The EPLF in contrast sought to build a truly Eritrean national movement that would overcome the territory's religious and ethnic divisions, through a Marxist-Leninist ideology that emphasised liberation struggle and the need for the revolutionary transformation of Eritreans. It, too, could draw on the authoritarian social values of Christian highland society, and it established a ferocious level of internal discipline, dedication and control that matched and indeed exceeded that of the *Derg*. When, in the aftermath of its victory against the Somalis in 1978, the *Derg* turned its attention to the war in the north, the EPLF was able to retreat in reasonably good order to a redoubt in the extreme north of the territory, leaving the ELF to bear the brunt of the Ethiopian attack, and subsequently to be driven out of Eritrea altogether.

Within its base area, the EPLF was then able to establish a quite astonishing level of not merely military but social organisation. This was not, in fact, a 'guerrilla' organisation, but one that depended on control of a zone which it was able to defend against all attack by the Ethiopian army, and from which it could then make forays into surrounding areas. Given total Ethiopian control of the air, not only workshops and weapons dumps but even schools and hospitals were tunnelled into the hillsides, and any significant movement of people and supplies had to take place by night. The lives of the 'fighters', both men and women, were rigorously controlled. In contrast to the stereotypical insurgent organisation that sees the guerrillas as swimming amongst the local population like fish in the sea, the EPLF was effectively withdrawn from the ordinary population of Eritrea, into a sparsely inhabited area where its members lived lives of military monasticism. It retained, however, an effective underground network in the more populated areas that served especially to provide military and political intelligence, and to exert enough pressure on the local population to ensure a steady flow of recruits – ostensibly volunteers – into the base area.

Just as on the Ethiopian side, the external factor was important but not critical. The EPLF maintained an image of itself as an entirely autonomous movement, fighting on its own without external allies of any kind, and sustained only by the support of the people and the heroism of its fighters. This image incorporated a heavy dose of mythology. The perennially fraught relations between Ethiopia and Sudan, whose government was fighting an insurgency in the south of the country that received substantial tacit support from the Ethiopians, meant that the EPLF had constant access across a frontier that the Ethiopian army was never able to control. At worst, during normally brief periods of Ethio-Sudanese rapprochement, Sudanese support for the EPLF was merely reduced and hidden. There was no overt military engagement on the Sudanese side. The EPLF indeed regarded the Sudanese armed forces with some contempt, and maintained effective control over much adjacent Sudanese territory itself. Sudan figured largely as a land bridge, across which the EPLF could bring people and supplies into Eritrea. The EPLF had its own dock and warehouse facilities in Port Sudan, and use of a nearby Sudanese airfield, from which supplies were taken by truck into Eritrea, operating by night as they approached the frontier. Weapons were not the most important of these supplies, and there is reason to believe the EPLF claims that they captured most of their arms from the Ethiopians: in the later stages of the war, very large quantities fell into their hands, including tanks and even anti-aircraft artillery, which the Ethiopians deployed in Eritrea even though their opponents had no air force. Ammunition was more often needed, but food was critical, since it was quite impossible to grow enough in the base areas, as were medical supplies and other requisites.

Food was obtained to a significant extent through Western NGOs concerned with famine relief in the perennially food insecure Horn of Africa. Though the Ethiopian government tried to ensure that famine relief entered Ethiopia under its own control, many NGOs – especially at the time of the great famine in 1984–85 – conducted operations both through the 'front door' (official food aid, delivered through the Ethiopian government), and through the 'back door' (unofficial aid, ostensibly to Sudan, delivered through the insurgents). A few agencies, notably War on Want, sided publicly with the insurgents. The EPLF for its part established its own 'NGO', the Eritrea Relief Association (ERA), through which to maintain the fiction that this aid was delivered on a people-to-people basis, separate from military operations. The ERA was in fact closely controlled by the EPLF: its staff were for the most part disabled ex-fighters, and cash supplied by relief agencies for local purchases of food was diverted to military uses.

A further important source of external assistance was the Eritrean diaspora. As invariably happens in conflict situations, a large number of Eritreans had taken refuge abroad, not only in neighbouring states such as Sudan but in Europe and North America, and these communities overwhelmingly supported the struggle for independence. The EPLF pioneered their mobilisation into an active constituency. In addition to local fundraising and propaganda, Eritreans abroad were expected to pay a given percentage of their own salaries to the Front: the EPLF was far more effective in taxing fellow nationals over whom it had no direct control than most African regimes were in taxing their own resident citizens. Doctors, engineers and other qualified professionals spent their vacations working within the liberated areas. Annual Eritrean get-togethers in Europe and North America promoted solidarity among scattered refugee populations, and were addressed by senior commanders from the field. ERA offices abroad served as de facto Eritrean embassies. The EPLF behaved in many ways like a state, long before it actually became one.

The Tigray People's Liberation Front was for over a decade very much the junior relation of the EPLF, a legacy which was to cause problems once it emerged as the dominant force in the government of Ethiopia, while the EPLF ruled the much smaller and poorer territory of Eritrea. Unlike the Eritrean movements, it had no existence prior to the 1974 Ethiopian revolution, and it was formed by a small group of Marxist students who fled to their home region of Tigray, immediately south of Eritrea, from the brutal suppression of dissident revolutionaries in the major towns. Unlike Eritrea, Tigray has no history of separation from Ethiopia – it is indeed the region in which that state originated some two thousand years ago – and it had no basis for a claim to independence. It does, however, have a sense of its own distinct identity, reinforced by a language, Tigrinya, which it shares with the Christians of highland Eritrea but which differs from Amharic, the language spoken to the south, and it has long had a truculent relationship with the authorities in Addis Ababa. It also has a topography admirably suited to guerrilla warfare, and a history of banditry.

For some years after the TPLF's formation in 1975, its members were preoccupied merely with staying in existence, and a determined effort on the part of the government – which faced its own struggle for survival at the time – would probably have destroyed it. Its most immediate foes were other guerrilla movements in the area, notably a 'white' organisation, the Ethiopian Democratic Union, formed by the aristocrat who had governed Tigray under the emperor, and a rival Marxist faction. For it to achieve 'movement hegemony' within Tigray was a triumph in itself, and it remained dependent for weapons and training on the EPLF to the north, which was of course happy to create a buffer zone between Eritrea and the rest of Ethiopia. It nonetheless developed differently from the EPLF, and at times in opposition to it. The exigencies of its military situation forced it to operate in a guerrilla mode, emphasising the close links with the population that the EPLF often lacked; and while the EPLF had the straightforward goal of independence for a sovereign Eritrean state, the fate of the TPLF was much more closely bound up with that of Ethiopia as a whole. In place of the EPLF's insistence on a centralised state directed by a single monolithic movement (itself), the TPLF articulated a vision of Ethiopia as a multi-ethnic confederation in which each ethnic group or 'nationality' would have rights to internal self-government – a programme that enabled it to make common cause with other dissident groups within Ethiopia.

These differences were expressed in divergences in Marxist ideology which, however stultifying they seemed to outsiders, had a real importance for the leaderships of the movements themselves. A moment of particularly sharp disagreement coincided with the great famine of 1984–85, at which point the EPLF refused to allow the TPLF to transport food across Eritrean territory to feed its starving people within Tigray. This caused lasting bitterness within the TPLF, which responded by moving as many of its people as it could to famine relief camps in Sudan, rather than have them take advantage of the food supplies offered (through the global NGO community) by the *Derg*. Though an alliance of convenience was patched up between the two movements, which lent one another considerable military assistance during the key battles against the *Derg* in the late 1980s and very early 1990s, a sense of alienation remained.

The Warfare of Attrition

The Ethiopian government's counter-insurgency operations in both Eritrea and Tigray were always in essence military. Although the *Derg* frequently insisted that its campaigns were 'multi-faceted', their non-military elements had no viable political component, but consisted merely in undertaking economic development projects which were intended to win over the 'hearts and minds' of the populations of the areas in which they took place. The peasants of northern Ethiopia and Eritrea have long experience of the need to knuckle under to whoever rules them, and would the regime have removed the military threat from the insurgents, it could doubtless have achieved the grudging acquiescence if not the enthusiastic support of the local population: a local proverb, 'the sun that rises tomorrow will be our sun: the government that rules tomorrow will be our government', readily expresses the sense that government is something that has to be accepted and endured, but which cannot be changed. To the insurgents themselves, however, the regime had nothing whatever to offer. The only card that it could put on the table was the promise of full participation in the revolutionary order already established to the south – and this was precisely the card that the insurgents had already rejected. Even had they acquiesced, moreover, the *Derg*'s ruthless treatment of its own internal rivals left them with little more than the prospect of similar treatment once they laid down their arms. The wars in Eritrea and Tigray therefore fell into the familiar Maoist logic of protracted conflict: for so long as the insurgents could maintain a credible threat, they denied the government the ability to establish itself; the government, however, had to win.

The wars therefore took the classic form of a series of campaigns in which the government forces attempted to dislodge the insurgents from their base areas, while the insurgents in turn sought to maintain the existence of their forces, establish themselves as the legitimate force in the eyes of the local population, respond flexibly to government attacks, and hold themselves in readiness for a decisive strike against demoralised government forces when the opportunity arose. Until very late in the day, the regime's principal efforts were devoted to Eritrea: it took the view that this was the decisive front, and that could the EPLF be militarily defeated, the situation in Tigray could readily be resolved. In the early years of the Ethiopian revolution, the *Derg* was heavily preoccupied with its own survival, and with only the pre-revolutionary army of 45,000 at its disposal, was in no position to undertake decisive military operations. In the most catastrophic government initiative of the period, the 'peasants march' of early 1976, some 30,000–40,000 landless peasants from northern Ethiopia were encouraged to March on Eritrea to seize land there; not only was the operation defeated with massive loss of life, but it convinced Eritrean peasants that their use of their own land was threatened by the new regime in Addis Ababa, and that their only hope of salvation lay with the insurgents. In the chaos inseparable from the outset of any revolution, and with the withdrawal of much of the Ethiopian army from Eritrea to meet the Somali threat in 1977–78, the Eritrean insurgents – then still divided between the ELF and EPLF – were able to take over the whole territory, save only a small number of garrison towns, and it seemed as though the quest for liberation was on the point of success.

This hope was rapidly quashed by the Ethiopian defeat of the Somali invasion in March 1978, and the transfer of much of the now greatly expanded army to the north. The insurgent successes were rolled back, in the process effectively destroying the ELF, until the entire territory was restored to Ethiopian control, save for the northern triangle, bordered by Sudan and the Red Sea, centred on the town of Nakfa. By early 1982, after extensive preparation and reinforcement, the Ethiopian army was ready to launch what proved in retrospect to be the decisive action of the war: the 'Red Star Multifaceted Revolutionary Campaign'. A well-equipped government army of over 84,000 men sought to dislodge an insurgent force estimated at 22,000 through a co-ordinated three-pronged attack. Opinions differ on how close this came to success, and the attackers came within 3 kilometres of the symbolic target of Nakfa, but eventually the assault bogged down, with appalling loss of life on both sides, and the EPLF survived.

Over the next five years, the conflict in Eritrea turned into a war of attrition, in which – to an extent that would only become apparent later – the initiative gradually shifted to the EPLF. Much of this shift derived from developments behind the front line, including the frustration of the political leadership in Addis Ababa at the failure to gain a decisive victory, and an increasing level of often ill-judged interference in the conduct of operations on the ground. In the country as a whole, too, the enthusiasm that had greeted the early years of the revolution was fading. Peasants who had rejoiced at gaining control over their own land found that the tax burden imposed by the new regime (and far more efficiently collected than before) outweighed the exactions of their former landlords. Military conscription, by which each peasants' association was obliged to yield up its annual quota of recruits, became increasingly burdensome: mothers, lamenting beside the buses that took their children away, were all too aware that they were unlikely to see them ever again. An army renowned for its high level of professionalism was eroded by the steady loss of experienced soldiers, and their replacement by progressively less well-trained and less-dedicated recruits. Morale dropped, the desertion rate increased, and the EPLF and TPLF found themselves for the first time having to cope with prisoners of war. The TPLF in particular trained some of these as cadres, with whom to create allied ethnic organisations in other parts of Ethiopia, under the umbrella of the Ethiopian People's Revolutionary Democratic Front

(EPRDF), as part of its programme to establish a confederation of different 'nationalities' to displace the *Derg*. Its Amhara subordinate started to operate in areas immediately to the south of Tigray that had previously been secure.

The end, when it came, was dramatic. Following a preliminary victory in December 1987, which led the *Derg* to execute its competent but contumacious commander in northern Eritrea, Tariku Ayne, the EPLF launched a stunning assault in March 1988 that overran the Ethiopian army's principal base in Eritrea, at Af Abet. The army corps stationed there, *Nadew* (Destroy), was cut off and destroyed. The veteran British sympathiser, Basil Davidson, who happened to be on the spot during a visit to the EPLF, hailed it correctly as the greatest insurgent victory since Dien Bien Phu. Massive quantities of military equipment fell into the EPLF's hands, as did, more embarrassingly, three senior Soviet advisers. Ethiopian forces were compelled to abandon the whole of northwestern Eritrea to the enemy, retreating to the core area of central and southern Eritrea around the capital, Asmara. From then on, the EPLF's ultimate victory could not be in doubt.

Less than a year later, in February 1989, a similar disaster befell the army in Tigray. An ambitious plan to seize western Tigray from the TPLF, which had steadily extended its control over the region while the army's principal focus had been on Eritrea, led to the Third Revolutionary Army being surrounded and annihilated around the town of Inda Selase. As at Af Abet, the fighting was intense, and some units of the Ethiopian army continued to fight with great courage, but the timely arrival of two mechanised EPLF brigades in support of the TPLF helped to turn the tide. Though the regime's forces pulled out of Tigray and were only able to supply their remaining forces in Eritrea by air, it was to be two further years before the insurgents reached Addis Ababa, as they moved out of the terrain in which they had fought for the previous fifteen years and steadily advanced south. In May 1991 Mengistu fled, and simultaneously the TPLF took Addis Ababa while the EPLF occupied Asmara. The EPLF declared the independence of Eritrea, to be formally confirmed by a referendum conducted in 1993, while the EPRDF regime (in which the TPLF held a dominant place) was installed in Ethiopia.

The Aftermath of Insurgency

These victories confirm the ability of insurgent forces to defeat even the largest, most disciplined, and best equipped military in the whole of sub-Saharan Africa. They resulted more than anything else from the exceptional levels of organisation, discipline and cohesion of the insurgents themselves, directed by skilful and experienced commanders, who despite their lack of formal military training came to match the leadership of a highly professional army. This discipline and experience in turn enabled them to take over the government and run a highly effective state – in sharp contrast to the shambles that followed insurgent victories in Somalia and the Democratic Republic of the Congo, but analogous to Rwanda, where the Rwandan Patriotic Front had a similar coherence, in 1994. In Eritrea, the EPLF simply became the government of a newly independent state: inheriting no bureaucracy, since the government of the territory had been in Ethiopian hands, it took over all the functions of government itself. The centralised command structure of the insurgent movement was replicated in the Eritrean state.

The TPLF had a far more complex task. The existing Ethiopian state bureaucracy for the most part transferred its allegiance to the new regime, providing it with a cadre of experienced administrators, and greatly easing the task of extending its control over a large national territory, but was at the same time wedded to a concept of Ethiopian statehood at variance with the TPLF's programme of ethnic devolution. Politically, too, the TPLF could not simply govern a country in which Tigray accounted at most for no more than 10 per cent of the population, and about which its own leaders, immured for fifteen years in their own mountainous homeland, knew very little. They were obliged to form alliances with other groups, where possible within the framework of the EPRDF, and to extend their support through the establishment of the Federal Democratic Republic of Ethiopia, which at least in principle granted autonomy to every 'nation, nationality and people' within the country. Governing a country as large as Ethiopia was in any case a much more difficult business than imposing control over a small one like Eritrea, and the TPLF/EPRDF for the most part managed it very skilfully. Nearly twenty years after their triumphs, both the EPLF and EPRDF regimes remain in power.

The principal problems that they faced related not to the difficulties of rebuilding effective state structures after long years of warfare, but to the attitudes that they brought to the task. These were most intense in the case of Eritrea. For the surviving EPLF cadres who took on the construction of the newly independent state, the 'struggle' was the defining experience of their lives, sanctified by the blood of the 'martyrs' who had died to achieve victory. Branded into their minds was the memory of the long years during which they had fought against seemingly impossible odds, and of the discipline and sacrifice that had led to success. The assumption that the new state should be run in accordance with the values that had brought it into being was automatic, and indeed these values had much to offer, not least in contrast to the chaos and corruption of so many other African states. Equally automatic was the sense of entitlement: that those who had been prepared to fight and die for Eritrea were those who had the right to run it. No mere vote cast by those who had not participated in the struggle could compare with the claims of those who had. They had won because they had fought, and anyone or anything that stood in their way could be removed by the same means.

Within a very short period of time, the confidence and elation with which Eritreans greeted independence soured. Relations with the outside world were among the first signs of trouble. Intensely aware that this had signally failed to offer them much help when they needed it, and determined to maintain complete control over their own state, the new Eritrean government treated all foreigners with suspicion. Well-meaning aid donors were rebuffed as soon as they sought any leverage over the way in which their money was spent. Fellow African states were castigated for their failure to challenge Ethiopia's assertion that its 'territorial integrity' precluded the possibility of secession. Relations with neighbours, constantly (and sometimes accurately) suspected of encroachment on Eritrea's affairs, were especially tricky. The national territory was sacrosanct. But exactly the same attitudes applied to relationships within the country, where any questioning or even discussion of the dictates of the leadership was instantly equated with treason. The assumption that the state had the right to control every aspect of its subjects' lives was transferred from the battlefield to everyday existence.

The new Ethiopian government was by no means as rigid. Partly because it had taken over a much larger and more complex state in which it had to build alliances with other groups, and partly because its new leader, Meles Zenawi, was vastly more intelligent and open-minded than his Eritrean counterpart, Isaias Afewerki, the EPRDF was able to preside over an opening up of political space after the stifling authoritarianism of the *Derg* years. Meles, charming and articulate, became one of the most sought after African leaders on the global stage, and became a leading proponent – publicly at least – of the post-Cold War ideals of democracy, development and good governance that donors sought to advance. Much of this was a façade: the sense of entitlement to rule was as strong among TPLF cadres as for their EPLF counterparts, and when in 2005 a fairly conducted election appeared to be heading for an opposition victory, the results were swiftly falsified and protests suppressed to keep the regime in power. The practical limitations to the formal grant of autonomy and self-determination to each of the country's ethnic groups likewise became apparent.

Most catastrophically of all, the two post-insurgent regimes became locked, in 1998, in a vicious and costly war over the demarcation of their common frontier. The origins of the dispute were simple: at the time of colonial partition, the Italians had incorporated into their maps of Eritrea territory that was administered on the ground by Ethiopia. The new Eritrean regime, inheriting the former Italian colony, insisted on its right to control territory that it felt to be legally its own. The Ethiopians demurred. The Eritreans then seized the disputed area – a narrow strip of negligible economic value – and the Ethiopians went to war to eject them. After two years and the loss of over 100,000 lives, they succeeded, leaving Eritreans locked into a siege state, in which the unthinkable defeat of their once invincible army reinforced both the international isolation and the domestic repression that proved to be the tragic legacy of one of the most heroic wars of liberation ever fought.

PEACE-BUILDING IN PRACTICE: A PERSONAL PERSPECTIVE ON LIBERIA AND THE DRC
Alan Doss

In his 2009 report to the UN General Assembly and the Security Council on peace-building in the immediate aftermath of conflict, the Secretary-General emphasised the need 'to provide basic security, deliver peace dividends, shore up and build confidence in the political process, and strengthen core national capacity to lead peace-building efforts. If countries succeed in these core areas early on, it substantially increases the chances for sustainable peace – and reduces the risk of relapse into conflict.'[1] As the Special Representative of the Secretary-General of the United Nations (SRSG) in Liberia and the Democratic Republic of the Congo (DRC), I was deeply involved in the efforts to build a framework of enduring peace in both countries along the lines traced in the Secretary-General's report.

Of course, SRSGs come and go, and so I was not on the ground for the entire period of the post-conflict peace-building. In Liberia, I joined the UN peacekeeping mission (UNMIL) towards the end of the transition period in the run-up to the 2005 national elections. When I was appointed to head up the UN mission in the DRC (MONUC) in late 2007, the transition had already been completed, but conflict was continuing and intensifying in the eastern part of the country. What follows therefore is a partial and personal assessment of peace-building efforts in the two countries, both of which are works still very much in progress.

Liberia and the DRC: Similarities and Contrasts

In war and in peace, Liberia and the DRC present huge contrasts and some remarkable similarities. The DRC is one of the largest countries on Earth, and has a population approaching 70 million. Liberia is one of the smallest, with a population of just over 3 million.

The Congo is practically a continent by itself. What happens in the Congo – for better or for worse – can have an impact well beyond its borders. It is physically as well as metaphorically the heart of Africa with 10,000 km of frontiers and nine neighbours, most of whom have suffered from conflict and warfare in recent years. In the new 'scramble for Africa', the Congo with its cornucopia of natural resources – minerals, forests, water and biodiversity – is an obvious attraction for commercial and strategic interests. Should significant oil reserves be discovered, the Congo will become an even greater magnet for commercial (and political) attention.

Liberia is a postage stamp compared to the Congo. It does have large deposits of high-grade iron ore, some diamonds as well as considerable prime forest, abundant fresh water and arable land for agriculture and, possibly, some offshore oil. In strategic and commercial terms, however, it is obviously not in the same league as the DRC. But it does have one great advantage: its historical ties with the United States. This affords Liberia international exposure and access beyond what would normally be expected for a small and poor country on the coast of West Africa.

Where the two countries compare most directly is in the deadly conflicts that overwhelmed them for more than two decades. These conflicts created massive security and humanitarian crises. Both countries suffered from systemic state failure and were despoiled by warlords and assorted domestic and foreign armed groups. Both countries became embroiled in the internal conflicts of their neighbours and in turn suffered intervention by their neighbours. Both were profoundly affected by the end of the Cold War which depreciated their value as strategic outposts, leading former allies to withdraw material and political support. Together Liberia and the Congo became bywords for mayhem and violence characterised by child soldiers, sexual abuse and appalling atrocities.

In earlier times, Liberia and the DRC were among the wealthiest countries in Africa (judged only by GDP, which admittedly is a narrow measure); today they are among the poorest. In both cases, their collapse into chaos, accompanied by widespread destruction and capital flight, led to a huge drop in national wealth and the spread of absolute poverty. Their social indicators went into freefall with dramatic increases in mortality, especially among the most vulnerable. The national administrations – already fragmented and weak before the onset of all-out conflict – totally disintegrated with corruption taking on epidemic proportions. The security services broke up along regional and tribal lines and fragmented into militias and armed groups guilty of unrestrained abuse of civilians and the pillaging of their countries' natural resources. The rule of law vanished. There was a mass exodus of trained and talented people.

The End of War and the Beginnings of Peace

How a conflict ends shapes the way that the peace can be built. Or, as the Secretary-General's report states in more elaborate terms, there:[2]

> [N]eeds to be a basic level of political will, commitment and consensus among the main national protagonists, without which most peace building efforts will be futile. The extent to which a consensus can emerge depends heavily on the conditions under which violence ceases, the quality of the peace agreement, and the nature of the peace process. Some peace processes are robust and inclusive ... and peace building efforts ... benefitted from a detailed agenda to address the causes of conflict. However, many peace processes are more fragile and require careful reinforcement and determined efforts by international and national actors to hold the peace in the face of on-going violence and opposition from spoilers.

The conflicts in the DRC and Liberia did not end with decisive victory for one group or another. After prolonged conflict and much bloodshed, the warring factions in Liberia and the DRC signed off on peace agreements negotiated under the auspices of regional actors and institutions and endorsed by the international community through the United Nations.[3] In neither case was there an outright winner but rather a weary stalemate that forced the protagonists to the negotiating table. What emerged were compromise agreements that included a period of transition leading up to general elections.

Transition and Peace-building

Signed just over a year apart, the Pretoria Accord of July 2002 and the Comprehensive Peace Agreement signed at Accra in August 2003 aimed to end the conflicts in the DRC and Liberia respectively. They covered much of the same ground. Overall, however, the Accra agreement was more explicit and extensive than the Pretoria accord, notably in mandating a restructuring of the security services and designating partners to help lead that process. Also, and of crucial consequence, was the stipulation in the Accra agreement that former Liberian President Charles Taylor could not be a part of the transition. The Pretoria agreement did not prescribe any exclusion.

Both agreements focused heavily on the immediate security and institutional arrangements for the transition. These included: ceasefire, security and demobilisation arrangements; the distribution of ministerial portfolios and state jobs; representation in the parliamentary institutions; and provisions for the arbitration of disputes arising from the agreements.

Although the phrase 'peace-building' does not appear in either of the peace agreements (perhaps because it had yet to become an accepted part of the international lexicon of peace-making), some peace-building dimensions were clearly present in both. I will focus on three dimensions, broadly defined, of the peace process: elections and their aftermath, inclusion and reconciliation; disarmament, demobilisation and reintegration and security sector reform; and stabilisation and state-building. I do so because these were issues I was deeply involved with during my tenure as SRSG in both Liberia and the Congo but more importantly because they are critical parts of the peace-building puzzle.

Elections and Their Aftermath

National elections, although delayed, were held in both the DRC and Liberia as the culmination of the transition processes.[4] Both elections were considered generally free and fair by international observers.

President Kabila won the presidential election in the Congo but his party did not secure an absolute parliamentary majority. As a consequence, he was obliged to include disparate political elements in his government to ensure that the presidential coalition held together, and could maintain a majority in the legislature.

Sadly, early optimism that the DRC elections had marked an end to the country's troubles proved short-lived. The bloody fight in Kinshasa between Kabila forces and the bodyguard of opposition leader Jean Pierre Bemba in March 2007 soured post-election hopes of stability and forced Bemba into exile. The hostilities further alienated a large number of Bemba supporters – mainly in the western areas of the Congo – who had not voted for Kabila. Also critical to the ill health of the peace-building process was the failure of the RCD-Goma political party to garner much popular support in the eastern region of the Congo, the base area that it had largely controlled since the invasion of Rwandan and Ugandan forces. The Tutsi adherents of RCD (Congolese Rally for Democracy), in particular, felt excluded from the new political configuration; and its military wing under the leadership of Laurent Nkunda did not readily accept integration into the Congolese army. The integration effort fully fell apart in 2007 after an ill-fated attempt to create amalgamated brigades in a process called 'mixage' culminated in troops loyal to Nkunda walking out of the integrated units (with their arms). Subsequently, Nkunda launched a full-scale rebellion, which only came to an end with the DRC-Rwanda rapprochement of late 2008.

The Nkunda uprising was not the only source of post-election trouble in the DRC. In early 2008, the Bunda Dia Congo, an irredentist movement with mystical overtones operating in Bas Congo province, staged attacks on security forces. The movement was suppressed with considerable force and loss of life. And in late 2009, a group of armed tribesmen staged a rebellion in northwest Congo, the heartland of Bemba support. Although the hostilities originated in a local community dispute, they quickly spread – possibly aided by elements of the former Mobutu army – and became a vehicle for wider protestations of disaffection with the Kabila regime. Although the rebellion was contained, the embers of conflict were never fully extinguished and retain the possibility of conflagration if stoked.

The Liberian elections were conducted peacefully without significant disorder and adjudged to be free and fair, despite claims of electoral malpractice by the losing candidate George Weah. Fortunately, the ECOWAS mediator, former Nigerian President Abdulsalami Abubakar, was able to referee disputes arising from competing interpretations of the Accra agreement, ensuring that the electoral peace process was not derailed by potential spoilers.

The elections were undoubtedly made easier by the physical absence of the main actor on the Liberian political scene – Charles Taylor. Upon signature of the Accra peace agreement in 2003, Taylor was obliged to go into exile, which facilitated the transition to peace. Although the transitional administration (and legislature) did not run the country well and was accused of flagrant corruption, it successfully contained Taylor loyalists by including them, together with representatives of other political factions and armed groups, in the government.

In the run-up to the elections, there were persistent fears that supporters of Charles Taylor, allied to disgruntled former soldiers and combatants, would create trouble. This was prevented by the large UN peacekeeping presence in Monrovia (and other potential flashpoints), which discouraged attempts to upset the results by violent means; and the close watch over Taylor in exile in Nigeria.

Ellen Johnson Sirleaf was elected president in 2005, a result that was welcomed internationally and accepted locally as probably the best outcome. There was no significant post-election violence with the exception of some sporadic protests organised by supporters of George Weah (the presidential candidate and former football star), which did not go beyond the capital. As in the DRC, however, the party of the president did not gain a majority in parliament. President Johnson Sirleaf recognised that her electoral victory, substantial though it was, did not give her the power to rule by fiat.

Following the elections, Presidents Kabila and Johnson Sirleaf were both obliged to broaden their base in parliament and make appointments to their governments from outside the presidential party (although, to some extent, this was a reward to opposition parties that had backed them in the second round of the elections). Nevertheless, some observers believe that this kind of de facto power-sharing is healthy and in itself a contribution to peace-building because it generates a greater degree of political cohesion and stability than a 'winner takes all' outcome. Others decry what they see as collusion and which, by reducing political alternatives, is not in the public interest.

What is clear however is that the Liberian elections, in contrast to those in the Congo, did help the country turn the page on the violence that had devastated it for almost a quarter of a century. There was a clear-cut winner and no group or faction had the capacity to contest the outcome in a violent manner. Even so, the Liberian elections did not definitively resolve all of the longstanding political tensions in the country. Communal tensions still simmer. In Nimba County, for example, ethnic riots occasioned by the return of Mandingo refugees from neighbouring Guinea raised renewed fears of communal violence. Prompt action by President Johnson Sirleaf to bring the communities together and to reach out to the Muslim community helped diffuse the crisis and prevent the situation from getting out of hand.

A successful election is only one step in the direction of political co-existence and tolerance. It is not a panacea. However, it does bestow a degree of legitimacy which makes decisive and sometimes unpopular action possible – provided the leadership is willing to engage and use that political capital to solve, rather than postpone, problems.

Inclusion

The experience of Liberia and the DRC (and many other post-conflict countries) demonstrates that elections are but one plank in the broader platform of peace-building. While elections are an important benchmark of political legitimacy (assuming they are free and fair), they do not automatically bridge the fault lines that divide communities and cause states to falter. Unless there are determined post-election efforts to tackle unresolved tensions arising from identity, land ownership and protection, among other issues, there is a strong possibility that renewed conflict has only been postponed and not prevented. Rightly or wrongly, should a group feel excluded or marginalised, it is likely to resort to protest or violence if it has the means and the leadership to do so.

This has been the case in the eastern DRC. The Pretoria peace agreement and subsequent Goma accords[5] signed by the National Congress for the Defence of the People (CNDP) and other armed groups did not succeed in bringing the Tutsi minority into the political mainstream nor satisfy the other armed groups. They continued to seek redress through violence, distracting government attention (and resources) from reconstruction and creating a pretext for delays in security sector reform. The Congolese government seemed to lose interest once the accords had been signed, giving the impression – perhaps unfairly – that the accords were really just a tactic and not an article of good faith designed to achieve a lasting settlement. And indeed the CNDP was also guilty of bad faith on occasions by attempting to put new demands on the table after agreements had been signed.

The Congolese government frequently expressed great resentment at what it saw as international appeasement of the CNDP, emphasising its electoral legitimacy and the right to use force if need be to deal with an armed threat to the state. Lacking the military capacity to defeat the CNDP, however, the Congolese government finally recognised that the only way to diffuse the threat was to secure an arrangement with the Rwandan government to divide and then integrate the CNDP forces, while also committing the Congolese army to take on the ex-Rwanda militias (the so-called FDLR).

It remains to be seen if this strategy will work, able to finally bring to an end the conflicts that have convulsed the Kivus for close to two decades. Certainly the rapprochement between the DRC and Rwanda (and the earlier one with Uganda) was a long-awaited and vital step towards ensuring durable peace in the eastern Congo, illustrating again the truism that neighbours must be a part of the solution if they are not to be a part of the problem.

Nevertheless, there are still elements of the ex-CNDP that have not accepted integration (and the loss of their own positions of power and profit). Long-held grievances and grudges do not necessarily disappear with the end of open warfare. Reconciliation, protection and the promotion of human rights must be equally sturdy planks in the platform of peace-building.

Reconciliation

Reconciliation is often viewed through the prism of truth and reconciliation commissions (TRCs). Both the DRC and Liberia established national TRC bodies (although the one in DRC did not really get off the ground). The Liberia TRC has proved to be highly controversial and its recommendations are unlikely to be implemented in full because they call for bans on individuals who are currently active in public life, including President Johnson Sirleaf.

However, in several countries we have seen that TRC mechanisms have played an important role in post-conflict peace-building, notably in South Africa. They allow victims and survivors to tell their story, ensuring that the historical record is not silent on the anguish of ordinary people caught up in extraordinary events. But reconciliation has to go beyond a historical account of injustice and suffering. It has to be community- as well as nationally driven to achieve a lasting impact. This cannot be done by a commission sitting in or travelling periodically from the capital; this is work that has to be undertaken region by region, community by community, day in and day out, in the field itself.

The focus of post-conflict reconciliation should be on the local well-springs of conflict. This means working with communities on their particular concerns, helping them to find their own solutions to problems that sometimes reach back generations. Both in the DRC and Liberia, for example, the return of refugees and internally displaced persons has been a flashpoint triggering violent, xenophobic reactions which, if left unresolved, will provoke new bloodshed.

These kinds of issues have to be managed at the community level. At the same time, reconciliation requires engaged national leadership, sending the right signals and actively encouraging reconciliation on a continuing basis. Electoral legitimacy is important, but in deeply divided societies it is not enough. Post-conflict leaders must see peace as an ongoing process of persuasion, compromise and protection that does not end with an election or when political opponents may no longer be active on the national stage.

Here again there is an interesting parallel between Liberia and the DRC: Charles Taylor and Jean Pierre Bemba are both on trial in international courts for crimes committed not in their own countries but in neighbouring states (Sierra Leone and the Central African

Republic respectively). Their absence from the political arena has facilitated post-conflict peace-building by Presidents Kabila and Johnson Sirleaf by removing opponents capable of mobilising armed opposition to their governments. But whatever the fate of Taylor and Bemba, their respective regional and ethnic constituencies have not disappeared; they will need to be managed adroitly and humanely to preclude a relapse into violence.

Rights
This is a central dilemma of peace-building: how to arrive at a framework of governance that ensures inclusion, tolerance and equity but recognises that those elected have a right to govern in the name of all. A politically expedient arrangement that simply shares out privileges in the name of 'power-sharing', co-opting political elites and diluting or eliminating political alternatives, is not the answer if it leaves underlying grievances and tensions unresolved.

Contemporary peace agreements usually insert provisions on human rights because their flagrant abuse and violation has often been both a cause and a consequence of conflict. Both the DRC and Liberia peace and transitional arrangements called for the establishment of human rights monitoring and protection bodies. Only recently, however, has Liberia fully constituted its independent human rights commission; in the DRC, it is still a distant prospect. Without full autonomy and, crucially, independent funding, such bodies cannot work effectively because they can be easily controlled by the government of the day.

Sexual violence is a special concern. Women are victims in war and too often in peace as well. Liberia has taken on the problem head on; the DRC has yet to do so despite the horrific toll that sexual violence continues to exact in the eastern areas of the country. Ending the conflicts in the eastern Congo will help to reduce the violence against women and children as has happened in other parts of the country now at peace. Nevertheless, the DRC could usefully emulate some of the initiatives taken in Liberia such as creating opportunities for women to join the police and to lead judicial institutions.

DDR, SSR and National Security Policy

The most visible and dangerous manifestation of the collapse of law and order in the DRC and Liberia was the proliferation of militias and armed groups. Some of these groups were created for self defence but all too often they were means of advancing the interests of political leaders, warlords and even foreign powers. Many of these groups forcibly recruited child soldiers – although the economic disintegration that accompanied Liberia and the Congo's political implosion produced a ready (and cheap) supply of foot soldiers for the armed groups.

The 'standard' model of post-conflict stabilisation now usually includes a DDR package and a call for SSR. However, the DDR and SSR processes in the DRC and Liberia have differed quite radically, with profound consequences for peace-building.

All of Liberia's combatants, including soldiers of the former Liberian army, were demobilised under US and international supervision, even though the Accra peace agreement called only for reform and restructuring. No option of automatic re-enrolment in the Liberian army was offered to former soldiers or ex-combatants from the militia. Residual security functions were entrusted to the UN peacekeeping operation and the national police (which went through a vetting and demobilisation process as well). Critically for security reform, UN forces in Liberia were proportionally far greater in number than in the DRC and could therefore assume a much higher security profile. The national police were also subjected to professional competency and human rights vetting under UNMIL auspices, and a significant number of the active police retired as a result.

The Liberian DDR programme ran into some initial difficulties with logistics and benefits and had to be suspended for a few months before it got back on track and succeeded in demobilising the armed groups. The army demobilisation effort was funded by a group of donors including the US, UK, South Africa and the European Union, with the US picking up the bill for the recruitment and training of the new (and much smaller) army. The whole process was overseen by a joint committee headed by the Liberian government with the strong participation of donors, UNMIL and regional partners (the African Union, ECOWAS, Nigeria and Ghana); during this transitional period the army was headed by a Nigerian general on loan to the Liberian government (a somewhat similar approach to that used in Sierra Leone). Although there were numerous and sometimes violent demonstrations by ex-servicemen (usually linked to demobilisation benefits), President Johnson Sirleaf was willing to face them down and ensure that the programme for the reconstitution of the Liberian army was not disrupted.

The new Liberian army is brigade strength and its mission is focused on territorial protection with provisions for aid to the civil power in case of emergency. Given the past experience of military abuse, public opinion in Liberia is understandably anxious about the future role of the army and insists very strongly that it must be subject to civilian control through governmental and parliamentary oversight. The degree of control to be exercised by these two arms of the government was – and still is – the subject of debate.

Beyond the operational programmes designed to recast the army and police force, the international community was able to engage in a structured dialogue with the Liberian authorities on security policy and national security architecture. An exercise led jointly by the government and UNMIL was undertaken to map out risks and threats and potential 'hot spots', culminating in the formulation of a national security policy.

In contrast with Liberia, former Congolese combatants as well as regular soldiers were given a choice of demobilisation and reintegration into civilian life, or military integration. Many opted for military integration because it offered some economic prospects and the power that comes with owning a gun. As a result, tens of thousands of former militiamen were integrated into the army, including the officer corps. They were able to do so without any vetting for human rights violations or even basic military competence: this was the price of peace. It is a price that has been paid several times over in subsequent peace agreements, which continued this practice.

The consequences of the decisions to allow wholesale recruitment of ex-militias into the Congolese army (FARDC) are very visible today. It explains in part (but does not excuse) the misconduct and ill discipline of the troops, the poor performance of combat units and the low state of FARDC morale. The plethoric size of the army makes the demobilisation of a significant number of troops an essential step to improve performance and pay; it also makes it a risky political and security exercise. But without such a demobilisation the prospects for improving the functioning of the army are slim.

The decision of the World Bank and other donors to suspend their support for the DDR programme in 2007 because of financial irregularities complicated the search for stability through DDR. The disrupted demobilisation left many ex-combatants and demobilised army soldiers without promised benefits, creating a potential source of violent dissent – and a reservoir for recruitment by newly emerging armed groups.

Despite considerable international pressure, and the openly expressed frustrations of President Kabila, SSR has not moved very far forward in the DRC. Assistance for army reform has come from a variety of partners (Belgium, France, the US, South Africa, the UK, China, Angola and the Netherlands) and has been largely concentrated on the training of selected battalions as part of a rapid reaction force and the improving of military infrastructure (such as barracks). Some assistance has been provided, mainly through the European Union, to help improve the control and command structures with decidedly mixed results; while MONUC/MONUSCO has provided field-level support for operations against armed groups and military justice, again with mixed results.

Unlike in Liberia, there has been no systematic dialogue between the government and partners on SSR and security policy. I tried on many occasions to launch such a dialogue on the back of the government's own declared plans for reform but without success. It became clear to me that the Congolese government did not want a multilateral dialogue, preferring to handle army reform issues on a purely bilateral basis. There was more openness, however, to concerted action on police reform.

Security Reform

Security reform is a vital but complex dimension of peace-building that is best done early, when an incoming government still has credibility and international goodwill. Post-conflict countries, more than most, need effective and accountable security forces to deal with the myriad security challenges they face. This is not just about a stronger or more efficient army; it is about the way a country anticipates and prepares for threats to stability and the democratic order from within or outside the country. When crises erupted in the DRC, which happened frequently, the National Security Council's response was always reactive with little contingency planning – this was essentially management *by* crisis not *of* crisis.

The DRC's road to SSR has been quite tortuous. While I was able to engage freely with very senior Congolese interlocutors on national security concerns, I did not make much progress in organising a structured dialogue on national security policy. The post-election confrontation with Bemba, followed by the renewed outbreak of fighting in the east (and more recently in the Equateur province), undoubtedly discouraged President Kabila from taking the bold steps required to fundamentally reshape and redirect the security services. The manifest lack of confidence between the government and the international community compounded the problem, continuing to impede and inhibit a constructive discussion on security policy in general and on army reform in particular.

Other aspects of the SSR agenda have suffered as well. There has been some progress on police reform but this has not reached all levels in all regions. Inadequate support from the government side has delayed the deployment of police in areas freed of the presence of armed groups. The implication of senior police in the death of leading human rights activist, Floribert Chebeya, in June 2010 has led to a further loss of public confidence.

Both civilian and military justice in the DRC leave a lot to be desired. There is not much evidence of progress and donors are reluctant to commit significant additional resources without some assurance that reform will be pursued seriously. These kinds of difficulties are not unique to the Congo: post-conflict countries are by definition fragile and therefore much less able to pull off the reforms needed to establish credible state institutions, restore confidence and build stability.

Nevertheless, the ultimate success (or failure) of peace-building in the Congo will depend in large measure on the progress of security sector reform, including the revamping of the national security architecture and the criminal justice system. Without those reforms, lasting stability may prove elusive. This will require determined leadership, confident that it can overcome resistance to change and willing to remove senior officers who stand in the way. These changes will not happen quickly, and the president will be anxious not to forfeit the goodwill of the army in the run-up to the general elections scheduled for November 2011.

A more confident approach to SSR was possible in Liberia because President Johnson Sirleaf enjoyed a security guarantee from the UN Security Council and ECOWAS, giving her the political space to move ahead with the disbandment of the army and reform of the police. She welcomed external assistance and advice on the understanding that her government would be in the driver's seat and would make the final policy decisions. Most importantly, President Johnson Sirleaf came across as a strong and credible leader who could generate political and funding support from international partners.

State-Building and Stabilisation

Liberia is the oldest republic on the African continent, dating from 1847. It was a signatory of the UN Charter and later a founding member of the Organization of African Unity. The Congo is a much younger state, achieving independence from Belgium in 1960. Nevertheless, both states were artificial constructs emanating from colonial ventures.

In the 1980s, the two countries began to fail under the cumulative weight of longstanding, unresolved internal tensions and the misgovernment of the Americo-Liberian elite in Liberia and the Mobutu regime in then-Zaire. The end of the Cold War, and the withdrawal of loosely conditioned aid, was the proverbial nail in the coffin. Both regimes were overthrown by violent means, which in turn triggered the near collapse of the two states as functioning entities capable of ensuring protection of their citizens under the rule of law, a minimum level of basic social services, and the upkeep of essential infrastructure. State institutions fell into complete disarray, exacerbated by the flight of human and financial capital.

With the conclusion of the peace agreements and the start of the transition, attention turned to stabilisation and the revival of the state institutions required to direct and manage post-conflict reconstruction and development.

Rebuilding State Institutions

The 'comprehensive and inclusive agreement' for the DRC did not provide much guidance for this work beyond listing the institutions of the transition and demarcating the separation of powers between the executive, the legislature and the judiciary. The Accra agreement for Liberia contained similar provisions but went further, mandating the establishment of a good governance commission, a contracts and monopolies commission and an independent national commission on human rights. It also called for the establishment of an international stabilisation force. In addition, both included provisions for co-ordinated follow-up to the agreements with international participation and assistance.

The results so far in the DRC have not lived up to initial hopes. Despite significant donor support, the government is still struggling to put in place viable institutions that can effectively manage the fundamental responsibilities of the state.

This problem is by no means restricted to the security sector. The administration of justice is woeful and impunity flourishes. The public administration is plethoric, poorly paid (if at all) and generally unresponsive. Civil service reform is as much needed as security reform.

Unfortunately, corruption is omnipresent in the DRC, impeding the collection of much-needed state revenue and discouraging responsible investment. There is not much transparency in the way major concessions and contracts are awarded and monitored. So much so that the IMF insisted that a major contract/concession with Chinese interests be renegotiated before it signed off on the debt relief package.

There has been progress, however, in the management of public finances – or at least sufficient progress to satisfy the IMF, World Bank and the Club de Paris. The DRC finally reached the Heavily Indebted Poor Countries (HIPC) Initiative completion point in July 2010 leading to debt service savings worth about $12.3 billion.[6] To quote the IMF: 'Reaching the HIPC completion point demonstrates the significant progress that the authorities have made over the past several years in strengthening macroeconomic policy management and performance'.[7]

The Congo has also produced the mandatory poverty reduction strategy paper as part of its commitment to secure debt relief.

According to UNICEF, there has been progress in reducing the rates of infant and child mortality (among the highest in the world) and expanding access to basic education.[8] These gains are important but absolute poverty and deprivation remains the norm for the majority of the Congolese people.

The building of an effective administration that can lead the way on poverty reduction and lay the foundation for enduring peace is a task that will require many years of sustained capacity-building allied to the improvement of public servants' conditions of service. International partners have not really focused on this issue in a systematic manner. Aid remains largely project-based and delivered via foreign experts and consultants. None of the donors are yet willing to contemplate budget support despite the well-known constraints created by project aid.[9]

Regionalism and Decentralisation

The international community has also been highly selective in directing its aid to the eastern areas of the country, largely for humanitarian relief. This is understandable given the grim economic and social conditions that have resulted from the recurring crises in that part of the country. Other regions of the Congo have not attracted the same kind of support, despite the fact that the human development indicators for some areas like Equateur province in the west are much worse than for the Kivus, raising issues of regional equity. This is why the UN has been encouraging the idea of a peace consolidation programme for the western areas of the country to complement the stabilisation effort in the east.

The decentralisation of powers mandated by the constitution adopted in February 2006 should be a driving element of the peace-building agenda. Given the vast size of the DRC, its cultural diversity and poor infrastructure, some level of decentralisation is both managerially indispensable and politically desirable. With the adoption of the new constitution in 2006, a process of decentralisation was inaugurated with the objective of bringing government closer to the people. Provincial assemblies were created, with authority to elect provincial governors. Revenues were to be returned to the provinces on a proportional basis and service delivery devolved to the provincial administrations.

By common consensus, the outcome has been disappointing. Several of the assemblies have been paralysed by partisan disputes. Governors have become hostages of the assemblies, with some voted out of office when they did not meet their demands, especially on financial matters. Others have alienated the central government. Revenues have not been returned to the provinces as originally conceived and this has antagonised richer and poorer provinces alike. Service delivery, which was already marginal, has gone into freefall.

This experience has stalled the next phase of decentralisation. By May 2010, an additional fifteen provinces should have been created. This has not happened, and is unlikely to, despite a constitutional provision mandating this change. Predictably, this has created a political backlash in areas where the new provinces were to be established.

The whole construct of decentralisation in the DRC, including the electoral arrangements for the governorship, needs review and further debate. The desirable and the practical have to coincide otherwise decentralisation will remain an unfinished and unworkable project to the detriment of long-term peace-building in the Congo.

Stabilising the East
The eastern Congo stabilisation plan is an initiative aimed at focusing and decentralising peace-building in the country. The plan was originally requested by the Security Council, recognising that UN security support in the east needed to be backed up by a sustained and co-ordinated programme of economic and social assistance. Unfortunately, the renewed violence in the Kivus in 2008–09 slowed the momentum of stabilisation. The government's first priority was

security, not stabilisation. Donors, with a couple of exceptions, were also reluctant to commit resources, given the uncertain security situation.

The structures of the stabilisation programme (STAREC) are now in place. However, there have been delays in the assignment of state agents, especially the police and magistrates, due to a lack of funding, the reluctance of cadres to move, and continuing security worries in areas where the stabilisation programme should be most active: those areas that have been liberated from the domination of armed groups. These factors have undercut the impact of the programme.

The government's strong and continuing commitment is indispensable to overcoming bureaucratic obstacles and resource constraints. Without this engagement, momentum will slow and opportunities will be lost. The failure of the Congolese state to reassert its presence has already prompted the return of armed groups to isolated areas with disastrous consequences for local people who have been subjected to brutal reprisals including mass rape.

In my view, stabilisation should not be considered an add-on that becomes feasible only when conflict has run its course. It should be part and parcel of the peace process and an integral element of the overall security strategy.

In addition, jobs have to be a central concern of stabilisation. Roads, for example, are vital to security, especially in areas like the Kivus where isolated communities are most at risk of attack, but are difficult to reach and protect in an emergency. Hence road construction can be used to put ex-combatants to work and in doing so serve to improve security by providing economic alternatives to participation in the militias. It is a practical and relatively cheap way of creating work for conflict-affected communities. Such an initiative was undertaken in Liberia where labour intensive public works were launched with the support of UNMIL, the World Bank and the UNDP as a means of providing an alternative to militia recruiters. A similar effort is under way in the eastern DRC but it needs to be expanded to ensure visible impact and, in doing so, help change the perception that a relapse into conflict is inevitable.

The International Dimension

In the years since the Pretoria and Accra agreements were signed, 'peace-building' has become a familiar phrase in the vernacular of the international community. As a concept, it focuses very much on what national actors must do to end the recurring cycle of violence and destruction, but it does also create a framework for the engagement of international partners that goes beyond humanitarian relief.

Donors are now more willing to direct official development assistance to core pillars of peace-building such as security sector reform. They recognise that failed or faltering states cannot be turned around quickly and that structural weaknesses may require many years of consistent attention and support to remedy them. The DRC and Liberia provide another instructive contrast in how that assistance can be effectively sourced, co-ordinated and used for building peace.

In Liberia, the moment the election results were known, the international community, through the International Contact Group, sought to establish a dialogue with the incoming president, focusing on ways to provide an early peace dividend. A 150-day emergency programme was designed and funding mobilised.

Although the programme was probably too ambitious and could not be fully funded, it did give a sense of direction and purpose in contrast to the drift that had characterised the previous transitional government in Liberia. Some high-profile projects were included such as the re-electrification of Monrovia, a city bereft of electricity for more than two decades. Getting the lights back on in the capital was an economic and social priority, which also paid political dividends.

President Johnson Sirleaf also moved quickly to deal with contracts and concessions. She established a joint government/donor mechanism to review them and to make recommendations on their renegotiation or cancellation if need be. Given the poor track record of the transitional and previous administrations in this area, this was a move welcomed by the donors (and the Liberian public) who subsequently supported the government in its battles with companies that had benefited from lopsided contracts and concessions awarded during the Taylor and transition years.

The government is still haunted by serious allegations of corruption. Nevertheless, the willingness of the Security Council to lift sanctions on the export of timber in June 2006 was a sign that the international community was gradually gaining confidence that some progress was being made in tackling the endemic problem.

In fact, the concessions and contracts review was part of a wider initiative on economic governance that had been put in place in the final days of the transitional government. It was intended to improve accountability and transparency in the management of public finances and state resources as a counterpart to enhanced donor support. The initiative – known as GEMAP (Governance and Economic Management Assistance Programme) – was opposed by the outgoing administration as an infringement on national sovereignty and indeed initially opposed by then-presidential candidate Johnson Sirleaf.

On assuming office, however, Mrs Johnson Sirleaf revised her earlier opposition to GEMAP while making it abundantly clear that the programme would be nationally led, an approach that the partners again welcomed. This was done through two joint committees personally chaired by the president: the GEMAP steering committee and the Liberia Reconstruction and Development Committee, which was charged with co-ordinating the overall national reconstruction programme.

This openness to working with international (and regional) partners made good political as well as economic sense. It enabled Liberia, for example, to get on the track to debt relief fairly quickly even though it was one of the three countries that had originally been specifically excluded from the HIPC debt relief scheme. It also encouraged a substantial donor investment in SSR.

At the conclusion of the transition in the DRC, some consideration was given to launching a GEMAP-type initiative but the idea never materialised, probably because of the anticipated opposition of the new government. A quite elaborate, multidimensional co-ordination structure was put in place but this has not proven very effective in stimulating an active policy dialogue with the government.

The Congolese government at times seems quite allergic to co-ordination, perhaps fearing that its own prerogatives will be diluted. This may stem from previous experience with the co-ordination mechanisms set up during the transitional period, notably the International Oversight Committee for the Transition (known by its French acronym, CIAT), which President Kabila came to view as a paternalistic and intrusive group. Co-ordination has worked best in the DRC around limited objectives or programmes rather than through broad-based mechanisms.

This apparent reluctance to engage with the international community in a structured and open fashion has not helped the DRC peace-building agenda. While peace-building is first and foremost a national responsibility, it does require external resources and political support, which means framing and delivering messages to regional and international partners in a convincing manner that builds confidence locally and beyond. Donors also need to align and simplify their agendas. In the DRC and Liberia, as in other post-conflict states, government capacities are stretched to the limit and simply cannot meet all donor expectations. Ironically, donor demands are greatest on some of the weakest governments in the world.

Building Confidence in Peace

Peace-building is really about confidence-building: confidence that the future can be better than the past. As the DRC and Liberia emerge from protracted conflict and terrible violence, their governments and societies must work to build that confidence, emphasising and investing in human security and economic stability – the cornerstones of successful peace-building.

Without that confidence, citizens and international partners alike will not make the political and economic commitments that are needed to secure the state and protect the individual. Peace-building should not become a perverse reversal of the Clausewitz dictum: the continuation of conflict by other means.

The international community can and must help with resources and counsel. It should understand, however, the enormous political challenges and immense economic constraints that post-conflict leaders and their governments face as they try to rebuild their countries.[10] This does not mean turning a blind eye to systemic government failure or abuse but it does require conciliation and concession, recognising that in peace-building, as in most human endeavours, the perfect is usually the enemy of the possible.

Of course, the heavy lifting will have to be done by the leaders and people of the DRC and Liberia; only they can determine the course of peace and make the tough choices and uncomfortable compromises that will build and sustain peace. Not an easy job by any means, but an unavoidable and indispensable one.

THE MILITARY ROLE IN POLITICAL VICTORY: SOUTH AFRICA, NAMIBIA AND APARTHEID

David Williams and Greg Mills

> War is a political activity. Unless there is a valid policy for which it is being waged, and unless that policy governs the means applied to waging it, there is a vacuum of purpose.
>
> (General Sir David Fraser, in *Alanbrooke*)

'The Border', the shorthand term by which the war in Namibia and Angola from 1966 to 1989 was known, was at its simplest the line dividing the territories of the two countries (Namibia, until 1989, was known officially as South West Africa). From the Atlantic Ocean, at latitude 15 degrees south, this line follows the course of the great Cunene River eastwards across Africa for about 350 km. Then it becomes a straight line, drawn in the arbitrary fashion of colonial administrators dividing up a continent, running parallel to the equator for another 450 km. Then it follows the course of another river, the Okavango, for 300 km, and reverts again to a colonial straight line for another 350 km. It is a border of some 1,600 km – the distance from Johannesburg to Cape Town, or from Ireland to Scandinavia.

On the southern side of the Border, in the province of Ovamboland, are the exotic places that became familiar as bases and postings for thousands of South African Defence Force (SADF) troops: Ruacana, Ondangwa, Oshivello, Oshakati, Rundu, Katimo Lulilo, the Caprivi Strip. Further south was the major military base at Grootfontein, 600 km north from the capital Windhoek. By train,

Windhoek was in turn 2,143 km from Johannesburg via De Aar by train, a circuitous journey that took at least four days. By air from Pretoria, Grootfontein was 1,600 km or three hours away – longer by an hour than any air journey within South Africa.

Whatever the interpretations of history, we know that the Border was a long way from home, logistically and psychologically. Its geography was strangely unfamiliar, even to the families of the men who served and fought in SWA and Angola. 'Somewhere on the Border' became a coded term used by tens of thousands of white South Africans to refer to a war fought unevenly over a period of twenty-five years. The vagueness reflected the ambivalent, shadowy nature of the SADF's defence of SWA – a territory over which, the rest of the world believed, it had no sovereignty. Details of operations – time, place and objective – were seldom released, even when there had been resounding success. For example, Operation *Savannah*, the 1975 intervention by the SADF in Angola that involved dozens of units, was expressly denied by the South African government even when it was far advanced – and few details were released when it was over. Already loathed and increasingly isolated because of its apartheid policies, the government in Pretoria was anxious not to be perceived globally as the aggressor, and worried about the reaction of its own white constituency.

The Origins

South Africa's strategy in fighting the Border War had its origins in a much earlier conflict. At the outbreak of the First World War in August 1914, Britain asked the Union government led by Prime Minister Louis Botha to render 'urgent imperial service' by seizing control of German SWA, thereby denying Germany access to the colony's harbours. This was achieved in a campaign led by Botha himself – the first operation by the Union Defence Force, formed in 1912. After the war, as one of the victorious allies, South Africa was mandated by the League of Nations to administer SWA. It did so for the next seventy years. For much of that time this vast, sparsely populated territory – a population of less than a million, but larger in land surface than Britain, Italy and Germany combined – was in effect treated by Pretoria as a fifth province. Several MPs from SWA sat in parliament in Cape Town; the territory's rugby team competed in the Currie Cup; and Afrikaans was one of the dominant languages.

But Pretoria's authority over SWA was increasingly contested from the 1960s, after the United Nations revoked the mandate and South Africa's occupation was declared illegal. The most direct political and military challenge came from the South West African People's Organisation (SWAPO). This liberation movement had its origins in the Ovambo People's Organisation (OPO), which was formed in 1957 and renamed SWAPO in 1960. Two years later, it set up headquarters in Lusaka and founded a military wing, the People's Liberation Army of Namibia (PLAN). Several hundred members were trained in sympathetic countries like Algeria, Cuba and the Soviet Union.

In September 1965, the first six insurgents – 'terrorists' in the official South African lexicon – crossed the border from Zambia into SWA via southern Angola. Two other small groups followed them in February and July 1966. They carried out attacks on tribesmen and white farmers, and began recruiting in Caprivi and the populous northern SWA province of Ovamboland: a pattern that would be repeated in the next few years. By and large, though, these pioneering insurgencies were nullified by police action.

In 1968, the United Nations General Assembly decreed that SWA should henceforth be known as Namibia. In 1971 and 1972, the first landmines laid by SWAPO killed five policemen in the Caprivi Strip. By 1973, PLAN felt sufficiently strong and bold to launch attacks on police patrols, and even a police camp. At the end of that year, Pretoria decided that the police could no longer cope, and the SADF took over from April 1974.

Whenever casualties on the Border were incurred, only the names of servicemen killed were released, with no mention of the units involved and those wounded (or, of course, how they were wounded). It was an approach that, apart from seeming paranoid and callous, provoked rumours and undermined the legitimacy of the SADF's activities.

Though SWAPO had achieved some hit-and-run military successes, and had steadily built political support among the majority Ovambo tribe, their scope for infiltration into SWA had been limited for nearly a decade by simple geography. The only part of SWA that bordered on SWAPO's host country Zambia was the Caprivi Strip, a thin symmetrical corridor about 200 km long and 25 km wide, touching Botswana in the south. Insurgents could get to Ovamboland only through Caprivi and the remote southeastern corner of Angola. The SADF's early defensive efforts were hence focused on Caprivi, and were largely successful.

No End in Sight?

In the early 1970s, white rule in southern Africa – the Portuguese territories of Angola and Mozambique, the rebel British colony of Rhodesia, and of course South Africa itself – seemed set to endure for many years.

Then came the surprising collapse of the right-wing Caetano government in Portugal, and that country's sudden withdrawal from its commitments in Africa. Angola quickly descended into civil war. South Africa intervened through Operation *Savannah* for two reasons: it was secretly requested to do so by some other African countries, including Zaire and Zambia, and by the United States; and it intended to safeguard the water supply to Ovamboland by securing the hydro-electric station at Ruacana. When international support evaporated, the SADF withdrew, undefeated but embarrassed, with its military capacity exposed in many areas.

Strategically, the Portuguese revolution indirectly opened the way for SWAPO, with the support of allies in the Movimento Popular de Libertação de Angola (MPLA), to establish bases right across the long border of southern Angola. Now it would be much easier to attack and destabilise SWA. After a cautious wait of nearly two years after *Savannah*, the SADF's aggressive reaction was to determine the conduct of the rest of the Border War. Pretoria could also take no strategic comfort from the transition of Rhodesia to black-ruled Zimbabwe, completed in 1980.

After the collapse of the Portuguese empire and the granting of Angola's independence in 1975, the threat posed by SWAPO became considerably more effective and demanded the use of SADF troops to counter it. A large South African military presence was maintained in Namibia (which stimulated the economy in the north) and, in addition to intensive counter-insurgency patrolling, numerous raids were made against SWAPO camps in Angola. The SADF also co-operated for the entire period between 1975 and 1989 with Jonas Savimbi's UNITA (União Nacional para a Independência Total de Angola) rebels, who were engaged in a civil war against Angola's self-proclaimed Marxist MPLA government.

A crucial change in the nature of the war was in the support provided to the Angolan government by Communist Cuba, which first became involved in 1975 and by the late 1980s had an estimated 60,000 troops in Angola – more than ten times the number ever deployed there by the SADF. Pretoria portrayed this foreign Communist presence as the main stumbling block to a peaceful resolution of the Namibian conflict. The US government shared this view, as shown both by its military support for UNITA and its insistence that South African participation was a condition for a Namibian settlement. Until the end of the 1980s, the Angolan and Namibian issues thus remained inseparable for the makers of South Africa's domestic and foreign policy.[1]

Nearly 400,000 Cuban soldiers rotated through Angola in fifteen years. This massive involvement has to be understood in the context of Cuba's overall supportive relationship with African liberation movements, having started with assistance in the form of medical teams sent to Algeria in 1963. This was done partly in the zeal of socialist brotherhood, given Cuba's ancestral connections through its African diaspora. But such assistance was not without cost. Overall, from 1975 until their disengagement in 1991, 2,700 Cubans lost their lives in Angola in an operation that was principally paid for by the Soviets and, to a lesser extent, by the Cubans themselves.[2]

Understanding Operation *Savannah*

For much of the time, the Border War was a conflict of relatively low intensity, characterised by seasonal guerrilla insurgencies, aggressive patrolling by small groups of men, brief firefights, the laying and lifting (and detonation) of thousands of landmines, and sporadic rocket attacks. But there were occasional major conventional operations, involving large formations of mechanised infantry, special forces, artillery, armoured cars and (in the final campaign around Cuito Cuanavale in 1988) tanks, often with co-ordinated support from South African Air Force fighters and bombers.

Operation *Savannah*, the SADF's invasion of Angola in 1975 to attempt to install the Frente Nacional para a Libertação de Angola (FNLA) guerrilla movement in power (which, it was envisaged, would have been more pliant than a MPLA government), took them to the outskirts of Luanda. It also set the stage militarily and politically for what was to follow. General Jannie Geldenhuys, who at the time was the Chief of the South African Army, recalls that a few things bothered him about Operation *Savannah*.[3]

First, its clandestine nature: only an absolute minimum of senior staff officers were involved in the operational direction in Pretoria, and hence it took on the air of a special forces operation. One would rather conduct war in the open, with the whole defence force involved, and with public support. Moreover, the exclusivity of the group of staff officers in control of the operation was disturbing. With the wisdom of hindsight and seen purely from a military point of view, it might have been advantageous had the media been better informed; and the normal command and control structures implemented. But the politicians always have their considerations, and military objectives are always subordinate to the overall political strategy.

Second, the vastness of the combat zone. The distance between Bloemfontein and Cela in Angola is 2,386 km, and the distance to Cassinga (which two years later became the objective of Operation *Reindeer*, the biggest airborne operation since the Second World War) is 1,928 km – in other words, the operational environment was larger than the area between Paris and Rome.

A third aspect was the exclusivity of the group of staff officers who controlled the operation. Not only were the actual military actions of Operation *Savannah* kept secret, but there was inevitably no appreciation in South Africa of the scale of the action, the distances involved, and the horrendous logistical difficulties. The incursion took place a few years after the imposition of a total arms embargo. Much SADF equipment was obsolete, and doctrine and tactics had hardly been tested by the limited scale of counter-insurgency operations. The degree of self-sufficiency that would be achieved through Armscor, the state armaments corporation, still lay in the future. Making matters worse, the operation's clandestine nature meant that the war was being fought on a peacetime budget.

Political sensitivities created additional difficulties. Commanders were told to use no more than 2,500 men, and there was heavy pressure not to take casualties or to lose equipment. Limitations were placed on the kind of troops that could be used, on the type of equipment, and on the use of aircraft. A maximum of 600 vehicles was allowed, of all kinds and for all purposes. In the end, vegetable-lorries were commandeered to make up the shortfall, and it was almost impossible to find spare parts and workshop facilities when vehicles, many of them old, broke down.

Indeed, serious equipment shortfalls were identified. There was a need for new trucks to replace the ubiquitous army Bedfords, especially mine-protected vehicles, which led to the range of Buffel,

Casspir and Ratel vehicles, the basic design of which has been replicated by those fighting three decades later in Afghanistan. The South Africans found themselves outgunned by the Cuban rocket-launchers, when they came into the war in force in November. The systems of co-operation between different corps of the army, and between the branches of the service, were also in dire need of review.

With the date for Angola's independence set as 11 November 1975, and with the failure of the Alvor Accord to unite the three liberation movements (FNLA, MPLA and UNITA), the Cubans stepped up their assistance to the MPLA which had started tentatively in August with a small financial donation. The Cubans, like the South Africans, realised that whoever controlled Luanda controlled Angola.

Their efforts were bolstered by the presence of some sixty Soviet advisers from early November. However, the turning point of the operation that led to the withdrawal of South African troops was the law passed by the US Congress forbidding US military support to any Angolan party. This was the so-called Clark Amendment, named after Senator Dick Clark. South Africa was not prepared to defend Western interests alone.

Without US official support, the South African military commenced their withdrawal in February 1976, just as Cuba's troop levels increased from 5,500 in December 1975 to 11,000 in February 1976. FNLA forces were defeated by a joint Cuban-Angolan attack on Huambo in January 1976, the southern-based remnants of the FNLA fleeing to South West Africa where they later formed the core of the 32 Battalion, the crack counter-insurgency unit of the SADF. UNITA also fled southwards, ensconcing themselves in the southeast where they could be most easily supported logistically and, as the situation demanded throughout the 1980s, militarily.

The debriefing conferences on the South African Army's participation identified and formulated the lessons learned and made substantial changes and adjustments, which, Geldenhuys notes, 'proved invaluable later on'. The improvements affected battle techniques and procedures; hardware projects, such the 127mm multiple rocket launcher; and closer co-operation between different corps of the army and between the arms and branches of the service.

Twenty Per Cent Military

March 1976 is thus seen by many as the start of a serious insurgency in Namibia. SWAPO was now potentially in a stronger position than before. For the first time, they had a prerequisite for successful insurgent campaigning – namely, a border that provided safe refuge. In addition to the change of power in Angola, the front-line states – especially Tanzania and Zambia – were directly or indirectly supporting the insurgency.

The PLAN (SWAPO's military wing) established an extensive network of training camps and bases in southern Angola, and they stepped up their incursions considerably. Though the intensity of the Border War was still very low, a series of intermittent contacts, mine incidents and hit-and-run attacks with mortars and rockets increased the casualty rate.

It has often been said that the Border conflict was a war of lieutenants and corporals, and so it was unless there were major conventional operations. Authority was devolved to the junior leader on the spot, who was expected to make decisions and take responsibility. To equip him for this, there was rigorous training that involved extensive theory and practice, drawing both on the evolved body of military knowledge and tough practical training. The SADF consciously drew on a tradition of 'training hard and fighting easy'.

By this time, the South African police had been withdrawn from counter-insurgency duties. They had been in the first line of those deployed both in South West Africa and then Rhodesia. But the South West Africa Police developed its own counter-insurgency unit, officially named the SWA Police Counter-Insurgency (SWAPO, though more infamously known by the term *Koevoet* or 'crowbar'. In August 1980, the SWA Territory Force was also set up as a local army unit, which came to assume an increasing role in operations against PLAN during the decade.

The SADF, according to Geldenhuys, realised that every sector was unique. Thus the SADF tried not to issue instructions of a general nature to be followed by all. Each sector had to have its own design for operations.

The SADF also developed an approach during the planning process. The first challenge often posed was to attempt to find an answer to the question: who holds the initiative, you or your opponent? The basic truth in an insurgency war is that the insurgent, potentially and often in practice, has the initiative. For the SADF, it was therefore imperative that ways and means of obtaining the initiative and keeping it are found. One example of such offensive action was in so-called 'search-and-destroy' operations. The SADF attempted to make more troops available for this purpose. Similarly, there was an effort made to allocate an increased number of troops for night operations. And the SADF tried to use more troops in areas just across the border – and the decision to cross the border was a political one.

There were two kinds of cross-border operations: specific and general. The first kind was a pre-planned operation, 'in and out', on selected bases of PLAN. During such operations the SADF, General Geldenhuys says, lost on average only one man for every hundred insurgents killed. The general operations had the aim of dominating an area and destroying insurgents. In these cases, the SADF lost an average of one man to every thirty of the enemy. More than thirty such operations of both types included Operations *Sceptic* (1980), *Protea* (23 August–4 September 1981), *Daisy* (1 November 1981), *Super* (March 1982), and, by the end of the campaign in 1987/8, *Moduler*, *Hooper* and *Packer*.

Geldenhuys believes that it was the SADF's sustained operations that distinguished this campaign from other COIN wars. According to this view, a mixture of conventional and counter-insurgency tactics succeeded in preventing infiltration by SWAPO insurgents into Namibia on any significant scale, and in stopping the advancing Angolan, Cuban and Soviet forces in the late 1980s. This created the space for an equitable diplomatic settlement for Namibia and, later, South Africa. Over the decade after *Savannah*, the SADF doctrine successfully emphasised firepower, mobility, and decentralisation of tactical authority. Geldenhuys notes that in the process South Africa achieved a world-leading capability in mine-resistant vehicles and in night-fighting.

Of course, success on the battlefield cannot be measured by head counts and ratios alone. Senior SADF soldiers accepted, from the minister of defence (and former chief of the SADF) Magnus Malan[4] down, that the ultimate solution was always going to be '80 percent political and 20 percent military'. Malan's quick rise through the ranks into politics reflected the relationship he enjoyed with President P W Botha (himself formerly minister of defence and prime minister), who came to rely on the military strategic guidance. The military's increasingly predominant role in decision-making during the 1980s explains the focus on a combination of domestic political reform (the ending, for example, of 'petty' apartheid restrictions) and the installation of the (coloured, Indian and white) tricameral parliamentary system in 1983, along with renewed efforts to counter South Africa's international and regional diplomatic isolation. The security dimension to this effort, which despite the '80 percent political, 20 percent military' mantra came to overshadow the political aspects, took the form of increased cross-border raids against PLAN and the ANC, support for military proxies (including UNITA, RENAMO in Mozambique and the Lesotho Liberation Army), and an increase in manpower, equipment and spending. And within South Africa, decision-making on policy was increasingly militarised through the National Security Management System, with the State Security Council at its apex.

By the mid-1970s, white South Africa had found itself outgunned militarily and increasingly diplomatically isolated (not least as a result of the 1977 mandatory UN arms embargo), and under considerable pressure at home and abroad due to the Soweto student uprising. The following expenditure and re-organisation of the defence force among other state agencies under the 'Total National Strategy' developed in response to the 'Total Onslaught' bought the white regime ten more years. During this time, the SADF increased in size to a peak more of than 150,000 active-duty and 455,000 reserve-duty troops by 1989, achieved partly by increasing the duration of mandatory national service to two years. Six nuclear weapons were constructed and a chemical and biological weapons programme developed. Furthermore, the SADF re-equipped with the products of a burgeoning domestic arms industry – from long-range artillery to fighter aircraft. By the mid-1980s, the (full-time) SADF comprised one-quarter so-called Coloured (mixed-race), Indian and Black (African) troops, even though its command structure and attitudes mirrored the prejudices behind white rule.[5]

By the late 1980s, there was again growing domestic unrest resulting in a State of Emergency, increasing military pressure in Angola with ongoing efforts by the Soviet/Cuban/MPLA force to unseat Savimbi's UNITA from its southeastern Jamba base, and a range of new, largely financial sanctions in place, including the US Comprehensive Anti-Apartheid Act. In particular, despite routine military success in Angola, the South African Air Force lost air superiority to the Cuban and Angola-flown Mig-21s and Mig-23s working in concert with an extensive air defence system. White South Africa also remained acutely sensitive to any increase in casualties, not least given the national service component. Whatever these challenges, the SADF was central to creating the diplomatic space which led South Africa and Cuba out of Angola and, in the process, negotiations from their focus on ending Angola's civil war to ending apartheid.

Conclusion: War is Politics by Other Means[6]

The 'Border War' ended with the series of major battles around Cuito Cuanavale in 1987 and 1988. The engagement around that southern Angolan town, which has become the focus of an extensive debate in South Africa over its winners and losers, ended in a tactical stalemate at the end of a long run of victories for the SADF/UNITA coalition. It also represented a psychological victory for the MPLA/SWAPO/Cuban/ANC alliance. It proved to Pretoria that there were strict limits on how much they could achieve in Angola; and that they had to consider what losses the white public back home was prepared to accept for distant, indistinct and undeclared objectives. Add a dose of machismo on the part of Castro by his raising of the military stakes, coupled with the SADF's until-then near-invincibility, and you have a 'victory' – which was how anything other than a major defeat must have looked at the time to the Angolans and Cubans. As the then-US Assistant Secretary of State for African Affairs Chester Crocker observes, 'While Castro was waging a political contest, the SADF leadership concentrated on battlefield logic'.[7]

In a sense, it was a victory, in that it was *not a defeat* for the Cuban and Angolan government forces. Or, as a former South African foreign affairs official summed up:[8]

> Cuito Cuanavale was a stand-off with an inconclusive military result but with a realisation that a military victory was not possible or only at a price that neither side was prepared to pay. Thus it led to a renewed sense of urgency to find a political solution and to establish linkage between what was happening in Angola to events in Namibia.

Cuban officials maintain that they had great respect for South African military prowess, particularly the G5 and G6 howitzers. These were accurate and 'kept them underground', with the result that their artillery was outranged 'and did not hit its objectives'. Yet, according to Crocker, when Pretoria 'emerged from its long night of diplomatic hibernation … to find that these artful military tactics were not good enough', the South Africans converted the SADF's position at Cuito into a 'bargaining chip'. Cuban bravado kept the South Africans engaged at Cuito, while the SADF would not withdraw until 'concrete, reciprocal agreements' had been reached.

South African diplomats had little respect for the diplomatic skills of the principal Cuban delegate (and Central Committee member) to the negotiations, Jorge Risquet. At the Cairo meeting, he reportedly nearly brought the entire diplomatic exercise to a halt with his confrontational and doctrinaire approach. Nevertheless, they did endorse the veteran Cuban revolutionary's observation that the SADF's obsession with detail was at the expense of the bigger picture. While the South African Department of Foreign Affairs regarded the SADF as undoubtedly more organised and disciplined – and with much greater budgets and resources at their disposal – they argued that many of the South African soldiers also suffered from 'tunnel vision'.

Cuba's chief negotiator, Carlos Aldana, was, however, widely respected by the South Africans, being seen as a warm and forthcoming man who had the knack of looking past the positions that various delegations took and working out what his interlocutors really wanted or feared. The chemistry between him and Neil van Heerden was viewed as contributing significantly to the success of negotiations. 'Carlos Aldana and I had a particularly warm personal relationship,' recalls Van Heerden:

Without him I am not sure we could have had the outcome we reached – certainly not in the timeframe in which it happened. He was a man who made you feel he was genuinely pursuing a path of peace. In the midst of the negotiations he said to me: 'Why don't we go somewhere to meet offshore – somewhere in the Cape Verde Islands?' So just the two of us went there with an interpreter. It was a very interesting experience as we were outside the atmosphere of the formal negotiations. We enjoyed long walks together and spoke about the melting pot aspect of Cuba. He thought that it was something Cuba could help South Africa with in the inevitable future melting pot we faced.

The South African military had a number of face-to-face meetings with their Cuban counterparts, mostly on Sol Island in the Atlantic. They were usually cordial and productive affairs – the military people appeared to understand each other. At one meeting, the Cuban delegation called for a short break as they wanted to introduce someone to the South African delegates, one of whom recalled: 'The doors burst open, and an imposing fellow walked in. It was the Cuban Commander-in-Chief in Angola, General Arnaldo Ochoa Sánchez. With General Geldenhuys leading our delegation, this was the first time we had the two commanders of the opposing sides in the same room at the same time.'[9]

The Namibia-Angola agreement also linked the end of SADF support for UNITA (which nonetheless continued for some time beyond this period and into the early 1990s) with the closure of the ANC's Angolan bases. But this fact is relegated to a footnote of history by the liberation movements in their appraisal of the events in and around Cuito in 1987–88, which has become the stuff of legend. After all, all sides need at least one military victory to cement their credentials. This explains why Nelson Mandela said, when he visited Havana in July 1991: 'We come here with a sense of the great debt that is owed to the people of Cuba. What other country can point to a record of greater selflessness than Cuba has displayed in its relations with Africa?'[10]

For the Angolan government, the Cubans and the South Africans, it was a strategic victory. Moreover, the impetus led to the conclusion of the Angolan-Namibian peace accords (hastened by the disintegration of the Soviet empire), an event which, critically, added impetus to democratic change within South Africa itself. In the end, military engagement helped, with assiduous diplomacy, to bring political change and victory in Namibia and South Africa.

WHO DARES, LOSES? THE RELEVANCE OF RHODESIA-ZIMBABWE

Greg Mills and Grahame Wilson[*]

Pound for pound, the Rhodesian security forces may have been the most effective fighting force in the last century.[1] Numbering at their peak 15,000 troops,[2] pitted against an opposition likely at least three times as strong within and without the country by the war's end,[3] and employing increasingly aggressive tactics taking them into the neighbouring countries, they were able to keep in check their numerically much larger guerrilla opponents, despite having to operate across a country bigger in area than Germany and over terrain practically impassable in many locations. But still the war was lost with the advent to power of Robert Mugabe's regime in 1980 – or was it? If so, why? This chapter revisits the Rhodesian strategy, assesses what mistakes were made in the conduct of the war and identifies lessons for contemporary counter-insurgency campaigns.

A Brief History

Much has been written about the Rhodesian 'bush war' – otherwise known as the 'Second Chimurenga'[4] [liberation struggle] – lasting from 1964 to 1979. A lot of these writings are popularised accounts of the war, focusing in the main on the catalogue of fighting experiences.[5] In so doing they risk, at worst, mythologising their

---

[*]   A version of this chapter appeared in the *RUSI Journal* (Vol. 152, No. 6, December 2007), pp. 22–31.

conduct, and at best of removing them from the political context of the time.[6]

The Rhodesian bush war involved atrocities and dirty tricks on both sides. The weight of international public opinion on these actions has, by and large, condemned the Rhodesians on account of the political system they were fighting to uphold – one committed to a disproportionate role for the white minority (numbering at its peak probably 300,000) over the black majority (then some six million). That much is undeniable in a war that cost the lives of an estimated 25,000 civilians,[7] 954 Rhodesian security force personnel, and over 8,000 guerrillas.[8] It should also be noted, however, that history is decreasingly kind to the actions of the Zimbabwean liberators, realising in the twenty-first century the ruthlessness with which they have been willing to conduct their politics, not just against hated colonial racists, but against their own people.

The war progressed through four stages. The first phase can be delineated from the time of the start of civil disobedience campaigns in 1957 through the creation of the two dominant African political movements in the early 1960s: Joshua Nkomo's Zimbabwe African People's Union (ZAPU), and its armed wing, the Zimbabwe People's Revolutionary Army (ZIPRA); and Robert Mugabe's Zimbabwe African National Union (ZANU), and its Zimbabwe African National Liberation Army (ZANLA).[9]

A second stage can be identified by the intensification of the conflict following the Unilateral Declaration of Independence (UDI) by Ian Smith's government on 11 November 1965 and the subsequent imposition of international sanctions. The start of this phase of the war – now commemorated in Zimbabwe as Chimurenga Day – occurred on 28 April 1966 between Rhodesian security forces and seven ZANLA insurgents near Sinoia. During 1967 and 1968, groups totalling more than 300 insurgents crossed into Rhodesia from Zambia. They included members of the military wing of South Africa's African National Congress, encouraging Pretoria to commit police forces in support of the Rhodesians.[10] The act of UDI sparked the insurgency by granting the black national movements the cause and timing; and in so doing it undermined the fundamentally political basis of the counter-insurgency by both de-legitimating the Rhodesian government and making the search for a credible if moderate black government partner much more difficult.

And at the same time, the Rhodesians battled to deal with the effects of international arms and oil embargos. These were met partly through South African supplied fuel and weapons, along with a dose of local engineering ingenuity, especially in the development of mine-protection vehicles. The launching of successful Rhodesian security force operations against the guerrilla incursions, such as Operations *Nickel, Cauldron* and *Griffin* in the late 1960s, represented a shift away from police control of the counter-insurgency through the British South Africa Police (BSAP), which still remained a continuous source of army/police friction among their respective leaderships until 1980.

A further significant up-shift marked a third phase in the war, around the time of the fall of the Portuguese colonial regime in Mozambique. Even before the formal transfer of power in Mozambique on 25 June 1975, the conflict had ratcheted up with guerrillas operating from bases in Kenneth Kaunda's Zambia and from those areas controlled by the Front for the Liberation of Mozambique (FRELIMO) in the neighbouring Portuguese colony. FRELIMO had already become convinced of the necessity to 'liberate' Rhodesia.[11] By this time, major operations (such as Operation *Hurricane* in the northeast) were under way and the shepherding of the African population into Protected Villages started, as was the establishment of a *cordon sanitaire* minefield along the border. Many of these concepts were borrowed from successful British-led operations in Kenya and Malaya. The Rhodesians hoped that by using similar tactics they would win the war. But there was a big political difference. The British had fought to enable the peaceful transfer to and consolidation of indigenous power; the Rhodesians aimed to maintain the white status quo.

Yet white casualties remained low, and most of the white Rhodesian public (save those in the farming community) were largely blissfully unaware of the deterioration in the security situation. In 1972 Prime Minister Ian Smith had stated on the radio that the security situation was 'far more serious than it appears on the surface, and if the man in the street could have access to the security information which I and my colleagues in government have, then I think he would be a lot more worried than he is today.'[12] As fighting intensified and responsibility for dealing with the insurgency moved from the police to the military, this stage saw the increasing professionalisation of the armed forces. For example, the Rhodesian Special Air Service (SAS) had shrunk from 150 to just thirty men by 1975 in an effort to get away from the ethos and image of the 'Special African Safaris' that it had become. But this set the stage for a large-scale expansion. By the war's end, the SAS had expanded to 270 'badged' (divided equally between regulars, national servicemen and reservists) and 200 'unbadged' personnel (clerks, cooks, drivers, guards and so on).

With the guerrillas massing over the borders in ever-increasing numbers and using a mix of terror and political inducements to 'win' the support of local civilians, the Rhodesians first countered by announcing a 'hearts and minds' campaign in April 1977, increasingly employing 'Fireforce' quick-reaction interdiction teams and, most tellingly, conducting large-scale raids into Mozambique and Zambia. In May 1977, the Rhodesian commander of combined operations, Lieutenant General Peter Walls, informed the public that Rhodesian forces were changing tactics from 'contain and hold' to hot pursuit 'search and destroy' operations 'when necessary'. In November 1977, around 200 Rhodesian troops[13] crossed the border in the biggest 'pre-emptive' cross-border raid yet. With air bombardment provided by the Rhodesian Air Force (RhAF), the Rhodesians attacked the 4,000-strong ZANLA base at Chimoio in Mozambique.[14]

Such raids were replicated with increasing frequency, including the attack on Joshua Nkomo's home in Lusaka, Zambia in April 1979 (Operation *Bastille*), along with regular air joint-force bomber raids on encampments and assembly areas in Mozambique and Zambia (with logistical and reconnaissance support often provided by South Africa). For example, the joint-force action on the ZIPRA camps in Zambia in October 1978 accounted for upwards of 2,000 ZIPRA soldiers. In addition, there were ongoing clandestine attacks on regional infrastructure by Rhodesian Selous Scouts[15] and SAS forces. And most notably, employing the wave of dissatisfaction over the governance performance of the self-avowedly Marxist-Leninist FRELIMO government in Mozambique and utilising both covert and overt support, during this time the Rhodesian government also assisted in forming, arming and replenishing the Mozambique National Resistance Movement (RENAMO). The development of such proxy forces reached its zenith as apartheid South Africa

Figure 3: Annual Deaths of the Zimbabwe War, 1973–78.

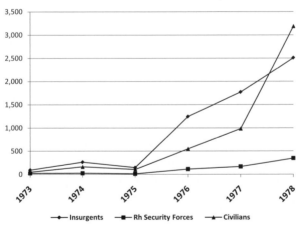

Source: Official Rhodesian Sources cited in Cilliers, *Counter-Insurgency in Rhodesia*, p. 242. Note that the figures only refer to the insurgents killed within Zimbabwe. The wounded can be computed on the ratio of 6.5:1.

invigorated RENAMO after the creation of Zimbabwe in 1980, replicating the model of its relationship with Jonas Savimbi's UNITA movement in Angola. Similarly, the pre-emptive cross-border attacks also became a feature of South African Defence Force actions in the 1980s, into Botswana, Zimbabwe, Zambia, Lesotho, Angola and Mozambique, sometimes aimed (as the Rhodesians had done) at guerrilla bases, on other occasions at regional infrastructure. A notable difference between the Rhodesians and South Africa, however, was in admissibility: the South African politicians mostly denied extra-territorial operations; the Rhodesians were largely allied around what was openly acknowledged as an internal and external enemy.

This third phase lasted from 1975 until March 1978, the date of the internal settlement between Ian Smith's government and the moderate United African National Council led by Bishop Abel Muzorewa,[16] leading to the (temporary) creation of Zimbabwe-Rhodesia in June 1979 following elections in April that year. The internal settlement followed the failed South African-brokered effort with the Zambians in August 1975 and the later Anglo-American peace initiative, which culminated in the ill-fated Geneva conference in 1977. During this new phase, the South Africans, on whom the Rhodesian security forces had relied a great deal not only for oil and funding,[17] but also for supporting troops (mainly police) and helicopters, largely pulled out in order to give more weight and credibility to the political process. In the field, this translated into increasing numbers of foreign recruits, notably Vietnam veterans from Australia, New Zealand and the United States, but also others from Canada, Portugal and especially the United Kingdom.

This phase ended with the failure of the government to capitalise on the relative success of the security forces in the political arena, with the inability of the Zimbabwe-Rhodesia administration of Bishop Muzorewa to secure international recognition, notably from the Carter administration in the US following his visit there in July 1979. More importantly, both Mugabe and Nkomo also rejected the arrangement, and the war continued unabated.

The fourth and final stage from 1978 until the end of the war saw increasing regional and international pressure on the parties to settle. The Rhodesians, although continuing to perform well militarily in the field, were weak politically at home and outside. These constraints were exacerbated by the disproportionately large effect of white casualties on its small population, who increasingly viewed themselves to be under siege. Moreover, the economy was faltering, weakened by large-scale white emigration[18] and tightening sanctions. The South African government was stepping up pressure on the Muzorewa-Smith government to negotiate an end to the crisis, presumably for various reasons including delinking its own future from the white Rhodesia, currying a degree of international favour and also reflecting the Afrikaner-dominated ruling National Party's deep-seated antipathy towards British colonial and settler regimes. Then, as now, the Rhodesian regime was vulnerable to South African sentiment – the military had assessed that absent Pretoria's acquiescence, the country would collapse in two weeks.

At the same time, the guerrilla armies had also changed their own tactics, their greater numbers reflecting the extent of their regional and international support, and were visible in their brazenness and willingness to attack high-profile civilian targets whatever the international reaction. Most notable in this regard were the two surface-to-air (SAM) missile attacks on Rhodesian civilian Viscount aircraft in September 1978 and February 1979 by ZIPRA forces, killing a total of 102 passengers and crew. Ten survivors of the fifty-eight in the first aircraft shot down were killed at the wreckage site by the guerrillas. The Viscount incidents were more costly in that they made it impossible for the white government to be seen to be talking to Nkomo's ZAPU, undoing the main hope to politically engineer a viable anti-Mugabe non-racial coalition.

By 1979, Rhodesian forces were heavily stretched; and by March, white men in the 50–59 year age group were liable for call-up duties. The terrorism war now entered a final conventional phase, with the hopes for a peaceful transition via the Muzorewa internal settlement dashed by the outcome of the aforementioned Carter visit. The Rhodesian security forces mounted further raids into Zambia (in September destroying no less than ten bridges) and Mozambique (including a major offensive in September, again into Gaza Province). The actions against the Zambian bridges were to ensure that Zambian President Kaunda was forced to maintain his route dependence on Rhodesian rail routes that had been opened in 1978, in turn an attempt to ensure his support for a negotiated political settlement favourable to (white) Rhodesian interests.

At the same time, in September 1979, the Rhodesian government began negotiations with ZANU and ZAPU at Lancaster House, leading to the ceasefire that December and the reinstatement of British rule, with the arrival of the governor-general Lord Soames in Salisbury the same month. The process culminated in the elections of February 1979. On 18 April 1980, colonial Rhodesia became independent Zimbabwe with Robert Mugabe installed as prime minister, the advent of what comprises nearly three decades of increasingly ruinous rule.

Reflections on Rhodesian Military Strategy

Even though the Rhodesian forces were able to hold their own in security terms by the war's end, they had to face major challenges along the way.

Shortage of Manpower

The shortage of manpower overall was exacerbated by the slowness in recruiting Africans into the security forces. The vast reserve of black manpower was not effectively used until late in the war, recruitment being limited by both money and, especially, politics – the government being unwilling to have more blacks than whites in the military. Only by 1979 had two further battalions of the black-dominated Rhodesian African Rifles been created, bringing the total to three. Despite the racial nature of the struggle, the black troops that made up 40 per cent of the regular army at the war's end were both conscientious and loyal – in stark contrast, for example, to the varied loyalties of large chunks of the post-Saddam Iraqi police and army. The failure to recruit larger numbers of black troops into the army earlier must be viewed as a key mistake by the Smith regime. Personnel shortfalls were partly met through increasing national service: going from four-and-half months of initial service to eight months, to a year, then to eighteen months and finally two years; and by increasing the call-ups of reservists. The latter especially placed considerable strain on individuals and the economy.

Strategically, the Rhodesians also attempted to maintain control over the whole territory, rather than to focus on key areas; tactically, troop shortages were amplified by having to deploy large numbers of men in static positions to guard fixed installations such as railways and farms.

Equipment Deficit

This was especially notable in hi-tech items such as night-vision equipment, but overall in terms of the scarcity of essential air support. A number of coping strategies were adopted to deal with the shortage of aircraft and age of airframes of those in Rhodesian hands. Rhodesian strength was increased by pilot flexibility, most being able to fly all of the aircraft in the air force inventory. Pilots were continuously rotated through the various squadrons to this end. Aircraft and crew were also supplemented by South African secondments, though this was used as a political lever by Pretoria; the helicopters being withdrawn from Rhodesia in 1976 during the attempts by South African Prime Minister John Vorster to negotiate an end to the conflict. Most of the (ultimately totalling sixty-six) RhAF Alouettes were on loan from the South African Air Force, along with many of the helicopter aircrew. These men were 'sheep-dipped', operating in Rhodesian uniform, and becoming temporary RhAF personnel. During some of the larger external Rhodesian raids in 1979, South African Air Force Pumas and Super Frelons operated in support of Rhodesian forces, such as during Operation *Uric* in September 1979. Also, South African naval forces, notably its strike craft, were constantly used in support of operations into Mozambique, operating from their major base at Durban, though submarines were used on at least two occasions for incursions into Maputo. The shortage of equipment also influenced tactics. For example, ground patrolling was supplemented by the use of Cessna Lynxes using fragmentation and concussion bombs or napalm. A lack of troop-carrying helicopters (a 'stick' of only three or four troops could be carried in the Alouettes), led to the use of paradrops from Dakotas. Late in the war some eleven Bell UH-1 'Huey' helicopters, able to carry eight fully-equipped troops, were acquired from Israel, though these were in poor repair and only half the fleet was still flying by the war's end. But the availability of equipment was not the be-all and end-all of the war's course.

Intelligence and Counter-Intelligence

Although Rhodesian intelligence was usually accurate, on a number of raids this was countered by the forewarning of guerrillas. But the difficulty in predicting guerrilla activities and movements relates less to a failure of intelligence than a failure of local knowledge and, above all, of politics. Where there was a high level of expertise (for example, in some areas of the Special Branch), the sheer volume of work was overwhelming.

In the area of counter-intelligence, it has long been suspected that the Rhodesian security forces were penetrated at a senior level, though the evidence is anecdotal. If so, some of the tip-offs may have been deliberate. One possible example is the likely leak to ZAPU announcing the SAS retaliation raid (for the Viscount downings) on Joshua Nkomo's Lusaka residence in April 1979 – his death would have obviously been contrary to the need to strike a political bargain with the veteran black nationalist, though Salisbury clearly needed to be seen to be taking action against ZIPRA. Care was taken with radio transmission, given the known presence of an East German-manned intercept station in Nampula in Mozambique. It has also been suggested that the Rhodesians may have been vulnerable to foreign (i.e. Russian) satellite intelligence. Certainly no precautions were taken in this regard, though little lead time was given in operational decisions and there was little public build-up to give outward warning.

Troop Morale

Continuous action for those on the front line took its toll in casualties and in growing social problems within the military. For example, before 1975, SAS personnel would be on operations for six weeks with just a five-day rest between rotations. As Chris Cocks observes after his three-year stint in the Rhodesian Light Infantry, 'such habits, formed during the war that was their *raison d'être* proved hard to break. Many of my comrades still tend to drink too much. I am an alcoholic. All of us started at the top of the mountain, young and full of hope. But our parents' war changed all that. There was no glory – just drink, drugs and death.'[19] Such sentiments reflected rising casualties. According to official statistics, between 1972 and 1976, 215 members of the security forces and 1,917 insurgents died; in 1977 alone, the casualties were 197 security personnel and 1,774 rebels.[20] Problems with morale both reflected and were aggravated by absenteeism and emigration.

Social Problems

Aside from the obvious dangers to white farmers targeted by the guerrillas to drive them off the land and the constant tensions involved, the strain of the war resulted in increases in social breakdown among the white population, including alcoholism, illegitimacy and divorce.

These problems were also reflected in the difficulties of military discipline: as the strain of operations increased, so the officers needed to be tougher in their application of discipline in key units.

Finances and Economic Impact

In absolute terms, Rhodesian defence expenditure remained low. By 1979, it was just a million Rhodesian dollars a day (around US$470 million annually). But in relative terms, the load increased dramatically during the 1970s: defence expenditure rose 610 per cent from 1971/72 to 1977/78, and on the police by 232 per cent over the same period. Put differently, in 1976, defence expenditure consumed 25 per cent of the total budget; by 1979, it was 47 per cent.[21] In spite of South Africa subsidising about half, these increases had to be funded partly by tax increases (such as the 12.5 per cent surcharge on income tax imposed in July 1978).

Coupled with sanctions, the war saw a decline in Rhodesia's gross national product by 1.1 per cent in 1975, 3.4 per cent in 1976 and 6.9 per cent in 1977. Income from tourism, for example,

Figure 4: Rhodesian Security Expenditure, 1971–77, Rh$.

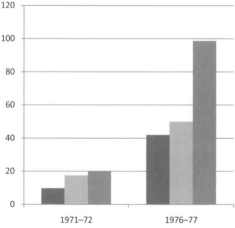

a chief economic contributor, declined by some 74 per cent from 1972–78.[22] The numbers of tourists declined from 240,000 in 1972, for example, to 88,000 in 1978.

Protecting the Population

In line with the aim of protecting (or separating) the population from guerrillas to prevent infiltration, resettlement was also utilised *à la* Malaya, of which the Rhodesian SAS 'C Squadron' had direct experience. This initially took the form of an extension of the 'no-go' area declared along the northeastern border areas in 1972.[23] The total population gathered into the Protected Villages is estimated at around 750,000 Africans in 200 villages. As Ian Beckett notes though, 'Too frequently, however, Protected Villages were regarded purely as a means of population control rather than as a basis for winning "hearts and minds"'. Conditions varied, but many lacked sanitation and other basic facilities. The villages were also inadequately defended, with the result that the population that may have collaborated with the security forces was frightened by the possible consequences.[24]

Losing Hearts and Minds

The winning of hearts and minds of the African population 'left much to be desired', and reflected the Rhodesians' preference for control rather than concessions, such as the extension in the use of martial law to govern, its application increasing to over 70 per cent of the country by September 1978 and to over 90 per cent one year later.[25] The original scheme to 'win hearts and minds' was first developed by Lieutenant Ian Sheppard in 1973. The so-called 'Sheppard Group' aimed to 'sell' the Protected Villages to the Africans through a variety of projects such as an African Development Bank, the inoculating of cattle, and the granting of land title to resettled Africans. However, the majority of the thirty-eight projects proposed met insurmountable opposition from the Ministries of Internal Affairs and Information and the group collapsed in November 1974. It was not until just under three years later, in July 1977, that a Psychological Operations Unit was established, yet this foundered on continued rivalry with the police Special Branch and resistance from senior military personnel. Similarly, a Directorate of Psychological Warfare was established in 1979 but proved ineffectual, in spite of some reported success in using spirit mediums (witch doctors). The major problem was that the government's 'concentration of increasing African political representation meant little to the average African', Beckett notes, 'and rarely offered a viable alternative to guerrilla intimidation'. No government, especially one lacking legitimacy and lateral thinking such as the Smith regime post-UDI, was ever going to be able to effectively counter the terror tactics employed as a deliberate weapon of war by the insurgents. For many Africans the war had tremendous costs, in terms of the creation of internal and regional refugees, and loss of livelihoods.[26] Before the war, African farmers had produced 70 per cent of national food requirements. This had fallen by one-third by 1977. As Beckett notes, 'Africans were caught in the real sense between intimidation both by security forces and guerrillas, the ratio of black civilian casualties caused by the protagonists running at 40:60 by 1978'. By 1979, over 900 African primary and secondary schools had closed, leaving around 230,000 pupils without access to education, while over ninety rural hospitals and clinics had also been shut and rural bus services cut by half.[27] The population was also not fooled by the creation of internal alternatives (such as Muzorewa's internal Zimbabwe-Rhodesia option), which lacked credibility. It is thus unsurprising that the adoption of a 'carrot and stick' approach to the obtaining of information, through direct financial rewards to amnesties (offered in both December 1977 and March 1979), met again with only limited success.

Character of Operations

Time was never on the Rhodesians' side. As Malaya and Northern Ireland illustrate, countering insurgency requires a long-term approach, a duration implicit in tactics such as the Protected Villages and in the engendering of the tenets of trust, law and order, and political inclusivity on which a resilient and successful society is based. Instead, the security forces took their lead from their political masters who were politically bankrupt and irrevocably tainted, thus favouring expediency over long-term strategy.

In spite of the abovementioned issues, even by the start of 1980, militarily the situation was not lost, even though resources were stretched and the military were struggling, in particular, with the effects of white emigration. Despite active and ongoing contestation and the direct involvement of FRELIMO troops ('Freds' as they were known by Rhodesian troops) in Rhodesia and Tanzanians on the border area, the Rhodesian security forces had not surrendered any major territory. As one indicator, the guerrilla forces, in spite of stretching the Rhodesians over two fronts, had not succeeded in establishing any uncontested 'liberated zones'. To the contrary, to the east RENAMO had achieved rapid success, prompting the question as to whether the Rhodesian high command should have used the rebels to attempt to establish its own such liberated zones within Mozambique, splitting the country in half.

Rhodesian success was partly the result of guerrilla ineptitude, and partly the result of the adoption of some distinct tactics by the Rhodesian security forces to address their manpower and other resource shortages, including, for example, the development of the aforementioned 'Fireforce' rapid deployment concept. Seeking to offset a lack of men through the concentration of firepower and mobility, four Fireforces, comprising thirty men each, were constantly available, two being manned by the Rhodesian Light Infantry and the other two by the Rhodesian African Rifles. By mid-1979, the Fireforces accounted for 75 per cent of all guerrilla casualties inside Rhodesia.[28] The Fireforce idea worked well in taking the fight directly to the insurgent and in reducing exposure and risk along logistics routes, but it placed an inordinate strain on troops. There was one instance of these units being used three times in one day in different engagements. The flexibility of Rhodesian forces was improved by the wide freedom granted to operational commanders. The constraints on operations were seldom political, even in calling in cross-border strikes. This degree of latitude demanded strict discipline, outstanding junior leaders, good training and careful debriefing. The high quality of school-leaving recruits into the Rhodesian forces, and their simple but thorough training focused on getting the basics right, showed in combat – notably in the elite units.

The Rhodesian security forces also attempted to deal with the shortage of manpower both by pre-emptive strikes into the host countries and the use of a *cordon sanitaire* of border minefields from May 1974 onwards. Eventually nearly 900 km of minefields were laid along the Zambian and Mozambiqan frontiers. But the costs were great, the system demanded high maintenance, and it certainly did not present an impassable barrier to the insurgents. On the other side, the guerrillas' widespread use of landmines also led to the development of a range of specially designed mine-resistant troop-carrying vehicles such as the Rhino, Hyena and Hippo, featuring a V-shaped body to deflect blast, and also novel local counter-measures such as the use of water in the tyres of transports. These vehicle types later spawned a similar range of South African vehicles including the Buffel and Casspir.

The cross-border raids were responsible for the bulk of insurgents killed during the war. Although effective in a military sense, they had political costs. The Rhodesians had few political allies, notably their South African quartermaster, but the latter was largely unprepared to tolerate the international fallout resulting from sending armed forces into a neighbouring country with which it was not at war. The military value of the operations also had to be weighed against the perception of 'every such action … as the wanton murder of innocent refugees who have fled from an oppressive regime.'[29]

The Rhodesians also attempted to assassinate political foes, in operations mostly led by (police) Special Branch members, but sometimes involving elite military units, most notably in the attempt on Joshua Nkomo's life in Lusaka in April 1979. From the perspective of those involved in these acts, there was hardly a strategy behind this though. It was mainly a tactical level response to circumstances, sometimes being motivated by revenge (the Viscount incidents).[30] Where these attacks were apparently more strategic was in an effort to push the insurgents to the negotiation table, most notably in the case of the recalcitrant Mugabe – though this may be giving the Rhodesian politicians more strategic credit than is due. There were at least five attempts on Mugabe's life, including two in Mozambique (where Rhodesian special forces were landed by South African submarine), and three in Rhodesia itself. In one instance, Mugabe's vehicle only narrowly missed being blown up in Fort Victoria (now Masvingo) while crossing a bridge. In each case, he was apparently tipped off beforehand – it is presumed either by a (suspected British) spy in the senior echelons of the Rhodesian government or as part of a co-ordinated attempt to coerce him to negotiations. The same 'tip-off' suspicion applied to Operation *Quartz* – the name given to the April 1980 post-election Rhodesian plan whereby attacks would be launched on ZANU and ZAPU assembly points. A simultaneous attack – Operation *Hectic* – would be carried out with the aim of assassinating Mugabe and the other leaders at their campaign headquarters, carried out by 'A', 'B' and 'C' squadrons of the SAS, supported by armoured cars and T-55 tanks (which had been part of a shipment from Libya to Uganda's Idi Amin seized by the South African authorities in Durban).[31] Troops of the SAS, Rhodesian Light Infantry and Selous Scouts waited eagerly for the code word 'Quartz' to be given as the elections drew to a close. But the signal never came, the operation being cancelled three hours before Mugabe was declared the winner.

The Rhodesians had some successes with so-called 'pseudo operations', in which members of the security forces as well as captured guerrillas 'turned' by the former were employed to infiltrate guerrilla organisations sowing discord and gaining information, originally formed along the lines of the British pseudo-gangs in Kenya during the Mau Mau emergency of the 1950s. From its initial start in the mid-1960s, the concept later developed into the formation of the Selous Scouts as a reconnaissance, tracking and, ultimately, commando fighting unit. By the war's end, the Scouts comprised around 1,800 men, three times the size of a normal infantry battalion, hardly allowing them to be the secret, covert force they needed to be.[32] The 'pseudos' – or *skuzapu* as the insurgents knew them – were ultimately to largely (but not entirely) abandon their pseudo rationale for a cross-border strike role.

The Scouts and other units were initially able to make great strides in the supply of tactical intelligence. But the use of the observation posts they employed depended fundamentally on studying local patterns – of the use of food and water and the movement of people – to ascertain whether guerrillas could be present. Successful counter-insurgency campaigns need to be cerebral rather than physical.

Nonetheless, the intelligence supplied never could be a complete picture. The insurgents, through a mix of empathy, race, language, cause or terror, achieved at least the passive co-operation of local inhabitants. After the conflict ratcheted up in the early 1970s (around the time of Operation *Hurricane* commencing in December 1972), it became a 'new' war. In this war there was little space for neutrals, and Rhodesian efforts to entice (or even terrorise) the African population into co-operation were mired in issues of race and legitimacy. Such an intrinsic political advantage, as Iraq and Afghanistan have also shown, is sufficient to allow insurgents to overcome considerable tactical weaknesses in combat skills and weapons.[33] Hence many in the local population would certainly know who and where the insurgents were and where they stored their explosives and weapons, but in most cases they were reluctant to tell. Technical and technological means can do little to overcome this political deficit, even if the Rhodesians had possessed them. Of course, insurgents seldom expose themselves, unless it is on their terms. And just as the insurgency itself took covert forms including bombings, sabotage and assassinations, so did the Rhodesians use such dirty tricks. But even the killing of the insurgents' leaders and heroes had little perceptible impact on the final outcome since these tactical actions could not overshadow the overall political process or negate the guerrillas' immutable racial advantage, granting them a local, regional and international legitimacy that they never lost sight of or failed to employ to their advantage.

Conclusion: Lessons for Others?

There are a number of differences between the insurgency faced by Rhodesia and those today under way in Iraq and Afghanistan. Nonetheless, there are relevant aspects and lessons.

There are many legacies of the war in Rhodesia's transition to Zimbabwe, not least the ethno-political rivalries of the various nationalist movements, to which the war had been midwife, left festering and unresolved. This war was not just about democracy and liberation, but was fundamentally concerned with racial identity – essentially of the role of black citizens in their country. This struggle has wider regional ripples today, notably for South Africa's own democratic maturation and, indeed, in its relationship with its northern neighbour. The immediate transfer of power to the guerrilla movements also illustrated that the considerable level of solidarity and ingenuity displayed by the white settler community was itself insufficient to defeat the guerrilla armies. So, too, were attempts to infuse African ownership through internal political accommodation at one level, and significant African representation in the security forces at another.[34]

It is apparently callous, yet sadly debatable in terms of human development, whether the war overall created more or less hardship for Zimbabweans, especially in the light of recent post-independence economic and political choices and developments. But the two events are not unrelated. For example, it is moot whether the Rhodesian forces hung on too long (thereby setting the stage for and fomenting the divisions besetting Zimbabwe today) or whether they did not hang on long enough, thus enabling transition to a different type of leader in improved global and national political circumstances. The answer to such questions lies in the realm of theory. What we do know in assessing Rhodesia's counter-insurgency strategy is that a plan is important – the white regime possessed little in the way of an overall political plan in which the military was employed as a decisive element. Much was made up along the way. A political solution with moderate black leaders depended on international recognition and this, in turn, demanded involving black leadership who possessed the necessary legitimacy. The UDI, itself a product of short-sighted leadership, fatally scarred the search for credible black partners.

We know too that development is crucial to winning a population over. In Rhodesia there was too little attention focused, both before the war and (as we know now in the light of the disastrous land redistribution scheme subsequently engineered by Mugabe) after it on improving the access of Africans to the better farming lands and to the economy overall. It is also possible to conclude that winning hearts and minds has to go beyond political representation and instead revolve around understanding the needs and insecurities of the population most contested – here the Rhodesians' efforts were constantly at risk of being undermined by arrogance, lack of understanding and empathy, often born of paternalism and racism. It remains unclear why the population at large was so passive. Unlike South Africa in the 1980s, the Rhodesians had to place almost no resources on domestic policing. The black townships were not sources of political unrest, or even threat. This may have been key to why the Rhodesians did so well for so long and, in today's context, why President Mugabe has remained in power.

Yet the military successes enjoyed by the Rhodesians also demonstrate a number of key elements – that technology, including air assets, is not vital if there is a great enough appetite for danger and sufficient stomach for casualties on the part of those countering the insurgency. In some operations, a 25–30 per cent casualty rate was deemed acceptable in the planning of the mission. Also, the delegation of responsibility to and development of junior leadership were key assets in the prosecution of the war from a Rhodesian standpoint. This demanded thorough training and a willingness to risk both mistakes and lives in building this confidence and capability. Technology cannot be a war winner on its own.

Assassination was used by both sides; by the guerrillas to coerce the local population, and by the Rhodesians apparently as a lever for negotiations. The latter aspect may, at least temporarily, have encouraged Mugabe to be more accommodating, and both to attend and concede at the (Lancaster House) negotiation table, but in the longer term may have hardened his resolve and deepened schisms and hatred. While counter-insurgency strategy suggests that military means have to shape the political process and ensure that it leaves behind people with whom to negotiate, the question of whether Zimbabwe would have been a more peaceful and prosperous country had Mugabe been killed before 1979 is moot.

Finally, and perhaps most controversially, the real reason for Rhodesia's difficulties and eventual transition was not, however, to do with the capability of its security forces, no matter how hard pushed they were by the war's end, but rather the absence of an effective parallel political strategy. This only occurred with the Lancaster House settlement. It is conventional wisdom that insurgencies can only be countered by a political deal – indeed, it is the failure of politics that result in the military's involvement in countering insurgencies in the first instance. At best, military means can pressure and shape this outcome. In the case of Rhodesia, it was the prevailing political rather than security considerations that eventually determined the outcome. While the Rhodesian security forces performed well with meagre resources, they facilitated an outcome that few of them had anticipated and wished for, the conclusion of which was the result of unimaginative, ineffectual and often dour political leadership. Very few, if any, military officers had the time (if indeed they possessed the will) to question the absence of political direction. For the key question in countering insurgency – 'What can we do to make the enemy's life more difficult and to improve our own?' – should be asked constantly by both the military and politicians.

Rarely do insurgents, in Rhodesia as elsewhere, lose the political aspect of their struggle in spite of their performance in the field; the latter often a function of the superior equipment, training, technology, mobility and operational coherence of those countering the insurgency. Thus the Rhodesian experience should teach us, above all else, that what is required to counter insurgency are superior *political* tactics and strategy, from the local to the global level.

RWANDA: PUTTING THE INSURGENCY BOOT ON THE OTHER FOOT

Greg Mills[*]

Most writings on countering insurgencies are written on behalf of those attempting to do just that. Very seldom have the insurgents used the opportunity to write about the strategy and tactics pursued by their opponents. If they did, they might be able to help answer a key question befuddling militaries, governments and development agencies from Afghanistan to the Sudan: what can better be done to counter insurgencies and enable peace?

The army of the Rwanda Patriotic Front (RPF) is a case in point.[1] Not only did the Rwanda Patriotic Army (RPA) fight as insurgents in the four-year 'revolutionary' war against the Juvenal Habyarimana regime in Kigali, but many of its cadres fought as members of Yoweri Museveni's National Resistance Army (NRA) in deposing Milton Obote's regime in Uganda, and then as members of the Ugandan Army from 1986 fighting various anti-government insurgencies.

When Yoweri Museveni's band of twenty-seven companions attacked the Military School at Kabamba in Uganda in February 1981 to snatch some weapons, Rwandan exiles Fred Rwigema and Paul Kagame were among their ranks. By January 1986, when Museveni's by-then 13,000-strong NRA guerrillas stormed Kampala, there were around 4,000 Banyarwanda among them, though they comprised a

---

*   A version of this chapter appeared in the *RUSI Journal* (Vol. 153, No. 3, June 2008), pp. 72–78.

higher percentage of the officer corps. Many members of the Tutsi diaspora had joined in 1982–83 and worked their way up through the ranks. But when Rwigema, by then deputy army commander and deputy minister of defence of Uganda and a major general, was removed by President Museveni from his post in 1988, the Rwandan exiles realised their fight to end their condition of 'statelessness' had not ended.

Since taking power in Kigali in July 1994, bringing the genocide to a stop, the RPA – now the Rwanda Defence Force (RDF) – has fought a war against Hutu extremist insurgents in Rwanda and the Congo, along with a more conventional nine-month conflict which ejected President Mobutu Sese Seko from his Zairean throne in May 1997. The RDF now also provides a large component to the Darfur peacekeeping mission in the Sudan.

It is likely that no army has fought more battles in recent times, and certainly none so often both as insurgents and as counter-insurgents.

Lessons from a 'Popular War'

During the struggle against Obote's government, the National Resistance Movement learnt the importance of co-operation between the various anti-government forces, notably the Uganda Freedom Movement (UFM) and the federalist FEDEMU forces. While they might not have been able to agree to fight together, at least they agreed not to fight each other. By treating prisoners of war and local communities with respect, they were able to win converts more easily, notably among the Baganda (who make up a fifth of the Ugandan population), many of whom were dissatisfied with a northern-dominated army and were prepared to cross government lines to join the NRA. The rebels, Major-General Frank Mugambage[2] observes, had to remember all the while that 'the bad behaviour of just one or two soldiers could make your life very difficult – discipline was imperative'. They had also learned the importance of capturing and holding territory; making it impossible for the government to deny their cause. These principles were translated across to their campaign to liberate Rwanda. Three overall lessons stand out for the RPA as insurgents against the Hutu regime.

First, it was an immensely difficult struggle, fraught with setbacks. It took the RPF four years of heavy and costly fighting to advance the 75 km from their Ugandan base; but just nine months to fight their way more than 2,000 km across the Congo to remove Mobutu from power. The opposition Rwandan government forces were well-armed and supported, especially by their French allies, and believed that they were fighting a life and death struggle. The insurgent had to make them believe they were not.

The *justness* of its cause was immensely important in galvanising both the RPA and its supporters. Initially, their struggle was in part motivated by the 'homelessness' of the Tutsi diaspora, ejected and marginalised after continuous pogroms before and after Rwanda's independence from Belgium in 1962. More than that, the RPF's cause was about a vision of a Rwanda where politics was inclusive, and the aim was a society free from sectarianism and poverty. This demanded the need for vigilance and discipline within the movement against 'ethnic' bias, and created ownership and participation by Hutus and Tutsis alike of and in the struggle.

Second, tactics changed to suit the circumstances. The initial 2,000-strong RPA incursion into Rwanda in October 1990 ended in virtual defeat. With the recall of then Major Paul Kagame from the United States (where he was enrolled on a command and staff course at Fort Leavenworth as a Ugandan officer), which involved a harrowing journey through Mengistu Haile Mariam's Ethiopia, the RPA changed tactics to avoid direct battle with the government Forces Armées Rwandais (FAR). The RPA retreated to the volcanic Virunga region to the northwest where it regrouped, but where the 5,000-metre-high altitude and cold cost the lives of several fighters. Supplies and food – mostly beans, maize and sorghum – had to be ferried up at night along slippery, difficult tracks from supporters among the local population. All the time the RPA kept another front open in the east forcing the FAR to divide its forces and avoid concentrating on the Virunga contingent.

On 23 January 1991, the RPA moved down at night from the Virunga range to carry out an attention-grabbing strike on the nearby *préfecture* of Ruhengeri, President Juvenal Habyarimana's seat of power and the heartland of the Hutu regime. Akin to a Rwandan Tet Offensive, this caused a national upheaval. The RPA also cut the road to Uganda, forcing traffic to use the more difficult route through Tanzania. As a front developed countrywide thereafter, the RPA would deliberately snipe around the edges, trying to draw out the FAR and catch them off guard, aiming to liberate areas as it went. The tempo of the campaign ensured that Habyarimana's government could not claim that the insurgency was simply a Ugandan ploy aimed at creating a Tutsi empire in the Great Lakes region, and aimed to stoke support within Rwanda for the RPA's cause. Its tactical battles against the government were aimed at the strategic goal, in Kagame's words, of 'a popular protracted war'.[3] Kagame's disciplined approach and tactical and strategic 'nous' was central to the success of the campaign. Lieutenant General Romeo Dallaire, the Canadian head of the UN peacekeeping force to Rwanda (UNAMIR) at the time of the genocide, observes, 'They [the RPA] had won all recent contests because of their superior leadership, training, experience, frugality, discipline and morale. If Kagame was responsible for mobilising their force he was a truly impressive leader and perhaps deserved the sobriquet that the media had given him: the Napoleon of Africa.'[4]

All this time, the FAR was growing at an exponential rate: from 5,200 in 1990 to 50,000 by 1994, and buying weapons on the international market (including from Egypt and apartheid South Africa). It also received support from around 600 French troops deployed after October 1990 to Rwanda where they were, *inter alia*, involved in directing artillery support and logistics, flying helicopters and providing airport security. The RPA increased fourfold to around

15,000 men by the time of the genocide in April 1994, recruiting heavily from the population inside Rwanda, its ammunition and weaponry coming from captured and other stocks, and funding through its diaspora.

Third, the regime in Kigali did not give the RPA much alternative but to fight on, at least until the Arusha peace agreement of 1993. When the Arusha negotiations stuttered at the start of 1993 over the issue of sharing power in the military, the RPA launched an offensive that took them to the outskirts of Kigali at Shyorongi and cut the Kigali-Ruhengeri road at Base. 'By reaching the road', recalls one senior officer, 'we proved that we were a force to be reckoned with in military terms and capable of taking the capital'. Power-sharing was institutionalised under the terms of the final Arusha Agreement signed in August 1993, though this set the stage for the rise of extremist Hutu elements intent, instead, on a 'final solution'.

'Negotiations were never accepted by the government', says Patrick Mazimhaka, a lead negotiator for the RPF,[5] 'since negotiations would expose the ills of the regime and defeat them politically. However, since many European countries were supportive of the Habyarimana government, with the neighbourhood insisting that we negotiate, and given our lack of much material support, we had little option but to go to the table at that time.' Under the terms of this agreement, the RPA withdrew its forces north of the capital, creating a 120-by-20 km demilitarised buffer zone. 'We certainly overestimated what the international community could do to ensure the agreement would stick', observes Mazimhaka, 'though we could never have expected genocide – even though whenever the regime was weakened and felt threatened, it responded by massacring Tutsis'. The shooting down of President Juvenal Habyarimana's executive jet[6] on the outskirts of Kigali on 6 April 1994 sparked a meticulously planned, 100-day orgy of violence, costing the lives of an estimated 800,000 Tutsis and moderate Hutus. UNAMIR, deployed under the Arusha deal, was powerless to intervene in terms of its mandate, numbers and equipment, though its presence gave false assurance to the international community. Dallaire had said bluntly from the outset that he could do more with the necessary means, but, as he noted, 'There was a void of leadership in New York. We had sent a deluge of paper and received nothing in return; no supplies, no reinforcement, no decisions.'[7]

The genocide made a RPA military victory both imperative and, ironically, more likely given the FAR's – and the Hutu extremist Interahamwe (literally, 'those who stand together') militia's – shift in focus to social annihilation rather than military defence, even though it had stacked considerable forces around the capital. One lesson of Arusha is not only that without a political deal including even your most implacable opponent, a counter-insurgency campaign is a lost cause; it is also that such an agreement can, if it does not carry all constituencies, set the stage for greater violence. In their rush to ensure peace, international actors have to be sure to understand the roots of the conflict and to discern, as accurately as possible, the intent of the parties involved.

Now the boot is on the other foot, what has Kigali under the RPF's rule learnt from countering its own insurgencies in the DRC and elsewhere?

Countering Insurgency after the Genocide

The three-hour, 160 km journey northwest from Kigali along the Ruhengeri Road to the town of Gisenyi on the border with the DRC is a mesmerising overload of colour and activity, winding through spectacular passes and cuttings, over and around potholed roads splitting dirt-poor villages, along a patchwork quilt of fluorescent green fields wending their way up and over steep hills, and dodging a continuous stream of trucks, cyclists and people. Not for nothing is Rwanda Africa's most densely populated country – people line the road at virtually every stage, all going somewhere or carrying something, from sacks of food, ubiquitous yellow plastic water-containers, charcoal, chickens, bananas, sorghum, wood and tin for shelters.

It is along this route that as many as two million Rwandans fled towards Zaire in the aftermath of the Rwanda genocide. Nearly all were Hutu, some fearing retaliation from the RPF, others taken as hostages *en masse* by the perpetrators of the genocide. Having jumped the Rwanda-Zaire border at the Gisenyi crossing on Lake Kivu, they temporarily turned the neighbouring Zairean town of Goma into a seething, cholera- and violence-ridden tented refugee camp.

From then on, Rwanda's relations with first Zaire and, since 1997, the DRC were strained – with little respite. Two invasions led by Rwanda followed, the first removing Zairean strongman Mobutu from power in May 1997. Both incursions happened ostensibly because Kinshasa was seen to be turning a blind eye to the activities of Hutu extremists on its territory. The same charges have since been levelled at Kabila's son, Joseph, who took over rule following his father's assassination in January 2001.

The November 1996 operation was not originally designed and planned to remove Mobutu, but developed that way according to several phases.

Phase One

The Rwandans planned to engage ex-FAR/Interahamwe forces at the southern and northern ends of Lake Kivu, respectively, around Bukavu and Goma at the Kavumu and Mugunga refugee camps, in order to remove the military constraints preventing the refugees from returning to Rwanda. At this time, the Rwandan authorities estimated that there were 300,000 armed and trained Hutus in Zaire, 50,000 in Burundi and Tanzania each, and around 100,000 in Rwanda itself. By defeating the ex-FAR/Interahamwe defence positions, the refugees would, as proved true, be able to return. General James Kabarebe, at the time in charge of the Congo operation, recalls:[8]

The original brief and mission was to try to separate the population from the armed soldiers. This was very difficult to do in the refugee camps where their logistics, food and medicines were being supplied by the Red Cross, UNHCR, etc, and their army by the French and Mobutu. The NCOs and officer corps of this defeated army were not only more or less intact but they were, because of this support, in better shape and more secure than they were before.

In an operation involving just two Rwandan battalions (3rd Battalion to the north; 101st battalion to the south), more than a million refugees were able to return.

Phase Two

Following the success of this operation, the *genocidaires* reorganised to move deeper into the DRC, driving with them a smaller part of the refugee population. Mobutu also flew in reinforcements and equipment, including his elite Presidential Guard (Division Spéciale Présidentielle). 'When they formed a front to attack us, we kept on pushing and defeating them. As a result', Kabarebe says, 'another dynamic developed.'

Phase Three

Given the levels of threat to their own security both from Kinshasa and the presence of increasing numbers of *genocidaires* in their territory, the Rwandans were joined by Tutsis from North and South Kivu provinces (the latter known as the Banyamulenge[9]). Out of these recruits and the inclusion of other Congolese, including from the Mai-Mai militia 'who had grown tired of Mobutu and the situation but were stuck with what to do', the Alliance of Democratic Forces for the Liberation of Congo-Zaire (AFDL) was formed. The spokesperson for the AFDL was Laurent Kabila, a one-time 'Simba Rebellion' revolutionary colleague of Ché Guevara turned, over three decades, small-time Dar-es-Salaam trader and smuggler. One of Ché's close associates in the Congo in 1965, 'Benigno', said of Laurent Kabila: 'With leaders like that Africa can expect to have long centuries of slavery and colonialism'.[10]

Rudimentary infantry training schools were established at Matere in the north and Remera to the south, with Rwanda providing the command, logistics and leadership, their Congolese allies the bulk of the fighting forces.

Phase Four

As the AFDL advanced on foot across the country, Mobutu's demoralised and poorly (if ever) paid troops also joined the cause. These groups were simply integrated, as there was no need to retrain them. By this time of the war, in March 1997, the AFDL faced the tactical challenge of capturing Kisangani, which had been mined and fortified by Serbian mercenaries recruited by Mobutu. However, there was little alternative for the Rwandans to take the Congolese town since Mobutu had signalled his intent on bombing Kigali by two raids on Bukavu. Kisangani and, to the south, Kindu, were the only likely launching airfield points for such a raid. The Serbs 'who were trying to fight a conventional war against our guerrilla operations' at Kisangani were defeated by an attack on their rear, fleeing through the Garamba forest into Sudan. This was before the Katangese 'Tigers', a group of Congolese fighters exiled to Angola, had suffered heavy casualties as part of the anti-Mobutu coalition. 'They were made up of so many generals and colonels', one Rwandan officer remembers, 'that we seemed to have suffered a great defeat when these senior officers were killed in the advance on Kisangani'. Kindu capitulated shortly thereafter, after a night crossing of the great Congo River on canoes.

The invasion had now changed fundamentally from dealing with the immediate threat of the *genocidaires* to a Congolese campaign: 'the marrying', as Kabarebe puts it, 'of our interests of security with the interests of our Congolese partners in power'.

Phase Five

The final phase involved the attack on Kinshasa along two axes; Kikwit on the west and Bandundu on the east, and all the time the front line becoming narrower and narrower. The last big engagement was against Jonas Savimbi's Angolan UNITA forces, long-time allies of Mobutu, at Kenge, about 190 km south of the capital in early May. 'We defeated them', Kabarebe remembers, 'and marched on Kinshasa from two directions. We treated Kinshasa like the refugee camps at Goma – we did not want to go in fighting and cause mass casualties. So we fought at the airport and went into the city at night for a soft landing. When they discovered we were in town, Mobutu's forces surrendered without a shot being fired.' It was 17 May 1997, just six months after the intervention started.

The bulk of the Rwandan forces walked the entire campaign in their gumboots, one battalion (the 101st) moving in this way from Cyangugu in the south on the border with the Congo and Burundi to the Atlantic Ocean, more than 2,000 km in a straight line. The Rwandans used small aircraft (De Havilland Twin-Otters and a Britten-Norman Islander) to ferry logistics and commanders. 'We would look for old airfields on our maps, find them, and clear them.' Not only did they have to walk across 'an entire continent', but the biggest menace was 'the sun, heat and mosquitoes – big and hungry enough to bite you through your hair and clothes'.

The underlying motives for the intervention were strategic and enduring. Notably, they were partly to deal with the *genocidaire* forces in the Congo being granted sanctuary by Mobutu and succour by the international humanitarian community. They were also intended to dissipate the anti-Tutsi ethnic dimension in regional relations. Further, they aimed to build an African alliance against these negative international forces, which were seen not only to have sponsored the genocide, but as assisting both indirectly through Mobutu and directly with the ex-FAR/Interahamwe in the camps, laying the conditions for a further round of violence.

On to Kinshasa

'When we captured Kinshasa', Kabarebe says, 'I called Laurent Kabila on my sat-phone. He was in Lubumbashi', in the southern mineral-rich province of Katanga,

> [S]taying in one of Mobutu's villas – he always moved from town to town staying in Mobutu's former houses. I said he should come to Kinshasa. He was surprised. But he quickly called the media in Lubumbashi – remember he was only the spokesperson of the AFDL – and without consulting the AFDL, proclaimed himself president of the Democratic Republic of Congo.

Zaire was no more.

> The next day he flew into Kinshasa as president. He said to me: 'Young man you have done a great job. You are not Rwandan, you are a real African nationalist. With you we are going to achieve so much. We will build a force of 600,000 soldiers and liberate Africa from Cape-to-Cairo.' I wondered who we were supposed to be liberating who from. He said he would talk to President Kagame to allow me to stay on as chief of staff. I said I wanted a Congolese as my deputy and asked him to appoint his son, Joseph.

Kabarebe had originally encouraged the younger, untrained Kabila to joint the fighting in Kisangani.

Yet any hope that Laurent Kabila's rule would lead to a more prosperous and stable period in the Congo's history quickly soured as his own regime was characterised by large-scale corruption, human rights abuse and a renewed round of warfare. Kabila soon turned against his Rwandan and Ugandan patrons as he sought to reverse Congolese impressions that he was simply a foreign stooge and cement his domestic support base, showing little heart and plenty of darkness as he went easy on the *genocidaires*.

Following his dismissal of Kabarebe as chief of staff and his overtures to new partners, including the various local Mai-Mai and foreign militias who had fled Rwanda in the genocide's aftermath in 1994 to set up base in Zaire, Kabila's former Rwandan and Ugandan allies turned against him. 'Kabila resented the fact that he acceded to power with the help of Rwanda', says Patrick Mazimhaka. 'He saw us as a tiny country, very inconsequential. We also had a totally different outlook in terms of what we considered acceptable behaviour, such differences being obvious at the beginning in the way his forces looted Goma. He resented the fact that we were trying to tell him how to behave in his country.' Kabarebe remembers that shortly before the fall out with Rwanda, Kabila said to him: 'Go and tell Kagame that Congo is like a very, very huge rock. We are going to take a tiny portion of it, and lay it on Rwanda, and construct a big airport in its place. Even when they are in total trouble', he observes, 'the Congolese think they are very huge and powerful.' Or as Mazimhaka puts it, 'Kabila resented the fact that his country was great and rich while Rwanda, Kabarebe and others had won the war for him'.

'Kabila II', as it is known in some Kigali circles, began in August 1998 when Rwandan forces again attacked Bukavu and Goma, driving Kabila's forces out, sponsoring a new rebellion. A dramatic attempt to take Kinshasa followed, involving an airlift in chartered Russian aircraft of three battalions of Rwandan and allied Congolese troops – coalesced into the Congolese Rally for Democracy (RCD) – to Kitona on the Atlantic coast. After swiftly advancing east on the capital, the force was defeated around the N'Djili International Airport 25 km southeast of Kinshasa, when the Angolans attacked from the rear and the lightly armed Rwandan-Congolese fighters were confronted with Zimbabwean armour and helicopters. The Rwandan force made its escape into Angola via the DRC's Bas Congo province before being exfiltrated by air. Until that point the Zimbabweans' support for Kabila was wavering given Kinshasa's failure to pay for arms supplied by Zimbabwe Defence Industries.

Nonetheless, this round of conflict was not over, lasting until the negotiation of a peace settlement via the Inter-Congolese Dialogue held at South Africa's Sun City in April 2002, being variously labelled the 'Second Congo War' or 'Africa's First World War', drawing in combatants from virtually all the surrounding countries, including Angola, Zimbabwe, Namibia, Uganda, Rwanda, Chad, Sudan, the Central African Republic and Libya along with foreign mercenaries. Further engagements between Zimbabwean and Rwandan forces followed, including in Kasai and at Kabinda near the diamond-rich town of Mbuji-Mayi in the centre of the country as the Zimbabweans sought to secure its riches. However, today the Rwandans maintain respect for the Zimbabweans as 'good soldiers' (a number of Rwandans had been trained in Zimbabwe in the 1994–96 period), though their Angolan allies less so, with some of their generals 'businessmen preferring to be making deals in Kinshasa' and the army 'heavy and slow, heavily mechanised'. Erstwhile allies Rwanda and Uganda also famously clashed several times between August 1999 and June 2000 in the town of Kisangani, violent encounters from which bilateral relations have not since fully recovered.

At the heart of the war (and the subsequent peace process) costing an estimated 5.4 million lives (mainly from disease and starvation) was the very future of the DRC as a state. At the time of the UN-sponsored Lusaka ceasefire 'putting an end to the mutually-hurting military-stalemate' in mid-1999 which preceded the Sun City political deal, Kinshasa's remit roughly covered 40 per cent of the western sector of the country while foreign troops and guerrilla groups occupied the remainder mostly in the eastern half.

Today, Rwanda still faces threats from a hotchpotch of some 7,000 militia and ex-government forces, grouped into the Democratic Forces for the Liberation of Rwanda (FDLR) based in the eastern DRC, and whose stated aim is to overthrow the government in Kigali. With a mindset that could not only justify but carry out the genocide, the FDLR – labelled a 'terrorist' organisation by the United States

– believe it is victory or death. The Rwandan government's options are thus to put diplomatic (and failing that, military) pressure on their host bases. It also has to allow the political and social space for them to return, even if to face the justice system at home. Such space involves, over time, the depolarisation of society from the perceptions of Tutsis or Hutus, victims or *genocidaires*, them or us, to one of a Rwandan nation.

Dealing with Domestic Insurgents

General Kabarebe, promoted in 2010 to minister of defence, argues that Rwanda was able to deal with those remnants of the ex-FAR/ Interahamwe *inside* Rwanda 'in record time' after the genocide 'simply because we employed unconventional means'. Given that an 'insurgency thrives on one thing – the one that has the support of the population wins', it is necessary to 'go deep into what they believe and turn them around'. To achieve this 'one has to be strong and show strength, but this is not enough. One also has to be willing to give in, otherwise one will fight them to the last man.'

In the case of Rwanda, this required 'thinking like an insurgent and their supporters. What are their basic needs and values? Why are they fighting?' There is no point, he argues, in attempting the scorched-earth tactics employed by the Ugandans, for example, against the Lord's Resistance Army, destroying food supplies and herding the population into camps. Instead, 'we did not underestimate the power of the peasants whose children were enrolled in the forces of the genocide, and used this to fight the insurgency'. Kabarebe offers one example in the case of an ex-FAR divisional commander whose children and wife, a schoolteacher, remained in Rwanda. Instead of carrying out reprisals against the family, he went out and identified the wife. Although scared at first, he asked her how she was coping and how her children were. 'She showed me the children. They are Rwandans. I had a responsibility towards them as a Rwandan officer. I gave them money for school fees. I sent the lady for further studies.

I provided food for the family.' The news soon reached the husband, and 'broke him as a human being. He was convinced to return home and was integrated into the military.' The individual is now a general officer in the Rwanda Defence Force in the intelligence corps – a 'poacher turned gamekeeper' if ever there was one.

'To defeat them', Kabarebe maintains, 'we had to convince them that we would not take them to a small Guantanamo Bay. I needed to understand what they were running from. You need to be both a psychologist and a soldier to win this struggle.' And the African peasant has been the centre of gravity of this process. 'They are not complex like Al-Qa'ida. For them the basics like food, clothing and care are important. We used this to win them over as a force for the reconstruction of Rwanda.'

The Rwandans argue that strenuous efforts have been made, through such 'diplomatic channels', to encourage ex-FAR forces to return home to Rwanda. The return of two million Hutu exiles virtually *en masse* from camps around Goma in the Congo from November 1996 assisted these political efforts, signalling to the insurgents that the returnees had much to gain, not only by leaving the Zairean camps, but in returning to help rebuild a new Rwanda in which they would have a place and a role. Of course, this process has not been entirely successful. Those members of the FDLR still operational in North and South Kivu in eastern DRC have continued to wage war against minority ethnic communities and entrench insecurity in that vast territory. Kinshasa's failure to act decisively against this group (and, to the contrary, to work alongside the FDLR in operations against renegade Tutsi general Laurent Nkunda's National Congress for the Defence of the Congolese People) has exacerbated regional fears and suspicions. Until the forces of genocide are seen to have been properly dealt with – disarmed, cantoned and preferably returned to Rwanda – then these insecurities will remain. But all this, more than anything, as General Kabarebe says, 'takes patience', though the closer relationship struck between Rwanda and the DRC in bringing the FDLR and, in parallel, Nkunda to heel at the start of 2009 in Operation *Umoja Wetu*, was certainly a diplomatic step in the right direction.

Morphing into Peacekeepers

In 2007, the Rwandan Army was one of the largest contributors to the African Union mission in Sudan (AMIS); afterwards, it went on to join the UN-AU peacekeeping mission in Darfur (UNAMID). By April 2008, Rwanda had 3,500 troops in the western region of Sudan where only 7,000 hybrid UN-AU peacekeepers out of the mandated 26,000 had been deployed to try to stop the violence which has so far killed an estimated 200,000 people and displaced 2.5 million others.

Labelled a genocide by the US government and human rights groups, the continuing conflict in Darfur has defied even the latest ceasefire attempts and is driven by a complex combination of factors, none of them easily resolvable and few – if any – under the control of the peace-makers. These include decades of drought, overpopulation and desertification forcing camel-herding Baggara nomads further south into land occupied by non-Arab farming communities in their search for water, all overlaid by Arab-African and Muslim-Christian dichotomies. The two main rebel groups – the Justice and Equality Movement and the Sudan Liberation Movement – accuse the government of oppressing mainly land-tilling non-Arabs from the Fur, Zaghawa and Massaleit ethnic groups directly through its support of the Baggara-recruited Janjaweed militia. Whatever its exact cause and label, the conflict and resultant devastation has caused the deaths of upwards of 300,000 people since 2003.

President Kagame likened the Darfur mission to his country's genocide. 'Our forces will not stand by and watch innocent civilians being hunted to death like here in 1994', he said in 2004 as the first Rwandan detachment of 150 troops arrived in Sudan. 'I have no doubt that they will intervene forcefully to protect civilians.'[11] Strategically, the Darfur mission is thus a rallying point for national unity in a post-genocide Rwanda. It also provides a professional challenge to the RDF to again prove its worth, first to Rwandans but also to the international community, and to exercise leadership in an African context, not as a state but rather as an actor on key issues concerning peace, stability and development.

At a tactical level, the lessons from the deployment stress the importance of a clear and viable mandate and the need to equip troops accordingly, the need for troops to be flexible and diplomatic in their responses to local needs, and the importance of good leadership. The personal involvement of the president with the troops before, during and after the mission is seen as critical to their morale, the relationship of the mission to Rwanda's own circumstances, and the mission's success.

But Rwandan commanders are less than sanguine about the prospects for mission success. The splintering of the opposition Sudanese Liberation Movement into various smaller entities fractured their adherence to the May 2006 Abuja peace agreement on Darfur. The peacekeepers believe that more must be done to coalesce these rebels as a first step to creating a lasting settlement, a unification that may not, of course, be in Khartoum's best interest.

From Rwanda to Darfur, the overall lesson is clear on both sides of the insurgency coin: without giving the insurgents an attractive alternative to fighting, a counter-insurgency strategy can at best hold the ring with no victory possible. Divisive – rather than inclusive – politics cannot ultimately win. But the wrong political strategy – based on a misunderstanding of your opponents' strengths and weaknesses – along with the absence of a just cause, will not take you anywhere except, as with Rwanda in 1994, further down a violent path. And never overestimate what the international community can and will do to assist a peace process.

SIERRA LEONE: 'PREGNANT WITH LESSONS'

David Richards[*]

More than a year before the civil war in Sierra Leone was officially declared over, one distinguished British military analyst described it as a conflict 'pregnant with lessons'.[1] Ten years later, his observation is no less valid. Whether one is examining the reasons why Sierra Leone descended into the abyss it did in the 1990s, the role of the Economic Community of West African States (ECOWAS) and its armed monitoring group (ECOMOG) in nearly bringing order to the country on three occasions, the UN's initial inability to stabilise the country, the role of the British, or the persistent failure of the international community to build on an improving security environment, there is certainly no shortage of relevant topics to study and from which to learn.

At a time when our operation in Afghanistan is proving difficult and expensive, it is too easy to surmise that overseas intervention will always be difficult and expensive; that we will always be resisted by a significant proportion of the local population; and that we will always struggle to adapt to local conditions and find a winning formula. Sierra Leone stands as an important example where overseas military intervention was not only justified, it was also successful and, equally importantly, relatively inexpensive. Yes, we need to learn the lessons

---

[*] This chapter draws upon the author's contribution to RUSI *Whitehall Paper* No. 62, 'Global Challenges and Africa: Report of the 2004 Tswalu Dialogue' (2004).

from Iraq and Afghanistan; but in doing so we must not forget those learnt in Sierra Leone.

Background

Sierra Leone, founded in 1787, was Britain's oldest colony in West Africa. With a university, Fourah Bay College, established in 1827, it developed into a small but relatively prosperous territory, with a distinguished educated elite, and at independence in 1961 seemed set for a stable future as a democratic and developing state. What went wrong? The most important factor was that diamonds, source of much of the country's wealth, deeply undermined its social and political stability. As farmers abandoned their fields to flock to the diamond areas, so these tiny but fabulously valuable stones provided cash enough to corrupt anyone who needed to be bought off, from top politicians to local policemen. When the then prime minister refused to step down after losing an election in 1967, the military stepped in, only to be overthrown by a further coup led by NCOs a year later: the spectacle of the entire officer corps, dressed only in their underpants, being marched off to jail vividly symbolised the collapse of the only national institution capable of maintaining public order. Though the new president, Siaka Stevens, succeeded in restoring a semblance of stability, this was achieved only at the price of a thoroughly corrupt body politic, increasingly alienated from the people it governed. When Stevens stepped down in 1985, he nominated the army commander, Major-General Joseph Momoh, as his 'elected' successor. One result of this depressing record was that the former colonisers, the British, were remembered with respect. Life for ordinary Sierra Leoneans had been so much better in colonial times that the arrival of a UK intervention force did not arouse the hostility that it sometimes had done elsewhere.

Sierra Leone's civil war began in March 1991 when a small armed group known as the Revolutionary United Front (RUF), accompanied by Liberian fighters and Burkinabe mercenaries, entered southeastern Sierra Leone from Liberia. Their stated aim was to overthrow President Momoh's corrupt government and they claimed their larger goal was a radical, pan-African revolution based upon the Libyan Gaddafi model. Foday Sankoh and other leading figures in the RUF were heavily dependent on Charles Taylor of Liberia. They had all met in the mid-1980s while undergoing guerrilla training in Libya and Burkina Faso. Taylor launched his own attack on Liberia in 1989 but was thwarted in large part by ECOMOG, the Nigerian-led West African intervention force sent to Liberia. Taylor's support for the RUF was reputedly motivated by a desire to punish the government of Sierra Leone for its participation in ECOMOG. More importantly, he aimed to prevent Sierra Leone from being used as a base by his Liberian opponents, the United Liberation Movement for Democracy (ULIMO), as well as to acquire diamonds and other plunder to finance his own campaign and subsequent regime.

The next nine years of civil war in Sierra Leone consisted of immensely complex and fluid forming and reforming of alliances among the different parties striving to control the spoils of the state. For present purposes it is not necessary to track all the twists and turns of these years, but the broad outline is needed in order to understand how the international community in general, and the British in particular, came to the aid of President Kabbah in May 2000.

On 29 April 1992, a group of young Sierra Leone Army (SLA) officers, disillusioned with his government, overthrew President Momoh in a military coup. However, the new National Provisional Ruling Council (NPRC) administration, consisting of eighteen military officers and four civilians headed by Captain Valentine Strasser, soon adopted a style reminiscent of its predecessors. It also suffered a series of military defeats at the hands of the RUF. Despite military government and the expansion of the SLA from 3,000 to over 13,000, the RUF advanced to within a few kilometres of Freetown, the country's capital. Moreover, it became increasingly apparent that the SLA often avoided fighting the RUF. Some army and rebel commanders even reached informal understandings not to confront one another. Both sides lived off the countryside, murdering, plundering, looting and abusing the civilian population. Militarily, neither side was able consistently to achieve an advantage.

Valentine Strasser was ousted in January 1996 in a bloodless coup led by Brigadier General Bio. Bio undertook to permit the elections scheduled for February 1996 to go ahead. The oldest political party in Sierra Leone, the Sierra Leone People's Party (SLPP), won 36.1 per cent of the legislature vote. Its presidential candidate, Ahmed Tejan Kabbah, a UN development worker[2] and veteran politician, won 59.49 per cent of the presidential votes in a run-off second round election in March. This election and these figures are important because, along with the evidence of the infringement of fundamental human rights (through torture, mutilation and the recruitment of child soldiers), it underpins the international case supporting Kabbah rather than any of the other factions competing with him.

At the end of 1996 a peace agreement was made between Kabbah and Sankoh, but in name only. Kabbah was doubtful of the loyalty of the SLA and used irregular Kamajor 'hunters' and mercenaries from the South African company Executive Outcomes[3] to wage bush war against the RUF, in which good progress was made for the first time. The Kamajors could match the RUF in knowledge of the forest tracks and so block their supply routes. However, in May 1997 frustration in the armed forces resulted in another coup, led by Major Johnny Paul Koroma. Kabbah was forced to flee to Guinea and the Armed Forces Revolutionary Council (AFRC), with Koroma at its head, entered into a power-sharing arrangement with the RUF.

There was widespread international condemnation of the coup. The United Nations mandated ECOMOG to intervene in order to restore Kabbah. The Nigerians, who provided the greatest part of ECOMOG, launched a fierce attack on Freetown in September 1997. In October, the AFRC/RUF government conceded. At

Conakry a deal was struck which would provide immunity for Koroma, a 'role' for Sankoh and a six month period of transition to restore the Kabbah government. But the Conakry agreement did not hold. ECOMOG continued to fight Koroma's regime until it was overthrown in February 1998. Kabbah was restored in March that year.

However, the violence continued intermittently and with growing intensity. In January 1999 the AFRC/RUF invaded Freetown and only narrowly failed to secure the city, killing and mutilating thousands in the process. A counter attack by a combination of ECOMOG, loyal SLA and Sierra Leonean irregulars including the Kamajors, known collectively as the Civil Defence Forces (CDF), pushed the AFRC/RUF back into the countryside before the fighting subsided into months of indecisive stalemate. There were allegations of atrocities committed on all sides. Britain provided material assistance to the pro-Kabbah forces who, assisted by considerable international pressure, were able to force the RUF to negotiations that ended in the Lomé agreement of 7 July. At Lomé, the RUF dropped their demand for the removal of ECOMOG forces, which made way for an agreement to permit power-sharing. The terms gave the insurgents four key government posts and effective control over the country's mineral wealth. Also, significantly, there was to be a total amnesty for the RUF and the death sentence imposed on Sankoh was lifted.

Before being too critical of the government and international community's role in the Lomé Agreement, it should be emphasised just how low the country had fallen in the early part of 1999. The functions of state had practically collapsed with ministries in confusion and officials lacking any direction. The Ministry of Defence staff, for example, comprised three officials. Most businesses and government offices had been looted and vandalised during January's AFRC/RUF attack. There was no water, electricity or any other public services operating in Freetown. Large numbers of armed military, paramilitary, ex-SLA, civilians and CDF roamed the city, occupying buildings, manning checkpoints throughout the town and extorting money from the populace to permit passage. The Sierra Leone Police Force (SLP) was totally ineffective, untrusted and seemingly corrupt at every level. There was no communication to towns outside Freetown other than via radio and satellite telephone, and no safe road access to the interior. To quote *The Economist*, 'Sierra Leone manifests all the continent's worst characteristics. It is an extreme, but not untypical example of a state with all the epiphenomena and none of the institutions of government. It is unusual only in its brutality: rape, cannibalism and amputation have been common, with children often among the victims.'[4]

The life expectancy of the population was only forty-nine years. That population was desperate for peace and, albeit cautiously and with a sceptism born of previous failure, was prepared to give Sankoh a chance.

United Nations Involvement

The international community welcomed the Lomé Agreement, because at least it appeared to have stopped the fighting – an assumption that soon proved wrong – but the amnesty was heavily criticised and seen as a major victory for the RUF. On 3 October 1999 Sankoh and Koroma returned to Freetown and held a joint press conference with President Kabbah. They apologised for the atrocities carried out during the eight years of the civil war and promised to strive for a speedy implementation of the Lomé Agreement. On 22 October the Security Council unanimously adopted Resolution 1270 to establish a 6,000 member peacekeeping force to be known as the UN Mission in Sierra Leone (UNAMSIL) with a six month mandate to oversee the implementation of Lomé. In December, the International Monetary Fund (IMF) approved 15.56 million SDRs (Special Drawing Rights) for post-conflict reconstruction. The wider international community at last appeared to be paying serious attention to Sierra Leone.

Following the Security Council Resolution, the process of putting together the force elements for UNAMSIL began. In February 2000, as it became apparent that there would be a security vacuum with the phasing out of ECOMOG, the Security Council voted to increase the force from 6,000 to 11,000. But UNAMSIL forces[5] encountered difficulty as soon as they entered Sierra Leone; the RUF prevented Indian and Ghanaian elements from deploying to the eastern Bendu region. Furthermore UNAMSIL, despite a Chapter VII mandate, interpreted its brief in a traditional UN peacekeeping manner, as one of neutrality between the parties. This seriously impeded the development of close relations with the democratically elected Kabbah government it had been sent to help, and ensured little co-operation between the latter's army and the UN.

Matters did not improve for UNAMSIL. On the very day that ECOMOG officially transferred its duties to the international force, the RUF attacked Kenyan UN soldiers. On 4 May 2000, 208 Zambians who had been sent to relieve the Kenyans were taken hostage and their thirteen armoured personnel carriers were captured. On 6 May, 226 Zambians surrendered to the RUF, bringing the total number of hostages now held by them to over 500. The same day the Secretary-General of the UN requested that the United Kingdom and other countries act to improve the situation. On 6 May the RUF, using the captured APCs, began to advance on Freetown. Lunsar, on the approach road, fell to them and on 7 May the RUF were only 40 kilometres away from the capital.

The UN mandate for UNAMSIL and Kofi Annan's urgent request must be seen in the context of acute and general recollection of the international community's failure to act in Rwanda. The UN report on general failures over the crisis, including by its own organs, was widely praised for its candour. Annan in particular was applauded for ordering the enquiry since his own role at the time was subject to criticism. One of the decisions following the Rwandan crisis had been to establish a high-readiness brigade known as the Multinational

Standby High Readiness Brigade for United Nations Operations (SHIRBRIG), but it was not to be seen in Sierra Leone. The analyst Richard Connaughton cites a letter, which he received from the military adviser to the United Nations Department of Peacekeeping Operations, Lieutenant-General Giulio Fraticelli, explaining that SHIRBRIG at that time was only available to Chapter VI (embargo and sanction) operations and that the Sierra Leone mandate was under Chapter VII (enforcement).[6] Since Chapter VI peacekeeping is initiated after due diplomatic process and with the consent of the parties involved, it is arguably the precise circumstance when there is no requirement for rapid reaction.

The British Intervention

The UN appeared powerless to stop the RUF and indeed started to evacuate their civilian staff from the country. The government and UNAMSIL seemed, and indeed believed themselves to be, on the verge of collapse. Into this deteriorating situation, on 5 May 2000 I was ordered to lead a British military team to assess the situation and to recommend whether or not to respond to Annan's request. I advised in favour of intervention initially to conduct a non-combatant evacuation operation (NEO), but using the whole Spearhead Battlegroup with significant helicopter support: in my judgment such a force was necessary given the geography and the strength of the approaching RUF force and the UN's inability to stop it.

Within thirty-six hours a sizeable British military force, that at its height grew to 5,000 people, started to arrive. It became clear to me that such a force could achieve much more than a NEO if we were able to stiffen the resolve of the better UN contingents and turn the loyal rump of the SLA and the Kamajors into an effective fighting force. So we secured Lungi Airport and much of the Freetown Peninsula, including the site of UNAMSIL's headquarters. With their vital ground secured for them, UNAMSIL was given a chance to regroup and reorganise.[7] Although dysfunctional for weeks, it was an opportunity to which, under great pressure from the UN headquarters in New York, they started to respond. Their evacuation was curtailed and confidence slowly started to return.

What UNAMSIL could not, and would not, do was push the RUF back from their positions close to Freetown. To do this we, the British, co-ordinated and sustained the efforts of a disparate grouping of Sierra Leoneans, largely CDF and ex-SLA, who remained loyal to their president. Guided at every level by British officers and NCOs, over the next few weeks they succeeded in securing much of the inland road route between Freetown and Lungi, relieving the military and political pressure on Freetown and its beleaguered government. The British themselves fought few battles directly although when we did our overwhelming firepower left no room for doubt in the minds of the RUF rank and file in particular. The RUF started to splinter into different factions and Taylor began to lose his grip. This at first ad hoc twin-track operation by the British, giving support to the UN on the one hand and assistance to the government of Sierra Leone on the other, soon became official strategy. To give it further effect, the UK deployed additional forces including a sizeable amphibious force.[8] The result was total psychological ascendancy over the RUF that bought the government and the UN the time they needed to reassert themselves. And perhaps more important, in a different psychological sense, was the impact of the UK's role on the mood of the people. They at last felt the glimmerings of genuine hope for the future, a feeling reinforced when many RUF leaders were detained, including Foday Sankoh himself, taken into custody on 17 May while trying to escape from Freetown.

By mid-June 2000 the security situation had stabilised sufficiently to allow the British operation to be terminated, although we agreed to provide additional military support in the form of financial and training assistance to the new SLA, now renamed the Republic of Sierra Leone Armed Forces (RSLAF). Suspicion of the UK's motives dissipated with the departure of the main force. A German journalist who had arrived sceptical of the British a few weeks earlier caught the prevailing mood in Sierra Leone well:[9]

> Intervention in the fate of Sierra Leone has also awakened suspicion of re-colonization. That may be. But this kind of intervention does have a certain charm – especially as the locals have given the Whites such a hearty reception whilst they fear their own soldiers and regard the Blue Helmets as useless. The withdrawal of the main British contingent has allayed any suspicion of over-presumptuousness – and makes the operation appear all the more justified.

The Sequel

For a while, the security situation continued to improve as UNAMSIL finally began to deploy troops outside Freetown. But it soon became clear that they had neither the will nor the capability to push home their advantage. Nor, at that stage, was the fledgling RSLAF in a position to do better.

In early October 2000, the situation was deteriorating again. UNAMSIL, far from gaining strength and authority, appeared to be in danger of moving backwards, especially when India announced the withdrawal of its contingent. The RUF remained in control of over half the country and were strengthening their grip on some key areas, including the diamond producing regions needed to finance their operations. They showed no sign of returning to negotiations, and were beginning to expand their operations into Guinea. Charles Taylor continued actively to support them and seemed impervious to ill co-ordinated attempts by the international community to bring him into line. The UK's efforts with the RSLAF were beginning to bear fruit but lacked a powerful co-ordinating headquarters to bring coherence to the work and to develop a plan to defeat the RUF, harnessing and informing other work at the strategic level.

So I was sent back to the country with the same team that had succeeded in May, this time explicitly charged with development of a coherent plan that would ensure the RUF's defeat while devising a long-term solution that would ensure stability into the future. The work, combined with some bold initiatives by UNAMSIL's civilian and new military leadership, forced the RUF to sign a ceasefire agreement at Abuja on 10 November. The RUF's new leader, Issa Sessay, publicly conceded that the British commitment to Sierra Leone, and the opportunity it had provided the UN, was the distinguishing factor in their decision to seek a peaceful outcome. They had succumbed to the British aim of 'persuading the RUF of the inevitability of defeat'.[10] Although too much time was taken exploiting the agreement, this was a conspicuous success for the UN, the Sierra Leonean government and the UK. It signalled the end of the conflict and an opportunity to start bringing a real improvement to the lives of the long-suffering people of the country.

That process is still in train. Some 18,000 United Nations peacekeeping troops were on the ground in Sierra Leone from October 1999 to December 2005 at a cost of US$2.3 billion. During that period the country made vital progress in a number of areas with the help of the international community and in particular Britain: the disbandment and rehabilitation of former combatants; the complete overhaul, retraining and equipping of the armed forces by a British-led International Military Assistance and Training Team (IMATT); the establishment and training of a new police force; a massive influx of international aid and assistance, plus foreign expertise embedded within key government ministries; the demobilisation and reintegration of child soldiers into their communities; the revival of the minerals sector and the clamping down on illicit smuggling of diamonds; the introduction of various measures to promote investment and tackle corruption and money laundering; and the 2007 elections – won by the opposition leader Ernest Bai Koroma with 54.6 per cent of the final vote against Vice-President Solomon Berewa's 45.4 per cent in a run-off – and thereafter the peaceful transition to a new democratic government led by President Koroma.

Sierra Leone's largely peaceful and fair election in September 2007 marked an important step forward in its democratic development. Disconcertingly, however, at the time of the election Sierra Leone was, according to the UNDP Human Development Index, the poorest country in the world. For all the foreign expertise and huge sums of international aid, nowhere in sub-Saharan Africa were sanitation, water supplies and the provision of electricity worse than in Sierra Leone. The same goes for infant and maternal mortality rates, as well as unemployment. The country produced almost no exports and had little manufacturing. Perceptions of elite mismanagement, corruption and enrichment remained very high among ordinary Sierra Leoneans.

In the UN development report released in October 2009, only Niger and Afghanistan ranked lower than Sierra Leone. Today it receives more British aid money per capita than any other country in Africa. And despite some recent positive steps forward – perhaps none more important than the introduction of an entitlement to free health care in April 2010 – on most indicators of development Sierra Leone is not significantly different from how it was when the guns fell silent nearly a decade ago. Endemic unemployment among the country's youth and acute inequalities mean that a return to violence and instability can by no means be ruled out. As ever, much will depend on the situation in neighbouring Liberia, whose own conflicts have often spilled over into Sierra Leone. Interestingly, the most obvious visible change from the war-shattered country of ten years ago is the Chinese presence in today's Sierra Leone. Hotels and casinos with Chinese names have sprung up in Aberdeen Peninsula, once the base for UN peacekeeping operations. The Chinese, scenting the opportunities afforded by Sierra Leone's rich mineral wealth, are leading an essential infrastructure works programme and have built (desperately needed) new roads as well as made numerous investments in the country's agriculture and fisheries industries.

It is an ineluctable fact of the early twenty-first century that the 'Chinese factor' will inevitably feature in post-conflict reconstruction and development situations, so we would do well in the West to incorporate this into our planning and thinking about how best to assist the countries subject to international intervention and stability operations.

Lessons

The reader will have drawn many lessons from the above account, ranging from the essentially military through to broad issues of international behaviour and competence. In his memoirs published in 2010, Tony Blair, Britain's prime minister at the time of the intervention, wrote that after the experience of Sierra Leone he 'became ever more convinced that there had to be a proper, well-equipped standing force for Africa, preferably African in nature, with a mandate to intervene and be deployed in situations such as Sierra Leone.'[11] My purpose is not to examine the military *per se*, although there is clearly a huge overlap with other areas. For those who do want to focus on this aspect, Richard Connaughton[12] and Professor Gwyn Prins[13] both offer penetrating and highly readable analyses. How the UN's approach to peacekeeping might improve further is a fertile theme that they both explore well.

The remainder of this chapter instead looks at the broader issue of how the international community might better go about assisting deeply failed states such as Sierra Leone. How is it that even when the international mission gets so many of the basics right, the outcomes in terms of economic growth and development can nevertheless prove so unsatisfactory? My thesis is that in essence the international community is guilty of too much talk and not enough coherent and timely pre-emptive action. There is no shortage of analysis, but implementation is something in which we are far less expert. Why are things moving so slowly in Sierra Leone and in many other countries whose populations deserve better? Finding the answer requires a stern examination of how, firstly, to produce a coherent multidimensional plan tailored to the long-term needs of a particular country and, secondly, how to implement that plan energetically and coherently to ensure success. This absence of coherence has been a key failing in Sierra Leone and other failed or failing states.

But, before proceeding to offer solutions, what immediate lessons can be gleaned from Sierra Leone's experience?

First of all, the right security environment (and thus 'the military') is as much a *sine qua non* for success in Africa as it is in any other region of the world. Conflict resolution may just be the start. If there is not enough money spent on a country's army and police – and this means investment in the round, not simply on equipment – then that army will soon bite the hand that inadequately feeds it.

Secondly, and self-evidently, a good military creating a secure environment will not alone solve a country's problems. It is fundamental to progress, but it must be part of a much broader effort across a range of interdependent dimensions – political, diplomatic, legal, economic, industrial, humanitarian, as well as military. Whilst this is well understood, too often the actors in these different areas work narrowly within their own discipline, even parochially; blind to the requirement to ensure their work remains coherent with the overall effort. This need for much greater intra-government and agency coherence is critical to future success.

Thirdly, when solutions are eventually agreed they are applied far too slowly. In the military, the concept of tempo – acting relatively quicker than one's opponent – is recognised as vital to success. When one fails to achieve this, the initiative is lost and the enemy will surely win. In Sierra Leone it became clear too often that well-intentioned solutions were being overtaken by events. Applied too late, they would become irrelevant, often aggravating the new problem.

Fourthly, bureaucratic inertia and incompetence is endemic and positively inimical to progress. Worse, it is clear that sometimes those responsible for solving problems deliberately take longer than they might because the problem they are charged with solving is their working life, income and even raison d'être. This is a recurring criticism of many UN workers.

Lastly, NGOs are often less effective than they should be because they suffer from the same institutional rivalry and bureaucratic inefficiency as government agencies. They too pull in too many directions, undermining each other and failing to see the big picture.

Whilst these broad observations apply to many states at all stages of development, in Sierra Leone they are especially applicable. For example, in 2000, the following specific criticisms applied:

- Massive international investment by West African standards was focused on the slow implementation of an unimaginative security plan that was very poorly integrated with the wider political, diplomatic, legal, economic and other issues; without which any military success would be, at best, transient
- There was open and almost anarchical inter-agency rivalry
- There was no coherent, multidimensional plan. Too often organisations that should have been acting in concert were, often unwittingly, undermining each other
- A bewildering lack of urgency and of tempo.

But such was the severity of the situation that for once a single actor, in this case the UK, could impose solutions on all the others involved. The Sierra Leonean government, UN and the few NGOs that continued to function needed British help too much and were in no position to argue. The result was the flowering benefits of coherent multidimensional action based on a widely understood and firmly directed plan. President Tejan Kabbah, certainly charitably but with some justification, described the British Army as 'the architects of Sierra Leone's salvation'. Indeed it is he who first encouraged me to expose the approach taken in Sierra Leone more widely.

Two issues are key. How, firstly, does one devise a recovery plan from scratch that ensures coherence over time across all dimensions? And secondly, how does one ensure the plan is implemented efficiently, remaining adaptable and responsive in the process? Here, the military have something to offer their civilian colleagues. When confronted by novel operational or strategic problems, military commanders employ a rigorously logical and deductive analytical tool to produce a coherent plan. By necessity, in recent years it has become highly sophisticated. The result of the analysis in Sierra Leone was a plan in which a number of inter-dependent lines of development (political, humanitarian, economic, financial, reconstruction, and humanitarian) were actively pursued, through a number of necessary way points or 'decisive points', to a defined end-state. Success in achieving these points ensures continuing coherence across and through the life of the plan. They are also useful indicators of the pace and depth of progress.

But how does one ensure that something so complex remains relevant to developments as they occur and is implemented with the necessary tempo? The key is devolving responsibility to talented, empowered people who understand the big picture, work to clear intent and are authorised, indeed required, to use their initiative and energy to ensure that what they are doing meets their narrow objectives and yet remains compatible with a clearly understood overall plan. But should we expect a country to do all this for itself? Many think not. On a visit to Guinea in 1999, the finance minister showed me yet another sophisticated and highly technical blueprint for recovery he had received. 'I hardly understand it', he said, 'and certainly my team does not. What am I meant to do with it?' One possible solution is to develop a concept of 'embedded support', where a team of highly-motivated practical people with proven track records – bankers, industrialists, diplomats, civil servants, doctors and soldiers – drawn from both inside and outside the country is put together to work with and alongside the host government's departments and agencies over a period long enough to teach and train indigenous successors.

Donors would agree to devolve responsibility for helping the country to this single team working throughout the government. Crucially, this demonstration of long-term and coherent commitment by the international community, and the high quality of the implementation team, would serve as a vital confidence-building catalyst to inward commercial and industrial investment.

An intellectually rigorous analytical and planning tool, accompanied by the dynamism and leadership of an embedded support team throughout the implementation phase, has considerable potential to accelerate progress when applied to the most undeveloped states in Africa. The era of muddled aims, inertia, confusion, and contradictory action could be a thing of the past. And it must be emphasised that external assistance of this type and 'African-based solutions' are not inimical; indeed the opposite is true. This is to do with teamwork, playing to people's strengths and, most importantly, the laying of long-term foundations. It offers the real promise of inducing external investment and sustainable growth. The era of fine analyses but inadequate practical help must come to an end. It is time for the practitioners to join the team. The international community's watchwords, and its benchmark, must become implementation and delivery. To paraphrase Winston Churchill, a little 'less jaw-jaw' and a little 'more war-war' is required if the failed or failing state is to recover in a time frame that will satisfy its people and our consciences.

SOMALIA: INSURGENCY AND LEGITIMACY IN THE CONTEXT OF STATE COLLAPSE

J Peter Pham

In the two decades since 1991, when in January that year the dictator Muhammad Siyad Barre ignominiously fled Mogadishu inside the last functioning tank of the country's once-proud military, leaving behind a capital in ruins and in the throes of uncontrolled street violence, Somalia has been the prime example of what Robert Rotberg has termed the 'collapsed state':[1]

> [A] rare and extreme version of the failed state ... a mere geographical expression, a black hole into which a failed polity has fallen ... there is dark energy, but the forces of entropy have overwhelmed the radiance that hitherto provided some semblance of order and other vital political goods to the inhabitants (no longer the citizens) embraced by language or ethnic affinities or borders.

Somalia has stubbornly resisted no fewer than fourteen attempts to reconstitute a central government and the fifteenth such undertaking, the current internationally-backed[2] but chronically weak 'Transitional Federal Government' (TFG), just barely manages to hold on to a few districts in the capital. And this much only thanks to the presence of the 8,000 Ugandan and Burundian troops who make up the African Union Mission in Somalia (AMISOM).

In contrast, insurgents spearheaded by the Harakat al-Shabaab al-Mujahideen ('Movement of Warrior Youth', henceforth Al-Shabaab), a militant Islamist movement – declared a 'specially designated global terrorist' by the US State Department in 2008,[3] a 'listed terrorist organization' by the Australian government the following year,[4] a 'proscribed organization' under the British Terrorism Act in early 2010,[5] and a 'listed terrorist group' by the Canadian government[6] – effectively control wide swaths of Somali territory and operate more or less freely in areas where they do not exercise actual day-to-day governance (the exception being the Somaliland and Puntland regions, discussed below).

This chapter makes the argument that the failure of Somalia's TFG and its predecessors to prevail over their opponents and bring an end to the conflict has little to do with the complaints often voiced of lack of outside assistance, especially of the military kind, than other factors over which external actors can have little positive effect. Specifically, if the regime fighting an insurgency is unable or unwilling to achieve internal political legitimacy, no outside intervention will be able to help it to 'victory', as even a cursory review of the relationship between legitimacy and military force in civil wars will confirm. In examining how such has been the case in Somalia, it is necessary to also look at the nature of political legitimacy in Somali society, deriving pointers from the success not only of the Islamist insurgents of Al-Shabaab and their allies, but also the two relatively stable polities which have emerged in the northern part of the territory of the former Somali state. The conclusion draws out the implications of engaging these alternative centres of legitimacy, an approach that the international community has come around to embracing amid the failure to otherwise check the progress of the insurgency and ensure a modicum of stability and security in the geopolitically sensitive Horn of Africa.

Legitimacy and Military Force

It is a principle that, in civil wars, while military force is vital for insurgents – without it, they pose no threat to the state – it is less important to the governments opposing them. For the latter, while having capable armed forces and the political will to use them is not unimportant, unless the governments achieve legitimacy their counter-insurgency (COIN) operations will ultimately fail. As for the sustainability of any peace, it is dependent less on a government's military strength than on its ability to convince the population of its legitimacy: in other words, deriving its just powers from those it proposes to govern and providing them with reasonable opportunities for political, economic and social development.[7]

At a very simplified level, there are three types of parties in any civil conflict: the core group that supports any given faction, whether out of high-minded principle or mere material interest; those who support the opposing faction; and those, often in the majority, who are disinterested or indifferent to the competing claims of the rival factions.[8] The factions contend with each other to convince the disinterested populace of their legitimacy, which has been defined as 'the belief in the rightfulness of a state, in its authority to issue commands, so that those commands are obeyed not simply out of fear or self-interest, but because they are believed in some way to have moral authority, because subjects believe that they ought to obey'.[9]

The classic distinction by Max Weber listed 'three grounds legitimating any rule': traditional legitimacy ('the authority of the eternal past'), juridical right ('rule by virtue of legality'), and charisma ('the authority of the exception').[10] For a government, the provision of goods and services to the population offers another form of legitimacy, or at least often the first step to creating a system in which its legitimacy is accepted. Conversely, the failure to meet basic expectations weakens the same claim of legitimacy. For their part, insurgents can use terrorist tactics to underscore an incumbent regime's inability to protect its own population, thus de-legitimising it. More positively, rebels can garner support and legitimacy from the populace by providing it with the very political and social goods that the government has proven unable or unwilling to supply.

In this context, especially for governments, military power has its limits. While military action can remedy some of the symptoms of diminished legitimacy, force alone cannot restore it. It needs to be recalled that the very existence of an insurgency implies a base of support that, if it does not actively aid the insurgents, at least tolerates them and, in so doing, implicitly denies the government's claim to legitimacy. Consequently, the military components of a counter-insurgency must be carefully calibrated to avoid adding to the numbers of the disaffected and 'all actions, kinetic or nonkinetic, must be planned and executed with consideration of their contribution toward strengthening [the government's] legitimacy'.[11]

The effect of external interventions, whether to assist governments in defeating insurgents or to merely hasten the end of conflicts, also needs to be carefully weighed since they may actually exacerbate a regime's crisis of legitimacy, by drawing attention to its weakness and even making it seem to be but a pawn of the intervening force. Just winning, in purely military terms, 'may not be enough and, often, may be a mistake or deflect one from grasping the prize of legitimacy itself'.[12]

There is little that a foreign actor can do to buttress an allied regime's domestic legitimacy, unless the latter is truly committed to taking the necessary measures to maintain – if not enhance – political, economic and social development not only for its core supporters, but the disinterested portion of the population as well. If, on the other hand, the government under challenge manages to maintain its legitimacy with these two groups, the rebels will be reduced to struggling just to survive. All of this, of course, requires the commitment of not inconsiderable amounts of time and resources. As Henry Kissinger succinctly framed it, while 'the guerrilla wins if he does not lose', the regime he opposes 'loses if it does not win'.[13]

A Quick Primer on Legitimacy and Identity among the Somali

Somali identity is historically rooted in *tol* [paternal descent] meticulously memorialised in genealogies (*abtirsiinyo*, 'reckoning of ancestors'), which determines each individual's exact place in society. At the apices of this structure are the 'clan-families'. According to the usual division, the clan-families are five in number: Darod, Dir, Hawiye, Isaq and Digil/Rahanweyn (also known as Digil Mirifle). The first four, historically predominantly nomadic pastoralists, are considered *bilis* [noble] clans. The Digil/Rahanweyn, traditionally cultivators and agro-pastoralists, occupy a second tier in Somali society. The latter also speak a dialect of Somali, *af-maymay*, which is distinct from the predominant *af-maxaa*. A third tier also exists in Somali social hierarchy, consisting of minority clans whose members, known collectively as *sab*, historically carried out occupations such as metal-working and tanning which, in the eyes of the nomadic 'noble clans', rendered them ritually unclean.[14]

These genealogical groupings are traditionally too large and too widely dispersed to act as politically cohesive units – although, in modern times, the advent of instantaneous mass communications has resulted in rendering the segmentary solidarity of their members a significant factor in national politics – the clan-families are subdivided into clans and sub-clans by descent along the male line. Among these, the basic and most stable unit of political organisation is the 'diya-paying group' (from the Arabic *diya*, 'blood-wealth') consisting of kinsmen who collectively pay and receive damages for injury and death. The unity of the group is founded not only on shared ancestry, but also a formal political contract (*xeer*) between its members. I M Lewis observes that 'the vital importance of this grouping, in an environment in which the pressure of population on sparse environmental resources is acute, and where fighting over access to water and pasture is common, can hardly be overemphasized' since it is 'upon his diya-paying group, and potentially on wider circles of clansmen within his clan-family, that the individual ultimately depends for the security of his person and property'.[15]

Despite the efforts of the Siyad Barre regime to impose 'Scientific

Socialism' with the professed goal of uniting the nation by eliminating its ancient clan-based political culture, 'tribalism in its special Somali lineage version' merely 'waited in the wings, ready for emergencies and sudden changes of political fortune' to re-emerge.[16] After the dictator's fall and the successive failure of three international military interventions – the United Nations Operation in Somalia I (UNOSOM I, April–December 1992), the United States-led Unified Task Force (UNITAF, December 1992–May 1993), and United Nations Operation in Somalia II (UNOSOM II, March 1993–March 1995) – to secure more than ephemeral space for the flow of humanitarian assistance,[17] central and southern Somalia returned to the age-old pattern of armed clan factions mobilised by powerful figures. Referred to by Somalis with the traditional title formerly reserved for battle leaders, *abbaanduule*, they were thus quickly dubbed 'warlords' by foreign journalists – and sustained by the spoils of conflict vying with each other for control of territory and such economic assets as were to be found amid the ruins of the collapsed state.[18]

In the absence of anything resembling a functioning state and amid the multiplying divisions of society, Somalis returned to segmentary solidarity as the basis for organisation. Islam came to be seen by some Somalis as an alternative to both the traditional clan-based identities and the newly emergent criminal syndicates led by so-called 'warlords'.[19] Islamic religious leaders have helped organise security and other services, and businessmen in particular were supportive of the establishment of Sharia-based courts throughout the south in the 1990s. These offered a pan-Islamist identity as an alternative to other possible legitimising principles for political organisation among the Somali.[20]

Traditionally, the Somali subscribe to Sunni Islam and follow the Shafi'i *mahdab* [school] of jurisprudence, which, although conservative, is open to a variety of liberal views regarding its practice.[21] Prior to Somalia's independence in 1960, there were different movements within Sunni Islam, the most dominant of which were the Sufi brotherhoods, especially that of the Qadiriyya order (although the Ahmadiyya order, introduced into Somali lands in the nineteenth century, was also influential).[22] While traditional Islamic schools and scholars played a role as focal points for rudimentary political opposition to colonial rule in Italian Somalia, historically their role in the politics of the Somali clan structure was neither institutionalised nor particularly prominent. In part this is because Sharia Law has not historically been entrenched in Somalia, its pastoralist culture relying more on *xeer* than religious proscription.[23] Hence, Somali Islamism is largely a post-colonial movement which became active in the late 1980s and which was strengthened by the collapse of the state in 1991 and the ensuing civil war, international intervention, external meddling and Somali efforts at political reconstruction. Absent this chain of events, it is doubtful that militant Islamism would be much more than a marginal force in Somali politics.

The Travails of the Transitional Federal Government

Since the collapse of the Somali government and state in 1991, regional and international actors have tried repeatedly to find ways to reconstitute the Somali state by sponsoring lengthy 'peace processes' aimed at establishing a functioning government in Mogadishu. The current embattled TFG is the result of the fourteenth and fifteenth such attempts, the Nairobi (or Mbagathi) and Djibouti processes.

The 'Nairobi Process' began in October 2002 under the patronage of the subregional Inter-Governmental Authority on Development with international support, especially from the European Union and the United States. The discussions were protracted, with more than 400 self-appointed delegates, and it took just over two years to establish the TFG using the '4.5 formula'. According to this system, power was to be shared between four of the clan-families – Darod, Dir, Hawiye and Digil/Rahanweyn (the Isaq, centred in Somaliland, declined to participate) – with some space (the '0.5') for minority clans. The Transitional Federal Charter agreed in October 2004 gave the Transitional Federal Institutions of government a five-year mandate. Heading up this structure was a Darod warlord, Abdullahi Yusuf Ahmad, who had launched his political career with the proceeds of a $1 million ransom he had extracted from the Taiwanese after his militia seized the trawler MV *Shen Kno II* in 1997.

It was not until June 2005, and then only under heavy pressure from its long-suffering Kenyan hosts, that the TFG finally relocated to Somali territory. Even then, the putative government could not enter its capital – the prime minister, Mohamed Ali Ghedi, who, to his credit, at least made the attempt, narrowly escaped assassination for his trouble – and settled instead in Jowhar, a provincial town safely north of Mogadishu, under the protection of a local warlord who was a fellow Hawiye clansman and patron of the prime minister. When relations eventually soured with the warlord, the TFG was forced to move on and, in a turn of events that is particularly humiliating in the Somali cultural context, was forced to take shelter among the Rahanweyn in the backwater of Baidoa, some 250 km southwest of the capital. So undesirable was the location and so reduced were its circumstances that it was not until February 2006 that the TFG could muster a quorum to convene its parliament in a converted barn.[24]

Meanwhile, a new force was emerging in Somalia: the Union of Islamic Courts. It was composed of the militias of various local tribunals, set up by the Islamists who had taken control of Mogadishu in June 2006 after defeating a ragtag coalition of warlords and business leaders hastily thrown together by the United States under the banner of the 'Alliance for the Restoration of Peace and Counter-Terrorism'. The Islamists, far from being checked, actually prevailed and, for the first time since the fall of Siyad Barre, Mogadishu was united under a single administration. Moreover, the Islamists, who reorganised themselves into a governmental structure, the Council of

Islamic Courts (CIC), quickly extended their control over much of southern and central Somalia, from the southern border of Puntland in the north to the Kenyan frontier in the south, leaving the TFG barely clinging on in Baidoa under the protection of the Ethiopian military.[25]

The CIC was, in many respects, a mixed blessing for most Somalis. The Islamists cleared away the roadblocks that had been set up by rival militias over the years and reopened the port of Mogadishu. They organised some rudimentary services, including the first municipal rubbish collection in nearly two decades. On the other hand, these improvements went hand-in-hand with the imposition of Islamic strictures that were largely alien to Somali experience including a ban on watching the 2006 football World Cup (deemed 'un-Islamic behaviour').[26]

Neighbouring Ethiopia was alarmed by the rapid rise of the Islamists in Somalia; hardly unsurprising, given their own earlier experiences with Somali Islamist groups, especially Al-Itihaad Al-Islamiya,[27] and the emergence of many of the same extremists in positions of authority in the CIC. When a CIC attack on the TFG in Baidoa, which was being protected by Ethiopian units, provided the *casus belli*, Ethiopian Prime Minister Meles Zenawi launched a full-scale military intervention on Christmas Eve 2006. The heavily armed and well-trained Ethiopians quickly routed the CIC's forces, many of whose commanders made the mistake of deploying in open country where their units were slaughtered by the invading forces. 'On the coat-tails of the Ethiopian forces rode the TFG',[28] which assumed control over key government buildings in Mogadishu under heavy Ethiopian protection.

As the populace's sullen acquiescence to the new regime turned into resentment of what amounted to a de facto foreign occupation, an insurgency gathered strength. Seemingly impervious to his increasingly tenuous position, Abdullahi Yusuf was finally forced to resign as president of the TFG in late 2008. His intransigence had been increasingly viewed by Somalia's neighbours as an obstacle to the latest peace process they had launched earlier that year by reaching out to the regime's supposedly 'moderate' opponents, led by the former Islamic Courts leader Sheikh Sharif Sheikh Ahmed. Sharif Ahmed was himself installed as the new TFG president in January 2009 by an electoral assembly packed for that purpose, which convened in Djibouti under the sponsorship of the Nairobi-based UN Political Office for Somalia. The mandate of the new regime was extended until August 2011.[29]

Not surprisingly, given how it came into being, the new iteration of the TFG has basically been 'unable to expand its authority beyond Villa Somalia in Mogadishu, seat of the presidency' and 'has had little relevance'.[30] In the summer of 2009, when the insurgents attempted to encircle the TFG in Mogadishu, a number of analysts were surprised by the effectiveness of the Islamist push through territory controlled by Sharif Ahmed's own Harti sub-clan of the Abgaal clan – the reluctance of even his closest kinsmen to defend him was a most telling indicator of his near-total lack of legitimacy. The promising alliance in early 2010 between the regime and the Sufi movement, Ahlu Sunna Waljamaca, whose militias have opposed the Islamist insurgents in the central regions of Somalia, collapsed when Sharif Ahmed reneged on the terms of the power-sharing agreement. In fact, the incumbent TFG president seems as unwilling as his predecessor to engage in the sort of deal-making that would co-opt key stakeholders, extend his regime's political base, or prepare the ground for security operations that might break the continuous stalemate.[31] A March 2010 report by the United Nations Monitoring Group on Somalia was, for a diplomatic document, unusually candid in its assessment of the regime and was, for all intents and purposes, a scathing indictment not only of the TFG, but of any policy built on it:[32]

> The military stalemate is less a reflection of opposition strength than of the weakness of the Transitional Federal Government. Despite infusions

of foreign training and assistance, government security forces remain ineffective, disorganised and corrupt – a composite of independent militias loyal to senior government officials and military officers who profit from the business of war and resist their integration under a single command. During the course of the mandate, government forces mounted only one notable offensive and immediately fell back from all the positions they managed to seize. The government owes its survival to the small African Union peace support operation, AMISOM, rather than to its own troops…

The security sector as a whole lacks structure, organization and a functional chain of command – a problem that an international assessment of the security sector attributes to 'lack of political commitment by leaders within the Transitional Federal Government or because of poor common command and control procedures'… To date, the Transitional Federal Government has never managed to deploy regimental or brigade-sized units on the battlefield…

The consequences of these deficiencies include an inability of the security forces of the Transitional Federal Government to take and hold ground, and very poor public perceptions of their performance by the Somali public. As a result, they have made few durable military gains during the course of the mandate, and the front line has remained, in at least one location, only 500 metres from the presidency.

Not only has the TFG 'failed to generate a visible constituency of clan or business supporters in Mogadishu', its very survival 'now depends wholly on the presence of AMISOM forces'[33] since, out of the some 9,000 troops that three separate military missions – the United States, the EU and France – have trained and armed for the regime, no more than 1,000 remain.[34] Efforts to supply this miniscule force have also proven counterproductive. Despite receiving more than 80 tons of weapons and ammunition from the United States in May 2009, the TFG singularly failed to expand its territory in Mogadishu. In fact, about the only noticeable change caused by the arms transfer was the collapse of prices in the arms market operating within walking distance of the government compound, suggesting that a not insignificant part of the shipment was simply sold by corrupt regime officials.[35]

The Insurgency

While the Ethiopian intervention in 2006 ended the rule of the Islamic Courts, the latter's Al-Shabaab militia not only survived, but also emerged as the dominant force opposing the TFG and its international supporters. Al-Shabaab itself was born earlier under the leadership of one of the CIC's more hardline leaders, Sheikh Hassan Dahir Aweys, who wanted for the Islamist movement a military wing whose members were not only well-trained, but indoctrinated to a pan-Islamist identity that transcended clan allegiances. The initiative was entrusted to one of his young deputies, Adan Hashi Farah 'Ayro', who had travelled to and been trained in Afghanistan before the Al-Qa'ida attacks on the United States and the subsequent American-led invasion in 2001. Other prominent leaders of the group had also had experience in Afghanistan and/or Kashmir, including Muktar Robow Ali ('Abu Mansur'), Ibrahim Haji Jama ('Al-Afghani'), and Ahmed Abdi Godane ('Abu Zubair'), who eventually succeeded Ayro as the group's nominal leader after the latter was killed in a US airstrike in May 2008.[36]

After the Ethiopian invasion destroyed the CIC, Al-Shabaab began operating as an independent entity. Over time, the group – insofar as it can be said to be one – has shifted its emphases from a purely local focus on driving out the foreign forces to an increasingly international agenda that has occasioned both a twin bombing in Kampala, Uganda, in July 2010 and formal proclamations of its adhesion to Al-Qa'ida. Gradually gaining control over much of southern and central Somalia – in January 2009, it even achieved an objective that eluded its former parent organisation, the CIC, when it took control of Baidoa – it has established local governments in those areas, which administer its harsh version of Sharia Law as well as adjudicating more prosaic disputes. Since early 2009, Al-Shabaab forces have not only attacked the TFG, but also battled with AMISOM forces, drawing the peacekeepers deeper into the conflict and causing them to suffer increasing casualties with terrorist attacks. Attacks have included the suicide bombing of 17 September 2009, which killed seventeen peacekeepers, including the deputy force commander, Brigadier General Juvénal Niyoyunguruza of Burundi, and wounded more than forty others,[37] as well as more conventional offensives.

Al-Shabaab has also enjoyed some success reaching out to the Somali diaspora in North America, Europe and Australia. One young recruit, Shirwa Ahmed, perpetrated what was the first known suicide attack by an American citizen when, in October 2008, he drove a vehicle-borne improvised explosive device in Puntland. Others in the diaspora have been indicted by US prosecutors for sending funds to the insurgency.[38] Al-Shabaab has also provided training camps for foreign Islamist militants as well as safe haven for some higher-ranking Al-Qa'ida operatives in East Africa, including Abu Taha Al-Sudani and Saleh Ali Saleh Nabhan, who were subsequently killed by Ethiopian and US special operations forces, respectively.[39]

Generally allied with Al-Shabaab – although occasionally also competing with it for control of key towns and strategic resources like the port of Kismayo – is Hizbul Islam ('Islamic Party'), formed by Aweys and other exiled former CIC hardliners after the 'moderates' acceded to the Djibouti Process with the TFG in 2008. The group's primary difference to Al-Shabaab is that it does not place as much emphasis on global jihadist objectives. Rather, its two principal demands are the implementation of a strict version of Sharia as the law in Somalia and withdrawal of all foreign troops from the country. Although it lost control of the strategic central town of Beledweyne to Al-Shabaab forces in June 2010, Hizbul Islam still controls some territory in the southern and central Somali regions of Bay and Lower Shabelle. There have been reports of talks, allegedly mediated by foreign militants, between the two Islamist groups aimed at bringing about their merger.[40] Subsequently, during the Muslim holy month of Ramadan, the two groups co-operated on a joint offensive against TFG and AMISOM forces in Mogadishu.

Another insurgent group is the Mu'askar Ras Kamboni ('Ras Kamboni Brigades') led by Hassan Abdullah Hersi ('Al-Turki'), a former military commander for the Islamic Courts. Based in middle and lower Jubba Valley, where it gained control of several strategically located towns which control access to the Kenyan border, the Ras Kamboni Brigades were aligned with Hizbul Islam until the beginning of 2010, when it announced it was joining forces with Al-Shabaab and the two groups proclaimed their adhesion to 'the international jihad of Al-Qa'ida'.[41]

The insurgents' attacks have increased in both ambition and sophistication. For example, whereas the 17 September 2009 suicide bombing of AMISOM headquarters and the 3 December 2009 assault which killed three TFG ministers as well as sixteen other people attending a graduation ceremony at Mogadishu's Shamu Hotel both relied solely on explosives to inflict damage, the 24 August 2010 attack on the Muna Hotel (just blocks from Villa Somalia and frequented by TFG officials) involved Al-Shabaab fighters dressed in government uniforms who went through the building room by room killing their victims. They then fought arriving security forces for some time before finally detonating their suicide vests. Other attacks have brought critical facilities like the international airport, the road connecting the port to the rest of the capital, and the barracks housing the African peacekeeping force under increasing pressure. The often heavy-handed response of the AU force has caused it to be widely viewed as a party to the conflict, rather than a neutral peacekeeping mission – thus bolstering the insurgents' standing as 'nationalists' among a populace that is traditionally disposed to xenophobia. Overall, the escalating insurgency has underscored the inability of the TFG and its AMISOM protectors to secure even limited territory within Mogadishu, casting grave doubt on both the former's viability and the latter's mission.

'Bottom-Up' versus 'Top-Down'

The most damning aspect of the utter failure of fourteen different attempts (so far) to rebuild national-level institutions, and the current struggles of the fifteenth just to survive the daily assaults of the Islamist insurgency, is that there are ready examples elsewhere in the territory of the former Somali state of what is possible when a 'bottom-up' or 'building-block' strategy is adopted, instead of continually defaulting to a 'top-down' approach in the pursuit of a conflict resolution, peace-building, or, for that matter, a counter-insurgency agenda. The experience illustrates how a process that is viewed as legitimate and supported by the populace can also address the international community's interests about issues ranging from humanitarian concerns to maritime piracy to transnational terrorism.[42]

Although they differ significantly in their political development and the courses they have charted for themselves to date, the northern Somali regions of Somaliland and Puntland have both been relatively successful in avoiding not only embroilment in the violence that has consumed most of southern and central Somalia, but also major internal conflict.

After the collapse of the Somali state, clan leaders in the former protectorate of British Somaliland, which had been briefly independent in 1960 before uniting with the former Italian colony of Somalia, proclaimed the dissolution of the union and set about building a separate state. The new administration's successful demobilisation of former fighters, formation of national defence and security services, and the extraordinary resettlement of over one million refugees and internally displaced persons, fostered the internal consolidation of its renascent polity. The establishment of independent newspapers, radio stations, and a host of local NGOs and other civic organisations reinforced the nation-building exercise. The stable environment thus created facilitated substantial investments by both local and diaspora businessmen who have built, among other achievements, a telecommunications infrastructure that is more developed and varied than in any of Somaliland's neighbours.[43] The internationally monitored presidential election in June 2010 which resulted in the defeat of incumbent Dahir Riyale Kahin, the election of Ahmed Mohamed Mohamoud 'Silanyo', and a smooth transition between the two – an unheard of occurrence in the region – reinforced Somaliland's case for the international recognition that has thus far eluded it.

The Darod territories in the northeastern promontory of Somalia have also demonstrated the success of the building-block model for the country and the wisdom of working with the deeply ingrained clan identities of the Somali. In 1998, tired of being held back by the constant violence and overall lack of social and political progress in central and southern Somalia, traditional clan elders of the Darod clan-family's Harti clan – including its Dhulbahante, Majeerteen, and Warsangeli sub-groups – meeting in the town of Garowe opted to undertake a regional state formation process of their own in the northeast, establishing an autonomous administration for what they dubbed the 'Puntland State of Somalia'. After extensive consultations within the Darod/Harti clans and sub-clans, an interim charter was adopted which provided for a parliament whose members were chosen on a clan basis and who, in turn, elected a regional president, the first being Abdullahi Yusuf Ahmed who, in 2004, went on to become president of the TFG.[44] The current incumbent, Abdirahman Mohamed Mohamud 'Farole', was elected in January 2009 from a field of over a dozen candidates. Unlike Somaliland, which has opted to reassert its independence, Puntland's constitution simultaneously supports the notion of a federal Somalia and asserts the region's right to negotiate the terms of union with any eventual national government.[45] While the region has become the centre of Somali maritime piracy, an activity in which many of its leaders are believed to be implicated,[46] the Puntland government has been especially diligent in its efforts to root out Islamist extremism there.

By leveraging the legitimacy they enjoyed by virtue of deeply rooted kinship and geographic bonds, traditional leaders in both Somaliland and Puntland have managed to deliver to their constituents a relatively high degree of peace, security, economic progress, and the rule of law, despite the lack of international recognition or much involvement for that matter. Put another way, they have combined Weber's 'traditional legitimacy' and 'legal right' with service provision in order to establish a sustainable political arrangement, 'an order beside the state'.[47] As COIN theorist David Kilcullen has noted:[48]

> Somalia is virtually a laboratory test case, with the south acting as a control group against the experiment in the north. We have the same ethnic groups, in some cases the same clans or even the same people, coming out of the same civil war and the same famine and humanitarian disaster, resulting from the collapse of the same state, yet you see completely different results arising from a bottom-up peace-building process based on local-level rule of law versus a top-down approach based on putting in place a 'grand bargain' at the elite level.

Encouragingly, there have been indications that the international community may finally be coming to the same realisation. In autumn 2010, the US Assistant Secretary of State for African Affairs Johnnie Carson announced a 'dual-track approach' that included greater engagement with government officials from Somaliland and Puntland with an eye to 'looking for ways to strengthen their capacity both to govern and to deliver services to their people'.[49] Likewise, after long refusing to even acknowledge their existence, the African Union's Peace and Security Council directed AU Commission Chairperson

Jean Ping to 'broaden consultations with Somaliland and Puntland as part of the overall efforts to promote stability and further peace and reconciliation in Somalia'.[50]

Conclusion

The astonishing failure of the fourteen different internationally backed attempts at re-establishing a national government in Somalia and the diminishing legitimacy and increasingly untenable position of the current TFG in the face of the sustained insurgency led by Al-Shabaab and its allies show, once again, the profound error of privileging top-down, state-centric processes that are structurally engineered with a bias in favour of centralisation, rather than bottom-up, community-based approaches.

As one analyst has summarised it, 'The UN, Western governments, and donors have tried repeatedly to build a strong central government – the kind of entity that they are most comfortable dealing with – in defiance of local sociopolitical dynamics and regional history'.[52] This despite the fact that the contemporary experience of insurgency and counter-insurgency in Iraq and Afghanistan – confirmed by the different outcomes in southern and central Somalia and in Somaliland and Puntland – clearly suggests that bottom-up efforts, especially when they reinforce the connection between legitimate local non-state structures to state institutions, have a greater chance of success. The stubborn refusal to acknowledge this reality results in the repeated capture of otherwise well-intended efforts by the very spoiler elites – the type of individuals who are habitués of 'peace processes' – whose lack of legitimacy provoked the crisis in the first place.

The real shame is that this all-too-often repeated error has, in recent years alone, not only wasted billions of dollars, but also caused untold human suffering in some of the most vulnerable corners of the globe.

THE CAMPAIGN AGAINST THE LRA: OLD WINE IN NEW BOTTLES

Sandrine Perrot

'The LRA is on the verge of defeat.' Such predictions about the Lord's Resistance Army's (LRA) close demise have continually resurfaced over the past two decades. Yet the LRA has shown an intriguing resilience and capacity for regeneration. The armed group is indeed as notorious as it is mysterious; its nature, motivations and objectives are still some of the most controversial issues of the northern Ugandan conflict. The LRA is often construed as a bizarre, exotic and violent fundamentalist cult abducting children, turning them into soldiers or sexual slaves, and perpetrating random and senseless predatory attacks on civilians. The political evasiveness and constant references to the supernatural of its charismatic leader, Joseph Kony, feeds his image of irrationality bounding on madness.

And yet despite several military and non-military attempts to tackle the LRA, the insurgency shows no sign of abating. The Juba peace talks, opened in July 2006, came to a dead end and led to renewed violence. And the very last Ugandan-led regional counter-insurgency operations, launched in December 2008, had limited impact. Today, once-localised LRA operations have turned into a regional presence. Originally confined to northern Uganda, the LRA is now militarily active in a constantly widening area of insecurity, which stretches from the east of the Central African Republic (CAR) and north of the Democratic Republic of the Congo (DRC) to the west and South Sudan.

US President Barack Obama's signing of the LRA Disarmament and Northern Uganda Recovery Act in May 2010 reinvigorated the ever-growing group of academic, political, military and humanitarian actors searching for 'new' solutions to the LRA. Closed meetings have been organised. Reports have been published. Blueprints have been issued on the Internet.[1] While new solutions may very well be needed, they must be rooted in a better understanding of the previous attempts to address the conflict and the reasons for their failures. This chapter argues firstly that the polarised cognitive and analytical frameworks used for the LRA – in particular, its use of extreme violence – have shaped but also restricted the formulation and implementation of strategies and policies for conflict resolution. Secondly, it argues that in this framework, the LRA has been militarily and politically underestimated. Thirdly, the chapter argues that the growing number of military actors involved in the conflict-resolution process is likely to add little but more confusion to already unco-ordinated actions.

A Short History of the Conflict: Misconceptions about the LRA
The LRA left Uganda in 2006. It has undergone numerous transformations since and has developed far beyond its original cradle of Acholiland in northern Uganda. However, it is still imperative to consider the socio-political context that produced the LRA in order to understand its structuring effect on the movement, its military leadership and its self-definition, as well as to unearth the origins of common clichés about the movement. This does not aim at recounting a detailed history of the insurgency, but it will highlight some of the salient elements therein, and attempt to reframe the narrative in order to weed out some misconceptions and misunderstandings.

A Localised Insurgency 1986–93
The LRA emerged, as with dozens of other armed groups, in the wake of the National Resistance Army's seizure of power in January 1986,

led by Yoweri Museveni. But while most of the Ugandan insurgencies were soon neutralised by military means or peace agreements, the LRA has remained active all over northern Uganda for the last twenty-three years. The conflict has since alternated between lulls and waves of widespread violence, punctuated by a stream of ambushes, massacres and abductions.

LRA leader Joseph Kony was born in Odek in Acholiland (northern Uganda) in the early 1960s (the exact date and year is unknown). He was trained as a traditional healer after he dropped out from primary school. In 1987, while in his twenties, he joined the 'Black battalion' of the Uganda People's Democratic Army (UPDA) – a rebel group created by military officers of the defeated Uganda national army – as a 'spiritual mobiliser'. Shortly afterwards, he claimed to have been possessed by spirits who guided him in his fight against Museveni's regime. He broke away from UPDA in November 1987 along with staunch followers convinced of his supernatural powers. He founded his own politico-religious armed group from the defeated remnants of the Holy Spirit Movement, which had been led by another spirit medium, Alice Lakwena. They were later joined by dissident UPDA fighters who had been unwilling to surrender after their rebel group signed the Gulu Peace Agreement.

The LRA insurgency was originally rooted in the political and economic marginalisation of northern Uganda and in the north-south disparities of the late 1980s. The LRA claimed to be fighting against the authoritarianism of Museveni's regime and the Ugandan military. Its original message entailed the creation of a new society freed from corruption and authoritarianism; this was put forward as the main rationale for the use of violence. But war fatigue in northern Uganda and the disputed spiritual legitimacy of Joseph Kony deprived the movement of popular support. As early as the beginning of the 1990s, the LRA had to resort to abductions to swell its ranks, and to internal violence to prevent defections.

The common focus on Kony's religious repertoires and the LRA's use of extreme violence and child abductions has overshadowed examination of the organisation's inherent military capacity. Over the years, the LRA has built an efficient combat structure and developed professionalised know-how in guerrilla tactics. Joseph Kony is the overall commander of the military, political and spiritual structure of the LRA. The formulation of military strategy is shared with a high command (Control Altar). Kony conveys strategic directions that he claims to receive from spirits to his top field commanders, who are then in charge of passing on operational orders to the LRA's four brigades (Stockree, Sinia, Gilva, Shila). Each brigade is made up of several battalions that exert a strict control on troops through disciplinary surveillance mechanisms (including internal terror), religious rituals and food and sexual prohibition.[2] Their military operations rely on a very efficient intelligence structure and highly mobile troops. A group of 100 to 200 fighters usually infiltrate an assigned area and then split into smaller units of ten to twenty combatants, difficult to detect before they attack remote villages and small trade centres to find food, arms, medicines and new recruits.[3]

'Local Solutions to Local Problems'

Until the mid-2000s, the attention given to resolving the twenty-year northern Uganda conflict was very low. Well-circulated reports of LRA atrocities by former abductees amplified the international echo of the dominant Uganda People's Defence Force (UPDF) discourse. These portrayed the LRA as a 'backward bunch of thugs and criminals' that the Ugandan government could flush out in a matter of weeks with its own military means. Indeed, until the end of the 1990s, the LRA remained a peripheral irritant, nationally viewed as a mere localised ethnic conflict. Through this belittling discourse, the UPDF and the Ugandan government succeeded in denying the LRA's agenda any political content. In so doing, it bolstered advocates of military options, and sidelined the calls for negotiation from religious and traditional leaders and opposition politicians in the north. It also precluded external intervention in Ugandan government affairs and especially in northern Uganda, an opposition stronghold.[4] On the national and international scene, the LRA was viewed as a local problem requiring local solutions.

The UPDF has regularly carried out major counter-insurgency campaigns: in 1987 when northern Uganda was cordoned off from the rest of the country; in 1991 with the notoriously violent Operation *North*; in 1996 again; and finally between 2002 and 2005, with Operation *Iron Fist* on the LRA's rear bases in southern Sudan. These military operations had mixed impact. They certainly – for a limited time – militarily weakened the LRA. On the one hand, the operations noticeably persuaded Kony to take part in the first peace talks ever, in 1992–94, and then in the Juba peace talks of 2006. On the other hand, they spurred violence against civilian populations, from the LRA. Kony's troops launched a number of retaliatory strikes, such as a wave of maiming against alleged collaborators in the first half of the 1990s, which followed the mobilisation of Acholi civilians in local militias. But the counter-insurgency operations also included repressive actions from the military itself against Acholi civilians alleged to be collaborators of the LRA. The military resorted to scorched-earth policies, forced internal displacements, mass arrests (*panda gari*), detention of northern opposition leaders, and military exactions.[5] This heavy hand reinforced the antagonism between the local population and the Ugandan government. The militarisation of northern Uganda fed a growing opposition against Museveni that converged with the LRA's grievances and made the counter-insurgency operations more complex.

The Failure of the 1992–94 Peace Talks

The 1992–94 peace talks led by the minister of state for pacification of northern Uganda, Betty Bigombe, were a short-lived parenthesis in Museveni's military response. It is still difficult to clearly establish the sequence of events that led to the failure of these two-year negotiations. Questions remain as to whether the decision of President Museveni to give the LRA a seven-day ultimatum to surrender in 1994 preceded or followed the contacts initiated by Kony with the Sudanese government. In any case, the resumption of hostilities marked a turning point. The LRA shifted its rear bases from northern Uganda to southern Sudan.

The LRA established a clear strategy of exploiting the availability of external resources (either from the diaspora or from Khartoum) to open up or maintain supply lines. In Sudan, the LRA transformed its repertoire, tactics, strategies and target selection. The group was used as a proxy by Khartoum to fight against the Sudan People's Liberation Army (SPLA) in southern Sudan and to attack Sudanese refugee camps in Uganda. Taking advantage of porous borders, Kony's troops regularly infiltrated northern Uganda with mobile units using hit-and-run tactics. Via the Sudanese armed forces and other armed groups allied to Khartoum, the LRA gained access to logistical support, food and medicine, but also to more sophisticated weapons (including land mines) and military know-how.

The end of the 1990s saw the relative power of Khartoum increasingly constrained. Global anti-terrorism policies isolated Sudanese President Omar Al-Bashir's government on the international scene. Eager to lessen this pressure, Khartoum signed a peace agreement with Kampala in 1999. This accord restored their diplomatic ties and weakened Sudanese assistance to the LRA. In 2001, Bashir officially announced the end of support to the LRA and, six months later, allowed a UPDF-led military operation against LRA bases in southern Sudan.

Operation *Iron Fist* had mixed effects: during its first phase, not only did the UPDF fail to eradicate the LRA from southern Sudan (where the insurgents took advantage of its numerous ammunition caches), but it also enabled the LRA to cross back to northern Uganda and to expand for the first time in Teso, eastern Uganda, in search of new support. This prompted a major humanitarian crisis, with the displacement of 1.8 million people in northern Uganda. But from the end of 2003, *Iron Fist II* was more successful. Top LRA commanders were killed or captured, disrupting the armed group's chain of command. Isolated from the Control Altar, and short of medicine, food and ammunitions, a large number of fighters and commanders started to defect, a trend encouraged by an extended amnesty offer.[6]

Forced to move again, the LRA shifted its base of operations from southern Sudan to the northeastern DRC and established a new settlement in the Garamba National Park in 2006. The military pressure on the LRA, the indictment of five of its top commanders by the International Criminal Court (ICC) in July 2005 on one side, along with the worsening humanitarian situation in Uganda, Sudan and Congo, and fears of regional spillover of insecurity (in southern Sudan where a Comprehensive Peace Agreement had just been signed as well as in the DRC) on the other, converged into the Juba Peace Initiative.

The Juba Peace Talks 2006–08

The Juba peace talks were probably the first serious window of opportunity for direct peace negotiations between the LRA military leadership and the Ugandan government. Numerous low-key initiatives had been taken previously to establish contacts with the LRA. Some led to peace talks, as in 1992–94; some others to meetings (such as Kacoke Madit) in London in 1997–98 or Nairobi in 2000. But mediators came up against the absence of direct contact with the LRA's top military leadership, unreliable intermediaries and, once established, contacts difficult to sustain. Further, there were fears that the LRA would take advantage of peace talks and ceasefires to rearm and reorganise.

The failure of the Juba peace talks was attributed to Kony. However, one cannot but notice that mixed messages on commitment to the process were sent by both parties – the government and LRA alike. Moreover, a large range of international actors were then competing over leadership of the talks, and pursuing unco-ordinated efforts to engage the LRA. The pending arrest warrants against five LRA top commanders certainly put pressure on its military leadership to ask for peace talks, but also severely interfered with the negotiation process. The criminal responsibility of the senior commanders and the ambiguity of the government and international community on the matter has remained a cause of concern for the LRA high command. It also divided the actors along the unresolved dilemma of 'peace' and/or 'justice'. Two questions were at the core of the debates: could the LRA be negotiated with? If so, was it a good idea to negotiate with 'criminals'? From the international point of view, the whole issue revolved around the LRA's agenda and motivations. Despite the LRA's efforts to change its communication policy, its image of an irrational gang of violent criminals that could only be – not to say had to be – stopped by military means has remained dominant. After two years of negotiation, the LRA's inability to clearly list its demands, and then its procrastination and delays in signing the laboriously negotiated five-point agreements,[7] exhausted the patience of international actors. Reports of new abductions and killings in the DRC in September 2008 and the failure of Kony to show up for the signing of the agreement on 14 November 2008 led everyone back to the military option.

The LRA in the Regionalised System of Conflict

Officially planned to kill, capture or force Kony back to the negotiating table, the joint Operation *Lightning Thunder* (between Uganda, South Sudan, and the DRC) was launched in December 2008 with the logistical, planning and intelligence support of the newly created US Department of Defense's Africa Command (AFRICOM). But when the Ugandan military carried out aerial bombings of the LRA main camps in the Garamba National Park, they had already been evacuated. Analysts blamed a poorly planned operation and leaks to the LRA. The armed group immediately launched a series of new retaliatory attacks, massacres and abductions in the DRC and southern Sudan, killing more than 900 and abducting more than 160 children in a two-month period.[8]

From Localised to Transnational Insurgency
Following Operation *Lightning Thunder*, the LRA moved further west. The incursions into the CAR, initiated in February 2008, increased at the beginning of 2009. By mid-2010, the different LRA groups were militarily active in Haut and Bas Uélé in northern DRC, around Yambio and Ezo in Western Equatoria (southern Sudan), and in Obo in eastern CAR. In late 2010, there were reports of attacks and fighting as far north as Birao in northeastern CAR on the border with Chad and Sudan.[9] The insurgency is now deeply entrenched in a regional 'system of conflicts' that 'start resonating and fit into each other, transforming their reproduction conditions and, especially the confronting parties, the stakes of the struggle and the objectives pursued'.[10] Multiple factors now contribute to its persistence, and the multi-layered (and sometimes competing) logic and strategies of the actors involved make conflict resolution even more of a challenge.

The spillover into the DRC and CAR established the LRA as a major regional threat. Today, no fewer than eleven militaries are dealing with the counter-insurgency operations, not to mention dozens of other armed groups and self-defence militias: there are three UN missions (MONUSCO, UNMIS, MINURCAT and maybe UNAMID eventually, if allegations that the LRA is in Darfur are corroborated); six state or sub-state actors (Uganda, the DRC, South Sudan, CAR, the US, France); and one regional organisation (the African Union, which gathered at Bangui in October 2010 to allow the creation of a joint brigade between the CAR, South Sudan, Congo and Uganda).[11] It is the first time ever that so many entities have been involved militarily. But this multi-actor operation has raised a number of issues relating to limited governance and military capacity, a lack of co-ordination, and the protection of civilians.

(Un)Co-ordinated Military Operations and the Insufficient Protection of Civilians

The UPDF and its 7,000 officially deployed men is probably the only efficient military actor engaging the LRA. CAR troops are undermanned – a few hundred only, mainly deployed in southern CAR – who have to deal with their own insurgencies. The SPLA is in the process of building its military capacity, and has devoted itself to the January 2011 Sudanese referendum. The FARDC intermittently receive pay and food rations, and routinely resort to predation on the civilian population. On the UPDF side, despite reports of some predation, it seems that the military is being reactive and working in collaboration with the local population. Indeed, in late 2009, the UPDF scored some significant military successes, with the killing, defection or capture of LRA senior commanders Major Okot Atiak, Major Okello Kalalang, Brigadier Santos Alit, Lieutenant Colonel Charles Arop, and others. They also claim to have been close to capturing Joseph Kony himself during an attack in Djemah in the eastern CAR at the beginning of October 2010. Defections or capture of senior commanders certainly put the group's cohesion at risk. Because information is restricted to within the LRA's top hierarchy, the senior commanders are the only ones to share some of Kony's secrets. However, for the last few months, the military campaign has come to a standstill and the UPDF has also suffered setbacks and losses, creating internal tensions.[12] There are reports of infighting amongst the leadership of the UPDF expeditionary corps in the CAR; following a disagreement on military strategy, the force commander, Colonel Emmanuel Rwashande, was replaced by Colonel Peter Elwelu, a former commander of the African Union force in Somalia in June 2010.[13]

More generally speaking, there are indeed as many actors involved as there are diverging and sometimes competing agendas. Despite being presented as a joint operation, *Lightning Thunder* lacked effective co-operation and information-sharing between the UPDF, the SPLA and the FARDC. Even though Sudan and the DRC allowed the Ugandan military to engage the LRA on their territory, the counter-insurgency was launched with no preliminary consultation, thus reinforcing pre-existing tensions between the three armed forces. Today, the sole objective of the UPDF is to kill or capture Kony and his top commanders, and it is only marginally concerned with the side effects of this manhunt on the security of civilians. Moreover, the UPDF wants to withdraw. The LRA has not been militarily active on Ugandan territory since 2006, and the UPDF is already engaged in disarmament operations in Karamoja (eastern Uganda) and peace operations in Somalia as the main troop supplier for AMISOM. The UPDF already withdrew from its northern base in the CAR and the Ugandan government decided to remove 1,000 of its 7,000-strong force to redeploy them in Uganda ahead of the February 2011 presidential election.[14]

On the UN side, MINURCAT and MONUSCO have failed so far to respond to unrealistic expectations about civilian protection. Both missions are already overstretched and in the process of an eventual withdrawal. The UN removed its troops from Bas Uélé district in northern Congo in August 2010, despite uninterrupted attacks there by the LRA since March. And Security Council Resolution 1925, unanimously approved in May 2010, authorised the withdrawal of 2,000 troops in line with Congolese President Joseph Kabila's wish that MONUSCO withdraw before the November 2011 elections there. MINURCAT is also downsizing in Chad and the CAR has already announced its final withdrawal by the end of 2010. There is little belief that UNMIS could address the LRA issue in Western Equatoria in the context of the referendum on the secession of South Sudan.

Operation *Lightning Thunder* officially ended after three months. But today, UPDF personnel continue to operate alongside the Congolese and Sudanese armies with no official mandate, officially for intelligence purposes only (to no great enthusiasm from the DRC and South Sudan governments). And in the CAR, President François Bozize, in a tense pre-electoral context, also demanded the withdrawal of the Ugandan military, partly to get the benefit of military assistance from the US and France – obtained in August 2010 – for his own army.[15] These developments undermine the sustained – if not co-ordinated – military efforts required in the macro-regional zone of insecurity in which the LRA operates.

The Effect on the LRA

What has been the impact of Operation *Lightning Thunder* on the LRA? The refrain about the LRA being on its knees has been short-lived: similar to when the group lost support from Khartoum in 2002, or after the war of attrition of Operation *Iron Fist* in 2004, the LRA has shown an intriguing capacity for rejuvenation. It has systematically responded to counter-insurgency operations with renewed and more brutal reprisal atrocities and forced recruitment to recoup its losses. The ongoing military operation in the DRC and the CAR is not an exception to the rule. Violence is used to structure and discipline the group, but also to leverage a measure of balance of power. Through the retaliatory Christmas massacres (24 December 2008, and 17 January 2009), the Makombo ones (14–17 December 2009) in the Haut Uélé district of Congo, or massive abductions in Sudan, the DRC or the CAR, the LRA clearly intends to show that its strike force has remained intact.

The Ugandan military claims that the number of LRA combatants has been dwindling since Operation *Lightning Thunder*. From an estimated 3,000 combatants at the highest point of LRA recruitment, its total force was reduced to a few hundred, according to Ugandan military sources. These figures however must be considered guardedly. The strength of the LRA has remained a contentious issue during the whole war, and estimates have been influenced by unsubstantiated claims of near-victory by the military. The LRA's strength continuously fluctuates over time either through abductions, killings, capture or defections. Furthermore, we have no clear idea about the number of auxiliaries accompanying them (wives, children born in the bush, porters, domestic aides, and so on).

The LRA is now militarily active in a vast tri-border area for the most part deprived of road and telecommunications infrastructure and dotted with scattered and remote rural settlements that are easy to attack, but difficult to protect. It is taking advantage of its familiarity with the terrain of game reserves and rainforests whose canopy hinders satellite detection, and makes good use of technology like GPS, satellite phones and solar-powered laptops (including some acquired during the Juba peace talks).

Now that the LRA is cut off from the social and political conditions that produced it, its objectives and motivations appear more ambiguous. Moreover, for the first time, there is a growing proportion of non-Acholi forces inside the LRA, who do not share the same language, spiritual references, political background or loyalties. This seriously challenges the cohesion and co-ordination capacity of the LRA. So far, its top hierarchy is still composed of Acholi commanders or Acholi abductees who moved up through the ranks from the bush. But the recruitment of soldiers of other ethnicities will necessarily affect its internal reconstruction, transform its discourses, references and self-representation, and encourage the use of more internal violence to prevent defections. Additionally, the quality of military training is harder to sustain when on the move. And the level of skill of new, non-Acholi abductees remains unknown.

However, what was described as a survival move by a spent force on the run had actually been planned months before. The LRA crossed into the DRC in September 2005, and the first incursions into the southeastern CAR date back from February 2008, when a group led by Dominic Ongwen and Okoth Odhiambo attacked and abducted from a number of villages before going back to their base in Garamba National Park. The LRA is now exerting control over border areas to secure cross-border operations and escape strategies.

The option that it could be opening and securing transit points to potentially re-enter Uganda should not be dismissed *a priori*.[16]

Joseph Kony and his top commanders are certainly looking for an exit strategy to avoid being tried in The Hague (the proposal for alternative justice, made by the Ugandan government during the Juba peace talks, now having been withdrawn). But they are also looking for new sources of support. The description of the LRA as a puppet of Khartoum has often denied agency to the LRA. But the armed group has regularly made alliances to maintain supply lines.[17] Their territorial expansion only increases their opportunities for collusion in a region already riddled with many other Congolese, CAR and Chadian armed groups, including some linked to Khartoum.[18] There is clear evidence that Kony has tried to directly link up again with Sudanese armed forces over the past two or three years. After various failed attempts, Brigadier Cesar Achellam made contact with Sudanese army elements in south Darfur in October 2009. And recent reports even claim that the LRA was regrouping in south Darfur: a first LRA group entered in August 2010, and another one of 200 troops, led by Kony and second-in-command Okoth Odhiambo, in October 2010.[19] South Darfur is past the territorial limit allowed for the UPDF in pursuing the LRA. But the Darfurian savannah is also much more difficult terrain for LRA operations. Nevertheless, this new move renews fears that the LRA could leverage its capacity for nuisance in the volatile environment of the Sudanese referendum, as it could also in successive forthcoming presidential elections in DRC, the CAR or Uganda. However, despite these concerns, the Ugandan military's claims that Khartoum has resumed its supply of logistical support to the LRA still have to be investigated in detail.

The Way Ahead: A New Strategy?

In this context, can the new involvement of the US alter the course of the conflict and bring it to resolution? The disclosure of the

Obama administration's full strategy in November 2010 was a non-event. It basically appreciated and supported existing mechanisms and multilateral efforts, more than it came up with new, innovative proposals.

Obama's Challenges

In any case, there was no evidence that new forces with no specific knowledge of the terrain would have been a game changer. One can hardly imagine a massive US intervention in the CAR (very much part of France's sphere of influence) or in Darfur. And a major military offensive would, anyway, be prevented by internal constraints, namely the withdrawal from Iraq, troop commitments in Afghanistan, and counter-terrorism operations. Inter-agency wrangling over LRA policy between USAID, the Department of State and the Department of Defense (and the latter between the Office of the Secretary of Defense and AFRICOM, for example) would first have to be resolved. Politically and diplomatically, the US also has to build legitimacy as a peace provider in the region. It has to clarify the AFRICOM mission, which now blurs the lines between security, human relief and development, as well as its position towards the ICC.

Moreover, the US has almost constantly sided with the Ugandan government and the pursuit of its military option (apart from a freeze on aid between 2000 and 2003, but partly bypassed by Museveni's anti-terrorism policies). They have enhanced UPDF military capacity, and unofficially backed the Ugandan military in northern Ugandan and Teso (eastern Uganda) from as early as 2003. Further, the US dragged its feet in giving financial support to the Juba peace process and immediately got involved in the new military intervention in the DRC. Finally, it is an open secret that for the US – as for many international actors – the real purpose of intervention does not lie in resolving the LRA insurgency *per se*, but rather the stabilisation of post-referendum South Sudan and the possible distribution of military support to the South Sudanese administration.

Killing Kony?

More generally, the LRA Disarmament Act has reopened the debate about options for finally resolving the conflict. The exclusively military option has clearly shown its limits. Yet tracking Kony and/ or killing him remains the dominant strategy. But this tack is open to questions. First, despite hi-tech satellite images provided by US intelligence and a tight manhunt led on the ground, no one has a clear idea of Kony's whereabouts. There are now many LRA groups scattered and on the move in the DRC and the CAR, and it is difficult to know for certain which one is led by Kony.

Even if he is in the CAR, the LRA leader will not let himself be captured easily.[21] He can rely on very good intelligence networks, well-rehearsed diversionary strategies and highly loyal bodyguards. Second, it is by no means certain that the death of Kony would necessarily guarantee the end of the LRA insurgency and the effective and sustainable disruption of the armed group's command and control structures. Not only has the LRA shown a great ability to reactively restructure its hierarchy after the defection, capture or killing of its top commanders, but, since mid-2010, it has shifted to a 'zonal' mode of operation with semi-autonomous sub-groups operating under the supervision of Kony's most trusted commanders. Kony's brother, Major David Olanya, is in charge of the Maboussou-Gambala area in the CAR, while General Binasio Okumu oversees the Obo area.[22] This reinforces the capacity of LRA units to operate despite gaps between command meetings, and to carry out attacks without being in direct contact with Kony or with other units for up to months at a time, while still knowing exactly what they have to do.

Militias and Civilian Protection

The mobilisation of self-defence forces is an option currently being tried in Western Equatoria to improve the protection of the civilian population. But despite the familiarity of the civilian population with their area and their more effective and reactive response to LRA attacks, local militia forces remain a poor and unsatisfactory palliative solution to the problem of civilian protection. The quick military success of the 'Arrow Boys' in Teso is used to buttress their legitimacy and demonstrate the efficiency of self-defence groups. Undoubtedly, the increase in the number of actors hostile to the LRA will make its survival strategy more difficult. Some other armed groups – for example the Union des Forces Démocratiques du Rassemblement, a former proxy of Khartoum who rallied in Bangui after a peace accord signed in 2007, or the Liberation and Justice Movement in Darfur – have already militarily engaged the LRA. However, other experiences of militias in northern Uganda should urge a more cautious approach. The arming of civilians puts them at risk of reprisal attacks by the LRA. It is known that the LRA interacts with the civilian population, asking for collaboration (for food, agriculture and information).[23] But the civilians, if armed, immediately become targets of LRA attacks. Additionally, the wisdom of adding to the arms flows in the area is questionable, especially as it is a border area subject to disputed claims of authority. The creation of militias has been endorsed by many local leaders in the LRA-affected areas. But while some (such as the governor of the Western Equatoria state) have encouraged their formation and funding, and distributed guns, others are more reluctant to put their monopoly of force at risk.[24]

Lessons Learnt, Current Challenges

The representations, perceptions and analysis of the LRA's nature and motivations have shaped strategic thinking on how to end the insurgency and have restricted proposed solutions for resolving the conflict. The military solution is still the dominant approach, even though there is no clear evidence that it is likely to quickly put an end to the insurgency. There is only a slow realisation of the LRA's capacity for co-ordinated action, its intelligence network and strategic planning capabilities; the skill of its seasoned and hardened fighters; and the motivation of its high command, radicalised as they were by internal purges and reshuffles after the Juba peace talks. There is a need to take the LRA seriously, albeit cautiously. The LRA has effective guerrilla tactics, and its development and movement strategy on the margins of states where the central authorities are weak reduce the chances of a military resolution. Troop withdrawal is certainly not an option, its presence being indispensable, if only as a deterrent. A containment strategy to isolate the different LRA groups and hinder cross-border movements would be more realistic and effective than emphasising the protection of civilians – provided that a co-ordinated strategy of national military involvement and/ or an extension of UN missions with enlarged regional mandates is implemented. Additionally, there is a need to further investigate and inhibit the LRA's external support (be it from Khartoum or anywhere else). But even if fully implemented, this strategy is likely to fail if it is not combined with engagement of the LRA through dialogue.

The dialogue option is certainly not new. But it has never been given a serious chance through political or financial sustainment. If chosen, this option would prioritise trust-building policies through time-consuming, low-key contacts with LRA intermediaries and representatives. It would identify who would be the leader in peace negotiations, using experienced local northern Ugandan leaders who have worked extensively on establishing contacts with the LRA top military leadership for the past two decades. These talks must be unambiguously and unanimously supported by donors, multilateral institutions and, above all, the Ugandan government. Finally, opening new direct talks with the LRA would eventually require readdressing the issue of the ICC arrest warrants that undoubtedly obstructed negotiations in Juba. If these preliminary conditions are not met, then the new options proposed by officials will be nothing but old wine in new bottles.

COUNTERING THE TERRORIST INSURGENCY IN BANGLADESH

A N M Muniruzzaman

Bangladesh has generally been considered a stable, democratic Muslim state that has made great strides in economic and human development. But, over the past few years, Bangladesh has been hit by growing spectre of terrorism and extremism that threatens the harmony and tolerance in its society.

The risks and vulnerabilities posed by terrorism have become a serious threat to Bangladesh's national security. Targeted assassinations and bombings of public places, religious festivities and places of religious worship have shocked the country many times in the recent past and have become a threat to life, the economy and political and religious pluralism. Indeed, we may therefore consider that this level of terrorist activity amounts to an insurgency. After all, the tactics and aims are akin to what we would call 'insurgency' elsewhere, such as in post-occupation Iraq. Bangladesh therefore is an interesting case study for the reader.

In this case, the distinction between 'terrorism' and 'insurgency' may be semantic, and so for scholars and strategists considering the 'counter-insurgency vs counter-terrorism' debate, and whether 'hard' or 'soft' measures are necessary or sufficient for victory, then the disjointed terrorist insurgency that Bangladesh faces may provide some food for thought.

The Threat to Bangladesh

The activities of the terrorists, extremists and fundamentalists present a complex challenge to democratic life in Bangladesh. The populace is comparatively peaceful, accommodative and tolerant. But the presence of the radical groups and their anti-state activities are undermining the country's tolerant traditions and its developing democratic culture, thereby posing a significant threat to security and stability. Bangladesh is grounded in a tradition of pluralism and there are popular aspirations for sound democratic governance. But there is a concern that popular confidence in democratic values has receded in recent times. Islamists are actively seeking to further challenge and uproot these values: if they are successful, they will push Bangladesh away from the pluralistic values of a liberal order.[1] In this way, radical Islamic groups are undermining the tolerant social fabric of the country and posing challenges to the overall stability of the society. The political formula of the terrorist and extremist groups is negation of the existing system. They argue that the current order is illegitimate and needs to be changed: for them, Islam is the solution. In this way, they also undermine the legitimacy of the state and question the foundations of democracy.

Several attacks were carried out in Bangladesh by radicals in the 1990s. The first major outbreak was witnessed when, in response to the demolition of the Babri Mosque in India in 1992, riots broke out in Dhaka city; these saw over fifty people killed and the setting fire to hundreds of houses owned by minorities. Indeed, whenever there were attacks on Muslim populations – whether in Kashmir, Palestine, Bosnia, Afghanistan, Mindanao or Iraq – Bangladesh witnessed reactions such as protest rallies and gatherings, which saw incitement. There were incidents of grenade and bomb attacks on churches and Quadiani mosques in Khulna, Dhaka, Mymensingh and Barisal in the mid-1990s. Attacks were also launched against cinemas and on the cultural programmes of progressive organisations. These radical outbursts undermined the liberal and pluralistic forces in the country.

In the twenty-first century, the problem of militancy and terrorism in Bangladesh has become even more acute. The government publicly acknowledges the existence of Islamic militancy.[2] Countrywide bomb attacks in August 2005, including the simultaneous detonation of approximately 500 bombs across the country by Jama'atul Mujahideen Bangladesh (JMB), demonstrated the ability of the extremists to attack on a significant scale.[3] It showed that terrorists operating in Bangladesh are developing new methods of attack and improving the efficiency of existing ones, both of which increase the pressure on Bangladesh's counter-terrorist agencies. In August 2009, the Minister for Home Affairs Shamsul Haque Tuku claimed that citizens were at risk, whether they travelled by foot or by car. He warned at the inauguration of the Sher-e-Bangla Nagar police station, 'We are all being watched by the militants; this is the reality'.[4] He went on to state that 'Militancy is threatening the very existence of the country. Because of the activities of militants, war criminals, and anti-liberation forces, we are at a very high risk. They are moving Bangladesh toward a worse situation.'[5]

The radical organisations based in Bangladesh are also increasingly connected to international terrorist groups. For instance, HUJI-B has links to terrorist groups not only in the region, but also on an international level. It is itself a party that was first formed in Bangladesh with the direct help of Al-Qa'ida. For this reason, there is growing concern that Bangladesh is increasing in prominence as a potential sanctuary for international terrorist organisations. This has serious implications not only for the national security of the country, but also for regional security and stability.

The government of Bangladesh has tried various plans and strategies to counter the threat of extremist violence in the country. But, the continuing threat demonstrates the inadequacy of government counter-terrorist policy. Defeating this threat demands a comprehensive and holistic government approach. Indeed, the cumulative effect of this terrorist insurgency, if left unchecked, will present a long-term challenge to the survival of Bangladesh as a democratic polity.

Secularism, Religion and Radicalisation

Bangladesh is founded on secular, democratic values and is widely regarded as a moderate Muslim state. The preamble of its original constitution explicitly stated a commitment to secularism and democracy: political parties were banned from using religion as a basis for their activities.[6] But since independence, Bangladeshi political actors have tended to emphasise the religious belief of the majority in constitutional and other legal enactments.

While the secular identity of the constitution has not been completely shed, it is important to note that religion has come to play an increasingly significant role in affairs of state. The rise of Islamic fundamentalism was embedded in Bangladesh's post-1975 political evolution: secularism was withdrawn as one of the fundamental constitutional principles; a constitutional ban on religious political parties was rescinded; the Jammat-e-Islami party was legitimised and rehabilitated; Islam was declared the state religion in 1988. Further, the centre-right Bangladesh Nationalist Party (BNP) and centre-left Bangladesh Awami League have competed to woo Jammat-e-Islami and other Islamist political groupings, in order to pander to the Islamic constituency and gain electoral advantage. These factors have all blended into the context in which religious extremism has risen to its current level. When combined with the well-funded proliferation of about 64,000 madrassas (religious schools) – many of them allegedly the breeding ground for militants – the scale of the challenge becomes clearer.[7]

This tacit process of Islamisation has been accompanied by a heightened public profile for radicals, following a dramatic increase in violence attributed to radical Islamist organisations. The violence followed a pattern that indicated a radical footprint. There were concerns that madrassas were flourishing and even supplanting the modern educational system in parts of the country. There was an increase in displays of intolerance, including organised campaigns against 'heretic' sects such as the Ahmaddiyas, as well as the non-Muslims who constitute about a tenth of the population.[8]

As a result, Bangladesh is now under tremendous stress from this process of radicalisation.[9] The most visible and dramatic sign of the growth of extremism came five years ago when all but one of the country's sixty-four districts suffered bomb attacks.[10] The carefully co-ordinated campaign of terror shocked the nation, but it was just the beginning. Other terrorist incidents, including attacks on the Bangladeshi-born British high commissioner and members of the judiciary, and sporadic attacks on religious and ethnic minorities, are further indication of the presence of well-organised extremist networks.

Terrorism is a global menace, and as noted above Bangladesh is no exception.[11] Indeed, this kind of low-level insurgency using the methods of terror has destabilised the country. The terrorist insurgency is a lethal offshoot of political use of religion, a dysfunctional education system and the socioeconomic backwardness of the country. It has in turn become a grave threat to national security: it obstructs socioeconomic and political development, foments instability and undermines governance.[12] Despite many operational successes by the government of Bangladesh and its law enforcement agencies, only limited success has been achieved in combating terrorist planning, networking and their underlying motivation.

Major Terrorist/Insurgent Groups in Bangladesh

Harkat-ul-Jehad-al-Islami Bangladesh (HuJI-B)

Huji-B was established in 1992 with the assistance of Osama Bin Laden's International Islamic Front.[13] The primary objective of HuJI-B is to establish Islamic *hukumat* [rule] in Bangladesh by waging war and killing progressive intellectuals (natural opponents of their project). The group's slogan is '*Amra sobai hobo Taliban, Bangla hobe Afghanistan*' [We will all become Taliban, and we will turn Bangladesh into Afghanistan]. It is against liberal and secular practices, as well as non-governmental organisations (NGOs) and cultural activity that import, and spread, modern Western ideas (including women's rights). It is estimated that HuJI-B has 15–20,000 in its cadres, the majority having come from madrassas,[14] which tend to be composed of the children of lower-class and lower-middle-class families.

Huji-B mainly operates in the coastal areas of Bangladesh – Chittagong, Cox's Bazar and the areas bordering Burma. The group apparently has six camps in the uplands of Chittagong, where militants are trained in the use of weapons. Unconfirmed reports suggest that it also maintains six training camps near Cox's Bazar.

The HuJI-B intensified its activities after the Awami League formed the government in June 1996.[15] It was involved in a number of attacks, including the murder of Shamsur Rahman, a journalist, in July 2000 in Jessor.[16] It was then also revealed that HuJI-B cadres had planned to assassinate twenty-eight prominent intellectuals, including the academic Professor Kabir Choudhury and the writer Taslima Nasreen.[17]

Jama'atul Mujahideen Bangladesh

The JMB is reported to have been formed in 1998 in the Jamalpur district. The principal aim of the JMB is to establish Islamic rule in Bangladesh through armed struggle: it calls for the dismantling of democracy and establishment of Islamic law.

The organisation came to public attention in 2002 with the arrest of eight Islamist militants at Parbatipur in Dinajpur district, along with the discovery of explosive devices and documents detailing the outfit's activities.[18] Three years later in August 2005, the JMB claimed responsibility for a series of blasts through leaflets in both Bangla and Arabic. The leaflets, left at the sites of the explosions across the country, proclaimed:[19]

We are the soldiers of Allah. We have taken up arms for the implementation of Allah's law the way the Prophet, Sahabis and heroic Mujahideen have implemented for centuries. If the government does not establish Islamic law in the country after this warning and, rather, it goes to arrest any Muslim on charge of seeking Allah's laws or it resorts to repression on Alem-Ulema, the Jamaatul Mujahideen will go for counteraction, Insha Allah. It is time to implement Islamic laws in Bangladesh. There is no future with man-made law.

The JMB is thought to number 10,000 full-time and 100,000 part-time personnel in its cadres; in addition, it is believed to contain a 2,000-strong suicide brigade.[20] The cadres span across society, including members in universities, the madrassas and amongst the ordinary population.

Hizbut Touhid

Hizbut Touhid was established in 1994 in the village of Korotia, in the Tangail district of Bangladesh.[21] It is led by Bayezid Khan Panni of Tangail (also known as Selim Panni), who claims to be the 'Imam-Uz-Zamam'. Hizbut Touhid's goal is to establish a world under the leadership of the Imam. Its ideology is set against democracy and democratic institutions, considering them to be the 'rules of evil'. The group promotes armed struggle for the establishment of global Islamic rule. Written material, authored by Imam Panni, is the group's guiding force. CDs, books and leaflets are widely distributed throughout Bangladesh in order to recruit personnel. Through these leaflets, the group urges people to join them to establish Islamic rule, and reject 'man-made' laws.

The group is believed to consist of around 1,200 trained operatives.[22] Imam Panni left Bangladesh shortly after independence, and developed connections with extremist groups abroad: it is therefore likely that Hizbut Touhid enjoys foreign linkages.[23]

Islami Samaj

Islami Samaj is a breakaway faction of Jamaat-e-Islami, formed in May 1993 by Mufti Abdul Jabbar. The present leader is Syed Humayun Kabir, a former member of Islami Chhatra Shibir.[24] In common with the other groups mentioned, it ultimately seeks to establish Islamic rule in the country, and likewise rejects democracy as a man-made system and contrary to divine rule.

In August 2008, security forces recovered a leaflet containing an insight into the group's ideology:[25]

> The nation and the country are in grave danger and human rights in the country are severely violated as the country is being run by a manmade constitution that allows sovereignty and laws of the humans. At such a dreadful state of the nation and the country, establishing the sovereignty of Allah and Islam, a comprehensive lifestyle guideline of Allah, can only pull the country out of the crisis and protect rights of the people. Democracy and all other manmade laws are a curse on humans and if the manmade system remains in society and the state, good governance and justice will not be established, discrimination will not be eradicated and people's basic rights will not be ensured.

Islami Samaj is active in Bandarban. Its headquarters is located in Kushiara, in the district of Comilla, and the group is believed to have close connections with the JMB.

Hizb-ut-Tehrir Bangladesh

Hizb-ut-Tehrir Bangladesh is part of a global Sunni Muslim political movement that aspires to establish a global caliphate across the Islamic world, led in Bangladesh by Mohiuddin Ahmed. Most of its members are university students. Like its counterparts, it seeks to impose Sharia Law – in this case, in Bangladesh. Hizb-ut-Tehrir seeks to create a global Muslim order through working in various states and steering public opinion in the direction of Islamic parties, with the intention of having Sharia Law established through these new governments.

Hizb-ut-Tehrir published in 2007 an Islamic manifesto for Bangladesh, which included the following demands: establishment of a caliphate; rule 'by the Quran and the Sunnah'; rejection of interference by 'the imperialists' in the caliphate's affairs; rejection of private or foreign ownership of Bangladesh's 'national resources'; and a refusal to sign any agreements with India beyond a ceasefire.[26]

Alla'r Dal

Alla'r Dal is linked with the JMB, and wages a jihad to establish Islamic rule in Bangladesh. The organisation is active in the southwest in Kushtia, Meherpur and Chadanga, which border the Indian province of West Bengal. The organisation may be working to rejuvenate the JMB by holding meetings, raising funds and recruiting members. Alla'r Dal uses propaganda to entice recruits to join its jihad, and has occasionally used coercion to this end. Those who refuse to join the group are declared *kafir* [non-believers].

Underlying Factors

Chronic Poverty

Bangladesh is a poverty-stricken country; though the percentage of people living in poverty has declined in recent years, the absolute number of poor people is still increasing. For instance, while the proportion of those living in poverty fell by 7 per cent between 1991 and 2005, the total number of poor people increased by 4.4 million in the same period.[27] Indeed, poverty does not only prevent people from achieving their potential, it denies them any semblance of control over their destiny, and so may ultimately be a denial of human rights. It is perhaps the most serious factor promoting the rise of radicalism, terrorism, religious fundamentalism, ethnic hatred and political rivalries in Bangladesh. Poverty generates the feelings of helplessness that provoke people to resort to acts of desperation. As a result, the spread of radicalism in Bangladesh has a strong causal link to the prevailing conditions of poverty: with so little to lose, the poor can easily be motivated by ideological and economic factors to adopt the path of violent radical activities.

Madrassa Education

Madrassas in Bangladesh have a long history, and are an integral part of the educational system. Since independence, it has been the official policy of the government to promote madrassas as an informal or alternative system of education. In recent years, successive governments, in their eagerness to placate popular sentiment, seemed to have placed a premium on promoting Islamic education. As a result, the number of madrassas established, students enrolled and teachers recruited has grown at an equal if not higher rate than the equivalent figures for the general educational system, as shown in Table 1. This has added to the power of political Islam in Bangladesh.

But now there exists a serious concern about the rapid growth of the number of madrassas and the involvement of some of their students and teachers in extremist activities. They have been accused of being the breeding grounds of radicalisation and extremism. It is

Table 4: Growth of Madrassas and General Educational Institutions in Bangladesh, 1996–2005.

	1996–2000		2001–05	
	General Institutions	Madrassas	General Institutions	Madrassas
Institutions	28%	17%	10%	22%
Teachers	16%	13%	12%	17%
Students	33%	58%	9%	10%

Source: Adapted from Rejaul Karim Byron and Shameem Mahmud, 'Madrasas mushroom with state favour', *Daily Star*, 4 August 2005. Figures according to Bangladesh Economic Review.

also alleged that political leaders of the Islamic groups and parties have developed radical political views, contrary to the ethos of mainstream society, in such madrassas.

Poor Governance, Dysfunctional Democracy

The state itself is a major reason for the radicalised context of Bangladeshi politics. Perhaps the most compelling proximate cause of the emergence of militant Islam in Bangladesh is the state's failure to address endemic problems of unemployment, poverty and political order. As a result, large segments of the population have little faith in the efficacy of state institutions. In such a political milieu, religious groups and organisations providing basic social services assume an important role. They underscore the state's inability to perform the everyday tasks of maintaining public order, providing essential social services, generating employment and pursuing public works: the basics of governance. Government failure has served as a recruiting ground for the radicals and the extremists. Religious groups and organisations have actively taken advantage of this and recruited young Muslims into their activities to fight against the government apparatus.

Another root cause of terrorism and extremism in Bangladesh is the absence of solidified democratic traditions and institutions, which provides the violent and extremist actors a space in which to grow and flourish. Bangladesh adopted a democratic parliamentary system in 1991. But it has been a messy and dysfunctional democratic system. The most worrying feature is the two-party system, dominated by the Awami League and the Bangladesh Nationalist Party. The conflict between them has contributed to fundamental failures of governance. Indeed, their adversarial relationship has resulted in political chaos and instability across the country at different times, which has helped extremist groups and the terrorists linked to them expand their networks safely. Government failure, both in delivery and political conduct, has thus fomented an insurgency fought with the tools of terrorism.

Radicalised Diaspora

Bangladesh is the largest manpower-exporting country for the Middle East and a number of other Islamic states in the world. The major destinations of the Bangladeshi workforce are Saudi Arabia, Malaysia, the United Arab Emirates, Qatar, Oman, Bahrain, Libya, Kuwait, Jordan, Lebanon and the UK. The large number of Bangladeshi workers in the Middle East has prompted a process of assimilation into its rigid Islamic culture, to the detriment of the softer, more moderate Islamic tradition of Bangladesh. Bangladeshi workers in Saudi Arabia, Kuwait and other Gulf countries are vulnerable to more extreme influences: many of them have become indoctrinated in the radical Islamism of the Wahhabi and Deobandi lineages. As a result, returning workers from the Middle East, exposed to these more hardline strands of Islam, have started to generate a new and rigid Islamic culture in Bangladesh. This has encouraged others to adopt the path of religious radicalism.

Furthermore, these Bangladeshi workers are the country's key source of foreign remittances. In 2009–10, nearly $11 billion was sent home to Bangladesh by workers abroad.[28] Alarmingly, the government has very little control over such inflows of money. There is no reliable trail of evidence for how such money is or has been used in Bangladesh. In this regard, there is a legitimate fear of the possibility to use such remittances in terrorist financing and to support radical Islamic groups to carry out their activities, precluding the ability of the security services to monitor or sever funding flows – a problem faced by count-terrorists and counter-insurgency campaigns alike.

The Government Response

Overall, the Bangladeshi response to its insecurity has been a classic 'hard' counter-terrorism response. But this has not delivered. The government's early responses to the threat of radicalisation and terrorism were based on a systematic denial of the issue. Sometimes they accused opposition political parties of creating trouble to undermine law and order. For instance, in 2006, the then-prime minister blamed the 'bomb terrorists and the main opposition political party for creating havoc in the country and resolved that the "conspiracy against the country" would be ended'.[29] The government of the day even described JMB operations commander, Siddiqul Islam (also known as Bangla Bhai), as a mere creation of the media.

But the increasing level of terrorist activities by the Islamic militants in Bangladesh finally forced the government to confront the real problem. The government outlawed several terrorist and extremist groups, including JMB. The Rapid Action Battalion conducted large-scale counter-terror operations, arrested a large number of extremists from various Islamic militant groups, and recovered large stocks of arms and ammunitions. The government also took legal action against terrorist operators. Most notably, on 30 March 2007, six top militants, including JMB supreme commander Abdur Rahman and his deputy Bangla Bhai, were executed after trial.[30] In all probability, the executions marked the end of the country's first overt militant campaign that had rattled the nation through a series of co-ordinated blasts and suicide bombings in 2005.

The government has also enacted special legislation to counter the threat of terrorism in Bangladesh. It approved the 2008 Anti-Terrorism Ordinance enacted by the previous caretaker government, with provisions for the death sentence (as a maximum) or life imprisonment for offences such as financing or supporting terrorist activities and murder.[31] The latest anti-terrorism law reads, 'If any person is found guilty of carrying out terrorist activities, he or she will be awarded death sentence or life imprisonment or maximum twenty years and minimum three years' rigorous imprisonment.'[32] It also empowers Bangladesh Bank to freeze the accounts of a suspected terrorist and give directives to other banks concerned to take measures against monetary transactions related to the financing of terrorist activities. According to the ordinance, the government will be able to set up one or more 'Anti-Terrorist Special Tribunals' to deal with such crimes. However, punitive provisions for sponsoring terrorist activities and sheltering terrorists have also been laid down in the ordinance. According to the latest law, 'If anyone gives money for carrying out terrorist activities, a provision is there to award him or her maximum 20 years and minimum three years' imprisonment and also pecuniary punishment.'[33]

Nevertheless, despite enormous operational and legal efforts by the Bangladeshi government, religious militant groups still remain a major concern to the security and the stability of the country. Islamist militancy in Bangladesh is showing new signs of life, even in the face of continuous crackdowns on terrorist infrastructure and activity by counter-terrorism forces in the country.[34] It has also been reported that many of the outlawed terrorist groups including the JMB, Alla'r Dal, HuJI and Hizb-ut Touhid have been regrouping and reorganising. The indications that the JMB and HuJI are trying to forge an alliance – despite their differences of opinion – is an alarming and important development. And in the midst of this evolving terrorist scenario in Bangladesh, a new jihadi outfit has emerged under the name of Islam-o-Muslim, believed to be a dissident breakaway faction of JMB.

Taken as a whole, these developments reflect the inadequacy of the government's counter-terrorism strategy. The terrorist insurgency is still active; new groups are forming despite the tough measures taken by the government. If the present trend continues, the nation will inevitably slide further down the slope towards a regime with a clear Islamist agenda. What is necessary is a comprehensive strategy to forestall this: a new direction for the state response. Decisive change is vital in order to restore the founding principles of Bangladeshi secularism, democracy and equal rights. There is still a thriving civil society, with bold intellectuals, journalists and human rights activists willing to challenge radical Islamism – and that is a cause for hope. Bangladesh has not been lost to radical Islamism yet, but it will be if the alarm bells are not heard.

Recommendations

This chapter has outlined the nature of the insurgency against the Bangladeshi state, the grievances and state failures at the heart of its root causes and the tough, yet incomplete, response to it. What therefore should the government of Bangladesh do to counter the terrorist threat? In this, there are important parallels between an effective response to terrorism and a classical insurgency. How government openly labels the problem – whether as terrorism or insurgency – may matter less than the response itself. This response must be comprehensive. It must range from ensuring democratic institutions at the top of the state all the way to engaging with civil society at the grass-roots level. And it must include both purely responsive actions – such as improving law enforcement – and proactive policies that address structural inequalities.

First and foremost, the radicalisation of individuals or groups needs to be tackled by addressing the contributory structural problems at various levels of society. This includes tackling inequality, discrimination, youth unemployment; modernising the education system; and reforming democratic and electoral institutions to bring back public confidence in a secular and progressive political system.

The state must improve co-ordination between the intelligence and law enforcement agencies. To respond to the challenge of the terrorist insurgency effectively, Bangladesh needs to adopt a national counter-terrorism strategy and a detailed action plan.

Bangladesh needs to develop a comprehensively reformed political system that upholds democratic governance at both national and local levels: the lack of such system breeds political extremism.

Islamic organisations, religious leaders and organisations should be brought into the terrorism discourse in Bangladesh. They will be important actors in the fight against ideological fanaticism and the restraining of radicalisation – and they should be designated as such.

A great asset in Bangladesh's fight against terrorism is that people are strongly against it. But, this aversion needs to be converted into active resistance through awareness campaigns and enlightened religious education in public places, including houses of worship.

Intelligence and law enforcement agencies need to be modernised, especially in terms of human resources, equipment and technical competence.

Media, civil society and think tanks should work to mobilise public opinion against terrorism.

The religious education system must be modernised so that the students are not exploited or radicalised by extremist religious leaders.

It will be important to educate the younger generation about the ills of political violence and the dangers of radicalisation. Special modules can be taught at the high school and college level in order to educate the students.

Conclusion

The extent and nature of violent threats to states and populations have been changing around the world. Bangladesh is not immune to this challenge. It is clear according to the numerous indicators that the threat level is increasing in Bangladesh. The government has tried to respond. But the response so far to counter terrorism has demonstrated the limitations of the exclusive use of 'hard power', without addressing the root causes of the terrorist insurgency. To tackle these threats, Bangladesh must urgently deal with the shifting trends and tactics of terrorism threats, and focus on the micro-level actors and issues. Institutions must be reformed, and terrorists pursued: 'hearts and minds' matter in this campaign as much as with any classic counter-insurgency. For this is a battle for the legitimacy of the state in the eyes of the people. Owing to the multidimensional nature of the problem, it is important to explore thorough, viable and effective strategy incorporating short-term, medium-term and long-term goals. At stake is Bangladesh's security – now, and in the future.

COUNTERING INSTABILITY IN KASHMIR

Ved Prakash Malik

Jammu and Kashmir has been a cause of instability in South Asia ever since India and Pakistan became independent in August 1947. For Pakistan, it is a national obsession based on religious grounds. For India, it is a test case for its secular credentials and legal and moral principles. It is also a case of poor strategic thinking. Kashmiris, now divided by the Line of Control (LoC), view it, justifiably, on ethnic grounds. Four wars have been endured, yet the problem continues to fester with both external and internal dimensions. Its strategic location, the ongoing proxy war and insurgency, and the declared nuclear capability of India and Pakistan have propelled Jammu and Kashmir to the centre stage of regional instability: a potential flashpoint for a nuclear war.

Nestling in the lap of the Himalayan, Karakoram and Hindu Kush mountain ranges, the state of Jammu and Kashmir comprises several well-demarcated regions and sub-regions, with diverse topography, culture, religion, linguistic and ethnic identities; a truly pluralistic landscape. Amongst its more prominent regions, Ladakh is ethnically and culturally Tibetan. A majority of its inhabitants practise Buddhism. The central Kashmir Valley is overwhelmingly Sunni Muslim, with a small but influential Hindu minority called the Kashmiri Pandits. There has been a strong bond of Kashmiriyat and Sufism in the Valley which binds Muslim and Hindu communities in a cultural and religious fraternity. Jammu has a mixed population of Hindus, Muslims and Sikhs. Gilgit Agency, close to the Afghan border, has diverse tribes, most of which are Shia Muslim. The sparsely populated Baltistan region is ethnically related to Ladakh, but the people there practise Shia Islam. Poonch is comprised of Muslims and Hindus, with a different language and ethnicity to the people of Kashmir Valley.

Sir Owen Dixon noted, in his report to the UN Security Council of 15 September 1950, that '... The state of Jammu and Kashmir is not really a unit geographically, demographically or economically. It is an agglomeration of territories brought under the political power of the Maharajah. That is the unity it possesses ...'[1]

Currently, the state of Jammu and Kashmir is divided among three countries due to unresolved territorial disputes. India controls the central and southern portion (Jammu, Kashmir Valley and Ladakh, including the Siachen Glacier); Pakistan controls the northwest portion (Azad Kashmir or Pakistan Occupied Kashmir (POK) and Northern Areas); while China controls the northeastern portion (Aksai Chin and the Shaqsgam Valley). Of the total area of the state of Jammu and Kashmir, India controls 101,338 km^2, Pakistan 85,846 km^2 and China the remaining 37,555 km^2.

Division of Jammu and Kashmir

The External Dimension

When India and Pakistan became independent, the Maharajah of Jammu and Kashmir was, under the Indian Independence Act 1947, to choose between India and Pakistan or become independent. Before he could determine a choice, Pakistan cut off essential supplies to the state from its side and followed with a tribal invasion assisted by the Pakistan Army. The raiders massacred, plundered and pillaged their way to the very gates of the state capital, Srinagar. The Maharajah appealed for military assistance to the Governor General of India, Lord Mountbatten. The Governor General and the Government of

India agreed to provide military assistance on the condition that the state sign a formal instrument of accession with India to ensure a legal as well as moral basis for military intervention.[2] The Maharajah executed the Instrument of Accession on 26 October 1947 along with another appeal for help to Sheikh Abdullah, the most prolific Kashmiri leader of the time. Pakistan protested the accession, but India accepted and immediately sent in military forces. Along with acrimonious diplomatic exchanges between Delhi and Karachi, the first Indo-Pakistani war over Jammu and Kashmir lasted for about fifteen months. In the face of Pakistan's denials of involvement and its support to the 'freedom fighters', India took the Kashmir question to the UN Security Council. On 13 August 1948, the UN Commission for India and Pakistan passed a resolution wherein there was to be a ceasefire, followed by a truce and withdrawal of Pakistan forces, Pakistani tribesmen and other nationals from all parts of Jammu and Kashmir, and finally a plebiscite to ascertain the will of the people of Jammu and Kashmir.[3] A ceasefire was declared on 1 January 1949. Under the Karachi Agreement of 27 July 1949, Jammu and Kashmir was divided along a delineated and demarcated ceasefire line signed by Indian and Pakistani military commanders. However, the plebiscite could not be held, as Pakistan did not fulfill the essential precondition of the withdrawal of its forces and civilians from the territory occupied through aggression. Later, withdrawal became untenable.[4]

In the mid 1950s, China occupied Aksai Chin, the northeastern part of the state, to provide better communications between its provinces of Western Tibet and Xinjiang. The Sino-Indian war of 1962 did not resolve the dispute. In 1963, Pakistan ceded Shaqsgam Valley ($5,180$ km^2 and contiguous to Aksai Chin) to China as part of a boundary settlement.

The 1948 Jammu and Kashmir ceasefire line between India and Pakistan, and its subsequent conversion to the LoC with very minor modifications, seems to have set the status and future of Jammu and

Kashmir in stone. India now controls nearly 60 per cent of the area of the erstwhile state; Pakistan has control over 30 per cent; and China occupies the remaining 10 per cent. The Indian side of Jammu and Kashmir comprises the Kashmir Valley, Jammu, and Ladakh, with a population totalling 10.15 million.[5] It is roughly two-thirds Muslim, just under a third Hindu, 2 per cent Sikh, and just over 1 per cent Buddhist and others, including Christians. The Pakistani side, Azad Kashmir and the northern areas of Hunza, Gilgit and Baltistan, is entirely Muslim. This area is comparatively sparsely populated, relatively inaccessible and economically underdeveloped.[6]

As both the Maharajah and Sheikh Abdullah – the most popular leader of the state – had consented to the accession to India on 26 October 1947, what then were the reasons for Jammu and Kashmir becoming a territorial dispute between India and Pakistan?

First, Pakistan was created on a religious (Muslim) rationale and the 'two-nation theory'.[7] Its political leaders expected that as this Muslim majority state was contiguous to West Pakistan, it would join Pakistan. But Sheikh Abdullah, who on behalf of the Kashmiri people decided to join India, believed otherwise: 'In Kashmir, we want a peoples' government. We want a government which will give equal rights and opportunities to all men – irrespective of caste and creed … It will be a joint government of the Hindus, the Sikhs and the Muslims. That is what I am fighting for.'[8] His pluralistic ideals were closer to that of India, which espoused secularism.

Second, Pakistan suspected the Hindu Maharajah of the Muslim majority state. His procrastination and indecision for two months over the issue of sovereignty led to Pakistan losing patience and deciding to force the issue through a tribal invasion. And when the Maharajah and Sheikh Abdullah decided to join India, the prime minister of Pakistan declared, 'We do not recognise this accession. The accession of Kashmir to India is a fraud.'[9] This ultimately led to Pakistan's obsession with Kashmir, with its liberation becoming a seemingly permanent item on the politico-military agenda.

Third, Most Indians still blame India's first prime minister, Jawaharlal Nehru, for needlessly referring the bilateral issue over the province to the UN Security Council when the Indian Army could have easily resolved the issue of Kashmir by force: Nehru instead pushed it into the vortex of international politics, to India's disadvantage.

In 1965, Pakistan repeated what it had attempted in 1947–48. Under Operation *Gibraltar*, columns of Pakistani invaders entered Jammu and Kashmir, which was expected to coincide with an internal uprising. The uprising never materialised. In 1947, the intruders had been disorganised and unruly. This time they were carefully chosen, trained, armed and organised. The intrusion was followed up with a fully-fledged military attack in the Jammu sector. India reacted across the ceasefire line and international border. At the end of this war, both nations agreed to exchange territories captured by either across the ceasefire line, thus restoring the status quo *ante bellum*.[10]

The next Indo-Pakistani war in 1971 – fought mostly in the east – resulted in the emergence of Bangladesh, and both sides retained minor gains that were made across the ceasefire line. They also took the political decision, as part of the Simla Agreement 1972, to redesignate the resultant ceasefire line as the LoC. This change in the nomenclature signified its transition from a military line separating the two armies to a political dividing line, which was expected to eventually evolve into a permanent boundary.

The Internal Dimension
When India adopted its constitution, the province of Jammu and Kashmir under its control was given special status and autonomy, with its own flag and constitution, under Article 370.[11] Delhi retained control over defence, foreign affairs and communications. All other rights were given to the state of Jammu and Kashmir, recognising the separate and distinct identity of the people of the state and the circumstances under which they had joined the Indian

Union. However, soon thereafter, consistent erosion started taking place in the powers of the state. The jurisdiction of the centre was extended to all subjects thereto excluded. All Indian services were extended to Jammu and Kashmir. Many powers of the state were transferred to the federal level in the Concurrent or in the Central List of the Indian Union. The state leaders protested and demanded restoration of rights provided under Article 370. This assurance was given in 1975,[12] but nothing much was done on the ground. This grievance became a rallying point for the extremists and the politically conscious in the state.

The governments that came to power in the state after independence also failed to tackle the socioeconomic problems facing the people. There was little investment in infrastructure and limited employment avenues for the youth. Lack of any workable economic strategy and pervasive corruption fuelled frustration and discontent, particularly among the youth. The central government also failed to protect and develop the people's linguistic and cultural heritage and aspirations.

Another major contribution to instability arose from the Congress Party in New Delhi trying to play a role in the internal politics of the state, where it had neither standing nor experience. It tried to foist its own rule on the state with the help of some unpopular local political leaders. The Kashmiris accused the ruling political alliance of rigging the state elections in 1989. This worsened the political situation and led to prolonged agitation, rioting and the weakening of law and order and governance. The delicate political, social and economic situation in Kashmir Valley became a ready-made recipe for exploitation and intervention by Pakistan.

The Return of the External Dimension
Under the military ruler General Muhammad Zia ul-Haq, Pakistan initiated a proxy war in Jammu and Kashmir soon after the Soviet withdrawal from Afghanistan in 1989. The Pakistani Inter Services Intelligence (ISI), working in collusion with the CIA, had gained

valuable experience in waging guerrilla warfare with the mujahideen in Afghanistan. The ISI stepped up its efforts to subvert Kashmiri youth. Many young men were covertly exfiltrated into the POK through the porous LoC for religious indoctrination and arms training, as was done in Afghanistan. Wahhabi Islam was introduced into the Kashmir Valley through mosques and madrassas, which eroded Kashmiri Sufism.[13] The trained militants had already started pouring back into Kashmir in the late 1980s. The period 1987–89 saw a spurt in violence, prolonged strikes in the Kashmir Valley, and attacks on political leaders, police and paramilitary forces. In December 1989, the kidnapping and subsequent release of the daughter of the Union Home Minister, Mufti Mohammad Sayeed,[14] in exchange for five top militants showed that the state administration had lost control. The militants had become more popular than the elected representatives of the state. The elected Chief Minister Dr Farooq Abdullah resigned in January 1990. Gubernatorial rule was imposed in Jammu and Kashmir, which as per constitutional requirements became presidential rule in June 1990. After a spate of murders of Kashmiri Hindus by militants, there was an exodus of the Hindu community from the Valley. Nearly 200,000 Kashmiri Pandits left their land and property in the Kashmir Valley to take shelter in Jammu and other parts of India. In July 1990, the Kashmir Valley and a 20 km belt along the LoC in the Poonch and Rajouri districts were declared 'disturbed areas'. Additional army units were deployed in the state for counter-infiltration and counter-insurgency operations, and to assist the civil administration in maintaining law and order and restoring normalcy. The ISI, however, continued to provide training, sophisticated weapons, equipment and financial support to Kashmiri militants. Over the years, the number of militant groups – pro-independence and pro-Pakistan – mushroomed in the state. The ISI then began to introduce mujahideen from Pakistan and other foreign countries – indoctrinated and more brutal – into Kashmiri pro-Pakistan groups. In this process, the home-grown pro-independence militant groups (such as the Jammu and Kashmir Liberation Front) lost support from the local Kashmiris and Pakistan, and were gradually eliminated. With the introduction of foreign mujahideen, the armed conflict gradually changed from one of insurgency to increasingly one of terrorism. The ISI also encouraged creation of the All Party Hurriyat Conference to organise overground cadres to project a united political approach against the Government of India.

Thereafter, a number of significant incidents of insurgency and terrorism occured: the siege of the Hazratbal mosque (Srinagar) in October 1993 and again in March 1996; the declaration of Sopore as a 'liberated zone' in October 1993; the spread of terrorist activities to Doda district of Jammu after 1994; the burning of Charar-e-Sharif, a Sufi shrine, in May 1995; and the kidnapping and killing of five foreign tourists in 1995. The army and paramilitary forces carried out protracted operations to contain insurgents and terrorists and to create a safe atmosphere for governance and to restart the political process.

After seven years of gubernatorial and presidential rule, despite a desperate bid by ISI-backed insurgents and mujahideen terrorists to stall and subvert the political process, parliamentary and state assembly elections were held in 1996, paving the way for the installation of an elected government. Dr Farooq Abdullah's party, the National Conference, won a comfortable majority with a voter turnout of 40–50 per cent. This turn of events dealt a severe blow to the militancy and Pakistani-sponsored proxy war. With a newly elected government in place and people in the Valley showing signs of disenchantment with militancy, army units were withdrawn from Baramulla, Sopore, Srinagar, Badgam and Anantnag. Paramilitary units were deployed to assist the civil authorities and the police in maintaining law and order.

In 1997, Pakistan started focusing on the Muslim population in the interior areas of Jammu (Poonch, Rajouri, Naushera and Doda), south of the Pir Panjal range. The proxy war was spread to these areas in a bid to make up for the lack of success in the Kashmir Valley and once again to trigger a Hindu exodus from the Muslim-dominated areas. Additional troops were deployed into these areas. In the following months infiltration attempts and violent incidents declined, but exchange of small-arms fire, heavier direct-firing weapons and artillery duels along the LoC became more frequent and intense. Also, as the number of local militants waned, control of terrorism in Jammu and Kashmir passed into the hands of Taliban-trained jihadi mercenaries.

To conduct counter-insurgency/terrorist operations in the state, two unified commands were established under the chief minister: one each for north and south of Pir Panjal Range. By the summer of 1998, there was substantial improvement in the overall situation and terrorism appeared to have been effectively contained. The Kashmiri people had become disillusioned with this scourge. The civil administration started functioning more effectively, with civil courts, schools and dispensaries working regularly. There was a noticeable increase in commercial activity. The number of tourists visiting the Kashmir Valley rose sharply.

Sabotage of the Lahore Declaration

India and Pakistan conducted nuclear tests in May 1998. Strong international reaction and perhaps a greater sense of responsibility gave an opportunity to both countries to intensify political dialogue and improve relations. In February 1999, the Indian prime minister, at the invitation of his Pakistani counterpart, journeyed by bus to Pakistan to sign the Lahore Declaration. During his visit, Pakistani jihadi elements that had a longstanding alliance with the Pakistani military started riots in many parts of the city to protest against this political move.[15] Indian military intelligence also intercepted radio messages from across the border exhorting all jihadi elements inside Jammu and Kashmir to increase the levels of violence. There was a sudden spurt in terrorist activities all over the state. Between February and April 1999, there were 618 incidents of violence in which 487 civilians, security forces personnel and terrorists were killed.

After the Simla Agreement of 1972, the Lahore Declaration was an important turning point in Indo-Pakistani relations. Indian political leaders expected that after this declaration, the ISI would cease supporting cross-border infiltration and militant activities in Jammu and Kashmir, and violence perpetrated by the latter would taper off. But that was not to be.

In May 1999, Pakistan repeated the attempts of 1947–48 and 1965. Pakistan Army soldiers, many of them dressed as mujahideen, intruded across the LoC into the Kargil-Ladakh sector of Jammu and Kashmir. This sparked a limited war. In July 1999, unable to withstand India's military reaction, and under severe international pressure, the Pakistan Army was forced to withdraw to the LoC. The Kargil War demonstrated how the Pakistani political leadership was working out of synch with the thinking and the plans of its military command.[16]

Following the Kargil War, the ISI continued to support mujahideen infiltration, and militancy intensified in Jammu and Kashmir for some time. This was a reaction to the setback that the Pakistan Army had suffered in Kargil. However, the situation was gradually controlled by taking more effective counter-infiltration and counter-insurgency measures. These holistic measures, discussed below, and the people's yearning for peace, have led to a perceptible improvement of the security situation in Jammu and Kashmir.

Management of the Internal Dimension: The Multidimensional Approach

There was a great deal of learning in counter-insurgency and counter-terrorism in Jammu and Kashmir during the decade, 1989 to 1999. The Indian government realised that military force was necessary to prevent violence, physically and logistically isolate militants and thus put them under pressure to surrender, renounce violence and secessionism (and also deter their supporters). But there is no military solution to the problem of insurgency. The solution ultimately lies in the political domain: whether within the existing national constitution or a modified version. For conflict resolution, one has to deal with the hearts and minds of the populace. This requires a holistic approach wherein political, economic, social, perceptual, psychological, operational and diplomatic aspects require equal and simultaneous attention.

Based on experience in Jammu and Kashmir and other states of India, a multifaceted strategy was adopted which, apart from the various measures taken on the security front, included:

- Focusing attention on the developmental aspects and implementation of a macro-level reconstruction plan to strengthen infrastructure, create employment and income-generation opportunities and improve quality of life
- Ensuring the continuity of the democratic process in the state and provide a secure environment for political mobilisation
- Refusing to tolerate human rights violations and ensuring the use of minimum force in the maintenance of law and order
- Ensuring the primacy of civil administration and elected representatives in the maintenance of law and order
- Measures to improve the conditions of migrants in Jammu and a package of incentives for their return to the Kashmir Valley
- Taking necessary measures to facilitate interpersonal contact across the LoC.

On the security front, a system of unified command under the governor, and after elections under the elected chief minister, was adopted. The unified command monitored and reviewed the ground situation regularly with senior representatives of the state government, army, paramilitary forces and other security agencies. In tandem with the state government, the Union Ministry of Home Affairs and Defence also monitored the security situation.

Democratic norms, good governance and a secular and liberal mindset – making no distinction between the majority and the minority and treating everyone equally in the eyes of the law – were emphasised. Civil and military officials were asked to act with firmness and determination, tempered by civilised and democratic behaviour.

The security forces had to employ the principle of the minimum use of force necessary during operations – not the overkill necessary in a war. They were not only to fight militants, but also had to reassure innocent people feeling insecure or neglected due to inadequate civil administration. We learnt that tough measures lead to increasing alienation. Human rights have to be respected. It is counterproductive to alienate hundreds and thousands of neutrals in order to kill a suspect.

Conversely, attempts at appeasement carry the risk of being read as signs of weakening resolve. One has to find the right balance. Military visibility should be reduced, particularly in urban areas, when the situation can be handled by armed police or paramilitary forces. The rules of engagement are based on two forms of self-restraint: discrimination and proportionality. It is also recognised that in such operations, with unique stresses, where it is impossible to identify the difference between friend and foe, and with frequent provocations, it is not possible to rule out mistakes. These aberrations have to be dealt with through legal means, in as transparent a manner as possible. At no stage can a nation afford to give a full licence to the security forces to operate freely. There is a requirement to define clearly their responsibility, authority, legality and accountability.

During sustained operations in Kashmir, the security forces involved professionals and senior and respected citizens as a link between them and the locals. They formed citizens' committees to learn about their difficulties, and held meetings with them as frequently as possible. Along with sustained operations, small- and large-scale civic action programmes have to be undertaken. In areas outside the reach of the civil administration, the Army Development Group launched Operation *Sadbhavana* [Goodwill] to undertake socioeconomic work – medical, education and employment training – to benefit the locals.

With experience, it was realised that specially organised, equipped and trained, geographically focused security forces were needed to deal with insurgencies and terrorism. Special forces, the Rashtriya Rifles and 'home and hearth' battalions are some examples. These forces, and all those who worked alongside them, were given training for local terrain, people, language, customs and traditions. Special training schools were established for this purpose.

On the political front, timely and transparent elections under the autonomous Central Election Commission were conducted at the grass-roots (Panchayat), state and parliament levels. The central government adopted a co-operative rather than supervisory approach and restarted dialogue with political leaders on autonomy and special status, considered by many as the key to sustainable peace and stability in the state.

The central government also decided to liberally support and assist the state government in its efforts to bring about all-round economic development and provide possibilities for gainful employment for the youth, with a focus on planned and balanced regional development. Priority was accorded to building physical, economic and social infrastructure, thereby improving the productive potential of the state while also improving quality of life. The state government was financially subsidised for security-related measures so that it could muster adequate funds for socioeconomic programmes.

In November 2004, as a special initiative in this direction, the prime minister announced a long-term reconstruction plan for Jammu and Kashmir involving an outlay of approximately $5.3 billion, including projects aimed at expanding economic infrastructure, provision of basic services, employment and income-generation activities, and providing relief and rehabilitation for different groups affected by militancy. Emphasis was on upgrading educational institutions, increasing professional schools, extending railways into the state,[17] construction and maintenance of roads, and further development of trade, commerce and tourism. These projects are to be implemented by Union ministries in consultation with the state government. The progress of implementation is monitored by the Ministry of Home Affairs and Planning Commission.[18]

In April 2008, another package was announced by the prime minister for the return and rehabilitation of Kashmiri migrants to the Valley, worth roughly $358 million. This package included provision of housing, transit accommodation, cash relief, student scholarships, employment, assistance to agriculturists/horticulturists and a waiver of interest on loans.

The central government also took diplomatic initiatives to encourage personal mobility across the LoC by introducing bus services on Srinagar-Muzaffarabad and Poonch-Rawalakote routes. Limited cross-LoC trade was also started in 2008.[19]

Jammu and Kashmir state is currently one of the largest recipients of grants from New Delhi, totaling $812 million per year. Its poverty rate, at 4 per cent, is one of the lowest in the country. The Jammu and Kashmir Bank – listed on the Indian stock exchange – reported a net profit of $13 million in 2008.

The Present Security Situation

In the last two decades of severe terrorist and secessionist violence, sponsored and supported from across the border, more than 13,775 civilians and 4,690 security personnel have been killed (details are in Table 5).[20]

There has been a dramatic turn of the security situation in Jammu and Kashmir in the past nine years. Terrorism-related fatalities in the

Table 5: Kashmir Insurgency Casualties by Year, 2004–09.

Year	Security forces killed	Civilians killed	Terrorists killed	Incidents
2004	2,565	281	707	976
2005	1,990	89	557	917
2006	1,667	51	389	591
2007	1,092	110	158	472
2008	708	75	91	339
2009	499	64	78	239

state have declined continuously since their peak of 4,507 in 2001, to 381 in 2009. Taking into account the overall improvement in the situation, the central Indian government withdrew approximately 35,000 troops from Jammu and Kashmir.[21] The long-term objective for restoring normality in the state is, as mentioned previously, to entrust responsibility for law and order to the local police.[22]

However, from late 2009, terrorist attacks once again increased. In the first four months of 2010, there were sixty-five infiltration attempts and 126 militancy-related incidents. The composition of militant activity in Jammu and Kashmir continues to be dominated by foreigners. Of the 239 terrorists killed in 2009, 76 per cent were foreigners, generally coming from the then-North West Frontier Province (now Khyber Pakhtunkhwa), Punjab, POK and other areas of Pakistan. Street protests organised by the overtly pro-Pakistan political party Hurriyat Conference also increased. This change has been linked to turnover in the Pakistani military command. According to Indian intelligence assessments in April 2010, forty-two terrorist training camps directed against India are operating in Pakistan and POK. Of these, thirty-four are 'active' and eight are 'holding' camps. Some 300 militants are currently waiting for an opportunity to infiltrate India. This reflects the fragility of the political and security situation. The Indian successes so far in the state are not irreversible.[23]

On the political front, the Union Home Minister stated in Srinagar in October 2009 that the government would start a dialogue process including 'every shade of political opinion' in Jammu and Kashmir for the resolution of the Kashmiri issue. This would be a 'quiet dialogue' and 'quiet diplomacy, away from the media glare, till a political solution to the problem is arrived at.' He said the Centre would hold talks with all mainstream political parties and also 'other groups', which are not organised or are referred to as extremists.[24]

The increased attempts at cross-LoC infiltration, recurrent efforts to provoke mass disturbances in the Valley, a sustained separatist rhetoric, and cumulative evidence of Pakistan's unchanged intent and strategy despite a tactical downward calibration indicate clearly that militancy in Jammu and Kashmir is currently down – but not out.

Management of External Dimension: A Negotiated Settlement

After the Kargil War, India strengthened counter-infiltration measures by deploying additional troops and sophisticated ground surveillance equipment and constructing a fence along the 740 km LoC. The construction, electrification and surveillance of the fence have been a monumental effort considering the terrain and climatic conditions.

India seems to have realised that, post-South Asian nuclearisation, there can be no military solution for Jammu and Kashmir. The Indian government, despite undermining the Lahore Declaration and military takeover in Pakistan, continued its diplomatic efforts to persuade Pakistan to give up support and stop cross-border terrorism. In the January 2004 Islamabad Declaration, the Indian Prime Minister Atal Bihari Vajpayee and Pakistani President Pervez Musharraf agreed to work toward normalisation of relations, consolidate confidence-building measures, and to commence the process of a composite dialogue that would include the Jammu and Kashmir dispute. Musharraf reassured Vajpayee that he would not permit any territory under Pakistani control (including the POK) to be used to support terrorism in any manner.[25] As a major confidence-building measure, both countries agreed to observe a ceasefire along the LoC. A secret back-channel dialogue was also initiated to find a long-term political solution to the imbroglio. After three years of secret parleys, in 2007 an understanding was reached that envisaged gradual demilitarisation and loose autonomy just short of independence for Jammu and Kashmir on both sides of the LoC, and facilitatation of cross-LoC interpersonal contacts and trade. But these negotiations were derailed due to political turmoil in Pakistan, the sacking of General Musharraf, and inadequate political discussions in New Delhi.[26]

In May 2010, a Chatham House survey report prepared by Robert Bradnock showed that:[27]

- More than 58 per cent of respondents were prepared to accept the LoC as a permanent border if it could be more open for personal contacts and trade. Only 8 per cent voted against making the LoC a permanent boundary
- Only 2 per cent of the respondents on the Indian side favoured joining Pakistan
- 44 per cent of people in the POK favoured independence, compared to 43 per cent in Jammu and Kashmir
- 20 per cent of respondents in Jammu and Kashmir thought that violence would help, compared to nearly 40 per cent who felt that it was getting in the way of a resolution
- 75–95 per cent of respondents favoured *azadi* [independence] as a final resolution
- The study concluded that holding a plebiscite in Jammu and Kashmir is now irrelevant.

The evidence also suggests that there is plenty of reason for optimism. Talks between India and Pakistan on converting the LoC to a soft border were on the right lines.

Conclusion

In October 1947, the state of Jammu and Kashmir signed the Instrument of Accession with India because its most important political leader of the state, Sheikh Abdullah, felt that India was politically 'a much more progressive state than Pakistan, and Kashmir would have far greater scope for free development according to its own genius if she allied with India.'[28] Pakistan, with unconcealed support for the tribal invasion, played the most influential role in the accession drama. But four decades later, Kashmiris' disenchantment and frustration with state politics and governance spawned insurgency and a demand for secession. Pakistan, which has not reconciled to Kashmir's accession with India, found this a golden opportunity to nurture and intensify their demand with both overt and covert support to militants.

Six decades later, the Jammu and Kashmir dispute with its internal and external dimensions and continued violence in the form of insurgency and terrorism has developed into a complex – and perhaps the most serious – cause of instability in South Asia.

According to Ashutosh Varshney, writing in 1992, 'At its core, the Kashmir problem is a result of three forces: religious nationalism represented by Pakistan, secular nationalism epitomised by India, and ethnic nationalism embodied in what Kashmiris call *Kashmiriyat* (being a Kashmiri)'.[29] India recognises that unless the hearts and minds of the Kashmiris are on its side, Pakistan is unlikely to give up its political and military efforts to gain control of the territory. Priority, therefore, has to be given to the internal dimension. Kashmir is not a unidimensional security issue. A multipronged approach has been adopted towards insurgency, which treats the important internal dimension as a phenomenon with political, economic, social, perceptual, psychological, operational and diplomatic aspects, all of which need equal and simultaneous attention. The approach includes autonomy, which continues to be discussed between the central government and the state. This strategy has worked well and resulted in the decline of militancy.

The external dimension is also important. So far, the Indo-Pakistani dialogue has not resulted in denial of overt and covert support to insurgency and terrorism by Pakistan. The Pakistan Army and ISI have been controlling the support and infiltration from the POK as and when required. The terror infrastructure in the POK and other parts of Pakistan remains untouched. Pakistani-based terrorist action in Mumbai on 26 November 2008 caused a serious setback to the ongoing Indo-Pakistani dialogue, which was resumed after a two-year gap. Pakistan would have to be persuaded, at bilateral and multilateral levels, to close down terrorist infrastructure in the POK and elsewhere, and reconsider the loose autonomy, gradual demilitarisation, and cross-LoC travel and trade facilitation proposals on Jammu and Kashmir.

Given its historical, complex internal and external dimensions, the insurgency and terrorism in Kashmir is unlikely to be resolved soon. But if India and Pakistan can get over their trust deficit and work genuinely for peace and harmony, it is possible to find a workable solution on Kashmir. Until then, it will remain a worrisome cause for regional instability.

THE SOUTHERN THAILAND INSURGENCY

Alastair Leithead[1]

The two coffins were elaborately decorated with flowers, fairy lights and the photographs of the husband and wife who lay inside them. The Buddhist monks were chanting in unison, performing the nightly ceremony as they had every day that week. Earlier that day at the temple two other elderly members of the same family had been cremated. In the front row, her palms pressed together in prayer, was Sa. She was mourning the death of both her parents and her grandparents, shot dead by armed men, their rural homes set on fire. Her young cousins, just ten and eleven, had seen what had happened and were in hiding. Among the mourners that night were soldiers wearing camouflage fatigues, some of the 30,000 troops stationed in Thailand's three Muslim-majority provinces on the southern Malaysian border to bring security to the people and to try and protect them from what has been one of the world's most violent (but least well known) insurgencies so far this century. On this, like many other occasions, they had failed.

The heavy rain kicked up the ash from the ground making the fire smell fresh. Among the charred wooden beams was a bicycle, burnt where it had been standing when the attackers came. This was where Sa's grandparents had lived. Villagers heard gunfire shortly after dark, not long after the mosque down the road had fallen silent. They had seen maybe a dozen men wearing army uniforms. The men attacked the family's two other homes in the small village of scattered houses among paddy fields, rubber plantations and jungle. The family were the only Buddhists left in a Muslim village, but had lived here for years and were an important part of the community. Neighbours took in and hid the two traumatised children who had seen their great-grandparents killed. This was September 2010, and was just one of the many violent attacks that month blamed on Malay-Muslim separatists, despite their use of military uniforms. It was a period when there was a shooting, a bombing, or an act of violence on average twice a day. By then 4,300 people had died and 7,000 had been injured in the seven years since a historic battle for separatism had been re-ignited with increasing Islamic overtones. As Hamid Karzai was being elected first president of the new Afghanistan, and troops in 'liberated' Iraq still patrolled on foot and put on a friendly face to try and win hearts and minds, southern Thailand was already ablaze, but few people outside the country noticed.

The reason they did not notice was that this shadowy insurgency has had no strong links to global terror networks such as Al-Qa'ida. Most analysts do not even see evidence of a link to regional organisations in Southeast Asia like Jemaah Islamiyah, which was blamed for the Bali bombing in 2002. No group has publicly claimed responsibility for the Bali attacks, but the leaflets militants have previously left behind suggest this is a separatist movement based on geography and cultural identity. Attacks are rarely outside Thailand's three southern border provinces and parts of a fourth province, an area which for centuries was the Malay Sultanate of Patani, before being formally annexed into what is now Thailand more than a hundred years ago. The people in this area have an historic identity based on ethnicity and religion, and consider themselves Malay-Muslim, or *Nayu,* with their own language. In an area that is more than 80 per cent Muslim in a country which is nearly 95 per cent Buddhist, many in the community want greater practical recognition from the Thai state of their different cultural identity. Many argue that a failure to provide this has created a sense of being second-class citizens, and provided the space for insurgency to grow.

Thailand's Deep South has had rebellions against central authority for a century or more, but the global Islamic reaction to the invasions of Afghanistan and Iraq and the global War on Terror gave recruitment a new rhetoric. While this is not just a religious insurgency, the rise of Salafi jihad elsewhere in the world has provided it with inspiration, as a way to mobilise young people and through echoing the tactics of roadside bombings, beheadings and assassinations. Foreigners have not yet been targeted, even though tourist islands like Phuket are a relatively short flight away. The most extreme voices demand independence from the 'infidel' Thai state that invaded their Islamic homeland. Others call for varying levels of self-determination within Thailand. It is something Bangkok has not given them to their satisfaction for decades, and some argue it is the key to resolving this crisis.

Historic Patani

Patani's history is long and disputed. It was founded around the fourteenth century, a sultanate that grew rich on trade and was a centre of Islamic learning. Its greatest days are said to have been in the sixteenth and seventeenth centuries under the reign of four consecutive queens. Revisionists have clouded accurate accounts of Patani's past for propaganda purposes. Some described the historic kingdom as having been an Islamic state, a position embraced by insurgents who justify killings by claiming they are part of a holy war against the invading non-believers. After being overwhelmed by its powerful neighbour Siam and ruled by divided leaders, the area kept a level of independence in exchange for paying allegiance, like many similar sultanates, in a time before the emergence of strong nation-states. Patani was formally annexed in 1902 and seven years later officially became part of Siam, which escaped colonialism to be renamed Thailand.

The old Patani sultanate was broken up into the three Thai southern provinces of Pattani, Narathiwat and Yala, and along with four districts defined in neighbouring Songkhla, became part of Thailand's unity policy. A strong army and governors appointed from Bangkok assimilated the country's disparate corners, prioritising solidarity for the nation-state above local customs and traditions. Thailand is a multi-ethnic country comprising the central Thais; the northeastern Issan people, with linguistic and cultural links to Laos; the northern Lanna, based on another ancient kingdom around today's Chiang Mai; and the southern Malay. There is a strong Chinese presence and significant minorities such as the Khmer, Hmong, Karen and Mon in the border areas. The assimilation process broadly worked, encouraged by King Bhumibol Adulyadej, who has reigned since 1946 and become the icon of Thai unity and prosperity under the moniker 'Nation, Religion, King'. Most ethnic groups with a cultural history now see themselves as Thai above everything else, but those in the Deep South have always maintained a cultural difference. Malay-Muslims still speak a Malay dialect and a minority write in *jawi*, which is a Malay-Arabic script. Some people see themselves as culturally closer to the provinces of northern Malaysia than to Thailand.

Separatists

Around the time the Twin Towers fell, a dormant movement was stirring. It was a movement which had emerged after the Second World War when Haji Sulong Toemeena, a leading Islamic spiritual leader, presented a list of seven demands to bring changes that would give the region a level of self-determination through local governance. They were rejected, he was jailed and eventually 'disappeared'. In the 1960s, separatists began fighting a guerrilla war and strong-arm military action fuelled their support, and by the 1970s there were attacks across the south and even in Bangkok. At the same time, Thailand was trying to deal with an even more violent and disruptive Communist insurgency across the country – an insurgency which was eventually brought under control. The way it was dealt with has great influence on the way the government and the military has been trying to tackle the insurgency today, even if its cause and effect were different.

The Communist Party of Thailand appealed to the minorities who felt neglected and abused by the establishment in Bangkok. Northeastern Issan was fertile recruiting ground, and there was a fear it was hoping to break off from Thailand with the backing of China and North Vietnam, which provided weapons, insurgency training and propaganda. The military government countered this by sending in mobile units to provide what people wanted in order to improve the presence and image of the central authority. Education, health and the economy of isolated villages were targeted for improvement, but in many cases the government failed to deliver. There was a major rural development scheme, and US money was flowing in to support the fight against Communism, but the insurgency kept growing. By the mid-1970s hundreds of millions of dollars of unco-ordinated aid had failed to halt a growing insurgency, and the US stopped the flow of cash. Thailand went through a period of instability as the military government fell and elections were held, only for the army to take over again a few years later. Deals were done with China to stop them supporting the Communist Party of Thailand and the violence began to ebb.

With the southern Malay separatist insurgency still raging, General Prem Tinsulanonda took charge of the country and began the further democratisation of Thailand. He gave up his uniform for civilian rule, and developed a new policy for dealing with the militants. He offered amnesty to insurgents; formulated a plan to tackle the political, economic and social problems which had isolated them in the first place through a Southern Border Provinces Administrative Centre; and then launched a major offensive against insurgent heartlands in the hills. Thousands put down their arms and returned to their villages. Weakened support from abroad, an ideological split and aggressive military action dramatically reduced the violence.

His policy of blending security, amnesty and clever politics also brought peace to the southern provinces. The key was persuading Islamic and community leaders in the south to join the newly democratic Thai representative system in an effort to give Malay-Muslims a national voice. The moderates were co-opted into Thai politics and promised to bring returns to their people from within the system. They were rewarded with money for private Islamic schools. Some reached senior positions, but with one foot in government and the other in their Malay-Muslim homeland they failed to bring enough concessions home and lost touch with the grassroots. Some became mired in the trappings of office; Islamic leaders lost moral authority and national politics eventually diluted them. This failure made a contribution to what was coming next.

The Resumption of Violence

A new liberal constitution in 1997 brought a more representative democracy, and with it a billionaire telecoms tycoon and former police bureaucrat to the job of prime minister. Thaksin Shinawatra was very popular, and remains the only Thai prime minister to have been elected for a second term, but his changes to the way southern Thailand was run have been blamed for awakening anger. He reorganised security, swapping in the police for the army and dismantling the successful civilian bodies. He initially blamed criminals and bandits for the violence, launching his own brutal crackdown. A series of incompetent security operations and extra-judicial killings created anger that helped fuel the insurgency. Some academics argue, however, that this new generation of insurgents had been in the making for many years, from the ashes of the previous militants, and their coming of age had coincided with the arrival of Thaksin.

The invasions of Afghanistan, and then Iraq, angered Muslims across the world and led to a surge in Islamic radicalisation, and it was no different in Thailand. The underlying aims were separatist, but jumping on this sense of Muslim persecution across the world it became a jihad. The Islamic element of Malay-Muslim identity became the focus for recruitment and indoctrination centred on the fringes of private Islamic schools, but the movement was very different to the more globalised form of jihad.

Although some attacks began in 2001, it was 2004 when the violence really erupted. In January a large group of militants stormed an army base and stole dozens of weapons, both arming themselves and scoring a major propaganda victory. In April more than a hundred people died after an ill-planned and suicidal simultaneous attack on ten police outposts and a police station was crushed by soldiers – but the way it was handled by security forces again gifted a propaganda victory to the militants. Duncan McCargo, one of the most respected voices on southern Thailand, recounted from interviewees the unreal and naïve way 'groups of men rushed up to military and police post and district offices, with a few guns, some wielding knives but others unarmed, chanting Islamic phrases and apparently believing or hoping that magic spells and holy water would make them invisible, invulnerable, or both.' Most southern Muslims are Sunni, but with animist roots. Through a strange blend of Islam, the Malay belief in magic, and a cult-like following of a charismatic Patani separatist, they met a variety of fates. Some were shot immediately as they ran towards checkpoints, fifteen were found afterwards with a single shot to the back of the head, and thirty-two died inside the Kru-Ze mosque in Pattani province. Militants retreated to the mosque after attacking a nearby police post, and exchanged fire with troops. The military stormed the mosque, the most sacred site for Malay-Muslims, throwing grenades and opening fire – making martyrs of the militants and playing into the hands of the propagandists who blamed the 'kafir Thai government' for striking at the heart of Malay-Muslim symbolism.

A few months later the army's reputation plunged even lower after events in Tak Bai, Narathiwat, where a mass demonstration started in October 2004 after six local men were discovered with guns. Security forces killed a small number of people and arrested hundreds of protesters. Many were tied up and stacked, face down, on top of each other in the back of enclosed military trucks, some as many as five people high. After being driven several hours to an army camp, seventy-eight had died, most through suffocation. Along with revelations about systematic torture of detained militant suspects, it was a low point for the military, undermining its own efforts and having a big impact on encouraging the insurgency. Military tactics changed, but ongoing failings by the security forces, especially among police, reservists and local militia, continued to undermine efforts by the Thai authorities to win the trust and respect they put at the heart of their strategy to end the violence.

The attacks continued apace. There were drive-by motorbike assassinations and bombings, some with secondary blasts to hit the security forces. Civilians became targets, and Muslims suspected of informing were murdered as well as Buddhists. Bangkok-appointed teachers required protection to go to and from school, targeted as the symbol of the state and its insistence on lessons in Thai rather than the Patani dialect. There were gun battles and beheadings, and roadside bombs detonated by radio signal to avoid mobile phone blocking devices. The militarisation of southern Thailand became the norm, as did the daily attacks. A National Reconciliation Commission report urged a focus on 'justice', but said little of decentralisation.

While US troops surged into Iraq, the Thai military launched its own surge into the south to recruit and train local paramilitary forces who they felt understood the dynamics more accurately. It reduced insurgent mobility, led to the capture of some militant cells and local leaders, but while the number of incidents decreased by late 2007, the military admitted the intensity of car bombings increased with bigger blasts in urban areas and more casualties. The violence dipped, but then levelled off. Huge amounts of money were shipped south to try and buy people out of poverty in an effort to turn them against the militants, but the effectiveness of this strategy was questionable.

Changes in the military leadership brought some adaptations to the counter-insurgency strategy and bright young minds turned to the new international doctrine of COIN. The civilian body, the Southern Border Province Administration Centre, which had been abolished by Thaksin, was reinstated. 'What we follow is a mix of what we experienced in the 1960s Communist insurgency in Thailand, some elements from the British experience in the Malaya Emergency, and some we take from the modern US Counter Insurgency strategy of David Petraeus' said Colonel Songwit Noonpackdee, the deputy commander of the Narathiwat Task Force in September 2010, who trained officers in counter-insurgency. He is young, but very talented. The son of a former army commander, his English is flawless and his understanding of and ability to explain the military strategy contrasts with the army spokesman who could say little more by way of explanation than 'development and security with rule of law, not just with guns.'

Colonel Noonpackdee recognises the need to respect cultures, language and religion, and that local people want government officials in the south to come from the south. 'Eighty per cent of people say they are Thai citizens, but [also] ethnic Malays, and we have to accept their identity.' He estimates that 60 per cent of the Thai military effort goes into development rather than security, but is based around giving communities what they want by holding a public hearing and relying on the 'four pillars' of village life: the headman, the religious leader, an elected sub-district head and a local charismatic leader. 'The projects are offered by the top down but are approved from the bottom up and are not big developments. They are in line with the King's "sufficiency economy" of agriculture, house repairs and water resources.' Using that structure and putting forward operating bases out into the villages has brought better intelligence and the colonel believes the insurgents can only operate in half the villages they had three years before. The remote areas are the unstable areas.

With regard to continued accusations of corruption and human rights abuses he says checks and balances are now in place to ensure those caught are treated properly and soldiers keep their discipline. 'The solution will have to be political, but we want to do this through the democratic process, through decentralisation', which is in the constitution. 'It's the people we need to focus on, not the insurgents.'

Colonel Noonpackdee is dedicated to tackling the real problems of the south, but human rights activists and observers argue that for every soldier like him, there are many more in the security forces who come to the south for promotion or to make money through corruption, who show little respect for the local culture, and would rather go the route of targeted killings than gather the evidence to secure conviction in a court of law.

If a political solution is the only way, many believe the government needs to drive the process. Some of Thailand's civilian leaders came up with some good ideas, even breaking a taboo by suggesting some form of self-determination for the south. King Bhumibol Adulyadej is credited with keeping the country together. Criticism of him is illegal under strict and opaque *lèse-majesté* laws, so calls for some level of autonomy in the south have been seen by some as questioning the King's policy of one nation – hence the taboo. But domestic politics have been in disarray, distracting attention from the south, neglected by policy-makers in Bangkok.

Thailand's Big Distraction

In September 2006 Prime Minister Shinawatra was removed in a bloodless military coup, which left deep divisions in the country and marked the start of Thailand's recent period of instability. His populist policies had targeted the country's poorest people in northeastern Issan, with cheap loans and health care schemes winning him the support of millions in what some see as a personal battle for power against the traditional Bangkok elite of the military, the establishment and the bureaucracy. But he limited democratic freedoms ruling as the country's chief executive, and was accused of using his position to enrich his own family. He has since been found guilty of corruption in office, and towards the end of 2010 remained in self-imposed exile outside the country from where he still stirs up supporters by addressing mass rallies by video link and bankrolling their anti-government campaign.

Thai politics became polarised around Thaksin Shinawatra, and very colourful. The People's Alliance for Democracy (PAD) was a middle class group who wore royal yellow and held mass rallies calling on him to resign. They helped precipitate the coup and continued to demonstrate against a new, democratically elected Thaksin-backed ruling party, closing Bangkok's international airports and only stopping when a court banned the ruling party in late 2008, allowing a new coalition government to be formed by the opposition Democrats. Prime Minister Abhisit Vejjajiva, a British-born technocrat, came to power at the end of December 2008 telling parliament he was committed to tackling the violence in the south which was 'a national priority,' emphasising the need to lift emergency rule in the Deep South.

Enraged Thaksin supporters adopted the tactics of mass protest and wore red. The military broke up a demonstration in April 2009, but a year later they were back in even greater numbers. After two months of their blockading central Bangkok with bamboo and tyre barricades and some armed resistance, the military finally broke up the demonstrations firing live rounds. Protesters set fire to a shopping centre and other buildings as they left. In all around ninety people died, most unarmed civilians. The anger remained below the surface and further instability was threatened.

Prime Minister Abhisit Vejjajiva narrowly survived because of military backing. Despite the distractions he appeared committed to the south, using the King's catchphrase: 'Understand, Outreach, Develop'. In short the plan was to respect Muslim-Malay heritage, make local officials accountable, and improve social and economic conditions. The four-year development budget from 2009 was set at $2 billion and plans were laid to hand over some control to the civilian body – but critics call it a compromise, watered down from his initial idea of bringing back civilian rule. The strategy was justice first, better security second, but Mr Abhisit's dependence on the military seemed likely to discourage radical change to the policy in the south. A lot of cash was being given out, but so were a lot of guns.

Polarisation

The women had arrived early in the morning to the Buddhist temple at Trohgen village in Pattani. Most came by scooter. They were middle-aged, and laughed and chatted as the man running the training course prepared to start the lesson. It was September 2009 and the small group of community volunteers had gathered for a refresher course on how to clean their shotguns. Monthira Peng-Iad, a forty-year old farm worker, was the first to stand up in front of the open-air class and disassemble and reassemble the weapon. The interior ministry established thirty-strong volunteer forces in every village – that was a total of around 60,000 people. They were there to protect their communities – villages that were becoming increasingly polarised as minority Buddhists left predominantly Muslim areas and segregation began to draw lines around everyday life.

'It's getting more violent every day', Monthira told me. 'So many of my relatives have been shot and killed I feel bitter inside. I want to know how to shoot, so I can help people in the village.' In a community used to having Muslims and Buddhists living side-by-side in peace, her rhetoric illustrated how divisive the insurgency was becoming. 'It's time to fight otherwise all the Thai Buddhists will be killed. We used to be friends and relatives but now we are divided. Now Muslims see all of us as enemies. They kill us', she said. One human rights group said up to a hundred thousand civilian Buddhists and Muslims had been given guns to protect themselves in the three southern provinces of Thailand, but this is a figure the military denies.

Tit-for-tat violence had become commonplace. On the same day as the training course, there were more armed men on guard outside the Al-Furquan mosque in Ai Payae village, Narathiwat province, than there were at afternoon prayers inside. The group of Muslim men, armed by the government but who did not appear particularly well-trained in weapons safety, were brought in after an attack on the mosque three months earlier when gunmen opened fire, killing ten people and injuring twelve. The bullet holes were still in the glass doors and windows and sprayed in a line on the far wall inside, just above the heads of the kneeling men. Ayu Jeh-Ngoh was shot twice, once in the back and once in the leg as he prayed. He suspected the attackers were from a nearby Buddhist village, taking revenge after a Buddhist had been killed in the area. Others suspected a similar thing, and said everyone knew who was responsible but nobody had been charged with carrying out the attack, and they said the investigation did not appear to be going anywhere. Those close to the Thai military say intelligence has improved dramatically since 2007 at the smaller, district level, but has not led to a greater number of arrests or successful prosecutions. Human rights activists point to the number of assassinations and targeted killings and argue this adds to a sense of impunity over vigilantism and does little to build confidence in a justice system identified as so important to resolving conflict.

The cycle of violence complicates an already difficult picture. Deep South Watch, at the Prince of Songkla University in Pattani, has been keeping a close track of the deaths and injuries. Academic Srisompob Jipiromsri believes 60 per cent are directly linked to the insurgency, and a further 10–15 per cent are related to it in some way. The rest are personal or criminal, but are only possible because of the insecurity.

Violent insurgencies generate instability and lawlessness. This encourages and creates the space for criminals and warlords, drugs smugglers and gun runners, especially around international borders. The support industries for insurgency breed and spread their tentacles. An ideological battle turns into big business as the insurgents and the local mafia work with each other and sometimes against each other, creating more instability and blurring the lines between them. The counter-insurgency element of buying hearts and minds means there is a lot of money around. Poorly paid police, soldiers and local militia are corrupted by the opportunities to make money, and corruption is rife among Thailand's police. The financial incentive is to keep the insecurity going rather than stop it. The lessons from Afghanistan reflect this. The conservative Islamic roots of the Taliban, welcomed in the south amid civil war, became corrupted by power and ambition as they spread in an effort to take control of the entire country – something they almost achieved. Today, twenty years after their movement began, the insurgency has no single leader or specific demand. It is funded by opium profits; its weapons and explosives move back up the same smuggling routes the drugs move down. Corrupt local officials and a weak government push the people into the hands of the insurgents. Troops are lured into making mistakes – in Afghanistan's case foreign troops make this far worse. Money may flood in to try and lift people from poverty, but with no rule of law, no justice and no security, ending the violence and returning to peace and stability is incredibly difficult and cannot be bought.

Thailand has no foreign troop presence and a much smaller border. The insurgents limit themselves by geography and are not entwined with Al-Qa'ida or global terror networks. But the complexities surrounding the business of instability make it incredibly difficult to resolve without resorting to some form of concession to broad demands. Take away or dilute the underlying grievances among the majority, and you isolate the violent minority. This is where many academics agree the only way forward is this awkward question of some level of autonomy, and talking to the insurgents.

Give and Talk

An embattled prime minister, Abhisit Vejjajiva is a big fan of reconciliation. After the red shirt protests in 2010, he began a long national reconciliation process, setting up committees, investigations and a truth commission. Just as efforts were going on behind the scenes to stabilise Thai politics, negotiations were also taking place with people hopefully in a position to help broker peace in southern Thailand. The Thai and Malaysian governments, the military and international academic groups had all been in discussions, not necessarily with the same people.

The insurgents in southern Thailand do not publicly claim responsibility for attacks and equally do not make demands. Who, if anyone, leads them has divided opinion. There is a broad agreement they operate in a loose cell structure with some limited co-ordination. Evidence presented by the academic Marc Askew, based on months living and working in the south and interviews with arrested militants, suggests: 'there is a clandestine and nebulous network of groups with no distinct leadership where loosely structured and led groups decide targets for themselves.' He says those arrested appeared to know little of any structure outside their own cell, adding: 'this is a war of old men being fought by young men.' What he means is that the groups which led the violence in the 1960s and 1970s may have driven the rhetoric then, and claim a role now, but in reality they no longer have control over the fighters on the ground today, who have no credible political wing. The tactics of this new generation of fighter are different: the increased Islamic element to their recruiting; the targeting of civilians and Muslims suspected of collaborating; and a move away from fighting in the hills to running an insurgency from within the population. Journalist and southern specialist Don Pathan says there are cells of much younger fighters in 90 per cent of villages, and while he agrees they are a 'new generation with old grievances,' he insists a solution cannot be possible without the involvement of the old guard who are trying to reinvent themselves through this process. He has identified thirty leaders who go to and from Malaysia to meet the traditional power-brokers.

The old groups most discussed are BRN-Coordinate (a branch of the Barisan Revolusi Nasional, or National Revolutionary Front) and the Patani United Liberation Organisation (PULO) which is thought to have three factions. Since the violence began again in 2004 both have claimed a significant role, but in reality many observers argue they may only have lines of communication with the new fighters rather than control over them. That loose relationship has been enough for continuing talks to be held with BRN-C, but critics say there has been no evidence they have succeeded in getting any active armed factions to the table. The 'old guard', which includes an alphabet soup of other groups, do not work well together and the fighters on the ground are even more disparate. Media reports often talk of the 'RKK' which are a small guerrilla force sometimes linked to BRN-C, but most commentators agree there are many floating cells or groups that owe allegiance to nobody, and the longer the crisis goes on the more difficult it will be to bring them to the table. While it was clear there was co-ordination over the simultaneous attacks in 2004, the military surge and improved intelligence may well have cut those connections and forced each group to be more self-contained. It could also explain why the level of violence is not expanding or developing onto a new tactical level. One apparent step forward came in July 2010 when a new group, claiming to bring together BRN-C and PULO, announced a ceasefire had been held in three districts in the previous month, but doubts were cast as it had not been announced before and some violence did continue. Critical analysts have said it perhaps said more about how little control the old guard have, rather than how much, as it had intended.

Negotiations are one tool in the box, but opinion is moving towards giving the majority of people in the south a little of what they apparently want to starve the militants of – some form of autonomy.

Sunai Pasuk of Human Rights Watch is considered an authority on southern Thailand. He agrees that winning hearts and minds of the 1.8 million Malay-Muslims is the only way to end the insurgency, but giving them cultural and ethno-religious respect would be far more effective than using development projects. He says the military and security forces 'act with impunity and do not see themselves open to any accountability.' Teaching the Patani dialect in schools would be a start, as would apologising for how they have been treated and delivering on promises to maintain their identity within the Thai state. There are a range of suggestions for decentralisation, from changing the whole regional structure of government, to introducing a new ministry devoted to the southern provinces as Srisompob Jipiromsri from Deep South Watch has proposed. He also suggests devolution, using the model of Northern Ireland in the UK as proof that power can be devolved without destroying the unitary state, or looking at the regional example of Aceh in Indonesia. Aceh has been seized upon by academics as a good model Thailand could follow. What appears to be lacking is a stable and confident government able to make promises and to keep them over the medium term, without power changing hands.

Conclusion

Much of the current thinking says Thailand's southern insurgency has its roots in an historical struggle for separatism based on the cultural identity of being Malay-Muslim. The government's centralised and unitary policies have alienated an ethnic minority on the fringe of the state, who have been made to feel like second-class citizens. The tactics and objectives of the guerrilla war fought by organised groups in the 1960s and 70s have changed as radical Islamic teaching and rhetoric has gained importance for recruiting and operating small, self-contained militant cells. The global Islamic reaction to Western foreign policy (particularly that of the US) after 9/11 has helped provide a focus, but religion is used as a motivator as opposed to the core aim of the insurgency. Confined to three provinces of southern Thailand and apparently not willing or able to spread its violence further afield, or to target Westerners, the southern insurgency is very different from other groups linked to global extremist networks.

Over-confidence and aggressive use of violence by Thaksin Shinawatra's security forces gave the insurgency the space, at the right time, to build its support base and set up a violent network of militants. Efforts to improve justice and security to win the people's trust are still undermined by corrupt and self-serving elements within the security forces. Development money is widely seen as being wasted or creamed off, and only a fraction reaches those to whom it is promised. A political solution is seen by many as the only solution, but like Afghanistan, the problem is who to talk to? Traditional groups lack command and control of the disparate militant cells, which appear to be only loosely co-ordinated, so negotiations must take place with many different elements. Giving some form of active decentralisation, or self-governance, to the three southern provinces is now being seen as a better way to win the population's support and trust, isolating the insurgents by undermining and diluting their main grievance and perhaps encouraging them to the negotiating table. But all this depends on a strong government while Thailand faces more political uncertainty and instability as its revered but aging monarch remains in hospital and pro-Thaksin red shirt supporters continue their anti-government campaign. Meanwhile, the killings go on.

THE LESSONS FROM NORTHERN IRELAND: COMPARISONS WITH IRAQ AND AFGHANISTAN

Chris Brown

It has been argued that British soldiers were better prepared for the contemporary wars in Iraq and Afghanistan as a result of their experience from Northern Ireland. But were they? And how similar were these different campaigns?

There is little doubt that the British experience of counter-insurgency in Northern Ireland gave – or should have given – British soldiers an initial advantage over their US counterparts when it came to Iraq and Afghanistan. Thirty-plus years of fighting a tenacious insurgency in Northern Ireland, recognising the essential contribution of intelligence and developing appropriate intelligence architectures to deal with the threat, countering improvised explosive devices (IEDs) and working with the police, the judiciary, the population and the media on a day-to-day, face-to-face basis, had inculcated broad COIN skills in a generation of British soldiers, which the US Army could not claim to have. Residual Vietnam experience was distant and confined to the highest ranks. In any case, it had largely been expunged both institutionally and by more recent US experience, which had emphasised manoeuvre warfare at which the US had no equal by 2003. The US military had been reconstructed, largely by those who combined the experience of Vietnam with an intellectual rigour to create an all-arms war-fighting capability second to none, primarily to counter the Warsaw Pact threat, but capable of dealing with the unexpected, such as the 1990 liberation of Kuwait.[1]

And it was not just the British military that had the edge: Northern Ireland had created a broader COIN expertise within the police and the civil administration, which could have been utilised in Iraq and Afghanistan. But the British advantage was squandered. Instead of building on the foundation of Northern Ireland and taking the relevant lessons forward into Iraq and Afghanistan, discarding the elements which were irrelevant, the British Army was slow to adjust to the specific requirements of both theatres. The US, unencumbered by such baggage, transformed more quickly. Why was this?

Countering Insurgency from a National Perspective

The security forces in Northern Ireland were all working to a single plan. Yes, there was friction between the various elements, but differences were ironed out; mostly in the province under the auspices of the Security Policy Meeting, chaired by the secretary of state for Northern Ireland and comprising the heads of all elements of the security apparatus. Military and police boundaries, for example, which were different in the initial stages of the campaign – thereby leading to lapses in co-ordination – were made co-terminous once police primacy was established. Where reinforcement was required at the national level, Prime Minister Tony Blair invested considerable enduring personal commitment to the peace process after his election in 1997. And yes, there were external influences such as the role played by the Irish government in Dublin, US Senator George Mitchell and the Independent Decommissioning and Monitoring Commissions – but they were largely supportive of a single coherent strategy. In Iraq and Afghanistan, such coherence was more difficult to achieve, largely and simply because coalitions and alliances inherently work not only to a coalition or alliance strategy, but also to individual national agendas. And in 'coalitions of the willing' – and Afghanistan has shown that, even with the invocation of Article V of the Washington Treaty, the NATO ISAF presence is still fundamentally dependent on individual national will – the national agenda will invariably prevail.

All troop-contributing nations appoint representatives outside the NATO or coalition chain of command who articulate national policy, not least in the form of caveats on what their forces will and will not do. Each nation takes its own stance on tricky legal issues such as detention. This is nothing new – alliances have always been similarly beset – but if these differences are highlighted in advance, they are much easier to work with. Missions can be appropriately tailored; national sensitivities can be avoided. The real problems come when national reservations are declared at a late stage in the planning or even in the execution of an operation.

The challenge is not purely a military one. The attempt in Bonn to divide responsibility for various aspects of rebuilding Afghanistan led to unco-ordinated pillars of activity, epitomised by the disparity between the development of the Afghan National Army, the Afghan National Police and the justice system. That imbalance between police and military will be felt in Afghanistan for many years to come in a way which was evident in Northern Ireland from the outset (though it was an imbalance that eventually drove the return to police primacy by the mid-1970s, and the eventual removal of the military element from the policing role). The specific lesson is that a useful indicator of the ending of an insurgency is the ability of the police to cope with the residual security challenge. In Iraq and Afghanistan initial under-investment in the police has, and will, perpetuate reliance on the military, which both distorts the security balance and potentially cedes an advantage to the insurgents. The wider lesson is that a coalition or alliance needs a means of harmonising a COIN strategy. In Afghanistan, the North Atlantic Council (NAC) is designed to provide coherence of NATO strategy, but frequently proved unwieldy or side-tracked by tactical detail and individual national agendas. For Iraq, nations were reluctant to join a coalition in which they had no voice at the highest level. Coalition nations produced 'work-arounds': embedded staff with the US Central Command Headquarters in Tampa, Florida, and headquarters in theatre; but by mid-2009 it was a coalition of one. Partly in order to foster coherence, the US is overly polite in dealing with the delinquency of its allies. Wikileaks may expose real US feelings, but although US leaders in public will invariably champion the advantages rather than the disadvantages of coalitions and alliances, Iraq and Afghanistan have spawned a generation of middle-management US leaders whose poor opinion of allies will colour their judgment as they reach higher positions. 'The Coalition' is more often than not used by US speakers to denote nations other than the US.

Campaign Coherence

If strategic coherence between contributing nations was difficult to achieve for Iraq and Afghanistan, the lack of coherence between individual nations' organs of government added a further layer of complexity which did not exist in Northern Ireland. A single UK government minister responsible for Northern Ireland provided a COIN campaign focus. This did not exist in any nation involved in Iraq or Afghanistan, even the UK. At the theatre level all nations involved in Iraq or Afghanistan bemoan(ed) the lack of co-ordination within their national capitals.

In general, it is much easier to co-ordinate within theatre, where representatives of different government organisations are forced together and needs must, than in the comfortable isolation of a ministry in Washington, Whitehall or wherever. But for the military this failure to co-ordinate within national capitals gets to the heart of a COIN campaign: there is no purely military solution. The military can at best provide security and kill or capture terrorists. But without strategic co-ordination of the economic, political, social and judicial lines of operation, the military effort is doomed to failure. In Northern Ireland, the insurgency was never going to be defeated without changes to the social and economic fabric of the province which had been the primary cause of the Troubles. Likewise in Iraq, the Sunni minority would never have been likely to abstain from violence against a regime bent on excluding them. In Afghanistan, support for the Taliban is unlikely to diminish until the average villager in the south believes that it is economically and politically more attractive to pledge loyalty to the Kabul regime than the Quetta insurgency.

Herein lies a fundamental difference between Northern Ireland, and Iraq or Afghanistan, and care must be taken to draw the right lessons: as soon as Iraq and Afghanistan were endowed with democracy, their respective governments became a further cog in an already unwieldy machine. Although the Northern Ireland Assembly has been an additional factor,[2] its powers, indeed its very existence, remain in the gift of the British government. Nevertheless, the international aid effort in Iraq and Afghanistan (both governmental and non-governmental) has lacked coherence, both in itself and with security – something that never afflicted the social and economic lines of the COIN campaign in Northern Ireland. Creations such as Provincial Reconstruction Teams in theatre and the Post-Conflict Reconstruction Unit[3] in London addressed these shortcomings, but all took time to reach fruition. From a British perspective, countering insurgency within a multinational context, particularly in a US-led coalition, the creation of a National Security Council (NSC) in 2010 provides a focus not only for co-ordination between UK government ministries, but also a central mouthpiece to speak to other allies. This should address the US and US NSC's difficulty in locating a single point of contact with other nations, which has been evident since the planning for Iraq and Afghanistan in 2002.

Baggage

Purists might argue that, as with strategy, there should be a single coalition or alliance doctrine on COIN. But, as described above, there will invariably be differences of national legal interpretation. And in exactly the same way as British COIN doctrine at the start of the 'Troubles' in Northern Ireland had been shaped by post-Second World War colonial experience – early footage shows British soldiers, bayonets fixed, forming squares and training to roll out banners proclaiming rioting illegal followed by shooting 'the insurgent in the red shirt' in order to disperse the crowd – the British approach in southern Iraq echoed tactics from Northern Ireland.

British commanders felt comfortable with a 'soft' approach – epitomised by berets as opposed to helmets – in a way that many US counterparts considered reckless. When the first IED threats appeared later in 2003, the instinctive solution was to take 'Snatch' Land Rovers from Northern Ireland in order to provide protection in Basra. British pride was enhanced by being able to pass on experience of IEDs to US forces. But the insurgency proved fundamentally different and the IEDs were frequently initiated by suicide – something that had never intentionally occurred in Northern Ireland. Methods that work in one situation can actually do more harm than good in another. The key is to understand the situation itself and why a particular tactic was successful. In reality, Northern Ireland had been relatively benign since the mid-1990s so the Northern Ireland COIN baggage carried by the British Army into Basra and Helmand was in many ways a watered-down version of that which had brought success during the 1980s. Even so, some of NATO's simplistic *mutatis mutandis* approach to the planning for Kosovo in 1999 – applying the template used in Bosnia – had been rightly criticised in British circles.

It took the UK longer to shed the Northern Ireland COIN template than it took the US to work out COIN from scratch. Highlighting others' shortcomings is frequently easier than addressing one's own. In 2005, the UK Brigadier Nigel Aylwin Foster wrote a critique of the US approach in Iraq.[4] This was accepted in US circles with an openness unlikely to be seen anywhere else. It was one of a series of catalysts for a fundamental review of US COIN doctrine which led to the first update of US COIN doctrine for twenty years: joint US Army and Marine Corps doctrine. In contrast, although the need for updated UK COIN doctrine was highlighted as early as 2004, it was not until 2009 that it went to press, too late for Iraq. The lesson here is that intellectual rigour and mental agility are essential elements of a successful COIN campaign. It took time for the British security forces to work that out in Northern Ireland; similar delay resulted in the situations in both Iraq and Afghanistan getting worse before they got better.

Publication of erudite doctrine is one thing; the challenge is in achieving its widespread adoption. The increasing reliance in all armies, but particularly in those of the US and UK, on simulation in training has spawned a generation of junior commanders who look to doctrine for guidance and who are prepared to hold their hands up when they get it wrong in training – the simulator does not lie so complaining is pointless – in the desire to improve before actual combat operations. There is no equivalent of simulation at the strategic level; there is little pan-government strategic doctrine; and some UK government departments have no process with which to distil lessons. At the strategic level, it is much easier to defray blame than at the tactical level. The interesting lesson here is that the desire to learn from lessons and the willingness to embrace doctrine vary considerably across the UK COIN apparatus. Even as late as 2010 there was still disagreement within the Ministry of Defence (MoD) on the definition of strategy, let alone its articulation. Moreover, the objective measurement of campaign success has not been consistently applied by the UK to the campaigns in Iraq and Afghanistan in the way in which it was carried out by the US or the way in which it was applied by the UK in Northern Ireland. With Afghanistan, it has not helped that nations adopted different measures of effectiveness from NATO: an easy solution in comparison to achieving NAC consensus on a common set of criteria, but a cop out that only increases Alliance divergence.

Resources

The COIN security framework has to be sufficient to protect the population from the insurgents. For the counter-insurgency in

Northern Ireland was never discretionary; nor did the budget for the campaign ever look like breaking the bank. This is partly a question of scale; it is also a question of national resolve, which has been much weaker, particularly for Iraq. In Northern Ireland, because the British Army was sized to play its role in the defeat of Soviet aggression in Europe, the resources both in manpower and equipment already largely existed. Troop strengths reached almost 30,000 (overall a ratio to the population of around 1:50, but actually much more concentrated at the point of main effort), but a comparison of other missions shows a wide disparity of troop density, in relation to coverage of both ground and population:

The Iraqi figures in the table above mask the discrepancy between US and other nations' security forces. The UK's contribution reduced sharply after the initial combat operation. Political statements about

Table 6: Comparison of Peak International Troop Strength by Territory and Population, up to 2004.

Location	Number of international troops		
	At peak	per km^2	per head of population
Kosovo	40,000	1 per 0.3 km	1 per 50
Bosnia	60,000	1 per 0.85 km	1 per 66
East Timor	9,000	1 per 1.6 km	1 per 111
Iraq	155,000	1 per 2.8 km	1 per 161
Somalia	40,000	1 per 16.0 km	1 per 200
Liberia	11,000 MEF: 2,200	1 per 8.0 km	1 per 265
Sierra Leone	18,000	1 per 4.0 km	1 per 300
Haiti	20,000	1 per 1.5 km	1 per 375
Afghanistan	OEF: 20,000 ISAF: 6,000	1 per 25.0 km	1 per 1,115

Source: Michael Bhatia, Kevin Lanigan and Philip Wilkinson, 'Minimal Investments, Minimal Results: The Failure of Security Policy in Afghanistan', Afghanistan Research and Evaluation Unit briefing paper, June 2004.

continuing withdrawals reduced British force levels to a point where, by 2007 as US forces were surging, the UK had insufficient security force strength to carry out its mission in Basra effectively: visibility in the city, let alone control of insurgent activity, was lost. By early 2008 this led to a situation where Iraqi forces, supported by US assets, were brought in to re-establish security in Basra.

In Afghanistan in 2004 the 6,000 ISAF troops were largely deployed in Kabul. The relatively high concentration of forces in the capital created what became known as the 'the ISAF effect': a degree of security that was not evident outside Kabul. Extending the ISAF effect beyond Kabul became a goal frustrated at that time by nations' unwillingness to provide the manpower required, variously estimated at around 100,000 troops. NATO therefore embarked on an incremental approach addressing the relatively benign north, followed by the west, and only in 2006 the heart of the insurgency in the south and east. The irony is that ISAF now numbers around 140,000. The British presence has moved from a force of 3,500 covering the whole of Helmand province in 2006, to a force at the time of writing almost three times that size covering one twentieth of the area. Moreover, the Afghan National Security Forces are now making their own significant contribution. The lack of appropriate levels of security force presence during the intervening six years ceded to the insurgents an advantage, which will now take several more years to turn around. The common lesson here is that COIN frequently demands more 'boots on the ground' than war fighting. The equally important lesson is that force levels must be driven by operational objectives rather than any political impetus for reduction in troop numbers. In this context, the US and UK governments' commitment to a timescale for withdrawal risks a repeat of Iraq.

In Northern Ireland, the drawdown of British forces was genuinely driven by the operational requirement. Moreover, in Northern Ireland the police were effectively resourced, and the Security Service main effort was focused on Irish republican terrorism, undistracted by Islamic extremism for the majority of the campaign. The generic importance of intelligence in COIN is rightly deserving of its own chapter in this volume, but the specific requirements of Northern Ireland led to a sophisticated intelligence structure, previously unmatched in British history. The specialised equipment requirements of COIN in Northern Ireland were easily covered by drawing on Treasury contingency funds rather than the core MoD budget under the Urgent Operational Requirement (UOR) process. This process was adapted for the requirements of Iraq and Afghanistan, greatly expanded, but inevitably capped by both internal MoD reluctance to accept that existing COIN solutions, mostly procured for Northern Ireland, were inadequate in these new theatres, and by a Treasury that saw expenditure as more discretionary. The added challenges of operating in a foreign country, particularly counter-terrorist targeting, have required advances in surveillance and biometrics, the lack of which would have rendered such campaigns ineffective even a decade ago. Heavy reliance on US support in these areas has been necessary in order to operate effectively.

Northern Ireland never became the MoD's main effort in the way in which Iraq and Afghanistan did; and so a funding process designed to cope with minor requirements of a backwater campaign became the mainstay of funding equipment for the MoD's main effort. This has led to a significant mismatch between the state of the equipment which a British soldier uses on operations in Iraq and Afghanistan and the equipment to which he or she returns for training. The two processes – UORs and the core MoD budget – have yet to be fully harmonised to the extent that the British Army could guarantee being effectively equipped for likely future conflict.

The one area of the COIN campaign in Northern Ireland that distorted the economy was the creation of a bloated public sector to provide jobs for people who might otherwise be unemployed, and thereby more susceptible to the attractions of insurgent activity.

Northern Ireland remains the UK region most heavily subsidised by government central funds. 'Normalisation' in Northern Ireland and, with it, a real need to reduce public sector employment comes at a time when the 'Celtic Tiger' boom is over and unemployment throughout Ireland increasing, leading to a real danger that the benefit of this aspect of the COIN campaign could be undone. On a much larger scale, but similar in principle, the Afghan economy will be distorted for the foreseeable future by the requirement for the US to fund security forces patently unaffordable from within Afghan national resources.

Legitimacy

Northern Ireland marked a watershed in terms of the British Army's understanding of the need to retain legitimacy, in much the same way as the media exposure of US illegitimate action in Vietnam had changed US Army attitudes and procedures; rule of law 'expediency does not pay. Departing from international humanitarian law even just a little bit is like being just a little bit pregnant.'[5] The situation in Northern Ireland had deteriorated to the extent that republicans referred to the British Army as 'a party to the conflict'. The lost ground was never completely recovered; the past still dogs the reputation and preoccupation with 'the past' shows little sign of easing. And yet the principle was again breached in Iraq, both by US and British forces. In order to avoid this situation, or recover from it, sustained political engagement at the highest level is required.

Doing the Right Thing Right

British shortcomings in Iraq and Afghanistan were not confined to inappropriate tactics from Northern Ireland being applied – doing the wrong thing. In some cases, British experiences in Northern Ireland were perfectly appropriate to Iraq and Afghanistan. But the right lessons taken from Northern Ireland were applied in the wrong way. This was, and remains, particularly apposite in the context of personnel policy. Although at the tactical level most battalions conducted six-month roulement tours of Northern Ireland, this policy was supplemented at the tactical level with battalions based in Northern Ireland for two years. Although these 'resident' battalions might not have sustained the tempo of activity of their roulement counterparts, they provided essential continuity by reinforcing roulement battalions and holding ground in less troublesome areas.

No such system has operated in Iraq or Afghanistan. The US, partly in recognition of this and partly because force levels would have been more difficult, if not impossible, to achieve on the basis of six-month tour lengths, adopted a twelve-month roulement policy.[6] Whether by design or necessity, this immediately gave US forces an advantage in terms of continuity in conflicts where intelligence and personal relationships with local leaders are key. And, as the campaigns in both Iraq and Afghanistan transition to an indigenous lead, the mentoring role which is increasingly being played by external forces lends itself to greater continuity than can be provided by six-month tours. Moreover, the creation of the Ulster Defence Regiment,[7] locally recruited and living in the community, provided continuity in Northern Ireland, particularly in quieter areas, allowing regular roulement battalions to concentrate on pockets of insurgent activity.

The absence of effective Iraqi and Afghan security forces until relatively late in the respective campaigns again denied the security forces the advantages they had enjoyed in Northern Ireland. Even now, the majority of Afghan National Security Forces personnel deployed in Helmand are from the north of Afghanistan: to the Pashtuns, they are foreigners who neither have a detailed understanding of southern Afghanistan nor enjoy acceptance by the local communities. In Oman a similar transition was accompanied by longer British tours and a higher percentage of 'loan service' attachments.

The MoD's adherence to six-month tours in Afghanistan is as much to do with preservation of force structures as operational efficacy. The biggest disadvantage of a six-month standard tour length in COIN is felt at the operational level.[8] In Northern Ireland the formation headquarters, down to and including brigade level, were manned by personnel on two-year postings, on average. Campaign continuity was thereby ensured. On the other hand, in Iraq and Afghanistan, successive British brigade commanders, all on six-month tours, as a consequence perceive an opportunity to create the decisive campaign breakthrough on their watch and, in so doing, enhance their personal career prospects. In Afghanistan in 2005 the then-US Combined Forces Command-Afghanistan commander, Lieutenant General Barno, remarked that in his twenty-plus month tour, he had seen four separate NATO ISAF commanders, and their headquarters each spend two months learning the job, two months doing effective work, and then spend their final two months planning and looking forward to hand over. The continuity role which had been provided in theatre in Northern Ireland was assumed *faute de mieux* by the Permanent Joint Headquarters (PJHQ) in the UK national sense and by JFC Brunssum in the NATO role. Neither was designed or positioned to play such a role – both are geographically dislocated from the centres of strategic and tactical direction, and communication between the two and with US Central Command in Tampa, Florida inevitably led to divergence and skewed the command structure from what in Northern Ireland had been simple and effective.

This failure to apply the lessons of Northern Ireland to Iraq or Afghanistan undermined understanding of the insurgency. Though British commanders may have deluded themselves that they inherently understood the nature of the issues at stake in Northern Ireland, they nevertheless spoke the same language, and regular and prolonged exposure to Northern Ireland reinforced that understanding. But the Iraqi and Afghan campaigns demonstrated other essential tools of COIN: the need for a deep understanding of the society, culture and basis of the insurgency – together with a linguistic ability to communicate.

The Regional Dimension

An insurgency where both the insurgents and the affected state can operate in isolation from any wider context is now a rarity. To a certain extent this has always been the case – insurgents have frequently needed an external safe haven from which to operate – but the globalisation of such conflicts, particularly through modern media, has imparted a regional, if not global, dimension to most insurgencies. Northern Ireland, despite the government's categorisation of it as an internal security matter and initial reluctance to engage externally, was never going to be solved without the assistance of the Irish government.

It took time for Dublin to realise that republican terrorism was just as much a threat to peace south of the border as north, but that realisation, together with political and economic maturity, became a powerful combination that increasingly denied the terrorist moral support, safe havens and funding. Saddam Hussein's Iraq, so long the pariah of the Middle East, let alone the Western world, found its post-Saddam insurgency increasingly affected by regional factors.

The porosity of the Syrian and Iranian borders enabled both Sunni and Shi'a extremism to destabilise the fragile fledgling Iraqi state in the period from 2003. In Afghanistan the regional effect is even more pronounced. For centuries a buffer state for neighbours and colonial powers alike, the insurgency will never be defeated without addressing the wider, particularly Pakistani, dimension. The lesson therefore is a common one in the sense that COIN will seldom be bounded by the geography of the affected state: it is important to recognise the specific regional factors affecting a given insurgency and embrace them in the COIN strategy. In the case of Iraq and Afghanistan, the regional effect of Iran demonstrates not only the danger of failing to encompass that specific dynamic with regard to the specific insurgency, but also the potential to develop into a conflict in its own right.

Conclusion

There is no such thing as a standard insurgency. Each has its own distinct characteristics. If counter-insurgency is to be successful, the nature of the insurgency has to be clearly understood by those who practise COIN. Only with such an understanding can the insurgency be broken down into its constituent parts and defeated in detail. Without such an understanding the best outcome is stalemate: the more likely result will be elements of the COIN campaign undermining any successful tactical actions to the overall detriment of the campaign and the downward spiral to insurgent victory. In Northern Ireland it took less than three years, from 1969 to 1972, to achieve such a downward spiral and stare into an abyss where more British security forces personnel were killed than in the first five years of the campaigns in Iraq and Afghanistan. The main reason was the inappropriate campaign waged by the British security forces from 1969 to 1972. Northern Ireland, Iraq and Afghanistan have all shown that there is a limited honeymoon period within which the underlying causes of the insurgency need to be addressed. In all three cases, that honeymoon period was squandered. In Northern Ireland it then took more than thirty years of painstaking counter-insurgency – based on a detailed understanding of the insurgency and intelligence structures to match – to restore a semblance of normality. In Iraq, the nadir was also reached three years after the Coalition intervention. In Afghanistan, it took slightly longer to plumb the depths and, while today there is a sense of improvement, the jury is still out on whether the COIN campaign in both Iraq and Afghanistan will lead to long-term stability, not least when the external assistance, so vital to the campaign, is removed. The key question now is whether the experience of Iraq and Afghanistan will ensure that British and US forces are better prepared for the next COIN campaign.

COKE ISN'T IT: CHANGING A CULTURE AND IMAGE OF VIOLENCE IN COLOMBIA

Greg Mills[*]

> The world must understand that this conflict requires unconventional, imaginative and transparent solutions. ... We will start an administration which is honest, efficient and austere. It cannot work miracles, but it will work.
>
> (Alvaro Uribe, 8 August 2002)[1]

> This operation ... is a turning point, and I believe, with a good margin of confidence, that we can say this is the beginning of the end for the FARC.
>
> (Juan Manuel Santos, 26 September 2010)[2]

Cali, Colombia's third-largest city has a terrible reputation to live down – the Cali Cartel. Then US Drug Enforcement Agency chief Thomas Constantine described it in the early 1990s as 'The biggest, most powerful crime syndicate we've ever known'.[3]

---

[*] This article is partly based on research conducted in Colombia in December 2006, March 2009 and December 2010, including in Bogotá, Medellin, Cartagena and Cali. Some of the 2006 material appeared in Greg Mills and Lyal White, 'Killing Pablo's Image: Security and State-Building in Colombia', *RUSI Journal* (Vol. 152, No. 1, February 2007). Grateful thanks to Claudia Torres, Alejandro Eder Garcés, Juan-Carlos Pinzon, Juan-Carlos Echeverry and the others who helped the author in Colombia in December 2010.

Formed in the 1960s, at the height of its reign twenty years later, the Cartel controlled as much as 90 per cent of the global cocaine market, even though it had diversified into other front businesses and drug types. It was an extremely sophisticated enterprise, less paramilitary than Italian mafia, 'more likely to bribe rather than kill' according to Cali's former mayor Dr Rodrigo Guerrero, and with tentacles deep into the political hierarchy, including the funding of Ernesto Samper Pizano's successful 1994 presidential campaign.[4] The Cartel's business manager had a Harvard MBA, while its decentralised cell structure allowed it to operate akin to a guerrilla organisation, with military, narco-trafficking, political, financial and legal cells all operating virtually independently. After increasing US-led success at drug busts against a cartel once considered as above the law on account of its political connects, in 1995 six of the seven heads of the cartel were arrested and incarcerated.

Today Cali has regained its reputation as a principal commercial centre. Yumbo in the city's northern suburbs near the airport is a major industrial hub which includes the world's second-largest brewer SABMiller. Residential and commercial construction is booming, from shopping malls to corporate headquarters.

Although crime remains a serious problem, and remnants of the FARC (Fuerzas Armadas Revolucionarias de Colombia – Revolutionary Armed Forces of Colombia) rebel group roam the mountains of either side of the fertile Valle del Cauca region along with narco-trafficking *Bandas Criminales* (known colloquially as 'BACRIM'), much activity has returned to the pre-drug days, when Cali was famed for its sugar *haciendas* [plantations], today producing 2.6 million tonnes in sugar and 325 million litres of alcohol from 200,000 hectares, earning $2 billion in exports. Not only that, however, but other, more productive and valuable forms of farming activity are occurring, making renewed fighting ever less likely.

Established in 2000, VallenPaz [Valley in Peace] works closely with government and other institutions for the transformation of the rural southwestern zones in the Valle de Cauca and Cauca regions around and south of Cali. It focuses on transforming plantation agriculture into higher-value, commercially sustainable, diverse smallholdings, by 2010 working with 8,000 farmers. With higher incomes has come greater prosperity and peace, with the coca producers and drug traffickers moving higher into the mountains to the city's south. One of the farmers, Guillermo, had moved to the area from the violent eastern department of Caquetá seven years before, where he had worked as a coca farmer (and likely FARC member), earning never more than $60 monthly to support his family of five. The VallenPaz scheme in Caloto in Cauca department took 53 hectares of run-down cattle-farming land and divided it up between ten families into smaller *fincas* [farms]. Their average monthly income was now $1,200 from a diversified range of products, including cocoa, pineapples, yucca, plantain and grapes, where the farmers carefully reinvested in the land, plants, irrigation facilities and buildings. Both Guillermo and another farmer, Jorge, agreed: 'It has changed our lives. We are settled. We are never going to move.'

Cali is not the only place in Colombia which has changed dramatically in the 2000s. The hedonistic thespian Rupert Everett once wrote of the Caribbean tourist mecca, Cartagena, that 'there was a bar near the port where breakfast was known as *blanco y negro*: a line of coke and a strong cup of coffee'.[5] This has long been the popular image of the Latin American state – a country out of control, hooked on a cocktail of drugs, power, exotic women, brutal right-wing paramilitaries, and radical Marxist and Maoist guerrillas, all bent on making the country ungovernable. But it is an impression out of kilter with contemporary Colombia.

Take Medillin, once the home of the notorious drug lord Pablo Escobar, listed in the 1980s as the seventh-richest man in the world from his share of the global cocaine trade. Since the former car thief was tracked down and killed by police operating in concert with local vigilantes (supported by the then rival Cali Cartel) and US special forces in a local Medillin *barrio* [suburb] in December 1993, Colombia's second-largest city has become a booming metropolis. This reflects the national economic growth averaging 5 per cent annually since 2002, up from just 1.5 per cent before this time. There have also been marked improvements in education and health. The murder rate in Medillin, once the highest in the world, has fallen dramatically over the past decade, and nationally the figure was more than halved between 2001 and 2010. At its peak in the mid-1990s, Colombia experienced 36,000 murders annually (fifteen times the level of the United States), ten kidnappings daily, and seventy-five weekly political assassinations[6] as the military, police, guerrillas, drug lords and paramilitaries all wrestled for control. Some 3,000 police were killed during 1997–2001 alone.[7]

The improvement in security has enabled the Colombian economy to develop, creating a positive cycle of governance, growth and reinforcing stability.

Although the drug trade has helped to stoke criminal violence and, since the end of the Cold War, lubricate the contemporary insurgency, Colombia's political history has been a continuously violent one. From the time of the sixteenth-century colonial conquest through the period of increased resistance to Spanish rule in the eighteenth century to the war of independence led by Simón Bolivar between 1812 and 1819, the state experienced widespread violence. During the nineteenth century, Colombia experienced no fewer than nine civil wars, and more than fifty anti-government insurrections. The 1899 'War of a Thousand Days' left 100,000 dead and led to the loss of control over Panama as a result of Washington's fomenting of a Panamanian secessionist movement in a step to safeguard US control over the envisaged canal. In 1856, in 1860, in 1873, in 1885, in 1901, and again in 1902, sailors and marines from United States warships were forced to land in order to patrol the Isthmus. This was not always at its own bidding. In 1861, in 1862, in 1885, and in 1900, the Colombian government asked that Washington protect its interests and maintain order on the Isthmus with troops.[8]

It is said, as a result, that not only does Colombia have the longest-standing record of democratic rule in Latin America, but also more than 150 years of war. Colombians have had to live with 'democratic insecurity'.

Much of this violence traditionally centred on political differences between the two major Colombian factions: the Liberals (with federalist tendencies) and Conservatives (with centrist leanings). These political preferences also, however, synched with rural and urban divides, the system of landlords and peasants, and of elite wealth and grinding poverty: of oligarchs, unequal land distribution, and indigenous Indian and Afro-Caribbean underclass.

Colombia's 2009 Gini coefficient measuring inequality was 0.587, the highest in Latin America. Official figures show that nearly half (46 per cent) of Colombians live below the poverty line and one-third of this number (17 per cent) in 'extreme poverty', giving lie to the average per capita income of nearly $4,000 (or over $9,000 in purchasing power parity terms). This poverty gap is starkest between rural and urban areas where 62 per cent of the rural population are poor compared to 39 per cent in urban areas, causing socio-political unrest and feeding conflict. This relates to access to land: 0.4 per cent of landowners own 61 per cent of rural land.[9] It is a nation of haves and have-nots, a highly stratified society where the traditionally rich families of Spanish descent have benefited to a far greater degree than the majority, mixed-race Afro-Colombian and Indian population. And the scarcity of avenues for social mobility provides a constituency for radical insurgents – or the intent for those making a living from illegal means. The role that the Soviet Union and its allies also played in promoting a left-wing insurgency in Colombia during the Cold War should not be omitted, however.

Such historical divisions and political differences peaked in 1948 with 'La Violencia', the most destructive of Colombia's wars, which

left 300,000 dead. The spark was the assassination of Jorge Eliécer
Gaitán, a populist Liberal leader, followed by urban riots in Bogotá,
popularly known as 'El Bogotazo'. The end result was a 1953 military
coup, the only twentieth century Colombian military intervention
in politics, and a 1957 pact between Liberals and Conservatives to
share power for the following sixteen years. However, this set the
stage for the next violent episode as disillusioned Liberals established
their own independent rural communities, while wealthy landowners
(and later the drug-lords) raised their own paramilitaries. Fuelled by
an influx of weaponry, ideology and money, this quickly morphed
into armed conflict. By the 1960s armed self-defence groups of
communists had by then established their own local government –
the Marquetalia Republic – in a remote region, in addition to the
enclave of Sumapáz outside Bogotá. An attack on this area by the
Colombian Army led to the formation of the Bloque Sur [Southern
Bloc] which, in 1964, renamed itself the FARC. FARC-EP (Fuerzas
Armadas Revolucionarias de Colombia-Ejército del Pueblo – the
Revolutionary Armed Forces of Colombia-Army of the People) came
about in 1982 at the Seventh Guerrilla Conference. This saw a major
shift in strategy from rural areas and small-scale confrontations to
larger-scale and into the urban areas.

Also on the anti-government side stood the ELN (Ejército de
Liberacón Nacional – the National Liberation Army) founded
in 1965, and the M-19 (Movimiento 19 de April) urban guerrilla
movement created also in 1965; and on the side of the status quo,
the army supported by a variety of paramilitaries including, most
prominently, the AUC (Autodefensas Unidas de Colombia – United
Self-Defence Forces of Colombia), established in 1997. A 1984
ceasefire led to a successful peace process with the M-19 movement
(with the ELN and FARC a member of the so-called umbrella
Guerrilla Coordinating Board), though the FARC and ELN decided
to continue the struggle. With the tailing off of support from the
Soviet Union and Cuba, the guerrillas turned to the narco-trade. This

funding, which initially took the form of the revolutionary *gramaje* [weight] tax, bolstered by profits from kidnappings, bank robberies and other criminal activities, brought in what the Colombian police estimated at $3.5 billion annually by 2005, or 45 per cent of FARC funding.[10] Their right-wing *paramilitares* opposition similarly received as much as three-quarters of their income from the drug cartels.

This chapter argues, however, that such a violent history is not destiny, but has its roots in poor political leadership and bad choices – and consequently, as the 2000s have shown, can be significantly changed by better policies and leaders. Longer-term, sustained change is however dependent on more than the energy and intentions of political leadership, but a deeper adjustment to ensure a less unequal and polarised society. Economic growth is a key part of this formula, as is establishing the state and its attributes from infrastructure to the rule of law in the rural areas. The governments of Alvaro Uribe Velez (2002–10) and, subsequently, from August 2010, Juan Manuel Santos Calderón, have put Colombia into a better position in the twenty-first century to tackle the threat posed, in particular, by an entwined scourge of drugs, widespread criminality, the leftist insurgency and rightist paramilitaries. The way it has been tackled, from the outset of Uribe's presidency and into Santos', was through the concept of 'democratic security' – until then an oxymoron in Colombia.

Power, Drugs and Ideology

The oldest insurgent group in Latin America, the FARC-EP has proclaimed itself to be a revolutionary agrarian, anti-imperialist, Marxist-Leninist organisation, inspired by the Bolivarian revolution, claiming to represent the peasantry and rural poor in a struggle against the wealthy and against the United States.

Yet it should be no surprise that Bogotá and other Latin American governments believe that the insurgency and the drug business are too interlinked to deal with each separately. 'The rebels used to fight for ideology', a senior Ecuadorean diplomat observed in Quito in 2006. 'What does that mean today? Now they fight for money and power. This is why it is more difficult to separate the insurgency from the drug industry.' This is down in part to Colombia's geography. Andrés Peñate, from 2005–07 the head of DAS (Departamento Administrativo de Seguridad – Administrative Security Department), has described Colombia's strategic position in the 1980s as 'Between the cocaine laboratories in Peru and Bolivia and the nostrils of the Americans'. The first drug lords like Escobar were less focused on controlling production than routes, explaining much of the violence, too, between the government, FARC, and the various paramilitaries. Difficult terrain and topography (half the country is jungle; and one-third mountainous) coupled with a weak central government mortally wounded governance and security efforts to bring the insurgency under control before 2002. Insufficient governance was exacerbated by the influx of drug money, which created alternative power structures, undermining the economy and judiciary, with a negative impact on productivity along with human and physical capital – three critical components of economic prosperity.

But by the government's own admission, there is much more to the fighting and the insurgency than drugs. The rural areas are the basis of the insurgency, but the lines defining the supposed good guys from the bad are, at best, blurred, not least by the government's historical working alliance with the paramilitaries, a relationship which has created another set of problems. As one retired general put it about the insurgents' motivation, 'They fight because they do not have opportunities in life. The areas where they live were not taken care of by the state – simply, the government did not go there. There are few options for them but to pick up a gun, even though that is not an easy life. It is also partly about values. It is also not just about a lack of education: after all, everyone is a doctor in Cuba, but there is still no employment.'[11] He added, 'If there is space where the state is not present, then someone else will be – whether this be the delinquent, the terrorist, the drug-dealer, the guerrilla, or the paramilitaries'.

Two demobilised guerrillas, Mauricio (ex-ELN) and Javier (ex-FARC), explained in December 2010 the circumstances that had made them rebels.[12]

Mauricio, 18, whose guerrilla mother had left him as a baby in the home of 'a peasant woman', said that his involvement had started at the age of ten, as a worker in a base 'planting food'. When he was eleven he 'got a gun and started fighting at 15. I got wounded last year,' he said peeling back his sleeve to show a rough hewn scar down his elbow, 'and I had to go to Caquetá for medical treatment. Those who are wounded either go there, to Valledupar, Barranquilla or to Venezuela. When I was healthy I went back to the combat zone. The last action I had, was against the marines,' he smiled nervously, 'when we were cornered. I don't know how I saved myself. I had to jump into a river. That day was tough.' Mauricio eventually decided to leave 'for a better future for my daughter and myself'.

Javier, a short, wiry man with darting eyes dressed in ill-fitting clothes, also started young. He first came into contact with the FARC as a twelve-year-old *raspachín* [coca picker]. 'The guerrillas approached me and asked me if I wanted to join. I said 'no'. They came back a second time, and I said 'yes', and they explained the FARC to me. They showed me a rifle and I liked it. They gave me four days to think it over, and I went with them.' Javier had just nine days' training before he was thrust into the fighting. After seven years as a guerrilla he left because his girlfriend was forced to have an abortion. 'The commandant treated us terribly.'

But both emphasise that they were fighting for a cause. 'We were fighting for equality, for our families, for a better peace, for the peasants and against the rich people,' Mauricio says, 'and everything the government says against that is crap'. Javier: 'The FARC ideology is the same as the ELN. They ask you why you want to be a revolutionary. They give you ideological training. You join the guerrillas for change, for equality, so that there is no more corruption.'

In essence, the struggle in the rural areas is most akin, in the opinion of one Colombian minister, to the taming of the west in America in the 1890s. In this 'frontier society', land rights and the rule of law have to be extended in parallel with infrastructure, opening up markets and opportunities.[13] In this, too, it is necessary to disaggregate the motives of the guerrillas: of the *encuadrillados* [foot soldiers], the *Milicias Bolivarianas* (civilian logistics support, embedded in the population), and the political leadership, both fighting with the guerrillas and the sympathisers operating legally within trade union movements, political parties and in civil society. As Mauricio and Javier indicate, the former group, in particular, are motivated apparently less by politics than a sense of community and survival – a band of brothers.

In the 1960s the FARC had a term for their strategy: *La combinación de todas la formas de lucha* [the combination of all forms of the struggle]. While they would have left-wing politicians, unionists, students and others representing their interests in formal chambers, the guerrillas would take the fight to the government in the mountains and hills.[14]

By the late 1990s this seemed to be working. FACR-EP and the ELN reached their operational zenith around 1999 with an estimated 18,000–22,000 fighters organised into seventy *frente* [fronts] countrywide. The expansion of the drug trade was connected with a 'lost decade' of economic activity in the 1980s, when growth came off the 5 per cent average sustained almost continuously since the Second World War. The success of eradication programmes in neighbouring Peru and Bolivia, and the relative absence of state authority in the isolated savannah and jungle areas to the east of the Andean region in particular, set the stage for the cultivation of coca and a drug boom. This also fed off the smuggling mindset and expertise which had developed out of protectionist Spanish colonial practices. Initially, there was a perception that cocaine generated revenues to make *all* Colombians better off.

The realisation that, however, drugs made normal economic activity impossible and the failure of the ambitious peace process led by the government of President Andrés Pastrana (1998–2002) set the stage for a more security-oriented approach. Pastrana's inability to negotiate a lasting peace with the FARC showed Colombians – and the world – that the 'guerrillas were not', as a Medillin businessman put it, 'Robin Hood, but drug-dealers and criminals. But he [Pastrana] provided the foundations of the situation we enjoy today, not least through improving Colombia's relations with the international community.'[15] Pastrana broke off three years of peace talks with the FARC after the group hijacked an airliner and kidnapped a Colombian senator who was aboard, and formulated Plan Colombia, a US$10.6 billion initiative launched in 2000 to take the guerrillas on.

By that time, by the army's admission, 'We were about to lose it. The guerrillas had almost moved from their first two stages of warfare (guerrilla warfare and movement) to the third, conventional war. We were losing a lot of guys, with bases being overrun. We did not have the numbers or equipment to take them on, with C-47 [Dakota] gunships, Mirage [fighters} which made a wonderful noise but little else, and very few helicopters. There was also a big disconnect between the different arms of the service. And,' the general reminds, 'we were being spread very thin in the jungle, making ourselves very vulnerable big time'. By 2000, the guerrillas had 'deployed from Ecuador to Venezuela, had built themselves considerable infrastructure in the southeast around Caquetá and Meta, and not only had Bogotá surrounded, but had deployed guerrillas into the outskirts. Road transport between the major cities was very difficult, if not impossible. A change of strategy was necessary.'[16]

Pastrana's appointment of General Fernando Tapias Stahelin as chief of the armed forces was the signal event in the transformation of the Fuerzas Militares de Colombia. 'Not only did they start the re-equipment process by hiring helicopters and procuring Blackhawks, but they changed both the strategy and attitude of the Army,' recalled one general in 2010. 'Three initial objectives were set: clear Bogotá of the guerrillas; stabilise the Eastern part of Antioquia, around Medillin, where much of the country's electrical power is generated from hydro, and where, by 2000, as many as 100 pylons per night were being blow up, and to disrupt the guerrillas operations in the southeast, around Macarena and Meta, where the centre of the guerrilla movement was militarily.' Considerable success was achieved by the time Uribe took over as president in 2001. 'He inherited a well-prepared, well-oiled machine, with which we had already turned the tide in Meta,' as one general observes.

Enter Alvaro Uribe, the Oxford- and Harvard-educated lawyer, like Pastrana a conservative, but a man, in his predecessor's words, 'elected to do war – when I was elected to do peace'. Uribe built on the successes of Pastrana, but focused, too, on normalising governance and lifestyles. He wanted to demonstrate to Colombians that, far from being contradictory, strong authority and democracy cannot exist without each other. As one measure of the changes wrought during the decade, by 2010, the FACR-EP and ELN had reduced in numbers to around 8,000 fighters, while terror attacks had dropped by 60 per cent in 2010 from a figure of 2,400 in 2002.[17]

The Elements of Democratic Security

At the time of Uribe's inauguration under the sound of distant mortar fire on 17 August 2002, 120 (of 1,099) mayors could not govern from their municipal offices, and there were no police stations in 158 of these municipalities.[18] As his vice-president (and radio journalist) Francisco Santos Calderón put it: 'The security situation was like the parable of the frog which is slowly heated up in warm water, never realising that he is being cooked alive. Well, the population was the frog, and we did not realise how bad things had become as a society.'

With Uribe's arrival Colombia underwent a dramatic transformation from widespread insecurity to increasing normality. Born in 1952, the staunchly Roman Catholic Uribe was formerly mayor of Medillin and governor of Antioquia. Despite the death of his father at the hands of FARC rebels in the mid-1980s, Uribe, who himself survived a number of assassination attempts, said in office that his anger did not influence his policies. But he seized the security problem in a manner unlike any of his recent predecessors, creating a wave of national political support and unprecedented degree of consensus. Despite the ongoing national risk of terrorism,[19] the dramatic improvements in security and strong economic performance saw Uribe's approval rating at 85 per cent, even after leaving office.[20] By then the FARC's approval rating was just two per cent.

Uribe's officials spoke of his job in terms of three missions: protect the population; control national territory; and take the fight to the guerrillas and paramilitaries or, as one member of his government observed, 'kick the bad guys up the arse so hard that they negotiate, but we negotiate not from a position of weakness but force'. In so doing, he did not reinvent the wheel, but capitalised on Pastrana's start and, critically, his improvement in international relations, taking the fight to the guerrillas and paramilitary groups. To do so, he had to not only change tactics but also, more significantly, deliver the means necessary to establish a modern, stable Colombia. Through the policy of 'Democratic Security', he effectively turned the guerrillas' own *combinación* [combination] strategy against them. Colombia's success in turning the tide, however, shows that weak (or insufficient) states demand more than a change of policies, but a building of state institutions.

But the first step in the democratic security policy was taking the fight to the guerrillas.

Tactically, this was reliant on a more aggressive approach in the security sector – on more money, soldiers and police, a more powerful justice system, the spraying of coca fields, better intelligence and more aggressive government tactics. The money for this was procured under Plan Colombia. The armed forces have risen in number from 191,537 in 2002 to 246,784 in 2006 and 286,000 (240,000 army, 14,000 air force, and 32,000 navy) by 2010; the police have increased from 104,920 to 131,550 and 160,000 at the end of the decade. More importantly, the number of full-time professional (as opposed to conscripts who serve a mandatory two year period) soldiers went up from 55,220 in 2002 to 73,080 in 2006 and 90,000 in 2010. The defence budget has increased from 4 per cent of GDP to over 5 per cent, to over $11 billion, during the 2000s. The increase in security expenditure has partly been financed through a 1.3 per cent 'wealth tax' earmarked for national security issues. Quality and not just quantity has been another measure of transformation of the armed forces. New equipment – including Blackhawks, Super Tucano aircraft from Brazil, unmanned aerial vehicles, and the latest communication, surveillance, and command and control technology – has paralleled the creation of a dedicated special operations command and greater investment in troops and their training.

The security forces (and, indeed, the entire government) have pursued a counter-guerrilla strategy based on Clear, Hold and Build. While the military and police together have undertaken the lion's share of actions in the first phase, the follow-up actions have been closely integrated with other government departments, notably through the Centro de Coordinación de Acción Integral (CCAI – Co-ordination Centre for Integral Action). The presidency's Acción Social [Social Action] department has channelled more than $800 million dollars to priority vulnerable communities since 2004. 'The overall aim', according to one official, 'was to remove the bad guys, build roads, create schools and clinics, and bring these places into the Colombia where 75 per cent of the population already lives'. The areas where the guerrilla flourishes, he noted, are those with weak social and infrastructure development, extreme poverty, few state institutions and little hope.[21]

President Uribe originally concentrated spending on eight priority regions; by 2010 this number was up to fourteen. The civilian-led actions – which are aimed at a range of areas including reconciliation, development of income-generating projects, illicit crop eradication and alternative livelihoods, and infrastructure development – have been described as being 'To fighting terror what bright lights are to deterring robbers at night'. It recognises that security actions are not enough by themselves. 'If you were a small farmer in Guaviare department in the centre of the country planting potatoes, you will probably have no way of getting them to market – no power, no roads, no river transport and no airport. So even if you could grow them,' noted one official, 'you could not sell them. So you grow coca. The bad guys turn up in a plane or a helicopter, and give you $500 and leave again. We have to break this cycle, we have to connect Colombia,' he added.[22]

Not only is it better synched with civilian actions, but the military component of the strategy has developed and changed in the following notable ways.[23]

Permanent Presence

Instead of reactive in-and-out strikes against guerrilla areas, the military and police built permanent bases in the conflict-afflicted areas. Although very expensive, this made 'society believe that we are not going to leave them, building trust, and allowing us to integrate more closely with the locals, getting to know their issues, economy and concerns. It also helped us with intelligence.'

Infrastructure

The military not only built bases, but thousands of kilometres of gravel and tarred roads and a cellphone network. The latter has been unexpectedly successful. 'The first tower we put up,' reminded one general, 'was in a base, fearing that it would be bombed. But later we built them outside. No-one ever bombed a tower. Everyone takes care of them because they need them. I took the cell manager there [to Caquetá]. He said I will help you, but you won't be successful. In the first six months they produced 400 per cent better results than anticipated.' The aim behind the military's actions on infrastructure has, overall, been to 'focus on the things that would encourage private sector investment'.

Intelligence and 'Jointness'
This is a critical aspect, especially given the size and impenetrability of the terrain and forest, which does not lend itself to using radar and satellite coverage. But taking the fight to the guerrilla had, at the outset, to recognise the problems in the state's intelligence system: it was fragmented between the different arms of service and the police, there were extreme limitations in methods and assets, operational security was problematic, there was an imbalance between tactical information and strategic considerations and few priorities and means of achieving them, and everyone, in the words of one senior officer, 'wanted to be a protagonist'.[24] Today there are joint inputs from a variety of government departments, both in the planning and execution of operations. As the general in charge of the Joint Special Operations Command noted in 2010, 'In one operation, we used an army chopper which carried marine special forces and police, and an air force loadmaster. We all know how to do the job.'

Strategic Shifts: High-Value Targets
Until 2006, in forty years of counter-insurgency, the government had not militarily targeted the FARC leadership. Since then, 12 of 18 senior FARC commanders have been killed, including the organisation's spokesman and Southern Bloc leader Luis Edgar Devia Silva (also known as Raúl Reyes) in Ecuadorian territory (1 March 2008) and the FARC's number two commander and military head Victor Julio Suarez Rojas (aka Jorge Briceño Suarez, and best known as 'Mono Jojoy') in central Colombia's Meta Department

(22 September 2010).[25] The message behind such actions is simple. President Santos: 'To the rest of the FARC, we are going after them. We are not going to rest.'[26] These targets are selected for their national and international impact – even though there has proven, by 2010, no shortage of those willing in the FARC to step into these (dangerous) shoes. The focus on 'high value targets' has yielded an intelligence dividend. According to police intelligence, the computers of Mono Jojoy and Reyes contained 'seven terabytes of information. Today we know what the FARC are, and what they want. Before these two computers we never had such a clear understanding of what they are.'

Special Operations Forces

The military set up the Special Operations Joint Command in 2005, realising the need for integrated assets and action. Special forces are used extensively in operations against high-value targets, integrating closely with the air force and the use of smart weaponry. The pattern of attacks against high-value targets has usually involved the use of precision bombs, followed by the helicopter insertion of special forces. The rescue of kidnapped soldiers, police and civilians has, of course, required different and unusually innovative methods, such as in the freeing of Green Party presidential candidate Ingrid Betancourt along with fourteen other hostages in July 2008 in Operation *Jaque* after six years in FARC captivity.

Training and International Co-operation

This has included increased sensitivity on human rights issues, including international humanitarian law, as key assets in improving the legitimacy of actions. Realising, too, 'that others had the technology and skills that we needed, this process has included training with UK, US, Latin American, and other elements. However, over time, this relationship has, as the Colombians have gained experience and lessons of their own, shifted from "recovery to partnership".'

In summary, while the armed forces and, especially special forces, have been at the tip of this campaign, according to the former army commander, General Muis Ardila, 'If we had just focused on the military side of the operation, we would be there for a very long time'.

Achieving security has also demanded rooting out corruption: this included military and intelligence leadership taking regular lie-detector tests. A focused and determined fight against corruption also resulted in the expulsion, by 2009, of 10,000 security force members, with 700 also in jail for human rights abuses. As Francisco Santos observed, 'Success depends on a mixture of policies. But one cannot emphasise enough that the basis of everything is security.' Such arrests are, he says, 'a cost you have to pay, otherwise it will only lead to wider corruption'. To an extent, the Uribe government has also had to live and die by this particular sword: investigations started in 2010 into the Watergate-style wire-tapping activities of the former president's close associates, including his chief of staff and the former DAS head, which carried with them the prospect of long prison terms.[27]

Military and police deaths from combat action peaked at 700 during the mid-2000s.[28] This has not been one-way traffic. The government claims to have 'neutralised' 7,000 guerrillas between 2002–06 alone, of which 25 per cent were fatalities. However, this is not the only route out of the conflict. The military have taken care to improve the soldiers' understanding of human rights which, as President Santos' chief of staff (and former deputy defence minister) Juan-Carlos Pinzón notes: 'helps with demobilisation [of guerrillas] and capture' as opposed to fighting to the death. This helps to explain why, in addition to 31,171 paramilitaries who collectively demobilised between 2003–06, a further 22,879 FARC, ELN, 'other dissidents' and paramilitaries voluntarily 'came over' as individuals between 2002–10 in the voluntary disarmament, demobilisation and reintegration scheme run by the Ministry of Defence (in the first two stages) and the High Council for Reintegration.[29]

The biggest challenge is getting uneducated men such as Mauricio and Javier steady jobs in an economy where, while there is only 5 per cent formal unemployment, more than half the country of 45 million people is informally employed, five times the (already considerable) unemployment rate of 11.5 per cent.[30]

The Growth-Security Nexus

'The improvement in security has enabled the economy to develop', observed David Bojanini Garcia, the CEO of the Medellin-based Suramericana, Colombia's largest conglomerate controlling 60 per cent of the stock exchange in 2006. Or as Vice-President Santos argued at the same time, 'The economy has boomed ... not the result of a boom, as elsewhere, of oil or other commodities, but a boom in security.' Or as Pinzón put it in December 2010, 'The system has resulted in improvements in security, but has also fed the economy, motivated investment, and allowed people to return to a normal life and create further opportunities'.

Colombia's economic growth averaged 5 per cent from 2003–08, up from 1.5 per cent pre-Uribe. Touching 7 per cent in 2007, it slipped to half this figure in 2008 due to the global economic crisis, and fell just into negative territory in 2009 due to weakening demand for its principal (commodity) exports, but rebounded to over 3 per cent in 2010. While per capita income remains stable at a shade under $10,000, since 2002 pro-market economic policies helped Colombia reduce poverty by 20 per cent and cut unemployment by 25 per cent (from 15.7 per cent in 2002 to under 12 per cent in 2007). A reduction in public debt levels to below 1.5 per cent of GDP, and an export-led growth strategy together facilitated growth together with the improvements in the security situation, establishing a positive cycle. The government's economic policy and democratic security strategy engendered a growing sense of confidence in the economy, particularly within the business sector, a confidence encouraged by fiscal incentives (essentially tax holidays) worth as much as 1 per cent of the country's GDP of $250 billion. Uribe's former finance (and, earlier, the agriculture) minister Dr Roberto Junguito Bonnet in 2006 estimated the components of economic growth: 'I believe that around one per cent of the increase in economic growth has been because of improving security, one per cent because of the good international environment, and one per cent due to good economic policies'.[31]

In part this is also because of the raw material. 'Colombians are smart, educated and work like hell,' says Karl Lippert, the CEO of SABMiller, the largest investor in the country with a stake of $7 billion.[32] Furthermore, Colombia has always had *serious* economic administration and policies, never defaulting on or rescheduling, for example, its international debt obligations. Even though there has been a long tradition of political violence, 'No-one', former president (1990–94) Cesar Gaviria has asserted, 'has ever questioned the viability of the country'.[33] Colombia has the fourth-largest economy in Latin America, behind Brazil, Argentina, and Mexico.

Foreign investment more than doubled between 2000 and 2010. But change was not only about financial figures and riches. According to public figures, recipients of public health care surged from less than 400,000 in 2002 to a shade under 8 million in Uribe's first (2002–06) term, and 'basic and medium' education coverage from 7.8 million to 9.3 million scholars during the same period.

Democratic security's critics argue that while the violence has mainly affected poor people, decisions have been taken mainly in the cities by members of the rich elite. They have argued, furthermore, that the influence of the drug barons remains strong, extending over the borders in terms of trafficking routes and money laundering schemes, and into government and the Congress. Although there have been substantial improvements in social conditions, there is still widespread poverty, especially in the rural areas. This helps to explain Pablo Escobar's popularity in some of the poor *barrios* of Medellin. His funding of low-income communities led to El Patrón acquiring a Robin Hood status in Medillin where there is still, today, a suburb named after him.

This has required improving the aspect of counter-insurgency that most campaigns struggle with – linking security with sustainable employment creation, especially in the rural areas.

Roads and Jobs

An increased security presence means that Colombians can now travel by road throughout most of the country, something that was not possible in 2002. It was then, as one cabinet minister notes, 'like Europe in the middle-ages, a bunch of city-states'. But this has come with other costs. There is a continuous presence of patrolling army, police and private security on streets and outside and inside buildings. This is an intrusion that most citizens are happy to pay for given the improvement in the economy and security. The policies of Presidents Uribe and Juan Manuel Santos dramatically illustrate the link between leadership, policy and results, as well as the virtuous cycle of security and development.

Unsurprisingly with 85 per cent of the population urbanised, not much attention has been lavished on the rural areas. But the advent of India and China, in particular, as dynamic, hungry markets and the success of Brazil in profiting from feeding them has alerted Colombians once more to the possibilities of rural development. This requires establishing property rights, on the one hand, and getting roads in to get goods out on the other. Prosperity is not just about land: people can be equally poor with land as they are without it in the absence of security, technology, machinery and finance.

But absolutely key in realising the opportunities is the building of infrastructure. 'If you pave [roads],' one military office commented in 2010, 'you move the guerrilla out and business in. It brings down costs and increases opportunities.' This is easier said than done.

Take Mitú, the capital city of the Department of Vaupés in southeastern Colombia, nestling on the border with Brazil, deep in the Amazon jungle, the front line on the war with drugs and insurgency.

In November 1998 an estimated 1,900 FARC guerrillas attempted to seize the town of some 28,000 people by force. After a struggle lasting several days with 120 national police members reinforced by a battalion of the Colombian army along with the air force, the FARC were forced back, taking hostages as human shields, including 40-odd members of the Colombian military. It was an operation, according to one general involved, 'that could never have been done a few years before. We had to take troops and helicopters by C130 to Brazil, and stage from there into Mitú.' Two of these hostages, police colonels Luis Mendieta and Enrique Murillo, were freed by the Colombian army in a rescue operation in June 2010.

Still, today, everything that goes to Mitú has to be moved either by plane or by boat from Guaviare, a journey that takes ten days. As a result, costs of basic goods are very high. Fuel is five times the price in Bogotá for example. An estimated 95 per cent of land is 'indigenous' – that is, uncleared for agriculture. But now, there is a functioning airport, more investment and twenty-four-hour lighting. As the presence of the state has increased so has the presence of the FARC diminished.

However, transforming the lives of the farmers and realising the security and economic dividend from rural growth is a challenge. VallenPez has, among the twenty-one similar NGOs working with a total of 250,000 smallholders countrywide, been successful because it has placed rural assistance schemes on a commercial rather than emotional donor footing. As one of its beneficiaries, the abovementioned Guillermo, noted, 'I have seen [farming] schemes where people receive everything for free, and thus they don't make the effort. The secret of our success,' he smiled, 'is that we do not get everything for free'. The success of these schemes shows that the solution is, in Rodrigo Guerrero's words, '85 per cent economic and 15 per cent security'.

Even with improvements in agriculture, this does not provide a stake in the system for all Colombians, however, not least given the 85:15 urban/rural split. Instead of using fiscal incentives to attract companies (the Uribe plan), the Santos government is seeking to use tax breaks for companies to encourage first-time employment. This would save the state much-needed fiscal revenue, and focus company benefits on those who need the break the most.

Regional and International Diplomacy and Influence

Uribe also had to construct a strong, if regionally politically incorrect, relationship with Washington, continuing the work of his predecessor Pastrana, whose previously noted assiduous diplomacy laid the foundations for the creation of Plan Colombia. By 2010, this provided around $800 million in US aid annually for the Colombian Armed Forces, around 85 per cent which was spent on the security forces.[34]

Uribe, and his successor Santos, have swum against the regional political tide. While much of South America has lurched politically to the left in the 2000s and anti-American rhetoric abounds, notably from Venezuela's President Hugo Chávez, President George W Bush described his Colombian counterpart as 'a strong and principled leader'. In November 2006, the two countries signed a bilateral free trade deal; America's biggest in the Western Hemisphere since 1994's North American Free Trade Agreement with Mexico and Canada. At the time it was expected to make more than 80 per cent of US exports to Colombia duty free.[35] The US is already Colombia's biggest trade partner, bilateral trade reaching $14.3 billion in 2005 and touching $21 billion in 2009.[36] Colombian trade analysts believed that the agreement could boost their country's GDP by as much as 2–3 per cent even though, by 2010, it had still not been ratified by the US.[37]

Many view neighbouring Venezuela and especially President Chávez as being behind the FARC, even though the latter has said, 'The guerrilla war is history ... At this moment in Latin America, an armed guerrilla movement is out of place.' [38] How to manage regional politics in a manner that stresses co-operation and avoids confrontation has been very difficult in this environment.

'We need to keep problems from migrating across borders,' said one general, 'both through security and investment and better border facilities. But of course,' he added, 'with some neighbours, some things are not that "clean"'.[39]

On 10 August 2010 Presidents Santos and Chávez agreed to restore diplomatic ties, which were severed earlier in the year after Uribe had accused Venezuela of harbouring the FARC. This does not, however, mean that Bogotá is convinced that Caracas is now the nice guy, however. Rather it is a realisation – the maturation – that the previous strategy was antagonistic and not delivering what the Colombian government was elected to do: in the words of Pinzon, to 'Guarantee peace for its people'.

Next Steps, Future Challenges?
Pinzón has noted, too, that 'Our success has brought new challenges'. The guerrillas have been bowed but not defeated. Their access to income from drugs grants them buying power for weapons and, in the poorer regions, people.

While the government has aggressively pursued the guerrillas and continues widespread aerial spraying to eradicate the coca crops, cocaine production levels – if the stability in the street value in the US market is any judge – remains constant at around 400 tonnes annually. And while the government has successfully countered much of the paramilitary involvement in production through a mix of amnesty, the corruption crackdown, demobilisation and better policing, the vacuum has been filled by the guerrillas and a new group of so-called 'criminal bands'. Where there is money to be made, there will always be an opportunist, domestically and regionally, as Mexican and Peruvian actors have filled the space vacated partly by the Colombian cartels. As Alejandro Eder, the High Council for Reintegration, observes, 'With drugs, you remove one layer of leadership, and several more spring up. It's a multi-headed monster.'[40] As a result, the government's actions have shifted to dealing with the value-added part of the drug chain, including production facilities, and not just the crops.

The FARC and ELN have not only moved their operations around the country in response to government operations (the balloon effect), but there is also evidence to suggest that they have changed tactics from semi-conventional back to guerrilla warfare, employing hit-and-run attacks and improvised explosive devices *à la* Al Qa'ida. During 2006 the guerrillas lost their ability to fight in big units and instead reverted back to guerrilla warfare employing terrorist tactics primarily against the army. The use of the security sector to hold the ring while other governance and economic actors move in is, however, recognised by government.

When in office Vice-President Francisco Santos emphasised the need for a political dimension to the struggle. As he put it in December 2006, 'We have made it very clear that there is going to be a negotiation. Our security policy is not an end, but a means to an end. Yet success is being at the table at your own and not the guerrilla's conditions.' Bogotá thus recognised – *and still does* – the first law of countering any insurgency: security measures are *part* of the means to a political settlement. The timing and nature of this olive branch and the method will likely be only a few years down the line, once the FARC leadership has realised 'there is no alternative, and that the high-value targeting continues to take effect.' Even so, the lucrative nature of the narco-trade makes it unlikely that all guerrillas will prefer the route of political incorporation, but instead will morph into further BACRIM – of which, by December 2010, there were seven such criminal groups, comprising an estimated 2,795 armed personnel and 1,347 in support functions.[41]

Overall, thus, the question of 'what to do with Colombia's drug problem (and the United States' drug addiction) looms large in assessing future options available to the guerrillas. Currently, the cocaine business is worth an estimated $400 million to Colombian farmers, $2.4 billion to the Mexican middlemen, and $29.5 billion to the US traders.[42] The guerrillas could potentially win, and win big, by moving up the value chain from growing and manufacturing into trading. This will probably require more aggressive eradication strategies and renewed efforts to infuse state institutions into rural communities. As one police colonel noted, 'Where the state is present, there is no Coke'.[43]

The government realises this challenge. As Pinzón has observed, 'The aim of Democratic Security is not just to bring security, but to create what security is all about – economic opportunities and social stability. President Santos is committed to the reduction of poverty, through the creation of formal employment.' Indeed, Santos won the election in 2010 promising to attack Colombia's deep social problems. On taking office he immediately put agrarian reform and informal employment on the agenda unlike any other president since Carlos Lleras Restrepo in the late 1960s.[44] This new direction includes a realisation that the FARC/ELN are more than just drug traffickers and bandits as commonly portrayed by the government, but a 'political-military organisation, which is not a simple [drug] cartel, but one motivated also by ideology'.

Land reform, as envisaged, has two components. First, buying land for redistribution; second, taking land away from the paramilitaries and again giving it to smallholders. Of course, more is necessary to make land realise its true value, including the provision of infrastructure (especially roads), agriculture extension services, and access to finance.

Agriculture is *the* story of unrealised potential for Colombia. 'We need three things to solve the next stage of our security and development problem,' says Juan-Carlos Echeverry, President Santos' minister of finance. 'We need to keep the economy going at more than five per cent growth. This will provide the money. Second, we need to spread our own, Colombian version of a welfare state, including health care, free primary education, the SISBEN system of grants to the three million of the five million extremely poor not already covered, and third promote agri-business. That way,' he noted, 'we can develop and benefit fast, provide more security, and avoid all the dangers including Dutch Disease [highly-valued currencies] which come with a reliance only on mining and oil'.[45]

Conclusion: Someone's in Charge

For many Uribe was elected with 'very anti-Colombian ideas and speech' of establishing national authority with a mandate of law and order.

He played both psychiatrist and strategist in dealing with the security problems beyond Bogotá's suburbs – getting the elite to recognise that the state could not be weak on taxes but strong on security. The two, he successfully argued, were related. He also tackled long-held fears about the primacy of the security forces over the civilian government. As Pinzón argued in 2006, the war had to be '20 per cent military and 80 per cent state-building and political'.

While the civilian-military strategy has followed conventional counter-insurgency wisdom of clear, hold and build, the degree of planning, careful integration of civilian and military elements (through the Acción Social and the CCAI) has been impressive, as is the quality of the personnel in both the security forces and the civilian agencies. The government has sought to attract the best and brightest, and has recruited widely from academia and business. The realisation that any solution has to be Colombian-led and (largely) financed is at the centre of the strategy. And herein is an important feature of the war: it is Colombians who are fighting other Colombians, with very few foreigners engaged.

There have been other, critical aspects to improving governance and security, which have demanded a hands-on leadership approach – not to say high energy levels. Even in his second term, Uribe spent every Saturday staging all-day consultations across the country. These *consejos comunitarios* [community councils] were televised nationally, where the audience had a chance to pose two-minute questions to the president and a selection of ministers. This way he covered most of the 1,100 municipalities and thirty-two regions in his eight years. Though it portrayed the president in a positive light, reflected in his extraordinarily high ratings, it aimed at more than just public relations and there is evidence of a genuine feedback loop. Uribe was also willing to make return visits to report back on his promises. As his VP Santos said in March 2009, 'He [Uribe] is on top of security all the time. He spends for example his Friday nights calling police all over the country'.

The results are clear to see, and not just in the security statistics. Of those polled in the most vulnerable areas of the country in 2010, 83 per cent thought that security had improved, and 60 per cent said there was greater trust. Some 69 per cent expressed improved confidence in the army, 52 per cent in the police, and 72 per cent in the national government. More worryingly, just 13 per cent felt that governance and transparency had improved.[46] Both Presidents Uribe and Santos have recognised that a combination of geography, topography and colonial history had left the Colombian state too weak to govern an inhospitable and inaccessible territory, little over twice the size of Texas or of France. Colombia did, by the turn of the twentieth century into the twenty-first, not so much as have a failed as much as an 'insufficient' state.[47] To do so, he had to not only change tactics, but the strategic circumstances of the Colombian state. The weakness of the state helps to explain why Colombia has battled so long with its drugs problem, and why tactical military offensives will, ultimately, only prove part of the solution in changing this situation.

The demobbed ELN and FARC fighters, Mauricio and Javier, expressed wide-eyed hope for the future. The former wanted to be a professional football player with Barcelona and find his daughter; the latter just wanted to be with his family, having been able to locate only his sister since his demobilisation. Despite an endearing naiveté, both were at the early stage of their release unworldly and unsuited to the demands of a modern economy, having been schooled in insurgency and coca, not maths and computers. Old beyond their years, their dead eyes spoke of hardship and little to look forward to. 'I feel like I am betraying my organisation,' said Mauricio. 'They gave me love I never had from my parents.' Javier put it more starkly. 'I feel that death is very present. I left an organisation – and I am an enemy to them now.' Both said, given the opportunity, they would not make the same decision again to demobilise. 'We still have not got the projects they said they would give to us.'

Of course, it is early days into a reintegration process that takes up to six years. And a few kilometres away from where Mauricio and Javier were chatting in Bogotá was the site of a launch at Juan Valdez Café of a new 'reconciliation' coffee brand, made with beans from conflict regions. Sold at a premium of 30 per cent, the coffee should generate $50,000 for these rural communities, one of a number of schemes to draw the private sector closer to their needs. Juan Valdez is one of 600 firms engaging with the reintegration scheme in this way. As Hernán Mendez of the National Coffee Federation put it at the event, 'Having a peaceful Colombia is everyone's responsibility, not just the government.'[48]

Indeed, sustained success in countering Colombia's complex insurgency will be down to the country's ability to maintain a high-enough economic growth rate, and generate employment, all the while extending the state outwards into the ungoverned jungles and mountains. This may not make the insurgency disappear altogether, but it will assist in dissipating much of the sense of grievance which has historically fuelled it.

EL SALVADOR: WHEN THE INSURGENTS (FINALLY) TAKE OVER

Greg Mills[1]

Where did we hide? Among the people of course.

(José, former ERP guerrilla)

The mountainous region of Morazán in El Salvador's northeast was a guerrilla stronghold in the country's twelve-year long civil war, the fighters enjoying broad support then, as now, among the area's impoverished farms and *campesinos*. The territory is hilly, wooded and, for the farmer, hardscrabble, but a perfect guerrilla playground and the site of much bitter fighting as the rebels attempted to cut the country in two, north to south, along the Torola River. In 1980, at the war's start, the government identified seventy-six camps to the east of the river, 'with tunnels, shooting ranges, and intelligence and defence systems, housing no fewer than 2,500 Cuban-trained guerrillas'.

Now on the Irish Aid and US Millennium Challenge Corporation-funded Ruta de la Paz ('Route of Peace'), near the Honduran border nearly 1,200 metres up, Perquín was once the site of a rebel headquarters. Two decades later, the war-museum in the village details the origins of the insurgency and the weapons used by both sides. The radio studio for Radio Venceremos ('we will triumph'), at the centre of the guerrillas' success in the propaganda war, is also on public display. The guides are former FMLN fighters, now eking out a living from the tips of the sprinkling of tourists. José had taken four bullets in his left leg four years into fighting his war. After treatment and therapy in Germany, today he offers a mix of propaganda and self-reflection as he wanders through the fading photographs and peeling posters exalting great socialist victories, rusting rifles, mortars held together with bits of wire, bits of downed helicopter scrap and an assortment of surface-to-air missile launchers. 'Now I tell people not to fight wars,' he said. 'We only did it because there was a need to do it. But weapons don't solve problems'.

El Salvador's colonial history is one of oligarchic economic control and the envy, anger, unrest and, ultimately, violence it generates. In the 1700s, a small group descended from Spanish settlers – known as the 'fourteen families' – controlled the economy, especially the lucrative indigo trade. As synthetic dyes took over, coffee became the main export crop, and by the twentieth century it accounted for 95 per cent of foreign income, controlled by an estimated 2 per cent of the population. Uprisings against such inequity occurred sporadically throughout the century, including the infamous *La Matanza* (massacre) in 1932 of 30,000 opponents, including the opposition Socialist politician, Agustin Farabundo Marti, by firing squad. The Frente Farabundo Marti para la Liberación Nacional (FMLN – National Liberation Front), founded in 1980, bore his name.

In the 1960s and 1970s, the vehicles for leftist political mobilisation were the so-called mass or popular organisations, drawing their leadership from radical Roman Catholic groups known as Christian Base Communities (Comunidades Eclesiasticas de Base – CEBs). The largest of these organisations was the Revolutionary Popular Bloc (Bloque Popular Revolucionario – BPR), with nine constituent groups and an estimated 60,000 members. They sought to establish the conditions for a revolution through public demonstrations, strikes, property seizures and propaganda campaigns.

By the 1970s, the civil conflict had developed into a struggle between anti-government guerrillas on the one side and government, paramilitaries and private 'death squads' on the other – the beginning of Salvador's *tiempos de locura* – 'season of madness'.[2] In October 1979, a reform-minded junta overthrew President Carlos Humberto Romero. The Junta Revolucionnaria de Gobierno (Revolutionary Government Junta – JRG) was inspired by a brand of left-wing politics. Under a civilian-military leadership,[3] the JRG (which took the form of three different juntas, though the two military men – Colonels Adolfo Arnoldo Majano Ramos and Jaime Abdul Gutiérrez Avendano – remained the only constant members) devised a number of reforms during its tenure, which lasted until the elections of March 1982. These included expropriating landholdings greater than 245 hectares. It also nationalised the commercial banking, coffee and sugar industries, while disbanding the ORDEN paramilitaries (Organizacion Democratica Nacionalista – Nationalist Democratic Organisation).[4] But even as these reforms proceeded apace, the war escalated.[5]

In 2010, General Abdul Gutiérrez explained the motivations behind the coup: 'The conflict started getting worse in the 1960s from the start of the Cuban revolution in 1959... Tensions were increased with the Jesuits bringing liberation theology to El Salvador. They started to organise the peasants, and to defend their rights. You must remember, our economy was almost feudal at the time. Then, in 1969, we had the war with Honduras.'[6] Known as the 'football war' or '100-hour war', the conflict was sparked by the two June 1969 World Cup qualification matches that both turned angry, especially the second game after a Salvadoran 3-0 victory. Hondurans retaliated, attacking Salvadoran immigrants, of which an estimated 400,000 had set up in Honduras partly on account of their own country's economic woes and the opportunities present in the Honduran banana business. El Salvador invaded Honduras on 14 July, with a ceasefire called after six days of fighting in which around 2,000 Hondurans lost their lives, and thousands of Salvadorans had to flee home.

General Gutiérrez recalls: 'El Salvador was [diplomatically] isolated as a result. … Honduras sent 375,000 peasants back to El Salvador. … We also had educational reforms … one result of which teachers went on strike.' The threat from the export of revolution from Cuba and the improving organisation of the communists, especially among students, was heightened by the fall of Somoza in Nicaragua in 1979. 'That really scared us, as normally – apart from Algeria, China and Cuba – guerrilla struggles failed.' Three National Guard positions were overrun in the north, and the army was running scared. This, the general says, explains the killings of the three nuns from the Maryknoll Order and one lay missionary in December 1980 who were working in the same area as the Guardsmen, their 'bodies were mutilated, eyes taken out, and members hung around their necks.' These events prompted General (then Colonel) Gutiérrez to plan a coup. 'Our main objective was that we did not want to divide the army or get shot, and we wanted to unite the country.' Once the problems such as who was going to lead the *golpe de estado* were resolved, the 'strategic objectives were chosen: (1) Stop corruption; (2) Start the democratisation process; (3) Agrarian reforms; (4) Structural reforms to make society more egalitarian; (5) Peace and good relations with the rest of the world; and (6) Peace with Honduras. These were all apparently neutral', says Gutiérrez, 'and not in favour of the guerrillas.' Despite the wide-ranging land and other reforms, however, the violence not only continued, but escalated. The guerrillas were not interested in having reforms handed to them: they wanted power.

For this reason, General Mauricio Ernesto Vargas, who headed the crack Atonal quick-reaction infantry battalion and later became one of the five government negotiators to the peace agreement, questions whether the war was about issues (the structuralist interpretation) such as 'poverty, corruption, dependency, and opportunity of the population', or whether it was due to external ideological and martial instigation, notably by the Soviet Union, Nicaragua and Cuba (the interventionist interpretation).[7] That the end of the Cold War saw a change in the fortunes of the guerrillas runs against the traditional rationale given – of a peasantry fighting for its rights and to end poverty – in favour of one which takes into account the role of external factors. After all, the external factor is apparently deemed as key in assessing the role of the US.

The military's reaction to the reformism of the Juventud Militar ('Military Youth') junta was also mixed. Conservative officers saw the reformists as weakening the military, playing into the hands of the left and increasing the likelihood of extremists seizing power. The majority of Salvadoran officers apparently fell into neither the reformist nor conservative camp, instead opting for 'concerned neutrality and inaction', though this 'ultimately worked in favour of the aggressive conservative faction'.[8]

During this time, the assassination of popular opposition cleric Archbishop Oscar Romero while delivering mass in San Salvador on 24 March 1980 saw the country plunge into violent civil war. His funeral a week later resulted in a bloody clash between demonstrators and security forces.

The violence would cost 75,000 lives and caused 25 per cent of the population to be displaced, internally and externally, over twelve years. Various peace initiatives reaped little reward. The ruling Partido Democráta Cristiano (PDC – Christian Democratic Party), led by veteran politician José Napoleon Duarte, won a contentious 1984 election over former intelligence officer Major Roberto D'Aubuisson's[9] rightist Nationalist Republican Alliance (ARENA) party. (Duarte won the February 1972 election, but was denied victory by the military, which supported Colonel Molina.) But the PDC and the FMLN were unable to agree to peace terms, including the rebels' participation in the 1989 election, which elected businessman Alfredo Cristiani with a majority of 53.8 per cent, the start of a twenty-year period of rule by ARENA. With business interests in cotton, coffee and seed, Cristiani had been drawn into politics in the beginning of the 1980s when the FMLN's *campesino* followers began squatting on farms.

By this time, with D'Aubuisson's blessing, Cristiani had started discussions with the FMLN. Some aspects made peace most likely. First, there was the opening provided by the end of the Cold War and the advent of Alfredo Cristiani's leadership. Second, far from the populist portrayal of a regime out of control, there were strict external monitors on the behaviour of the government, notably from the US. And assiduous diplomacy helped, not least by the United Nations and the negotiators themselves. On this, General Vargas remarks, 'You had to have a good working relationship to get the deal done, not an emotional relationship or a friendship. You had to visualise the material interests of both, knowing that we all had to make sacrifices. And you had to have a good liver to negotiate with those guys for a long time!'

President Armando Calderón Sol (1994–99) says of that period:

> The transition was possible because of the election of ARENA, a centre-right party which had the credibility and the support of the armed forces to enter into a dialogue with the FMLN. Because D'Aubuisson supported Cristiani and the negotiations, it was possible. We had to change the country, and he was wholly supportive of this view. But really it was the fall of the Berlin Wall that provided the opening for peace. Central America was one of the last scenes of the Cold War.

And it proved very difficult to negotiate with the one-time enemy: '...it was very difficult. It was important, however, to create trust between the negotiators. That was a very long process, in which the country's friends, such as Colombia, Mexico, the US and Spain, helped a lot, and the UN especially.'[10]

Despite the ongoing talks, the FMLN initially responded to ARENA's election by launching their own 'Tet-style' military offensive, so-called *'ofensiva hasta el tope'* ('until the end offensive'), taking the war into the capital San Salvador, hoping that such a bold act would help to sway US public opinion in their favour. The ten-day offensive included a stand-off between twenty heavily armed guerrillas and twelve US Green Berets, part of an advisory team, who were holed up for more than a day on the fourth floor of the Sheraton Hotel in San Salvador's wealthy Escalon district in December 1989, where the Organization of American States Secretary-General João Clemente Baena Soares was staying.[11] It illustrated that the FMLN were far from a beaten force, and more powerful than the estimates of 6,000 soldiers indicated. President Calderón Sol recounts:

> This was a very difficult time for the process, for the dialogue. But we were convinced that no-one was going to win the war, and that our differences needed to be solved through an 'understanding'. Both the right and the left were convinced about the need for a democracy, and of the need not to have a military dictatorship. You must remember that there was a lot of resentment among the right towards the military, on account of what the junta had done.

Salvador's 'Tet' was mainly fought in some of the capital's poorest districts of Soyapango, Cuidad Delgado and Mejicanos. Although the guerrillas were badly battered by government forces, at the same time the army killed six Jesuit priests at the Universidad Centroamericana. This act prompted outrage in Washington, and raised doubts about the US approach. José Luis Merino, who as 'Commandante Ramiro' played an active part in the military struggle – and by 2010 was seen as the most influential member of the FMLN – explained that the Jesuits, long in opposition to the government on account of their liberation theology, were playing an important role between the guerrillas and key army officers, especially in the cavalry, trying to encourage them to mutiny at the time of the offensive. Rather than an act of mindless violence, the army's response was thus a clear message to both the Jesuits, and its own elements, to desist.[12] 'The guerrillas used to kill whole villages', argues General Gutiérrez thirty years later. 'But', he ponders, 'the death of the Jesuits is the great sin of the army, and has been used against us.'[13]

With the pressure of the withholding of US support on the one side, and the change in the Cold War context narrowing the FMLN's options on the other, a UN-supervised peace process began soon after in April 1990 (the process was ultimately monitored through ONUSAL – the UN Observer Mission in El Salvador). On 16 January 1992, the Chapultepec Peace Accord was signed in Mexico, under the terms of which the FMLN became an opposition political party. The government agreed to compensation for victims, and to the dismantling of various paramilitary groups along with military units, as well as the Guardia Nacional, Policia Nacional, Policia de Hacienda (Treasury Police) and Policia de Aduanas (Customs Police). A totally new police force was created, with an FMLN quota.

Conservative presidents followed in the elections of 1994 (Armando Calderón Sol), 1999 (Francisco Guillermo Flores Pérez) and 2004 (Antonio Saca), before former journalist Mauricio Funes achieved victory for the FMLN by taking power in June 2009. Funes, whose brother was a guerrilla who had been killed, was the first FMLN leader who, however, had not fought himself in the war. He ran a moderate campaign, promising the retention of the dollar as the official currency (dollarisation had taken place in 2001 under Flores) and more attention on health care and crime prevention.

How the War Was Fought
In May 1980, the year the civil war officially began, Salvadoran revolutionary parties met in Havana to form a consolidated politico-military command, the DRU (Dirección Revolucionaria Unificada – Unified Revolutionary Directorate). In October that year, with Fidel Castro's support, the FMLN was formed, comprising the Fuerzas Populares de Liberación (FPL), Ejército Revolucionario del Pueblo (ERP), Resistencia Nacional (RN), Partido Comunista

Salvadoreno (PCS) and Partido Revolucionario de los Trabajadores Centroamericanos (PRTC). As the military institutions of the left were getting organised into one body, the mass organisations were following a similar strategy. In April 1980, the Revolutionary Democratic Front (Frente Democratico Revolucionario – FDR) was established.

Their opposition came in the form of various paramilitaries and right-wing bands that came to be known as 'death squads'. Funded by the oligarchy and drawing on both active and retired military personnel, these squads targeted 'subversives' in order to discourage anti-government activities. The best known of these squads included the Wars of Elimination Anti-Communist Liberation Armed Forces (Fuerzas Armadas de Liberacion Anti-Comunista de Guerras de Eliminacion – FALANGE), the White Warriors Union (Union de Guerreros Blancos – UGB), Mano Blanco (White Hand) and the Maximiliano Hernández Martinez Brigade. These units followed broadly the tactics of the military regimes in Guatemala, Brazil and Chile. Public protest was outlawed by the Law for the Defence and Guarantee of Public Order in November 1977, which eliminated most restrictions on violence against civilians.

After the FDR leader, Enrique Alvarez, was killed along with five other members in November 1980 by a death squad, the front moved to formal unification with the DRU and, later, the FMLN. The first public announcement of the FMLN-FDR was made in Mexico City in January 1981, just four days after FMLN guerrillas initiated an operation that they optimistically and grandly dubbed the 'final offensive.'

This first major attack established control in most of the Morazán and Chalatenango departments in the north. Yet the guerrillas' logistical network was not sufficiently robust to support an almost countrywide operation. Neither were they well armed or trained; the Salvadoran armed forces, although initially taken by surprise, were able to beat back the attacks. The FMLN was not able to declare, as it had hoped, Morazán a liberated territory. The offensive also demonstrated the limited extent of the guerrillas' support among the Salvadoran population. But it did establish the FMLN as a formidable political and military opponent, with unintended consequences. The timing of the final offensive had in large part reflected the desire of the FMLN to take power before the inauguration of US president Ronald Reagan. It had the desired effect of convincing the US of the seriousness of the guerrillas' intent. But for them it had the wrong result.

US military assistance to El Salvador had totalled just $17 million in equipment between 1950 and 1979, less than that received by any other Central American country except army-less Costa Rica. Instead, Salvador was forced to purchase modern equipment primarily from Brazil, Israel and France. It had been forced to completely re-equip its infantry with G3 rifles from West Germany, source quantities of West German armoured personnel carriers, and obtain artillery pieces from Yugoslavia.[14]

On 14 January 1981, four days after the offensive began, President Carter announced the approval of $5 million in 'non-lethal' military aid; an additional $5 million was authorised four days later. This helped to establish a trend that President Reagan, fearing another Nicaragua, would build on when he assumed office on 20 January 1981. As Reagan put it in May 1984, 'San Salvador is closer to Houston, Texas, than Houston is to Washington, DC. Central America is America; it's at our doorstep, and it has become a stage for a bold attempt, by the Soviet Union, Cuba, and Nicaragua, to install Communism by force throughout the hemisphere.'[15]

Although annual American military assistance peaked at $197 million in 1984, it was far from a blank cheque. As General Vargas says, 'Our alliance with the United States was not very functional. Their objective was to stop communism; our objective was survival.' The US Congress required certification by the executive every six months of Salvadoran progress in such areas as the curbing of abuses by the armed forces, the implementation of economic and political reforms (especially agrarian reform), and the demonstration of a commitment to hold free elections with the participation of all political factions which renounced the armed struggle.

As the military and its agents targeted both rebels and their supporters including unionists, clergy, independent farmers and students, the FMLN worked across their *frente* (fronts) – Feliciano Ama in Occidente, Modesto Ramirez in the Central region, Anastasio Aquino in Paracentral, and Fransisco Sanchez in Oriental – to blow up bridges, cut power lines, destroy coffee and cotton plantations, and anything else to damage the economy that supported the government. Both the Cuscatlan and Golden Bridges over the main Rio Lempa (three-quarters of El Salvador's people live in its basin) linking the eastern part of the country with San Salvador were blown, the latter reputedly by Cuban special forces. The FMLN also murdered and kidnapped government officials. (In the space of a few months in 1989, for example, the FMLN murdered the Attorney General Roberto Garcia Alvarado (April), the Minister of the Presidency Jose Antonio Rodriguez Porth (June), and the daughter of Colonel Eduardo Casanova Vejar (October).) As time passed, guerrilla efforts became more advanced, as did their weaponry. At first, much of it was Western and Israeli-made, being sourced from surplus Nicaraguan and Vietnamese stocks. Later it became increasingly Soviet in origin. At the same time, their attacks became more strategic and better planned.

In 1981, President Reagan dispatched Green Beret trainers to El Salvador. Although their number was limited to fifty-five and they were ordered to avoid combat zones and to carry only side-arms for self-defence, twenty-one American soldiers died in the war, more than were killed in the 1989 invasion of Panama.[16] These soldiers were used to train four 1,000-man 'rapid reaction' battalions, the first of these being the Atlacatl Battalion. A five-member US advisory team helped the Salvadoran Army to reorganise its command structure, streamline planning, and develop intelligence and communications techniques. The same year, the first group of 500 Salvadoran officer candidates participated in a training course at Fort Benning, Georgia, while the US also began training Salvadoran non-commissioned officers in Panama. In 1982, US special forces provided counter-insurgency training to the Belloso and the Atonal Battalions. By late-1983, the US had trained 900 Salvadoran officers, around half the entire officer corps.[17]

The US also provided cash transfers to sustain the Salvadoran government and economy, aid to displaced people and assistance to rebuild infrastructure damaged by guerrilla sabotage. Aid was increased after the US National Bipartisan Commission on Central America (the Kissinger Commission) concluded in January 1984 that the 37,500-man Salvadoran Army was too small to break the military stalemate with the 9,000–12,000 FMLN guerrillas. During the next four years, El Salvador received an average of $100 million annually in US military assistance. In 1983 and 1984, about 3,500 Salvadorans attended US-run training courses at the Regional Military Training Center, operated by US forces, in Puerto Santo Tomas de Castilla in Honduras. Additionally, in 1982 Argentina supplied military advisers along with an order of Argentine-made infantry equipment. Israel reportedly also provided counter-insurgency training.[18]

Four Stages

In summary, the war developed through four stages.[19]

1979–81: The Army in Disarray

By the time of the 1979 coup, which had been carried out to separate the army's interests from those of the oligarchy so as to ensure the preservation of the former, the army possessed little over 12,000 men, putting it in no position to fight a guerrilla force of an estimated 6,000. It was also divided among itself (exacerbated by the coup), and without external assistance. As General Guitérrez puts it, 'There were three fundamental grave deficiencies in the armed forces – (1) a total lack of equipment, (2) lack of training, and (3) mostly it was not being prepared to confront the type of problems we were facing at the time.' He noted later: [20]

> Our military doctrine was mainly Chilean from World War II, to fight a conventional war. A guerrilla war was very different to what we had been trained for... The US told us: 'You have major problems. You are underequipped. You don't have a real intelligence apparatus. You make too many mistakes. You lack leadership. And you should not operate in big units, but in small units.

And he says of their opponents, 'By 1979, we discovered that the guerrillas had 600 tonnes of weapons in the country, and between 2,500 and 2,700 of them had already been trained.' But by the admission of guerrilla commanders such as Joaquin Villalobos (of the ERP), regarded as first among equals of FMLN commanders, the guerrillas then did not possess the necessary degree of unity or the logistics and numbers to 'break the back' of the army.[21]

1981–83: Guerrilla Ascendancy

With the unification of the guerrilla forces at Castro's urging in 1980, the guerrillas attempted to prove, in Villalobos's view, that 'we could win the war'. With notable successes in key points (including in Perquín, Corinto and Morazán with the loss of three army companies) and increasing urban activity, the focus now turned to targeting army morale. This period culminated with the last major sustained guerrilla offensive against San Miguel to the east, followed up with a three-month period involving some eighty-five separate attacks, many of them successful with a large number of government troops killed or injured. As Tom Pickering, the US ambassador to El Salvador from 1983–85 recalls: [22]

There were days at the end of 1983 when we wondered whether we would make it through the next two or three months ... One can well characterise my two years ... as the nadir of political-military activities, and all the consequences – political and negative economic effects – were being widely felt in the country.

1984–89: The Tide Turns and Stalemate

By this time, US-trained and equipped forces were starting to arrive. Although some guerrilla successes continued (notably the destruction of infrastructure), the government quickly became much more effective, especially the air force. Having no helicopters at the start of the war, the Salvadoran Air Force acquired eighty UH1H 'Hueys' and fifteen UH1M and Hughes 500 attack helicopters, plus Cessna A37 ground-attack aircraft and Fairchild C123 Provider and Israeli Arava transports. The political situation also started to change – first, with the election of President Duarte in 1984. The guerrillas, in the view of the then-commander of the US military group in El Salvador, had 'taken a step back in terms of the classic insurgency stages, and had gone back to smaller units, dispersed, with less confrontation with government forces ... . At the same time, the insurgency began to lose its people.'[23] During this time, General Vargas notes, the armed forces changed:

[By] 180 degrees. At the start of the war we did not have enough officers, or enough men. We had to reorganise totally. We borrowed the concept of the 'Hunters' from the Venezuelans, with whom President Duarte had a good relationship, to operate behind enemy lines. We also created the rapid-reaction battalions, along with the long-range reconnaissance patrols, known as PRAL. This was very expensive to do. People often think that the US was giving us money. But really they were giving us training and equipment. But probably the restructuring was the most difficult part of the process. We had to change from being stuck in static bases with no territorial control, to becoming very mobile and flexible, with the units able to be semi-autonomous, able to sustain themselves for between 90–120 days in the field. Only once they were engaged in combat would support come by air.

And the guerrillas' confidence almost caused, in his opinion, their undoing. 'They changed tactics to try and engage our units with the same size units of their own. They almost got wiped out, and had to go back to being small and mobile.'

1989–90: Pressure and Peace

By the time of the election of Cristiani in 1989 as the first ARENA president, the government had gained the upper hand. At the ceasefire on 1 January 1992, the government estimated that 12,000 of its own troops had died and 28,000 guerrillas.[24] But, Vargas contends, neither side was beaten:[25]

> You cannot defeat the guerrilla militarily. You can only neutralise them. It is also very difficult to measure superiority. You can defeat them in the field, but someone can drop a bomb in a hotel and make a lot of 'noise'. You cannot claim a victory, but rather try and achieve instead an unstable military equilibrium. Even if you can defeat guerrilla forces militarily, you will never get peace that way, as Peru, Guatemala, Uruguay, Colombia and especially Venezuela and Spain show us.

Ending the insurgency went hand-in-hand, too, with a host of concessions and reforms. A constitutional amendment prohibited the military from playing an internal security role except under extraordinary circumstances. The Treasury Police and National Guard were abolished, and military intelligence functions were transferred to civilian control. By 1993, the military had shrunk its personnel from a high of 63,000 during the conflict to the level of 32,000 as required by the peace accords. By 1999, uniformed and non-uniformed strength stood at less than 15,000, and it declined by 2010 to 4,800, around one-quarter of the strength of the police. All armed FMLN units were demobilised when the organisation became a legal political party.

At war's end, the Commission on the Truth for El Salvador registered more than 22,000 complaints of political violence in the country, between January 1980 and July 1991. Some 60 per cent of these acts involved summary killing, 25 per cent kidnapping, and 20 per cent torture. Around 85 per cent of the violence was attributed to state agents, including paramilitary groups and death squads. The FMLN was cited in 5 per cent of complaints, even though the FMLN continuously violated the human rights of many Salvadorans, notably those identified as right-wing supporters, military targets, pro-government politicians, intellectuals, public officials and judges. These violations included kidnapping, bombings, rape and killing.[26] The view of who was worse than the other depends, in Salvador at least, on one's politics. One's terrorist is another's freedom fighter; or taken to an extreme, one's 'death squad paramilitary' is another's defender of property and personal rights.

Regardless of the morality of the methods, it was a counter-insurgency campaign prosecuted with remarkable success by the military, in spite of the relatively small number of government troops. They were also operating with severe constraints. Not only were they expected to act according to human rights norms (though clearly they did not always do this) while the guerrillas were not expected to abide by the same 'rules'; in the process, the army was constantly fighting a losing battle in the propaganda war. Indeed, this was a front that 'they were never able to master', says General Guitérrez. 'There was a double-morality in the war. Everyone talks about the death squads on the right; but no-one says anything against the urban commandos of the guerrilla who were just assassins, who would come and kill businesspeople, intellectuals and others, and who never were demobilised.' And for diplomatic reasons, government forces were never able to tackle the guerrilla sanctuaries that existed across the border in Nicaragua, Honduras and elsewhere.

This was a war that, on close examination, belies many of the stereotypes. For one, the reason for the government's success in gaining a peace process out of a guerrilla struggle did not lie exclusively in the volume of aid and weaponry received from the US. As General Vargas reminds, '[The US] gave us what they thought we needed, not what we wanted. We were fighting three or four fronts at any one time, and only received enough to keep us alive, never to fight. And much of the equipment was Vietnam era, including our rifles and helicopters.'

Rather the reason for success may reside in the same reason given as to why the levels of violent repression in El Salvador have always been so high. Ambassador Tom Pickering remembers that 'It was a society heavily prone to violence. In large measure, alcohol, the machete, lack of education, frustration, all tended to produce an atmosphere of Saturday night massacre in the place... Violent methods of control were part of the repressive atmosphere...'[27] The level of violence is also attributed to population density, the highest in Latin America at 293 people per km^2, placing it in the top quintile worldwide.[28] Such density enabled the military to operate effectively with small units spread countrywide. There has also always been a strong sense of national identity, and local practices were 'more likely to resist than to comply with external pressures'.[29] Thus national control over these areas went hand-in-hand with the presence of the state. Such control strengthened the hand of the government, undermined the likelihood of a guerrilla victory, and ultimately steered the process, with external urging, to the negotiating table.

The Economic Pillar of Transition

Since 1992, El Salvador has shown how the past is not everything. It is possible to deal with a violent history, extreme political polarisation, skewed wealth distribution, high crime rates, a dependency on agriculture and deforestation. It shows that politics can quickly mature to the point that one-time insurgents can assume office free from immediate violence or economic disaster, even though divides remain including among their own ranks.

Until the land reforms of the early 1980s, El Salvador's economic structure was notable for the unequal distribution of land ownership, being dominated by large plantations producing cash crops for export, especially coffee. Economic development was also hindered by the drain on human and financial resources caused by conflict, frequent natural disasters, and adverse changes in the terms of trade.[30] Economically on a par in the early 1970s with Thailand, South Korea, Malaysia and Costa Rica, by 1982 it had fallen far behind. Between 1982 and 1986, El Salvador fell even further behind as it failed to diversify its exports away from agricultural commodities and into manufactured goods. In 1986 per capita GDP was almost half the level of 1977, with the country stuck in a period of disinvestment.

By 1987, El Salvador's economic output barely equalled 80 per cent of its 1978 level. Exports were only the third-largest source of foreign exchange, after foreign aid and remittances from Salvadorans living abroad. By mid-1987, it was estimated that the total cost to the economy of the war based on lost agricultural production, damaged infrastructure, and funds diverted from economic to military purposes was about $1.5 billion. GDP declined by 23 per cent between 1979 and 1982, recovering modestly to 1.5 per cent growth between 1983 and 1986.

Since 1992, a key pillar of the peace process has been economic stability and growth. A commitment to free markets and careful fiscal management, along with targeted programmes, saw poverty cut from 66 per cent in 1991 to 34.6 per cent in 2007. The banking system, telecommunications, public pensions, electrical distribution and some electrical generation systems were privatised; import duties reduced; price controls eliminated. On 1 January 2001, the US dollar became legal tender in El Salvador.

Despite the destruction of the civil war, agricultural production in El Salvador rebounded quickly, in part because of higher prices for coffee and sugar, and diversification into horticulture. Salvador also created new export industries through fiscal incentives for free trade zones, the largest beneficiary of which was the textile and apparel (*maquila*) sector, directly providing 70,000 jobs by 2008. By then, one-quarter of Salvador's eight million citizens lived in the US, and their remittances home have been an important source of income for many families. In 2008, more than one-fifth of families received remittances, totalling $3.8 billion.

Until the 2008 global recession, with the politics and the economic fundamentals restored El Salvador's annual GDP growth rose to nearly 5 per cent after many years of remaining stuck at 1.5 per cent. Back offices for giant US-based concerns were established, while the financial sector was sold to first-class international banks and many European and American investors bought strategic businesses such as the brewery, cement, pension funds, and insurance companies, in the process bringing in $5.3 billion in the 2000s.

The key outcome of the years of constant growth, supplemented by the flow of foreign family funds, has been the creation of a Salvadoran middle class, the glue that keeps society together and functioning.

Conclusion: *Hasta la Victoria Siempre?*

On 11 December 1981, US-trained soldiers of the government's elite Atlacatl Battalion massacred more than 750 residents of the northern hill village of El Mozote, about 10 km down a cobbled and dirt track from Perquín.

A simple wall of remembrance skirts the edge of El Mozote's main square alongside the Santa Katarina church where 146 children and two adults were taken outside and killed, among them Maria de la Paz Chicas's pregnant sister and four-year old child. 'They brought all the people here', she says today, 'from Guacamaya, and killed them here. They told them they were going to give them food. They took all the young pretty women to the hills and raped them there for three days. The children', she says beckoning to a garden, 'were killed there, where there is now the "Garden of Reflection of Innocence". Their ages were between two months and sixteen years. They killed the men behind the fence', she says pointing in the opposite direction. 'But they never found the bodies. They were totally burnt. And the women were killed behind there, in the doctor's house. They also burnt them, though some they were able to identify with bits of clothing.'

There was a sole survivor, Rufina Amaya, who fled through a pineapple plantation into a river. Her husband and four children were all killed. From her hiding place she could hear the screams of children, including that of her own son, crying out, 'Mommy! Mommy! They're hurting us! Help us! They're cutting us! They're choking us!'[31] She died of a heart attack in 2006, and is buried in front of the wall of remembrance.

Why did it happen? 'There are different versions', says Maria. 'Some say it was because the people helped the guerrillas. We would give them tortillas and water. But we would also do the same for the soldiers. I think it was because of *Radio Venceremos*, which was broadcasting nearby'. The perpetrator, the Atlacatl Battalion, was disbanded under the terms of the 1992 peace agreement. In a quirk of fate, its leader Lieutenant-Colonel Domingo Monterrosa Barrios, designated as a *'Heroe de Joateca'* by the Salvadoran Congress, was killed just kilometres from El Mozote in October 1984 when his helicopter, the remains of which are displayed in the Perquín museum, was brought down by a FMLN booby-trapped radio.

Many of the challenges that provided the social backdrop to the civil war remain. El Mozote has just one tiny inn, three small shops, and one place to eat. Maria and her friend are making a living by giving tours and selling a few wares, including locally-made hammocks. 'Things are not as good as before', she says. 'Everything changed and nothing is the same. We are poor. But', she smiles, 'we are happy.'

Despite the improving development trajectory led by ARENA, Salvador's parliamentary elections in January 2009 went the way of the FMLN. The party's leader, Mauricio Funes, apparently persuaded many voters that FMLN was willing to work not only with the centre, but also with Washington, in the process winning the 15 March 2009 presidential election.

The 2009 FMLN claimed to be different to the *Bolivarianistas* in Venezuela, Bolivia, Ecuador and neighbouring Nicaragua: instead, 'a revolutionary movement more in the mould of Barack Obama than Ché Guevara'.[32] The FMLN once boasted candidates and manifestos reflecting its Marxist origins. Its 2004, presidential candidate Schafik Handal was a long-time leader of El Salvador's Communist Party. Apparently concerns over crime, economic growth and unemployment won Funes the election, though ARENA's implosion and selection of candidate made the ruling party probably his best ally. But as the Wikileaks revelations of November 2010 illustrate,[33] Funes faced challenges within his own party to his leadership and policies. Some are critical, too, of the way in which the party elite have enriched themselves, notably through ownership schemes of investments such as ALBA Petroleos de El Salvador, formed in 2006 with a $1 million stake, 60 per cent from Venezuelan state oil company PDVSA and 40 per cent from ENEPASA, an association of twenty FMLN municipalities.[34] President Funes quickly learnt that politics is sometimes war by other means, especially among his own party. And the involvement of Hugo Chavez's Venezuela in El Salvador, as elsewhere, shows that there is scope, still, for external influences to meddle in and distort local politics.

From the right, Funes has been criticised for having no plan to deal with economic problems or fight El Salvador's increased criminal activity. Criminal statistics on homicides, robbery and extortion have increased. By the start of 2010, thirteen persons were murdered daily, making Salvador one of the world's most violent countries. The president's response was viewed as muted compared to the operations

– *Mano Dura* (Strong Hand) and *Super Mano Dura* – conducted by Presidents Flores and Saca respectively against the *maras* ('mara' being slang for gang), the two most notorious being MS13 and M18. The challenge of dealing with the *maras*, which employ many of the same methods as the insurgents did in the 1980s, including extortion, are placed into perspective by their number of 40,000, shading the challenge of operations against the 10,000 FMLN guerrillas.

The sophistication of the gangs' methods and involvement in more legitimate front businesses has furthermore complicated any approach, as has the increasingly martial aspect of criminal organisations generally throughout the region, such as Mexico's Zeta drug-paramilitary formed around disgruntled ex-special forces. Many see this as requiring greater use of repressive techniques to counter, especially in a country like El Salvador where force is the language apparently best understood.

Whatever the challenges, the lesson of El Salvador is thus: steady reforms and economic growth, even if not spectacular, are key to relieving the political pressures that give rise to violence, and can reduce the space for nefarious external actors. This has to be both expedited and matched by political savvy and compromise, as it was in 1992. But, as President Armando Calderón Sol reminds, the transition is not yet complete. 'The defeat of ARENA at the polls is a victory for the political process, for democracy and for El Salvador. But only when the FMLN cede political power to someone else can the transition process be considered as finished.'[35]

NOTES AND REFERENCES

Introduction: Contemporary Insurgency (pp. 1–13)

1. This section draws on Greg Mills, 'Between Trident and Tristars? On Future War and its Requirements', *RUSI Journal* (Vol. 155, No. 3, June/July 2010), pp. 28–30.

2. Human Security Centre, *Human Security Brief 2006* (Vancouver: Liu Institute for Global Issues, University of British Columbia, 2006), p. 9.

3. Colin S Gray, *Another Bloody Century: Future Warfare* (London: Phoenix, 2007).

4. See Rupert Smith, *The Utility of Force: The Art of War in the Modern World* (London: Vintage, 2008).

5. DCDC, 'Strategic Trends Programme: Global Strategic Trends – Out to 2040', January 2010, available at <http://www.mod.uk/DefenceInternet/MicroSite/DCDC/OurPublications/StrategicTrends+Programme/>.

6. *BBC News*, 24 November 2011.

7. *Visionofhumanity.org*, 'Global Peace Index', 2010, available at <http://www.visionofhumanity.org/gpi-data/#/2010/GINI>.

8. John Mackinlay, *The Insurgent Archipelago* (London: Hurst, 2010), p. 231.

9. *Ibid*, p. 142.

10. Discussion, World Bank representative, Copenhagen Aid Risk Management Event, 25–26 November 2010.

11. Cited in General Sir David Richards, 'Twenty-first Century Armed Forces: Agile, Useable, Relevant', Annual Defence Lecture, Chatham House, London, 17 September 2009.

12. With a nod to Rupert Smith, *op. cit.*

A Soldier's Perspective on Countering Insurgency (pp. 15–34)

1. Frank Hoffman, *Conflict in the 21ˢᵗ Century: The Rise of Hybrid Wars* (Arlington, VA: Potomac Institute, 2007), p. 8.

2. Frank Kitson spent much of his career countering insurgency, from Malaya to Northern Ireland, and his two books, *Low Intensity Operations* and *Bunch of Five*, shaped British military thinking for many years. Frank Kitson, *Bunch of Five* (London: Faber & Faber, 1997), p. 282. Emphasis added. See also Frank Kitson, *Low Intensity Operations: Subversion, Insurgency and Peacekeeping* (London: Faber & Faber, 1971).

3. See Richard Stubbs, *Hearts and Minds in Guerrilla Warfare: The Malayan Emergency 1948–1960* (Oxford: Oxford University Press, 1989), p. 2.

4. Rupert Smith, *The Utility of Force: The Art of War in the Modern World* (London: Penguin, 2006).

5. Bernard Fall, 'The Theory and Practice of COIN', *Naval War College Review* (April 1965).

6. J F C Fuller, *Reformation of War* (London: Hutchinson, 1926), p. 254.

7. Sir Robert Thompson, *Defeating Communist Insurgency: Experiences in Malaya and Vietnam* (London: Chatto & Widus, 1966), p. 51.

8. *Ibid.*

9. Tony Jeapes, *SAS Secret War* (London: William Kimber, 1980/HarperCollins, 2000), pp. 11–12.

10. Ministry of Defence/Command of the Defence Council, *Land Operations Vol. III – Counter-Revolutionary Operations*, 'Part 1 – Principles and General Aspects', Army Code No. 70516 (Part 1), August 1969; 'Part 2 – Internal Security', Army Code No. 70516 (Part 2), November 1969

11. 'Part 1 – Principles and General Aspects', *op. cit.*, p. 41.

12. Paddy Ashdown, 'After Iraq and Afghanistan – Shall We Ever Intervene Again?' The Hands Lecture, speech at Mansfield College, Oxford, 4 November 2008.

13. *Ibid.;* Kitson, 1997, *op. cit.* p. 283.

14. The phrase 'The legitimate object of war is a more perfect peace' is inscribed on Sherman's statue. B H Liddell Hart, *Sherman: Soldier, Realist, American* (London: Stevens & Sons, 1960), p. 425.

Countering Insurgencies by Preventing Insurgencies (pp. 35–51)

1. John Shy and Thomas Collier, 'Revolutionary War' in Peter Paret (ed.), *Makers of Modern Strategy* (Princeton, NJ: Princeton University Press, 1986), p. 817.

2. David Galula, *Counterinsurgency Warfare* (Westport, CT: Praeger Security International, 2006), p. 1.

3. This analysis relied on following works in particular: Galula, *op. cit.*; C E Callwell, *Small Wars: Their Principles and Practice;* Bard E O'Neill, *Insurgency & Terrorism;* Jeffrey Record, *Beating Goliath;* US Army/Marine Corps, *Counterinsurgency Field Manual* FM 3-24; T E Lawrence, *Seven Pillars of Wisdom;* Shy and Collier, *op. cit.* Important new works that have been added to this body of literature include David Kilcullen, *The Accidental Guerrilla: Fighting Small Wars in the Midst of a Big One* (London: Hurst, 2009), David H Ucko, *The New Counterinsurgency Era: Transforming the U.S. Military for Modern Wars* (Washington, DC: Georgetown University Press, 2009), and John Mackinlay, *The Insurgent Archipelago* (London: Hurst, 2009).

4. Galula, *op. cit.*, p. 24.

5. US Army/Marine Corps, *Counterinsurgency Field Manual* FM 3-24 (Old Saybrook, CT: Konecky & Konecky), p. 60.

6. FM 3-24, *op. cit.*, pp. 60, 64.

7. Bard E O'Neill, *Insurgency & Terrorism: Inside Modern Revolutionary Warfare* (Herndon, VA: Brassey's Inc, 1990), p. 59; Galula, *op. cit.*, p. 24.

8. O'Neill, *op. cit.*, pp. 59–61; FM 3-24, *op. cit.*, pp. 60–61.

9. O'Neill, *op. cit.*, p. 58.

10. C E Callwell, *Small Wars: Their Principles and Practice* (London: The Stationery Office, 1914).

11. *Ibid.*, pp. 57–70.

12. Carl von Clausewitz, *On War*, edited and translated by Michael Howard and Peter Paret (Princeton, NJ: Princeton University Press, 1989), p. 480.

13. Drawn from Galula, *op. cit.*, pp. 23–24.

14. O'Neill, *op. cit.*, p. 53. Clausewitz highlights the crucial role of infantry for operating in rugged terrain, *op. cit.*, pp. 348–51.

15. Galula, *op. cit.*, p. 23.

16. FM 3-24, *op. cit.*, p. 33.

17. O'Neill, *op. cit.*, p. 13.

18. FM 3-24, *op. cit.*, p. 33.

19. Galula, *op. cit.*

20. O'Neill, *op. cit.*, pp. 13–17; Galula, *op. cit.*, pp. 17–19.

21. O'Neill, *op. cit.*, pp. 13–17; Galula, *op. cit.*, p. 7.

22. See the reference to Algeria in Galula, *op. cit.*, p. 20. Alistair Horne, *A Savage War of Peace: Algeria 1954–1962* (New York, NY: New York Review of Books Classics, 2006) captures this evolution of violence well.

23. Kalev I Sepp, 'Best Practices in Counterinsurgency', *Military Review* (May–June 2005), p. 9.

24. Galula, *op. cit.*, p. 21. For highly adaptive insurgent tactics see, for example, T E Lawrence, *Seven Pillars of Wisdom* (New York, NY: Random House, 1991), p. 337.

25. FM 3-24, *op. cit.*, pp. 57–91; Callwell, *op. cit.*, pp. 43–56.

26. FM 3-24, *op. cit.*, pp. 67–68; O'Neill, *op. cit.*, p. 62.

27. FM 3-24, *op. cit.*, pp. 103–33.

28. Jeffrey Record, *Beating Goliath: Why Insurgencies Win* (Washington, DC: Potomac Books, 2007), p. xi. Chapter 2 specifically addresses this issue of external assistance.

29. Alan J Vick, Adam Grissom, William Rosenau, Beth Grill and Karl P Mueller, *Air Power in the New Counterinsurgency Era: The Strategic Importance of USAF Advisory and Assistance Missions* (Santa Monica, CA: RAND Corporation, 2006), pp. 83–93.

30. FM 3-24, *op. cit.*, pp. 179–81.

31. T E Lawrence, *Seven Pillars of Wisdom* (New York, NY: Anchor Books, 1991), p. 196; Shy and Collier, *op. cit.*, p. 839.

32. Galula, *op. cit.*, pp. 5–6, 20.

33. Horne, *op. cit.*, recounts this strategic miscalculation in detail.

34. Galula, *op. cit.*, p. 94.

35. Janet C Wylie and Joseph Caldwell Wylie, *Military Strategy: A General Theory of Power Control* (Annapolis, MD: Naval Institute Press, 1989), pp. 22–27.

From Insurgency to Stability to Development: In Afghanistan as Africa (pp. 53–86)

1. Interview, ISAF HQ, Kabul, 1 May 2010.

2. Discussion, Qalat, Zabul, 14 April 2010.

3. Kandahar City, 21 April 2010.

4. Interview, ISAF HQ, Kabul, 2 May 2010.

5. This was drawn for the authors by Brigadier Richard Felton, Lashkar Gah PRT, May 2010.

6. See, for example, Mats Berdal and Achim Wennmann (eds.), *Ending Wars, Consolidating Peace: Economic Perspectives* (London: IISS, 2010).

7. See US Army Corps of Engineers, 'Kandahar City Power Solutions: Key Opportunity to Produce Counterinsurgency Effects', April 2010.

8. *New York Times*, 'High Costs Weigh on Troop Debate for Afghan War', 14 November 2009.

9. According to the Ministry of Agriculture in Kabul, international funding to their sector alone in 2010 was over $2 billion, with USAID ($789 million), USDA ($151 million), DfID (£50 million) as the main donors.

10. Interview, Kabul, 1 May 2010.

11. Discussion, 3 May 2010.

12. Interview, USAID, ISAF HQ, September 2010.

13. Discussion, Forward Operating Base Walton, September 2010.

14. Discussion, Turquoise Mountain Foundation, Kabul, 1 May 210.

15. This section draws on US House of Representatives Subcommittee on National Security and Foreign Affairs, 'Warlord, Inc.: Extortion and Corruption along the U.S. Supply Chain in Afghanistan', June 2010.

16. Discussion, Kabul, 2 May 2010.

17. Survey conducted in Kandahar City, 2 May 2010.

18. *AOL.ca*, 'Let There Be Lights: Kandahar Residents Want Power Instead of Cdn Polio Shots', 25 April 2010.

19. Conducted on 3 May 2010.

20. Discussion at Gandamack Lodge, Kabul, 2 May 2010.

21. In 2004–05, the trade in opiates was the equivalent of 47 per cent of licit trade across the country; and an estimated 60–80 per cent of trade in Kandahar City was opiate-related.

22. Interview, Kabul, 2 May 2010.

23. See, for example, 'The potential for copper', produced by the Afghanistan Geological Survey, available at <http://www.bgs.ac.uk/afghanminerals/docs/copper_A4.pdf>.

24. Discussion, Kabul, 1 May 2010.

25. See Jean-François Bayart, *The State in Africa: The Politics of the Belly*, translated by Mary

Harper, Christopher and Elizabeth Harrison (London: Longman, 1993), especially p. 238.

26. Patrick Chabal and Jean-Pascal Daloz, *Africa Works: Disorder as a Political Instrument* (London: James Currey, 1999), p. 16.

27. Discussion, Forward Operating Base Walton, Kandahar, September 2010.

28. Discussions, Kandahar, September 2010.

29. Maureen C Ramsey, 'Micro-Hydro as a Practical Method to Build Energy', press release, US Army Corps of Engineers Afghanistan Engineer District, available at <http://www.aed.usace.army.mil/News/Releases/092006.html>.

30. DAI, 'Making a Difference—the Evidence of Success', available at <http://www.dai.com/work/success_stories_detail.php?stid=60>.

31. Interviews conducted in Weish, April 2010.

32. Discussion, Kandahar PRT, Kandahar, 22 April 2010.

33. See, for example, Greg Mills, 'Kandahar Through the Taliban's Eyes', *Foreign Policy*, 27 May 2010.

34. *Cgdev.org*, 'Good Aid, Bad Aid Quota Tracks How Donors Stack Up', 4 October 2010.

35. Overseas Development Institute, Evaluating humanitarian action using the OECD-DAC criteria: An ALNAP guide for humanitarian agencies' (London: ODI, March 2006). See also OECD, 'The DAC Principles for the Evaluation of Development Assistance', 1991; OECD, Glossary of Terms Used in Evaluation, in 'Methods and Procedures in Aid Evaluation', 1986; and OECD, '*Glossary of Evaluation and Results Based Management (RBM) Terms*', 2000.

36. See Belgian Development Agency, 'Aid Efficiency', available at <http://www.btcctb.org/aid-efficiency>.

37. *AU Monitor*, 'Aid Efficiency in Fragile and Conflict Situations', 9 August 2010.

38. Interview, 21 April 2010.

39. The upper house (Loya Jirga) comprises 102 seats; the lower house (Wolesi Jirga) comprises 249 seats.

Special Operations and Instability: A Military Investment Strategy (pp. 87–106)

1. Amy Belasco, 'The Cost of Iraq, Afghanistan, and Other Global War on Terror Operations Since 9/11', Congressional Research Service report, 16 July 2010, available at <http://www.fas.org/sgp/crs/natsec/RL33110.pdf>.

2. Anthony H Cordesman, 'US Casualties: The Trends in Iraq and Afghanistan', Center for Strategic and International Studies, 6 August 2008.

3. For several in-depth examples of the strategic utility of small military elements, see Robert Kaplan, *Imperial Grunts: On the Ground with the American Military from Mongolia to the Philippines to Iraq and Beyond* (New York: Vintage Books, 2005).

4. US Joint Chiefs of Staff, 'JP 3-05: Doctrine for Joint Special Operations', para. I-1.

5. For detailed definitions of each activity, see *ibid.*

6. Michele Malvesti suggests a complete restructuring of special operations forces doctrine to delineate between 'missions' and 'activities' and employ terminology that classifies the US role as 'unilateral' or 'in partnership' and the activities as 'disruption and defeat' or 'shaping and enabling of the environment.' Michele L Malvesti, 'Time for Action: Redefining SOF Missions and Activities', Center for a New American Security, December 2009.

7. In this case the terms 'overt' and 'covert' are used in their common definitional forms to portray activities as either open or concealed, and not a reflection of specific terms included in legal or policy guidelines for intelligence activities.

8. US Department of Defense, 'Building Partnership Capacity: QDR Execution Roadmap', 22 May 2006, p. 4, available at <http://www.ndu.edu/itea/storage/790/BPC%20Roadmap.pdf>.

9. Foreign Internal Defense is defined as 'operations that involve participation by civilian and military agencies of a government in any of the action programs taken by another government or other designated organization, to free and protect its society from subversion, lawlessness, and insurgency.' Unconventional warfare is 'the culmination of a successful effort to organize and mobilize the civil populace against a hostile government or occupying power ... and to synchronize their activities to further US national security objectives.' JP 3-05, *op. cit.* See also, US Joint Chiefs of Staff, 'JP 3-07.1, Joint Tactics, Techniques and Procedures for Foreign Internal Defense', 2004.

10. JP 3-05, *op. cit.*, p. vii.

11. This is the first of five 'truths' that have become tenets within the US special operations community: humans are more important than hardware; quality is better than quantity; special operations forces cannot be mass-produced; competent special operations forces cannot be created after emergencies arise; and most special operations require non-special forces assistance. *Ibid.*, para. II-4.

12. Robert G Spulak Jr, 'A Theory of Special Operations', Joint Special Operations University (JSOU), October 2007, available at <http://jsoupublic.socom.mil/publications/jsou/JSOU07-7spulakATheoryofSpecialOps_final.pdf>.

13. The White House, 'National Security Strategy', May 2010, pp. 22, 26, available at <http://www.whitehouse.gov/sites/default/files/rss_viewer/national_security_strategy.pdf>.

14. Department of Defense, *op. cit.*

15. The White House, *op. cit.*

16. There are, of course, potentially negative effects on the host nation and the perceived legitimacy of its government that must be considered along with the positive or negative reaction of the international community.

17. Eric T Olson, 'A Balanced Approach to Irregular Warfare', *The Journal of International Security Affairs* (No. 16, Spring 2009).

18. Kelly H Smith, 'Surrogate Warfare for the Twenty-first Century', *Contemporary Security Challenges: Irregular Warfare and Indirect Approaches* (Vol. 9, No. 3, 2009), pp. 39–54.

19. Critics may view the term surrogate as a connotation of a superior-inferior relationship. This is often not the case since surrogates are chosen for their ability to successfully negotiate political, cultural and operational challenges that may be insurmountable to the sponsor.

20. In his essay, Homiak describes 'with' as a relationship where external Actor A operates alongside host nation Actor B to accomplish mutual goals. 'Through' is a process whereby Actor A enables Actor B with training, equipment and other support, but does not actually participate in the operations. Finally, 'by' represents a relationship where Actor B, pursuing mutually defined goals and objectives, takes unilateral action to conduct operations that ultimately meet the requirements of both actors. Travis L Homiak, 'Expanding the American Way of War: Working "Through, With, or By" Non-US Actors', *Contemporary Security Challenges: Irregular Warfare and Indirect Approaches* (Vol. 9, No. 3, 2009), pp. 19–38.

21. Alister Bull, 'Obama, in Letter to Yemen, Stresses US Support', *Reuters*, 20 September 2010.

22. Sheila Carapico, 'Special Operations in Yemen', *Foreign Policy*, 13 May 2010.

23. In this example, the term 'unilateral' is intended to describe efforts that were conducted by foreign forces rather than with or through Afghans. Therefore, a

coalition effort could still be essentially unilateral.

24. T E Lawrence, 'Twenty-seven Articles', *Arab Bulletin*, 20 August 1917, pp. 126–33. Lawrence intended his twenty-seven articles to serve as advice for advisers to the Arabs. Whereas his advice is specific to the Arab Revolt of 1916–18, it remains sound, particularly considering that 'odd conditions' exist in all foreign countries.

25. For a very detailed analysis and tools for planning military COIN operations, see US Army, *Field Manual FM 3-24: Counterinsurgency* (Chicago: University of Chicago Press, 2007). For a simple yet valuable comparison of successful and unsuccessful COIN practices, see Table 1-1, pp. 1-29.

26. See S M Goode, 'A Historical Basis for Force Requirements in Counterinsurgency', *Parameters* (Winter 2009–10), pp. 45–57; John J McGrath, *Boots on the Ground: Troop Density in Contingency Operations* (Carlisle: Combat Studies Institute Press, 2006); James T Quinlivan, 'Force Requirements in Stability Operations', *Parameters* (Winter 1995), pp. 59–69.

27. For additional analysis of the unintended effects of counter-insurgency operations, see David Kilcullen, *The Accidental Guerrilla: Fighting Small Wars in the Middle of a Big One* (Oxford: Oxford University Press, 2009).

28. FM 3-24, *op. cit.*, para. 1-1.

29. Adrienne Mong, 'America's Forgotten Frontline: The Philippines', *MSNBC.com*, 1 October 2010. Abu Sayyaf is a militant organisation, founded by veterans of the Afghan jihad against the Soviets, with ties to Al-Qa'ida in the Middle East and Jemaah Islamiah in Indonesia.

30. The standing mission of the JSOTF-P illustrates the relationship between the US military and the Philippine government: 'The mission of the US Joint Special Operations Task Force – Philippines (JSOTF-P) is to support the comprehensive approach of the Armed Forces of the Philippines (AFP) in their fight against terrorism in the southern Philippines. At the request of the Government of the Philippines, JSOTF-P works alongside the AFP to defeat terrorists and create the conditions necessary for peace, stability and prosperity.' JSOTF-P Public Affairs, 'JSOTF-P Fact Sheet', 1 April 2009, available at <http://jsotf-p.blogspot.com/2009/04/jsotf-p-fact-sheet.html>.

31. Kaplan, *op. cit.*, p. 154.

32. See Herb Daniels, 'Keeping COIN Simple: The Outhouse Strategy for Security Development', *Contemporary Security Challenges: Irregular Warfare and Indirect*

Approaches (Vol. 9, No. 1, 2009), for a short but telling example of the positive effects of relationship building and non-standard special operations approaches.

33. Josh Scott, 'US Commander Leaves Lasting Impact in Southern Philippines', JSOTF-P Public Affairs, 2 July 2010, available at <http://jsotf-p.blogspot.com/2010/07/us-commander-leaves-lasting-impact-in.html>; Pia Lee-Brago, 'US Envoy Says Abu Sayyaf, JI, RSM Weaker Today', *Philippine Star*, 3 July 2010.

34. D P Fridovich and F T Krawchuk, 'The Special Operations Forces: Indirect Approach', *Joint Forces Quarterly* (No. 44, 2007), pp. 24–27.

35. For press releases highlighting the results of the military efforts, see JSOTF-P Public Affairs, 'DVIDS – Joint Special Operations Task Force – Philippines', available at <http://www.dvidshub.net/units/JSOTF-PH>.

36. The efforts of JSOTF-P are not without precedence. From 1950–54, US military advisers trained and supported – but did not materially participate in – the successful Filipino counter-insurgency against the communist Huks. For a comprehensive rundown of this and other US surrogate operations, see Richard D Newton, 'Seeds of Surrogate Warfare', *Contemporary Security Challenges: Irregular Warfare and Indirect Approaches* (Vol. 9, No. 3, 2009), pp. 1–18.

Intelligence in Low-Intensity Conflicts: Lessons from Afghanistan (pp. 107–26)

1. Characterising the war in Afghanistan is a complex exercise. One thing is clear: calling it a counter-insurgency falls way short of accurately characterising the war.

2. 'Battle space' is used here because the intelligence challenge goes beyond where the conflict physically takes place.

3. In this usage, resources include time, blood and treasure.

4. Because of the cultural diversification within the territory, even the utility of the label 'Afghan' is limited.

5. This is not to suggest that the US and Pakistan are not co-operating closely in some areas, but rather to explain that there are many levels to the US-Pakistan relationship: many co-operative, some counterproductive. In part, this is because Pakistan is not a singular nation-state with strong governance across all aspects of its national security institutions, let alone national life (broadly defined). Not only are there differences between the various peoples of Pakistan and the state, but both groupings have multiple sub-groups that often vie with one another for

power and thus have markedly different approaches to the US and its interests in the region. The modern elites in both public and private sectors tend to see Al-Qa'ida as a threat to Pakistan, while Islamist-leaning groups in both sectors see India as by far the greatest threat to Pakistan and the cultivation and support of *talibs* [students] in Afghanistan as vital to keeping India in check.

6. The Indo-US relationship is marked by a mutual struggle to overcome historical prejudices and misperceptions.

7. Some of the ethnic and tribal groupings include the following peoples (or nations): Pashtun, Tajik, Hazara, Uzbek, Turkmen, Nuristanis, Aimaqs and Balochis. In addition to these groupings, must be added sub-national tribes and clans, as well as political groupings (such as the Taliban), terrorist groups, warlords and various regional and international actors.

8. Bob Woodward, *Obama's Wars* (Simon & Schuster: New York, 2010), p. 77.

9. *Ibid.*, p. 150.

10. Dana Priest and William Arkin, 'A hidden world, growing beyond control: Top Secret America Special Report', *Washington Post*, 19 July 2010.

11. Woodward, *op. cit.*, p. 77.

12. Priest and Arkin, *op. cit.*

13. Woodward, *op. cit.*, p. 79.

14. *Ibid.*, p. 150.

15. *Ibid.*, p. 79. Woodward goes on to explain that Harvey created a colour-coded mapping system thus: ISAF was blue, insurgents red, Afghan security forces green and Afghan people white. This is noteworthy because in the Flynn report, discussed below, the authors refer to the pressing need to collect 'white' intelligence.

16. There are many questions about the programme, especially relating to career progression and development, especially given the proposed US drawdown in Afghanistan starting in July 2011.

17. Woodward, *op. cit.*, pp. 350–51.

18. Michael Flynn, Matt Pottiner and Paul Batchelor, 'Fixing Intel: A Blueprint for Making Intelligence Relevant in Afghanistan', Center for a New American Security, Washington DC, January 2010.

19. *Ibid.*, p. 7.

20. *Ibid.*, p. 4.

21. *Ibid.*, p. 9.

22. *Ibid.*, p. 10.

23. *Ibid.*, p. 13, for example.

24. Adrian Bogart, *One Valley at a Time*, JSOU Report 06-6 (Hurlburt Field, FL: JSOU Press, 2006); Jim Gant, *A Strategy for Success in Afghanistan: One Tribe at a Time* (Los Angeles, CA: Nine Sister Imports, 2009).

25. General Martin E Dempsey, commander of the US Army Training and Doctrine Command, quoted in Flynn, Pottiner and Batchelor, *op. cit.,* p. 23.

26. *Ibid.*, pp. 17, 12.

27. *Ibid.*, p. 9.

28. *Ibid.*, p. 21.

29. The source for the Pentagon office space is <http://pentagon.afis.osd.mil/facts.html>. Accessed 7 October 2010. See Priest and Arkin, *op. cit.*, but their calculations are off: they estimate that only two Pentagons equate to the same floor space (17 million square feet).

30. Walter Pincus, 'Intelligence Spending at Record $80.1 Billion in First Disclosure of Overall Figure', *Washington Post*, 28 October 2010.

31. Priest and Arkin, *op. cit.*

32. Although the legislation fell short insofar as key powers remain with the CIA, and these are a source of tension between the Office of the Director for National Security (ODNI) and the CIA. For example, the director of the CIA 'still had authority on covert actions and reported to the President on them', Woodward, *op. cit.,* p. 56.

33. It managed the National Intelligence Program budget, but not the Military Intelligence Program budget, which resides under the authority of the Secretary of Defense according to ODNI, 'National Intelligence: A Consumer's Guide', 2009. On the recommendations, see 'The 9/11 Commission Report: Final Report of the National Commission on Terrorist Attacks upon the United States', July 2004, pp. 407–16

34. Eli Lake, 'Intel Foiled at Al Qaeda Plot, DNI Chief Says', *Washington Times*, 2 November 2010

35. ODNI, 'Questions & Answers on the Intelligence Community Post 9/11', undated, available at <www.dni.gov/content/Question_and_Answer_IC.pdf>. Accessed 7 October 2010.

36. Woodward, *op. cit.*, p. 7.

37. Priest and Arkin, *op. cit.*

38. Quote by General Jack Keane as Army Vice Chief of Staff, 'Inside American Power: The Pentagon', *National Geographic* [TV], 13 May 2003.

39. Ernesto Londono and Haq Nawaz Khan, 'Pakistani Government Condemns NATO Airstrikes', *Washington Post*, 28 September 2010, p. 12.

40. Craig Whitlock and Greg Miller, 'Paramilitary Force is Key For CIA', *Washington Post*, 23 September 2010, p. 1.

41. Secretary of Defense Gates and Chairman Mullen are quoted numerous times in Woodward, *op. cit.*, as admitting that they failed to present alternatives when different options were specifically demanded of them. Their advice reflects their professional judgment and they are obligated to give the president their unvarnished opinions. However, aside from throwaway non-options, the fact remains they were unable to think of a different approach. Their thinking was supported by a tremendous amount of analysis and intelligence, which one assumes was equally unable to articulate an alternative.

42. Woodward, *op. cit.*, p. 116.

43. Lawrence Wright, 'The Rebellion Within: An Al Qaeda mastermind questions terrorism', *New Yorker*, 2 June 2008.

44. Noman Benotman, 'An Open Letter to Osama bin Laden', *Foreignpolicy.com*, 10 September 2010.

45. Karen De Younf *et al*, 'Taliban in High-level Talks with Karzai Govt, Sources Say', *Washington Post*, 6 October 2010.

46. *Der Spiegel*, 'Interview with Pervez Musharraf', 4 October 2010.

The Role of Media Operations (pp. 127–38)

1. David Kilcullen, 'New Paradigms for 21st Century Conflict', *Foreign Policy Agenda* (Vol. 12, No. 5, May 2007), p. 44.

2. Ayman Al-Zawahiri, July 2005. Letter intercepted by American intelligence.

3. British Army, 'British Army Field Manual: Countering Insurgency', October 2009, pp. 1–6.

4. *Ibid.*, pp. 1–6.

5. *Ibid.*, pp. 1–3.

6. *Ibid.*, pp. 6–4.

Failure to Communicate: 'Producing' the War in Afghanistan (pp. 139–55)

1.   Paddy Ashdown, 'We are Losing in Afghanistan', *Guardian*, 19 July 2007.

2.   Antonio Giustozzi, *Empires of Mud: Wars and Warlords in Afghanistan* (London: Hurst, 2009).

3.   Theo Farrell, 'Improving in War: Military Adaptation and the British in Helmand Province, Afghanistan, 2006–2009', *Journal of Strategic Studies* (Vol. 33, No. 4, 2010), pp. 567–94.

4.   Thirty interviews were conducted by the author, accompanied by Dr Kenneth Payne, Defence Studies Department, King's College London, with commanders and senior civilian and military officials responsible for Information Operations, Public Affairs, and Strategic Communications in HQ ISAF and ISAF Joint Command in Kabul, and in Kandahar in HQ RC-S, the Kandahar PRT, and the Office of the Governor of Kandahar between 27 August and 10 September 2010. The interviews were facilitated by the Prism cell, HQ RC-S. Where quoted directly, they are done so anonymously or identified only by position.

5.   Thomas Rid, *War and Media Operations* (London: Routledge, 2007); Alistair Horne, *Algeria: A Savage War of Peace* (New York, NY: New York Review Books Classics, 2006); Alex Marshall, 'Managing Withdrawal: Afghanistan as the Forgotten Example in Attempting Conflict Resolution and State Reconstruction', *Small Wars and Insurgencies* (Vol. 18, No. 1, 2007), pp. 68–89; and Lester Grau, 'Breaking Contact Without Leaving Chaos: The Soviet Withdrawal from Afghanistan', *Journal of Slavic Military Studies* (Vol. 20, No. 2, 2007), pp. 235–61.

6.   Quoted in Steven Livingston, 'Clarifying the CNN Effect', Research Paper R18, Joan Shorenstein Center, Harvard University, June 1997, available at <http://www.hks.harvard.edu/presspol/publications/papers/research_papers/r18_livingston.pdf>. Accessed 1 October 2010.

7.   Neville Bolt, 'The Leak Before the Storm', *RUSI Journal* (Vol. 155, No. 4, August/September 2010), pp. 46–51.

8.   Manuel Castells, *Communication Power* (Oxford: Oxford University Press, 2009), p. 49.

9.   David Richards, 'Future Conflict and Its Prevention: People and the Information Age', speech at the International Institute for Strategic Studies, London, 18 January 2010, available at <http://www.iiss.org/recent-key-addresses/general-sir-david-richards-address/>. Accessed 1 October 2010.

10. Robert Gates, Landon Lecture, Kansas State University, 26 November 2007, available at <http://www.defense.gov/speeches/speech.aspx?speechid=1199>. Accessed 1 October 2010.

11. Rupert Smith, *The Utility of Force: The Art of War in the Modern World* (London: Penguin, 2006), pp. 284–85.

12. Michael Vlahos, 'The Long War: A Self-defeating Prophecy', *Asia Times*, 9 September 2006.

13. David Betz and Anthony Cormack, 'Iraq, Afghanistan and British Strategy', *Orbis* (Vol. 53, No. 2, 2009), pp. 319–36.

14. An apprehension confirmed by research on the impact of aid on the insurgency. Due to the large amount of money involved, and the level of corruption endemic in Afghanistan, ISAF efforts may be destabilising, actually serving to exacerbate tribal, ethnic, political differences. In some instances, according to Andrew Wilder, research director at Feinstein International Center, Tufts University, aid is extending the reach not of governance, but rather predation, and 'creating vested interests to create insecurity.' See United States Institute for Peace panel, 'Opposed Development: Concept and Implications', 16 June 2010, available at <http://www.usip.org/newsroom/multimedia/video-gallery/opposed-development-concept-and-implications>. Accessed 1 October 2010.

15. Anatol Lieven, review of Antonio Giustozzi, *op. cit.* in note 2, and Alex Mullah Abdul Salam Zaeef, *My Life with the Taliban* (London: Hurst, 2009) in *Current Intelligence*, 6 September 2010.

16. Betz and Cormack, *op. cit.*, p. 327.

17. John Mackinlay, *The Insurgent Archipelago* (London: Hurst, 2009).

18. US House of Representatives Subcommittee on National Security and Foreign Affairs, 'Warlord, Inc.: Extortion and Corruption along the U.S. Supply Chain in Afghanistan', June 2010.

19. Morris Janowitz, *The Professional Soldier: A Social and Political Portrait* (New York, NY: Macmillan, 1971), pp. 21, 35 and 164.

20. Bolt, *op. cit.*, p. 49.

21. Mackinlay, *op. cit.*, pp. 192-96.

22. Anthony King, 'Hamkari and the Future of the Afghan War', *RUSI Journal* (Vol. 155, No. 6, December 2010), pp. 68–74.

23. See Antonio Giustozzi, *Decoding the New Taliban: Insights from the Afghan Field*

(London: Hurst, 2009); and particularly *Empires of Mud, op. cit.*

24. David Betz, 'Redesigning Land Forces for Wars Amongst the People', *Contemporary Security Policy* (Vol. 28, No. 3, 2007), pp. 221–43.

25. Thomas R Mockaitis, *British Counterinsurgency, 1919–60* (New York, NY: St Martin's, 1990).

26. Tim Foxley, 'The Battle for Hearts and Minds in Afghanistan: The Effectiveness of Taliban Information Operations and Related Communications Activities', unpublished paper for the Swedish Armed Forces, March 2009.

27. Donald Rumsfeld, 'New Realities in the Media Age', speech to the Council on Foreign Relations, New York, 17 February 2006, available at <http://www.cfr.org/publication/9900/new_realities_in_the_media_age.html>. Accessed 1 October 2010.

28. Sir Jock Stirrup, Annual Chief of Defence Staff Lecture to the Royal United Services Institute, London, 1 December 2008, available at <http://www.rusi.org/events/ref:E4905F2EFC2531/info:public/infoID:E49341B0484026/>. Accessed 1 October 2010.

29. Foxley, *op. cit.*

30. Neville Bolt, David Betz and Jaz Azari, 'Propaganda of the Deed 2008: Understanding the Phenomenon', *Whitehall Report* 3-08 (London: RUSI, 2008).

31. Bolt, *op. cit.*, p. 49.

32. A case in point is the report by Major General Michael Flynn, 'Fixing Intel: A Blueprint for Making Intelligence Relevant in Afghanistan', Center for a New American Security, 2010.

Peace-Building in Practice: A Personal Perspective on Liberia and the DRC (pp. 177–201)

1. UN General Assembly, 'Report of the Secretary-General on Peacebuilding in the Immediate Aftermath of Conflict', A/63/881 – S/2009/304, 11 June 2009.

2. *Ibid.*

3. Global and Inclusive Agreement on the Transition in the Democratic Republic of the Congo signed in Pretoria, South Africa on 16 December 2002, available at <http://www.reliefweb.int/rw/rwb.nsf/db900SID/MHII-65G8B8?OpenDocument>; Peace Agreement between the Government of Liberia, the Liberian United for Reconciliation and Democracy (LURD), the

Movement for Democracy in Liberia (MODEL) and the Political Parties signed in Accra, Ghana on 18 August 2003, available at <http://www.usip.org/files/file/resources/collections/peace_agreements/liberia_ceasefire_06172003.pdf>.

4. The elections were held in November 2005 in Liberia, and March 2006 in the DRC.

5. The Acts of Engagement signed in Goma, DRC in January 2008 and the agreement signed in March 2009.

6. International Monetary Fund (IMF), 'Debt Relief under the Heavily Indebted Poor Countries (HIPC) Initiative Factsheet', 30 July 2010, available at <http://www.imf.org/external/np/exr/facts/hipc.htm>. Accessed 6 December 2010.

7. IMF, 'IMF and World Bank Announce US$12.3 Billion in Debt Relief for the Democratic Republic of the Congo', press release, 1 July 2010.

8. UNICEF/Ministry of Planning, Joint Press Release, Kinshasa, 18 September 2010.

9. Liberia also suffers from the same lack of capacity in the public sector. Donors expect reform to be carried out by civil servants that have little interest, or incentive, to push forward reforms that might then put them out of a job or curb their ability to make some money from the services they sell to the public.

10. The budgets of the UN peacekeeping missions were larger than the Liberian state budget and not far below that of the DRC.

The Military Role in Political Victory: South Africa, Namibia and Apartheid (pp. 203–17)

1. For details on this historical background, see Greg Mills and Simon Baynham, 'South African Foreign Policy, 1945–90', in Greg Mills (ed.), *From Pariah to Participant: South Africa's Evolving Foreign Relations, 1990–1994* (Johannesburg: South African Institute of International Affairs, 1994), pp .10–36.

2. The Angolans supplied food on an intermittent basis, and partly paid for the demobilisation of Cuban forces. One chartered Soviet aircraft travelled weekly from Angola to Cuba. But the Angolan supply chains were unreliable. On one occasion Cuban troops went without boots, which the Angolans were supposed to furnish. Interview, Havana, June 2004.

3. This section is drawn from Jannie Geldenhuys, *On the Front* (Johannesburg: Jonathan Ball, 2009), and from several personal interactions of that author with David Williams.

4. See Gary Baines, 'Review Article: Magnus Malan: From Uniformed Technocrat

to Securocrat', *Historia* (Vol. 54, No. 1, May 2009), pp. 314–27.

5.   See Annette Seegers, *The Military in the Making of Modern South Africa* (London: IB Tauris, 1996).

6.   This section draws heavily on Greg Mills and David Williams, *Seven Battles that Shaped South Africa* (Johannesburg: Tafelberg, 2005).

7.   See Chester Crocker, *High Noon in Southern Africa: Making Peace in a Rough Neighbourhood* (Johannesburg: Jonathan Ball, 1992).

8.   These interviews were conducted in South Africa and Havana, Cuba in 2004.

9.   General Ochoa was later arrested and executed by Havana on charges of drug trafficking and other 'economic crimes', though it is widely suspected he was executed more for his potential as a coup plotter since he had challenged Castro's military policies in Angola. Javier Corrales, 'Gatekeeper State: Limited Economic Reform and Regime Survival in Cuba, 1989–2002', *Latin American Research Review* (Vol. 39, No. 2, June 2004).

10.   Cited in Piero Glenijeses, *Conflicting Missions: Havana, Washington and Africa, 1959–1976* (Chapel Hill, NC: University of North Carolina Press, 2002), p. 394.

Who Dares, Loses? The Relevance of Rhodesia-Zimbabwe (pp. 219–40)

1.   This chapter describes the forces, places and the authorities as they were then constituted and denoted.

2.   At the peak of 1979, this was made up of around 3,400 regulars with the remainder conscripts. This figure was supplemented by around 45,000 British South Africa Police (of which 8,000 were regulars, the remainder reservists).

3.   By the Rhodesian Security Forces' own estimates, the number of guerrillas operating inside Rhodesia grew from 350/400 in July 1974 to 700 by March 1976, 2,350 by April 1977, 5,598 by November 1977, 6,456 by March 1978, 11,183 by January 1979 and as many as 12,500 by the end of the war. At the time of the ceasefire in December 1979, an estimated 22,000 ZIPRA and 16,000 ZANLA guerrillas remained outside the country, although not all were trained. See Ian F W Beckett, 'The Rhodesian Army: Counter-Insurgency, 1972–1979', available at <http://selousscouts.tripod.com/rhodesian%20army%20coin%20 72_79%20part1.htm>. Last accessed 17 December 2010.

4.   The First Chimurenga is celebrated in Zimbabwe as the First War of Independence, also known as the Second Matabele War, referring to the 1896–97 revolt against

the British South Africa Company's colonial rule.

5. See, for example, Ron Reid-Daly as told to Peter Stiff, *Selous Scouts: Top Secret War* (South Africa: Galago, 1982); Barbara Cole, *The Elite: The Story of the Rhodesian SAS* (South Africa: Three Knights, 1984); and Peter Stiff, *See You in November* (South Africa: Galago, 1987). Some Rhodesians came to believe their own mythologies. *TIME* Johannesburg Bureau Chief William McWhirter quoted one senior non-commissioned officer in 1978: 'We have created a top-rate bush fighter. You can drop an average reserve troopie [private] anywhere in the country at night with a compass, and he can give you a six-figure grid reading which can put you within 100 yards of his position.' See *TIME*, 27 February 1978.

6. A notable exemption is Jakkie Cilliers's account of the conflict, *Counter Insurgency in Rhodesia* (London: Croom Helm, 1985), written originally as an MA thesis and the result of travel and interviews throughout Zimbabwe.

7. Including civilians in Mozambique and Zambia. Officially the war cost the deaths of 410 white and 691 black civilians, but these figures were clearly understated.

8. This does not include external casualties of the guerrilla organisations.

9. ZAPU was formed in 1962, and almost immediately banned by the Whitehead government; ZANU was formed in August 1963 as a result of Nkomo's expulsion from ZAPU of Ndabaningi Sithole, Robert Mugabe, Leopold Takawira and Washington Malianga, as a result of their opposition to his leadership.

10. *Umkhonto we Sizwe* [Spear of the Nation].

11. Cilliers, *op cit.*, p. 12.

12. Cited in *ibid.*, p. 13.

13. Made up of Dakota paratroop and helicopter-borne troops comprising ninety-seven SAS, and eighty-eight Rhodesian Light Infantry soldiers.

14. Some estimates put the base numbers as high as 12,000. The attack is vividly described in Chris Cocks' sobering account of his service in the Rhodesian Army, *Fireforce: One Man's War in the Rhodesian Light Infantry* (South Africa: Covos Day, 2001), pp. 144–46. The raid led to the largest air effort yet marshalled by the Rhodesians, though the age and serviceability of the aircraft indicated their problems: forty-two helicopters, eight Hawker Hunters, six Vampires, three Canberras, six Dakotas and around one dozen Lynxes (a militarised version of the Cessna Super Skymaster). At the peak of its strength during the insurgency, the Rhodesian Air Force had 2,300 personnel. Of these, only 150 were pilots actively involved in combat operations.

In the Chimoio raid, the largest such joint-force operation of the war, over 1,200 guerrillas and dependents, some of them women and children, were killed.

15. The name, after the nineteenth-century explorer Courtney Selous, was originally given to an armoured car unit constituted in 1961 and later relinquished to the special forces pseudo-guerrilla unit upon its creation in 1973.

16. Muzorewa was teamed in an alliance that included the Reverend Ndabaningi Sithole and Chief Jeremiah Chirau.

17. It is estimated that, by the war's end in 1980, the South African government was directly and indirectly footing the bill for around half of the Rhodesian defence expenditure.

18. Officially, in 1971 the country had 9,403 white immigrants; in 1976, 7,072 residents left, and in 1978, 13,709.

19. Cocks, *op cit.*, p. 272.

20. Ronald Weitzer, *Transforming Settler States: Communal Conflict and Internal Security in Northern Ireland and Zimbabwe* (Berkeley, CA: University of California Press, 1990).

21. From 1971/72 to 1976/77 the budget for the Ministry of Internal Affairs (previously the Department of Native Affairs) jumped from R$9.7 million to R$42 million; that for the Ministry of Law and Order (including police) jumped from R$17.5 million to R$50 million; and expenditure for the Ministry of Defence grew from R$20 million to R$98.7 million. See Government of Southern Rhodesia Report, 'Estimates of Expenditure', 1971/72 and 1976/77.

22. Beckett, *op. cit.*

23. For example, under Operation *Overload* in July 1974 over 46,000 Africans were removed from the Chiweshe area into twenty-one protected villages and some 13,500 people from the Madziwa area. Officially there were 116 protected villages by August 1976, 178 by September 1977 and 234 planned or built by January 1978.

24. Beckett, *op. cit.*

25. *Ibid.*

26. It is estimated that over one-third of the African cattle herd died during the war while, with only 1,500 out of 8,000 cattle dips still in operation in 1979, disease such as anthrax and tsetse again became rampant.

27. Beckett, *op. cit.*

28. *Ibid.*

29. Major General Arthur Bruce Campling, 'Pseudo-Terrorist Operations in Rhodesia' (undated mimeo).

30. After the first aircraft was shot down, Nkomo laughed and joked about the incident on television. In his memoirs, *Story of My Life* (1985), Nkomo however expressed regret for the shooting down of both planes.

31. Under the terms of this plan, 'A' Squadron of the SAS would assassinate Mugabe, while 'B' Squadron would mount an attack on Vice-President Simon Muzenda and the 100-man contingent of ZANLA based in the Medical Arts Centre. 'C' Squadron was designated to take out the 200 ZIPRA and ZANLA men with their commanders (Rex Nhongo, Dumiso Dabengwa and Lookout Musika) based at the Audio Visual Arts building of the University of Rhodesia. See R Allport, 'Operation Quartz: Rhodesia 1980', available at <http://www.rhodesia.nl/quartz.htm>.

32. See 'The Rhodesian Army 1977', available at <http://members.tripod.com/selousscouts/rhodesian_army.htm>.

33. On the parallels with Iraq and Afghanistan see, for example, Edward Luttwak, 'Dead End: Counter Insurgency as Military Malpractice', *Harper's*, February 2007.

34. By 1979 blacks comprised 40 per cent of the 15,000 army personnel and 60 per cent of the British South African Police. Most, however, apparently enlisted for economic reasons. See Weitzer, *op cit.*

Rwanda: Putting the Insurgency Boot on the Other Foot (pp. 241–57)

1. This article is partly based on interviews with serving and retired RPA/RDF officers during 2008, and members of the RPF.

2. As a colonel regarded as one of Kagame's deputies in the RPA, later chief of the cabinet of the Government of Rwanda, and from 2009 High Commissioner to Uganda.

3. See Gerard Prunier, *The Rwanda Crisis: History of a Genocide* (London: Hurst, 1995), p. 96. For details of the RPA's origins and *modus operandi*, see Prunier's chapter in Christopher Clapham (ed.), *African Guerrillas* (London: James Currey, 1998), pp.119–33.

4. Romeo Dallaire, *Shake Hands with the Devil: The Failure of Humanity in Rwanda* (London: Arrow, 2004), p. 67.

5. Later minister of youth in the RPF government, special envoy to the Great Lakes and until May 2008, deputy chairman of the Commission of the African Union.

6. The French-piloted aircraft – a gift from the French government to Rwanda – was returning from a regional meeting in Dar-es-Salaam. Its occupants included

Burundi's President Cyprien Ntaryamira who had hitched a ride in preference to taking his older propeller-driven aircraft.

7.   Dallaire, *op. cit.*, p. 290. Some 2,538 UNAMIR personnel were on the ground on 7 April 1994. On 21 April, the UN Security Council passed Resolution 912 stating that it was appalled at the large scale of the violence in Rwanda, but at the same meeting voted to reduce UNAMIR to just 270 volunteer personnel and to limit its mandate. As Dallaire notes (p. 322), 'The resolution's phrases were pure UN-ese: "… having considered … express regret … shocked … appalled … deeply concerned … stressing … expressing deep concern … condemns … strongly condemns … demands … decides … reiterates … reaffirms … calls upon … invites … decides to remain actively seized of the matter".' On 17 May, the Security Council (Resolution 918) moved to give UNAMIR a more robust mandate and 5,500 troops, even though, as Dallaire observes (p. 374), it remained vague on the genocide and the role the UN force should play in stopping it.

8.   General Kabarebe is the highest-ranking RDF officer among those political and military figures indicted by French and Spanish judges on separate war crimes charges. French Judge Jean Louis Bruguiere issued arrest warrants on 17 November 2006 implicating nine RPF members, including President Kagame and Kabarebe, in the downing of Habyarimana's jet. In February 2008, Spanish Judge Andreu Fernando Merrelles indicted forty officers of the RPA, including Kabarebe, and the deputy commander of the UN/African Union Darfur force Major General Emmanuel Karake Karenzi, on genocide-related crimes, linking them to the death of nine Spanish nationals during the mayhem before, during and after the genocide in Rwanda and the Congo. The Spanish judge also claims to be in possession of evidence implicating Kagame, but cannot indict him because of his immunity as head of state. Kabarebe compares the role of the dissidents' and enemies' evidence, on which the French and Spanish indictments are based, to 'George Bush being indicted by Al-Qa'ida'. He believes that this stems from Rwanda's military defeat of the French-sponsored Hutu army and Mobutu, the lack of credibility of the FDLR internationally, and the democratic and economic success of a post-genocide Rwanda. 'The French are humiliated, especially when you look at our progress after liberation from *Francophonie* influence, compared to those such as Chad, Ivory Coast, Cameroon and others who remain within that ambit. This judicial process is not different to the guerrilla war or to the [French] Zone Turquoise [established as a

safe haven for refugees at the end of the genocide, among them many *genocidaires*] – it is another tool of war, another frontline we must fight', says Kabarebe who believes that the process 'is also intended to serve the surviving *genocidaires*, to see them not as perpetrators but as victims.'

9. A minority community of mainly Tutsi Kinyarwanda speakers living in South Kivu, numbering, from recent election statistics, around 300,000.

10. Interview, *El Ché – and Tracing Ché* [documentary film]

11. *Daily Telegraph*, 'Rwandan Troops Spearhead Peace Force for Darfur', 16 August 2004.

Sierra Leone: 'Pregnant with Lessons' (pp. 259–75)

1. Discussion between the author and Richard Connaughton, Freetown, Sierra Leone, 28 October 2000.

2. Kabbah had worked for the UN for twenty-two years before returning to Sierra Leone in 1992.

3. These were the mercenaries who had restored Kabbah to power – a result which could not be deplored with conviction.

4. *Economist*, 13 May 2000.

5. Contributors of force troops were: Bangladesh, Ghana, Guinea, India, Jordan, Kenya, Nigeria and Zambia.

6. Richard Connaughton, 'Military Intervention and Peace-keeping: The Reality', *Joint Force Quarterly Review*, 26 July 2001.

7. By chance Bernard Miyet, the head of the UN's Department of Peacekeeping Operations, was in Freetown when the British arrived. There is no doubt that his presence and pragmatism eased the way for what potentially could have been a very difficult relationship between the UN and UK forces. 'The arrival of the British is good for us', said a UN spokesman, despite initial problems.

8. HMS *Illustrious* arrived off Freetown on 11 May and the HMS *Ocean* group on 14 May.

9. M Tkalec, 'Neocolonialism with a Human Face', *Berliner Zeitung*, 21 June 2000.

10. My direction to the force commanders, and specifically those officers with responsibility for the campaign's information operation – Freetown, 10 October 2000.

11. Tony Blair, *A Journey* (London: Hutchinson, 2010), p. 247.

12. Connaughton, *op. cit.*

13. Gwyn Prins, *The Heart of War* (London: Routledge, 2002).

Somalia: Insurgency and Legitimacy in the Context of State Collapse (pp. 277–94)

1. Robert I Rotberg, 'The Failure and Collapse of Nation-States: Breakdown, Prevention, and Repair' in Robert Rotberg (ed.), *When States Fail: Causes and Consequences* (Princeton, NJ: Princeton University Press, 2004), pp. 9–10.

2. It is significant that while the TFG and its predecessor entities have received various expressions of support from the international community, other states have been rather reluctant to actually accord it formal recognition.

3. Department of State, Office of the Coordinator for Counterterrorism, 'Designation of al-Shabaab as a Specially Designated Global Terrorist', Public Notice 6137, 26 February 2008.

4. Commonwealth of Australia/Attorney-General Robert McClelland MP and Minister for Foreign Affairs Stephen Smith MP, 'Listing of Al-Shabaab as a Terrorist Organisation', joint media release, 21 August 2009.

5. The Terrorism Act 2000 (Proscribed Organisations) (Amendment) Order 2010, No. 611, 4 March 2010.

6. Canadian Ministry of Public Safety, 'The Government of Canada Lists Al Shabaab as a Terrorist Organization', news release, 7 March 2010.

7. See Eliot Cohen, Conrad Crane, Jan Horvath and John Nagl, 'Principles, Imperatives, and Paradoxes of Counterinsurgency', *Military Review* (Vol. 86, No. 2, March/April 2006), pp. 49–53.

8. See John A Lynn, 'Patterns of Insurgency and Counterinsurgency', *Military Review* (Vol. 85, No. 4, July–August 2005), pp. 22–27.

9. Rodney Barker, *Political Legitimacy and the State* (Oxford: Clarendon Press, 1990), p. 11.

10. Max Weber, 'The Profession and Vocation of Politics' in Peter Lassman and Ronald Speirs (eds.), *Weber: Political Writings* (Cambridge: Cambridge University Press, 1994), pp. 311–12.

11. Cohen *et al*, *op. cit.*, p. 50.

12. Timothy J Lomperis, 'Vietnam's Offspring: The Lesson of Legitimacy', *Conflict Quarterly* (Vol. 6, No. 1, Winter 1986), pp. 26–27.

13. Henry A Kissinger, 'The Vietnam Negotiations', *Foreign Affairs* (Vol. 47, No. 2, January 1969), p. 214.

14. See I M Lewis, *A Pastoral Democracy* (London: Oxford University Press, 1961).

15. I M Lewis, *Making and Breaking States in Africa: The Somali Experience* (Trenton, NJ: Red Sea Press, 2010), pp. 8–9.

16. *Ibid.*, p. 102.

17. See John L Hirsh and Robert Oakley, *Somalia and Operation Restore Hope: Reflections on Peacemaking and Peacekeeping* (Washington, DC: US Institute of Peace, 1995).

18. See Virginia Luling, 'Come Back Somalia? Questioning a Collapsed State', *Third World Quarterly* (Vol. 18, No. 2, June 1997), pp. 287–302.

19. Abdurahman M Abdullahi, 'Recovering the Somali State: The Islamic Factor' in A Osman Farah, Mammo Muchie and Joakim Gundel (eds.), *Somalia: Diaspora and State Reconstitution in the Horn of Africa* (London: Adonis & Abbey, 2007), pp. 196–221.

20. See Shaul Shay, *Somalia between Jihad and Restoration* (New Brunswick, NJ: Transaction Publishers, 2007), pp. 93–127; also see Kenneth J Menkhaus, 'Somalia and Somaliland: Terrorism, Political Islam, and State Collapse' in Robert I Rotberg (ed.), *Battling Terrorism in the Horn of Africa* (Washington, DC: Brookings Institution Press, 2005), pp. 23–47; and 'Risks and Opportunities in Somalia', *Survival* (Vol. 49, No. 2, Summer 2007), pp. 5–20.

21. See I M Lewis, *Blood and Bone: The Call of Kinship in Somali Society* (Princeton, NJ: Red Sea Press, 1994), p. 167.

22. See I M Lewis, *Saints and Somalis: Popular Islam in a Clan-Based Society* (Lawrenceville, NJ: Red Sea Press, 1998).

23. See Michael van Notten and Spencer Heath MacCallum (eds.), *The Law of the Somalis: A Stable Foundation for Economic Development in the Horn of Africa* (Trenton, NJ: Red Sea Press, 2006).

24. See Lewis, *op. cit.* in note 15, pp. 188–94.

25. See Kenneth J Menkhaus, 'The Crisis in Somalia: Tragedy in Five Acts', *African Affairs* (Vol. 106, No. 424, July 2007), pp. 357–90.

26. See Oscar Gakuo Mwangi, 'The Union of Islamic Courts and Security Governance in Somalia', *African Security Review* (Vol. 19, No. 1, March 2010), pp. 88–94.

27. See Medhane Tadesse, *Al-Ittihad: Political Islam and Black Economy in Somalia: Religion, Money, Clan and the Struggle for Supremacy over Somalia* (Addis Ababa, 2002), pp. 16–24. The group 'Islamic Union' was established in the early 1980s, seeking the creation of an expansive 'Islamic Republic of Greater Somalia', and

eventually a political union embracing all Muslims in the Horn of Africa.

28. Menkhaus, *op. cit.* in note 25, p. 382.

29. See Kenneth J Menkhaus, 'Somalia: What Went Wrong?', *RUSI Journal* (Vol. 154, No. 4, August 2009), pp. 6–12; J Peter Pham, 'Peripheral Vision: A Model Solution for Somalia', *RUSI Journal* (Vol. 154, No. 5, October 2009), pp. 84–90.

30. Apuuli Phillip Kasaija, 'The UN-led Djibouti Peace Process for Somalia 2008–2009: Results and Problems', *Journal of Contemporary African Studies* (Vol. 28, No. 3, July 2010), p. 278.

31. See Andre Le Sage, 'Somalia's Endless Transition: Breaking the Deadlock', *Strategic Forum* (No. 257, June 2010).

32. UN Security Council, Report of the Monitoring Group on Somalia pursuant to Security Council Resolution 1853 (2008), S/2010/91, 10 March 2010, pp. 4, 12.

33. Bronwyn E Bruton, *Somalia: A New Approach*, Council on Foreign Relations Special Report 52, 2010, p. 10.

34. See Elizabeth Dickinson, 'How Much Turf Does the Somali Government Really Control?', *ForeignPolicy.com*, 23 September 2010.

35. See J Peter Pham, 'Somali Stability Still Poses Threat Even After Successful Strike on Nabhan', *World Defense Review*, 17 September 2009. The price of AK-47 rounds, for example, fell over 50 per cent to approximately $0.30 each.

36. See Roland Marchal, 'A Tentative Assessment of the Somali *Harakat Al-Shabaab*', *Journal of Eastern African Studies* (Vol. 3, No. 3, November 2009), pp. 381–404.

37. See *CNN*, '21 Killed in Suicide Attack on African Union Base in Somalia', 18 September 2009.

38. See Evan Perez, 'Case Shows Rise of Non-Bank Transfers to Fund Terror', *Wall Street Journal*, 17 November 2010.

39. Jonathan Stevenson, 'Jihad and Piracy in Somalia', *Survival* (Vol. 52, No. 1, February/March 2010), pp. 27–38.

40. *AFP*, 'Somalia's Top Islamist Leaders in Unity Talks', 10 July 2010.

41. Abdi Sheikh and Abdi Guled, 'Somali Rebels Unite, Profess Loyalty to al Qaeda', *Reuters*, 1 February 2010.

42. See J Peter Pham, 'The Somali Solution to the Somali Crisis', *Harvard Africa Policy Journal* (No. 6, 2010), pp. 71–84.

43. See Iqbal Jhazbhay, *Somaliland: An African Struggle for Nationhood and International Recognition* (Johannesburg: South African Institute for International

Affairs/Institute for Global Dialogue, 2009).

44. See Kinfe Abraham, *Somalia Calling: The Crisis of Statehood and the Quest for Peace* (Addis Ababa: Ethiopian International Institute for Peace and Development, 2002), pp. 445–63.

45. While the region's constitution still formally commits it to being a part of a future federal Somalia, the lack of progress in the southern and central parts of Somalia and the lacklustre performance of the TFG have caused Puntlanders to edge closer to outright secessionism. In late December 2009, the regional parliament voted unanimously to adopt a distinctive flag (hitherto the flag of Somalia had been used), coat of arms and anthem.

46. See J Peter Pham, 'Putting Somali Piracy in Context', *Journal of Contemporary African Studies* (Vol. 28, No. 3, July 2010), pp. 325–41; also see J Peter Pham, 'The Failed State and Regional Dimensions of Somali Piracy' in Bibi van Ginkel and Frans-Paul van der Putten (eds.) *The International Response to Somali Piracy: Challenges and Opportunities* (Leiden: Martinus Nijhoff, 2010), pp. 31–64.

47. See Dustin Dehéz and Belachew Gebrewold, 'When Things Fall Apart: Conflict Dynamics and an Order Beside the State in Postcollapse Somalia', *African Security* (Vol. 3, No. 1, January 2010), pp. 1–20.

48. David Kilcullen, *Counterinsurgency* (Oxford: Oxford University Press, 2010), p. 156.

49. Johnnie Carson, 'Remarks to the Press from the UN General Assembly', 24 September 2010, available at <http://www.state.gov/p/af/rls/spbr/2010/147922. htm>. Accessed 1 December 2010.

50. African Union, Peace and Security Council, Communiqué of the 245th Meeting, PSC/MIN/1 (CCXXXXV), 15 October 2010, p. 3.

51. Seth Kaplan, 'Rethinking State-building in a Failed State', *Washington Quarterly* (Vol. 33, No. 1, January 2010), p. 82.

The Campaign against the LRA: Old Wine in New Bottles (pp. 295–312)

1. See Resolve Uganda, 'From Promise to Peace: A Blueprint for President Obama's LRA Strategy', September 2010; Acholi Religious Leaders Peace Initiative, 'Response to "From Promise to Peace: A Blueprint for President Obama's LRA Strategy" by Resolve', October 2010; Jort Hemmer and Nikki Frenken, 'The Lord's Resistance Army: in Search of a New Approach', Conflict Research Unit, Clingendael Institute, 25 June 2010; International Crisis Group, 'LRA: A

Regional Strategy beyond Killing Kony', 28 April 2010.

2. For more details on the organisation of the LRA, see Chris Dolan, *Social Torture: The Case of Northern Uganda, 1986–2006* (New York: Berghahn Books, 2009); Tim Allen and Koen Vlassenroot, *The Lord's Resistance Army: Myths and Reality* (London: Zed Books, 2010); Sverker Finnström, *Living with Bad Surroundings: War, History and Everyday Moments in Northern Uganda* (Durham, NC: Duke University Press, 2008).

3. Even if portrayed as a predatory group attacking civilians, the LRA also regularly engaged UPDF, SPLA, hostile militia groups and even UN soldiers. It also gained the advantage over elite US-trained Guatemalan troops on a mission to track and kill Kony in the Garamba National Park in 2006.

4. Chris Dolan, 'Understanding War and Its Continuation: The Case of Northern Uganda', PhD dissertation, Development Studies Institute, London School of Economics and Political Science, 2005; Sandrine Perrot, 'Vers une Fin de Conflit au Nord de l'Ouganda? La LRA (1987–2005), Causes et Enjeux d'une Guerre Prolongée', *L'Annuaire des Pays d'Afrique Orientale* (2004), pp. 73–139.

5. Human Rights Watch, 'Uprooted and Forgotten: Impunity and Human Rights Abuses in Northern Uganda', 20 September 2005.

6. An amnesty was granted in 2000 under the pressure of local religious and parents' associations.

7. The five agenda items were: cessation of hostilities; comprehensive solutions to the conflict; reconciliation and accountability; formal ceasefire; and disarmament, demobilisation, and reintegration.

8. Human Rights Watch, 'The Christmas Massacres: LRA Attacks on Civilians in Northern Congo', 16 February 2009.

9. Birao houses a CAR military base, MINURCAT and many offices of international NGOs working in Darfur.

10. For a definition of the system of conflicts, see Roland Marchal, 'Tchad/Sudan: How Two Crises Merge', *Review of African Political Economy* (No. 109, 2006), pp. 469–82. See also Hans Peter Schmitz, 'Rebels without a Cause? Transnational Diffusion and the Lord's Resistance Army (LRA), 1990–2010', Peace Research Institute Oslo.

11. *Sudan Tribune*, 'Western Equatoria Welcomes Creation of African Forces to Respond to LRA Rebels', 18 October 2010.

12. The UPDF suffered losses in battles with the LRA, but also with other armed groups, for example in May 2010 northeast of Djemah when an estimated fifty-three soldiers were killed, reportedly by Sudanese militias. Ledio Cakaj, 'Disturbing Developments in the Hunt for Kony', Enough Project, 29 June 2010, available at <http://www.enoughproject.org/publications/field-dispatch-disturbing-developments-hunt-kony>. Last accessed 12 November 2010.

13. *Ibid.*

14. Henri Mukasa, 'British Army Chief, Aronda Discuss LRA', *The New Vision*, 9 February 2009.

15. *Voice of America*, 'La République centrafricaine veut en finir avec la LRA', 19 August 2010.

16. Ledio Cakaj, '"This is our land now": Lord's Resistance Army attacks in Bas Uélé, Northeastern Congo', Enough Project, 10 August 2010, p. 5.

17. Acholi Religious Leaders Peace Initiative, *op. cit.*

18. Some of these armed groups opportunely adopted 'LRA tactics', creating confusion about the identity of the attacking forces (see also the mind-shattering cases of rape reported during recent alleged LRA attacks that are at odds with usual LRA modes of operation).

19. International Crisis Group, 'The LRA in Darfur and Central African Republic', ICG podcast, 12 October 2010.

20. 'Lord's Resistance Army Disarmament and Northern Uganda Recovery Act of 2009', US Congress 1067.

21. Ledio Cakaj, 'On the Heels of Kony: the Untold Tragedy Unfolding in the Central African Republic', Enough Project, 24 June 2010.

22. Richard Vokes, 'The LRA on the March Again', *theafricanist.blogspot.com*, 14 October 2010.

23. According to an Enough Project report, in Bas-Uélé the LRA deported civilians, took their land, and forced some abductees to cultivate for them. Some villagers allegedly gave funds and guns to the LRA to protect their own communities from attacks. In Bas Uélé, the LRA sent letters to conclude non-aggression pacts with local communities. Ledio Cajak, *op. cit.* in note 16, p. 5.

24. Richard Ruati, 'Arrow Boys in W. Western Equatoria to be Armed against LRA – Governor', *Sudan Tribune*, 28 September 2010.

Countering the Terrorist Insurgency in Bangladesh (pp. 313–28)

1. Maneeza Hossain and Lisa Curtis, 'Bangladesh: Checking Islamist Extremism in a Pivotal Democracy', Heritage Foundation backgrounder, 15 March 2010.

2. Jahangir Alam Akash, 'State Confession Regarding Islamic Militancy', *UPI Asia. com*, 16 September 2009.

3. Bangladeshi Enterprise Institute, 'Countering Terrorism in Bangladesh: A Strategy Paper', July 2007.

4. *Daily Star* [Bangladesh], 5 August 2009.

5. *Ibid.*

6. Benedict Rogers, 'Bangladesh's Secular Democracy Struggles with Violent Radical Islam', *The Cutting Edge*, 24 November 2008.

7. Shahidul Islam, 'Revolt in the Rifles: Crisis Needs Very Careful Handling', *Holiday*, 27 February 2009.

8. Anupam Ray, 'Islamic Radical Ideologies and South Asian Security: The Case of Bangladesh', CSIS report, 27 October 2008.

9. A N M Muniruzzaman, 'Bangladesh at the Crossroads: Democracy, Radicalisation and Terrorism Amidst the Emerging Security Challenges of South Asia', speech given at the Henry Jackson Society, 22 December 2008.

10. Rogers, *op. cit.*

11. Bangladesh Institute of International and Strategic Studies, 'Countering Radicalization in South Asia: Bangladesh Perspective', roundtable discussion, 25 May 2009, available at <http://www.biiss.org/asia.pdf>.

12. *Ibid.*

13. Joyeeta Bhattacharjee, 'Understanding 12 Extremist Groups of Bangladesh', *Observer India*, 7 June 2009.

14. *SATP.org*, 'Harkat-ul-Jihad-al Islami Bangladesh (HuJI-B): Terrorist Group, Bangladesh', undated. Accessed 23 October 2010.

15. *Ibid.*

16. *Ibid.*

17. *Ibid.*

18. *Ibid.*

19. *Daily Star* [Bangladesh], 'Leaflets Ridicule Democracy', 18 August 2005.

20. Adam E Stahl, 'Jama'atul Mujahideen Bangladesh: Militant Islamist Terror', *Terrorism Watch*, 30 April 2007.

21. Sunita Paul, 'HuT Planning Offensives in September 09', *Modern Ghana*, 16 April 2009.

22. *Daily Star* [Bangladesh], '31 Hizb-ut Towhid Men Sent to Jail', 19 April 2009.

23. Bhattacharjee, *op. cit.*

24. *Ibid.*

25. A M M Quamruzzaman, *The Militia Movement in Bangladesh: Ideology, Motivation, Mobilization, Organization, and Ritual* (Saarbrücken: LAP Lambert, 2010).

26. Hizb-ut-Tahrir press release, 6 January 2007, available at <http://www.khilafat. org/newPages/PressRelease/Resources/PR_ENG_070106_01.pdf>.

27. SUPRO, 'Increasing Poverty and MDGs Achievement: Is a Poverty-free Bangladesh Possible?', *SUPRO Position Paper*, 15 July 2007.

28. *Xinhua*, 'Bangladesh Receives Record Nearly $11 bln Remittance in 2009–10 fiscal [*sic*]', 7 July 2010.

29. 'Weekly Assessment and Briefings', *South Asia Intelligence Review* (Vol. 4, No. 29, January 2006).

30. Julfikar Ali Manik and Shariful Islam, 'Six JMB Militants Hanged', *Daily Star* [Bangladesh], 31 March 2007.

31. *Daily Star* [Bangladesh], 'Anti-Terror, RPO Ordinances get Cabinet Nod', 20 February 2009.

32. *Ibid.*

33. *Ibid.*

34. Animesh Roul, 'Islam-o-Muslim and the Resilience of Terrorism in Bangladesh', *Terrorism Monitor* (Vol. 7, No. 22).

Countering Instability in Kashmir (pp. 329–47)

1. Sir Owen Dixon, an Australian judge and diplomat, was appointed by the UN as a mediator between the governments of India and Pakistan on Kashmir from May to September 1950.

2. See Burton Stein, *A History of India* (New York, NY: Wiley Blackwell, 1998).

3. UN Commission for India and Pakistan Resolution of 13 August 1948 (S/1100, Para 75) and Josef Korbel, *Danger in Kashmir* (Princeton, NJ: Princeton University Press, 1954).

4. In 1950, Sir Owen Dixon, the UN mediator, stated this towards the end of his talks with the prime ministers of Pakistan and India. He had asked them directly whether

they agreed that there was no prospect whatsoever of reaching agreement on any programme of demilitarisation leading up to an overall plebiscite. Liaquat Ali of Pakistan and Pandit Nehru of India answered categorically in the affirmative.

5. Population census of India, 2001.

6. Pakistan de-linked the Northern Areas from Jammu and Kashmir and absorbed it into the rest of Pakistan in 1982.

7. The 'two-nation theory', that Muslims and Hindus are two separate nations and therefore Muslims should have an autonomous homeland in the Muslim majority areas, was the basis for the Partition of India in 1947. The theory was undermined after East Pakistan became independent and called itself Bangladesh. India, with the second-largest Muslim population in the world, has remained secular.

8. Josef Korbel, *Danger in Kashmir* (Princeton, NJ: Princeton University Press, 1954).

9. Michael Brecher, *The Struggle for Kashmir* (New York, NY: Oxford University Press, 1953).

10. Tashkent Declaration, 10 January 1966.

11. Many leading parties in India did not, and still do not, favour extension of Article 370 of the Indian Constitution.

12. The Indira Gandhi-Sheikh Abdullah agreement of February 1975.

13. Sufism is an umbrella term for the ascetic and mystical movements within Islam, which reject worship motivated by the desire for heavenly reward or the fear of punishment. It insists on the love of God as the sole valid form of adoration. It encourages people of religions to live in harmony. From *The Columbia Encyclopedia,* Sixth Edition (New York, NY: Columbia University Press, 2000).

14. A Kashmiri, Mufti Mohammad Sayeed later founded the Jammu and Kashmir People's Democratic Party and became chief minister of the state from November 2002 to November 2005.

15. Nawaz Sharif stated in an interview to a weekend magazine of the Dawn Group: 'It was later revealed to me that the stone pelting on the cars of diplomats and processions against Vajpayee's visit to Lahore in February 1999 were stage-managed and orchestrated by the agencies through a politico-religious party (Jamaat-e-Islami).' *Times of India,* 11 October 2004. The Jamaat-e-Islami was referred to as the 'Army's B team in matters ideological' by Ayaz Amir in his article 'Retrieving the Lost Years', *Dawn* [Pakistan], 5 December 2003.

16. V P Malik, *Kargil: From Surprise to Victory* (New Delhi: HarperCollins, 2006).

17. This includes an ambitious Kashmir railways project worth $2.5 billion.

18. Ministry of Home Affairs Annual Report, 2009–10.

19. *Ibid.*

20. *Ibid.*

21. *Ibid.*

22. On 31 January 2010, India's defence minister A K Antony declared, 'As far as policy is concerned, we are very clear. Our ultimate aim is to bring normalcy in Kashmir and entrust law and order to Kashmir Police itself. The Army can safely safeguard the border. That is our long-term aim.' *Times of India*, 1 February 2010.

23. Statistics and assessment based on information collected from the Ministries of Home, Defence (Army Headquarters), and South Asia Terrorism Portal of the Institute for Conflict Management, New Delhi. On 18 March 2010, Jammu and Kashmir chief minister Omar Abdullah said that about 550–75 terrorists were presently active in the state.

24. Ministry of Home Affairs, *op. cit.*

25. The Islamabad Declaration, 6 January 2004.

26. Editorial in *Times of India*, 26 April 2010.

27. *Times of India*, 'Just 2% of People in Jammu and Kashmir Want to Join Pak', 28 May 2010.

28. *India News* (No. 22, Volume VIII).

29. Ashutosh Varshney, *Perspectives on Kashmir: The Roots of Conflict in South Asia* (Boulder, CO: Westview Press, 1992).

The Southern Thailand Insurgency (pp. 349–66)

1. The author would like to thank Marc Askew, an academic based in Australia, but with significant experience living and working in southern Thailand; Shawn Crispin, Asia Times Online; Don Pathan, Journalist; Sunai Phasuk, Human Rights Watch (Bangkok); Phanu Uthairat, Director of the Southern Border Provinces Administration Centre; Srisompob Jitpiromsri of Deep South Watch based at Prince of Songkla University, Pattani Campus, Thailand; Colonel Songwit Noonpackdee, deputy commander of Narathiwat Task Force and COIN trainer; Songaun Inrak, President of the Teachers' Federation of Narathiwat; Colonel Banphot Phunphian, Chief of Public Relations at the Internal Security

Operations Command 4th Forward Area, Sirinthon Fort, Yarang, Pattani. Many thanks to Marc Askew, Shawn Crispin and Don Pathan for reviewing the chapter, but suffice to say all errors are my own. Interviews were also carried out with relatives of those killed in the violence and others who did not wish to be named.

The Lessons from Northern Ireland: Comparisons with Iraq and Afghanistan (pp. 367–81)

1. For a background comparison of counter-insurgency lessons from British and US experience, see John Nagl, *Learning to Eat Soup with a Knife: Counterinsurgency Lessons from Malaya and Vietnam* (New York, NY: Praeger, 2002).

2. For example policing, and its budget, is a devolved responsibility exercised from Stormont: there is no separate police budget for dealing with terrorism or insurgency. National security, however, remains the responsibility of Westminster, but without the budget to finance police activity unendorsed by the Northern Ireland Assembly.

3. Now known as the Stabilisation Unit.

4. Nigel Alywin-Foster, 'Changing the Army for Counterinsurgency Operations', *Military Review* (November/December 2005).

5. Glynne Evans, valedictory dispatch, Lisbon, 2004.

6. Increased to fifteen months during the height of the 'Surge'.

7. Later known as Home Service Battalions of the Royal Irish Regiment.

8. Sometimes referred to as the theatre strategic level.

Coke isn't it: Changing a Culture and Image of Violence in Colombia (pp. 383–411)

1. *BBC News*, 'Extracts from Uribe's inauguration speech', 8 August 2002.

2. *BBC News*, 'Colombia's Santos hails "beginning of end" for Farc', 27 September 2010.

3. Cited in *TIME*, 'New Kings of Coke', 1 July 1991.

4. The Cali Cartel reportedly provided in excess of $6 million, delivered in paper bags normally used for birthday gifts.

5. Rupert Everett, *Red Carpets and Other Banana Skins* (London: Little, Brown, 2006).

6. See Steven Dudley, *Walking Ghosts: Murder and Guerrilla Politics in Colombia* (New York, NY: Routledge, 2006), p. 2.

7. Information supplied by the Policy Intelligence Division, Bogotá, 10 December 2010.

8. *GlobalSecurity.org*, 'Colombian Domestic Disturbances', available at <http://

www.globalsecurity.org/military/world/war/colombia.htm>. Last accessed 16 December 2010.

9. ABColombia (CAFOD, Christian Aid, Oxfam GB, SCIAF, Trócaire), available at <http://www.abcolombia.org.uk/mainpage.asp?mainid=76>.

10. Police Intelligence, Bogotá, 10 December 2010.

11. Discussion, Bogotá, 8 December 2010.

12. Interview, Bogotá, 7 December 2010.

13. Discussion, Bogotá, 8 December 2010.

14. Dudley, *op cit.*, p. 8.

15. Interview, Medellin, December 2006.

16. Discussion, Bogotá, 9 December 2010.

17. Information supplied by Colombian Police Intelligence, Bogotá, 10 December 2010. In 2007, then-FARC-EP Commander Raúl Reyes claimed that their force consisted of 18,000 guerrillas.

18. Ministry of National Defense, Republic of Colombia, 'Policy for the Consolidation of National Security', 2007.

19. According to Maplecroft, Colombia had the world's sixth highest risk of 'terrorism' in 2010. See Maplecroft, 'Somalia overtakes Iraq, Afghanistan, Pakistan and Colombia to become world's terror capital – Global study', 15 November 2010, available at <http://www.maplecroft.com/about/news/terrorism.html>.

20. *Reuters*, 'Popularity of Colombia's Uribe soars after rescue', 6 July 2008.

21. Discussion, Bogotá, 10 December 2010.

22. Bogotá, 10 December 2010.

23. This section is based on discussions with former and active security personnel in the army and police in Bogotá in December 2010, including former deputy army commander and head of the special operations group General Muis Alberto Ardilo.

24. Discussion, Bogotá, 9 December 2010.

25. See Derek Henry Flood, 'If a Rebel Falls in the Forest: The Steady Evisceration of the FARC Leadership in Colombia', *Militant Leadership Monitor* (Vol. 1, Issue 9, 29 September 2010).

26. *CNN World*, 'Guerilla leader killed in Colombia, president says', 23 September 2010.

27. See, for example, The Center for International Policy's Colombia Program, 'An overview of the DAS Scandal', 7 October 2009.

28. For example, 602 in 2000, 518 in 2001, 684 in 2002, 605 in 2003, 589 in 2004, and 710 in 2005. The bulk (528 in 2005) of casualties was from the Colombian Army.

29. This comprised 15,429 FARC, 3,205 ELN, 498 dissidents, and 3,347 paramilitaries, of which 3,683 were men, 4,196 women, and 3,015 minors.

30. Henry Mance, 'Waiting game for Colombia's informal workers', *BBC News*, 19 January 2010.

31. Discussion, Bogotá, December 2006.

32. Speech to visiting African group, Bogotá, March 2009.

33. Discussion, Bogotá, December 2006.

34. Will Grant, 'What future for US-backed Plan Colombia?', *BBC News*, 13 June 2010.

35. An additional 7 per cent of US exports would receive duty free treatment within five years of implementation. All remaining tariffs would be eliminated ten years after implementation.

36. In 2009, US exports were $9.45 billion, imports $11.32 billion: U.S. Census Bureau, 'Trade with Colombia: 2009'.

37. It was not approved by the end of President Bush's term in January 2009. Although President Obama asked the Office of the US Trade Representative to address outstanding issues in the agreement, during a visit from Uribe in June 2009, Obama said he did not have a 'strict timetable' for the agreement.

38. Cited in *Wikipedia*, 'Revolutionary Armed Forces of Colombia', available at <http://en.wikipedia.org/wiki/Revolutionary_Armed_Forces_of_Colombia>. Last accessed 16 December 2010.

39. Discussion, Bogotá, 7 December 2010.

40. Discussion, Bogotá, 6 December 2010.

41. Police Intelligence, Bogotá, 10 December 2010.

42. Information supplied by the Colombian government, December 2010. See also James Blitz, 'UN warns of gangs' global muscle', *FT.com*, 17 June 2010.

43. Bogotá, 10 December 2010.

44. Juan Forero, 'Colombia's Santos is elected president', *Washington Post*, 21 June 2010; Public Policy and Management, 'Can Colombia's New President Close the Inequality Gap?', 20 October 2010.

45. Discussion, Bogotá, December 2010.

46. CCAI survey, presented in Bogotá in December 2010.

47. Discussion, Bogotá, December 2010.

48. Bogotá, 6 December 2010.

El Salvador: When the Insurgents (Finally) Take Over (pp. 413–34)

1. This chapter is based on several research visits to El Salvador, in October 2005, March 2009 and December 2010. Grateful thanks are extended to Luis Membreno for his kind role in facilitating these visits, especially the meetings and interviews in December 2010, and to him and Michelle Parker for the insights they offered. All mistakes and opinions, however, remain the author's alone.

2. See Todd Greentree, *Crossroads of Intervention: Insurgency and Counterinsurgency Lessons from Central America* (Maryland: Naval Institute Press, 2008).

3. The first of the three iterations of the junta was lead by Colonels Adolfo Arnaldo Majana Ramo and Jaime Abdul Gutiérrez Avendano, along with Guillermo Ungo, Mario Antonio Andino and Román Mayora Quitós.

4. Previously, in the 1960s, the government of President (Colonel) Arturo Armando Molina had attempted to exert control by using the peasant-based ORDEN, which had been established earlier by General José Alberto 'Chele' Medrano. It functioned extremely effectively as a paramilitary unit, providing not only 100,000 troops by the late 1970s, but also an important source of rural intelligence.

5. *Global Security.org*, 'El Salvador Civil War', available at <http://www.globalsecurity.org/military/world/war/elsalvador2.htm>. Last accessed 17 December 2010.

6. Interview, General Jaime Abdul Gutiérrez Avendano and General Rinaldo Golcher, San Salvador, 13 December 2010.

7. Interview, San Salvador, 13 December 2010.

8. *Global Security.org, op. cit.*

9. On 7 May 1980, Major D'Aubuisson was arrested at a farm, where documents were found linking him to the death of the Archbishop and of plotting a coup d'état. Pressure from the right forced his release and that of his colleagues. He was described by Robert White, former US Ambassador to El Salvador, as a 'pathological killer', and was known widely as 'Major Soplete' ('Major Blowtorch') on account of his preference for that form of torture. D'Aubuisson died in 1992.

10. Interview, San Salvador, 15 December 2010.

11. David Brand, 'The Sheraton Siege', *TIME*, 24 June 2001.

12. See José Luis Merino and Roberto Regalado, *Comandante Ramiro: Revelaciones de*

un guerrilero y líder revolucionario salvadoreno (Mexico: Oceansur, 2011), p. 113.

13. Interview, General Jaime Abdul Gutiérrez Avendano, San Salvador, 13 December 2010.

14. 'El Salvador: Foreign Military Influence and Assistance', *Country-data.com*.

15. Televised national address, 9 May 1984, available at <http://college.cengage.com/ history/us/gillon/am_exp/1e/students/primary/contras.htm>.

16. Robert Parry, 'The USA's Secret War in El Salvador, 1981–1992', available at <http://flag.blackened.net/revolt/mexico/usa/secsal.html>.

17. *Country-data.com*, *op. cit.*

18. *Ibid.*

19. See Max G Manwaring and Court Prisk (eds.), *El Salvador at War: An Oral History* (Washington, DC: National Defense University Press, 1988).

20. Interview, Sal Salvador, 13 December 2010.

21. Manwaring and Prisk, *op. cit.*, p. 78.

22. *Ibid.*, p. 145.

23. *Ibid.*, p. 146.

24. Interview, General Golcher, San Salvador, 13 December 2010.

25. Interview, Sal Salvador, 13 December 2010.

26. The Commission on the Truth for El Salvador, 'From Madness to Hope: The 12-Year War in El Salvador', commission report, 26 January 2001, part IV; America Watch Committee, *Report on Human Rights in El Salvador* (New York, NY: Random House, 1982).

27. Manwaring and Prisk, *op. cit.*, p. 11.

28. Figures from UN Department of Economic and Social Affairs.

29. *Greentree*, *op. cit.*, p. 75.

30. Richard A Haggarty(ed.), *El Salvador: A Country Study* (Washington, DC: General Post Office for the Library of Congress, 1988).

31. Bill Van Auken, 'Images of El Salvador Carnage Reprised in Light of Iraq War', *Wsws.org*, 28 October 2005.

32. Bart Beeson, 'El Salvador's Revolution by Majority', *Foreignpolicy.com*, March 2009.

33. Michael E Allison, 'Wikileaks El Salvador', *centralamericanpolitics.blogspot.com*, 7 December 2010.

34. 'Venezuela and FMLN Mayors of El Salvador Form Joint Venture', *Venezuela Analysis*, 8 April 2006.

35. Interview, San Salvador, 15 December 2010.

ABOUT THE AUTHORS

Anthony Arnott

Major Anthony Arnott is a helicopter pilot in the UK Army Air Corps. He attended the Royal Military Academy Sandhurst in 2001 before serving for three years in Northern Ireland as an infantry platoon commander and pilot. He has been deployed to Afghanistan twice: in 2008 as the UK helicopter force operations officer, and in 2010 with the Prism strategic analysis group.

David Betz

Dr David Betz is a Senior Lecturer in the War Studies Department at King's College London, where he heads the Insurgency Research Group, and is Academic Director of the MA War in the Modern World Programme. He has advised the UK Ministry of Defence on counter-insurgency and stabilisation doctrine and cyber-security, and also ISAF on strategic communications, counter-insurgency and countering corruption. He has published articles on strategy, insurgency and counter-insurgency, information warfare and civil-military relations in *Armed Forces and Society*, *The Journal of Strategic Studies*, *Contemporary Security Policy*, *Orbis*, the *RUSI Journal* and *International Affairs*, as well as many chapters in edited books.

Chris Brown

A soldier for over thirty-six years, Lieutenant General Chris Brown saw operational service in Northern Ireland; the Falkland Islands; Western Sahara and Cyprus with the UN; Bosnia, Kosovo and Afghanistan with NATO; and Iraq as Deputy

Commander of Coalition Forces and Senior British Military Representative. He has commanded soldiers at all levels from platoon to division, including 7th Parachute Regiment and General Officer Commanding Northern Ireland. His final military appointment was leading the MoD's analysis of lessons from the Iraq campaign. He has since worked with the AU on contingency planning for the 2011 referendum on Southern Sudan. He read law at University College Cardiff and International Relations at Peterhouse college, Cambridge.

Adam Cobb

Dr Adam Cobb is Professor of International Relations, United States Marine Corps Command and Staff College. He researches and teaches culture and inter-agency operations, irregular warfare, strategy, cyber-warfare, energy security and Asia-Pacific security. He has advised the Joint Chiefs of Staff and was involved in weekly strategy sessions with General Stanley McChrystal. He is an SME for the US Navy, conducting strategic briefs for deploying amphibious squadrons. He is a senior war game designer for the Chief of the Air Staff's *Unified Engagement*. Dr Cobb has briefed the US National Intelligence Committee on China's military modernisation; the US China Economic and Security Review Commission; and the Tswalu Process in South Africa.

Christopher Clapham

Professor Christopher Clapham is editor of the *Journal of Modern African Studies*, and is based at the Centre of African Studies at Cambridge University. Until his retirement, he was Professor of Politics and International Relations at Lancaster University; he was President of the African Studies Association of the United Kingdom, 1992–94. His main interests lie in the politics and international relations of Africa, with a particular concern for the Horn of Africa. He has also worked on Liberia and Sierra Leone.

Alan Doss

Alan Doss is the former Special Representative of the United Nations Secretary-General and Head of the UN Missions in Liberia and the Democratic Republic of the Congo.

Alastair Leithead

Alastair Leithead has been the BBC's Asia Correspondent since February 2009, living in Bangkok but covering East Asia. He covered Thailand's anti-government protests. Before Thailand, Alastair was based in Afghanistan for more than two and a half years. He won the 2007 Bayeux Television Award for war correspondents and was shortlisted in 2008 for a BAFTA for best TV news coverage. Prior to Afghanistan, Alastair was briefly based in Miami and before that South Africa, periodically travelling to Iraq. Alastair Leithead was brought up in Newcastle-upon-Tyne where he attended the Royal Grammar School, before going on to receive an honours degree in Geography at Manchester University. He has worked at the BBC for fourteen years.

Michael A Lewis

Lieutenant Colonel Michael A Lewis US Army serves as the Special Operations Chair for the Marine Corps University in Quantico, Virginia, while concurrently pursuing a doctorate in conflict analysis and resolution from George Mason University. He has fourteen years' experience in the special operations community, including three years in the Pentagon working on Department of Defense and national-level counter-terrorism plans and policies. He has conflict experience in Somalia, Afghanistan and Iraq as an intelligence officer, operations officer and special operations aviator.

Ved Prakash Malik

General V P Malik was Chief of the Indian Army from October 1997 to September 2000. Concurrently, he was Chairman of the Chiefs of Staff Committee of India from January 1999 to September 2000. He planned, co-ordinated and oversaw execution of Operation *Vijay* to successfully defeat Pakistan's attempted intrusion into the Kargil Sector in 1999. After retirement, he was a member of the National Security Advisory Board for two years. He writes frequently for newspapers and professional magazines. He is the author of *Kargil: From Surprise to Victory* (HarperCollins, 2006) and written several papers on strategic affairs, defence planning and security issues.

Greg Mills

Greg Mills heads up the Johannesburg-based Brenthurst Foundation. He holds a BA (Hons) from the University of Cape Town, and an MA and PhD from the University of Lancaster. From 1996–2005 he was National Director of the South African Institute of International Affairs. He headed up the Prism strategic analysis group for General David Richards in Kabul in 2006, was seconded as Strategy Adviser to the President of Rwanda in 2008, has served as a member of the Danish Africa Commission from 2008, and during 2010 deployed twice to Regional Command (South) in Afghanistan in an advisory capacity based in Kandahar. He is the author, *inter alia*, of *The Wired Model: South Africa, Foreign Policy and Globalisation* (2000), *The Future of Africa: New Order in Sight?* (2003, with Jeffrey Herbst), *Seven Battles that Shaped South Africa's History* (2005, with David Williams), *From Africa to Afghanistan: With Richards and NATO to Kabul* (2007), and *Why Africa is Poor – And What Africans Can Do about It* (2010). He serves on the Advisory Council of the Royal United Services Institute, is a trustee of the SA Military History Museum, and is on the visiting faculty of the NATO Higher Defence College in Rome.

A N M Muniruzzaman

Major General Muniruzzaman (Rtd) is a career military officer with thirty-eight years' active duty, including various senior command posts. An experienced peace keeper, he was a member and head of the country contingent to UNTAC in Cambodia. He also has the distinction of heading the post-election UN Mission in Cambodia. General Muniruzzaman is currently the President of the Bangladesh Institute of Peace and Security Studies, a leading think tank in South Asia.

Sandrine Perrot

Sandrine Perrot is a Senior Research Fellow at the Centre for International Research (CERI) at Sciences-Po. She joined CERI after a two-year postdoctoral fellowship at the Center for International Studies at the Université de Montréal. Dr Perrot specialises in Uganda and in armed conflicts and violent phenomena in sub-Saharan Africa. Her PhD was titled 'The Reversibility of Chaos? The Rebuilding of a Political Order in Uganda (1986–2001)'. She has worked extensively on northern Uganda and the Lord's Resistance Army. Her current research focuses on militias and paramilitary groups. She has written numerous journal articles and contributions to edited volumes. She is also the Co-director of *Research in Question*, a member of the editorial board of *Politique Africaine* and *Critique Internationale*, and an Associate Researcher at the Centre d'Etudes des Mondes Africains.

J Peter Pham

J Peter Pham is Senior Vice President of the National Committee on American Foreign Policy and Associate Professor of Justice Studies, Political Science and African Studies at James Madison University. Specialising in African political and security issues, he frequently advises the US and other governments as well as the private sector.

David Richards

Born in 1952, educated at Eastbourne College and University College Cardiff, David Richards was commissioned into the Royal Artillery in 1971. He has served in the Far East, Germany, East Timor, Sierra Leone and Afghanistan, where he commanded ISAF between May 2006 and February 2007. A graduate of the Staff College, Camberley (1984), his staff appointments include being Chief of Staff of the Berlin Infantry Brigade, an instructor at the Staff College, Colonel Army Plans in the UK Ministry of Defence, Chief Joint Force Operations, Assistant Chief and then Chief of the General Staff. He commanded 3rd Regiment Royal Horse Artillery, 4th Armoured Brigade, and the Allied Rapid Reaction Corps. He was appointed Chief of the Defence Staff in October 2010.

Paula G Thornhill

Dr Paula G Thornhill retired as an US Air Force Brigadier General in 2009 and joined RAND later that year as the Director of Strategy and Doctrine (Project Air Force). Her last air force assignment was as Commandant of the Air Force Institute of Technology. Other assignments included Principal Director of Near East and South Asian Affairs (Office of the Secretary of Defense) and special assistant to the Chairman of the Joint Chiefs of Staff. She holds a DPhil from Oxford University.

Christopher Vernon

Colonel Christopher Vernon has been an officer in British Army since commissioning in the Queen's Own Hussars in 1977. His early service saw time as an armoured officer in Germany and tours in the infantry role in Northern Ireland, as well as two tours in the Ministry of Defence in London. He worked as the military spokesman for the commander of the UN Force in Bosnia in 1995. He then commanded the Queen's Royal Hussars, an armoured regiment in Germany, from 1998–2001. Promoted to colonel in 2001, he was the military spokesman in Iraq for the US/UK coalition intervention in 2003. Since then he has been Commandant of the Land Warfare School (2003–05), Chief of Staff of Regional Command (South) in Kandahar, Afghanistan in 2006, and Deputy Commander of the International Military Advisory and Training Team in Sierra Leone in 2007. He is currently Commander of the British Peace Support Team in South Africa.

David Williams

David Williams is a South African journalist and broadcaster with more than three decades of experience. He currently serves as Director of the King Edward VII Educational Trust, and is the author, *inter alia*, of *Great Games* (Penguin, 1998), *Toughest of Them All : The Springbok-All Black Rivalry* (with Grant Harding, Penguin, 2000), *Seven Battles that Shaped South Africa* (with Greg Mills, Tafelberg, 2005) and *On the Border 1965–1990* (Tafelberg, 2008).

Grahame Wilson

Major (Rtd) Grahame Wilson is the most decorated officer to have served in the Rhodesian Army. After the transition to Zimbabwe, he served as Officer Commanding Special Air Service from April 1980 to the unit's disbandment in December that year.